8.50 - 347   5-67 (Sweeninger)

A HISTORY OF SOUTHERN RHODESIA

Early Days to 1934

A HISTORY OF
SOUTHERN RHODESIA

Early Days to 1934

by L. H. GANN

LONDON
CHATTO & WINDUS
1965

Printed in Great Britain by
Robert MacLehose and Company Limited
The University Press, Glasgow

PREFACE

Few countries in the world have made more progress over the last seventy years than Rhodesia. Its people can look back on considerable achievements, but the country is still in search of a national identity. This in turn must derive from a better knowledge of the past, and Rhodesians have therefore stood in need of a general history that would meet the canons of scholarship whilst throwing some new light on the creation of our plural society. Some good works have of course already appeared in print. H. Rolin's *Les Lois et l'Administration de la Rhodésie* (1913) is outstanding from the legal and constitutional point of view, but it only goes up to just before the First World War and has now become almost a bibliophile's treasure. H. M. Hole's *The Making of Rhodesia* (1926) which deals with the pioneering period, has likewise long been out of print and has in many ways become outdated. The Institute of Race Relations' important trilogy *The Birth of a Dilemma* (1958) and *Year of Decision* (1960) by Philip Mason and *The Two Nations* (1960) by Richard Gray is mainly concerned with the more specific problems of race relations. Dr L. H. Gann, formerly Editor at the National Archives of Rhodesia and Nyasaland and now Research Associate at the Hoover Institution, Stanford University, has filled the gap, the present volume mainly concentrating on the period between the first arrival of the Pioneer Column in 1890, and 1834 when Dr Godfrey Martin Huggins (later Lord Malvern) formed his National Government and thereby opened a new chapter in the Colony's political history.

This work is the second volume in the history of the territories which formerly comprised the Federation of Rhodesia and Nyasaland, the first being *A History of Northern Rhodesia: early days to 1953*, published in 1964. A further volume carrying the history of Southern Rhodesia from 1935 to 1953 is in course of preparation. It is intended that the volumes can be read in isolation from one another, each forming a complete entity of its own. To record the more ancient history of this part of the world will of course as yet require a great deal of additional research, the subject forming a fruitful field for co-operation between tribal historians, anthropologists and archaeologists; already the National Archives has made a start in this direction and has, with the co-operation of the Centro de Estudos Históricos Ultramarinos in Lisbon, published several volumes in the Documents Series which will eventually cover the period 1497–1840. But the author has given us what he set out to do, a well-planned record of the British impact on an underdeveloped country which will hold the interest of general readers and serve as an introduction to more specialized works.

The opinions expressed by the author on past events and on personalities are of course his own, and do not in any way commit any Government.

In conclusion, I should like to express my gratitude to the Anglo-American Corporation, the Rhodesian Selection Trust, The British South Africa Company and the Rhodesian Printing and Publishing Company who helped to make this venture financially possible.

T. W. BAXTER
Director
National Archives of Rhodesia

CONTENTS

INTRODUCTION

Southern Rhodesia as we know it today, is little more than seventy years old. Like all emergent states of Sub-Saharan Africa, the country owes its boundaries to the late nineteenth-century 'Scramble for Africa' when diplomatists and civil servants in the capitals of Europe drew lines across the map to demarcate the spheres of influence claimed by the various powers. Southern Rhodesia nevertheless possesses a geographical 'personality' of its own which has profoundly affected its past.[1] With its 150,333 square miles it is about three times as big as England, but its population is not very much more than three times that of Birmingham. It lies between the Limpopo river in the south and the Zambezi in the north, and constitutes part of an enormous plateau. Almost the whole region rises above 1,000 feet, more than four-fifths above 2,000 feet, while many parts are higher still, so that the people of Salisbury, the capital, live at an elevation greater than that of Ben Nevis, the highest mountain in Great Britain. Rhodesians who dwell on the main watershed enjoy a fine Californian type of climate; the Eastern Highlands are cool and rainy, whereas the plains of the Limpopo, Zambezi and Sabi are hot and dry. The veld is broken by rivers which flow for the most part in an irregular fashion, depending on the rains, which usually start in November and continue to about March, transforming the parched veld into a sea of green. Visitors to the Highlands on the eastern border can admire splendid mountain country, reminiscent sometimes of Scotland and sometimes of Central Europe. On the main watershed, from north-east to south-west, the rainfall becomes less, but still suffices for savanna or open woodland which stretches endlessly to the grey-blue horizon beyond. The rolling veld once teemed with herds of game and generally offered few obstacles to newcomers, whether white or black. Vegetation becomes sparser in the *acacia* and *terminalia* country further west, where precipitation decreases, the trees are more stunted, but grasses still flourish and cattle find excellent pasture. An outer rim of low-lying *mopane* country encircles much of Rhodesia, stretching along the Zambezi valley in the north and the Limpopo river in the south; great herds of kudu, antelope

[1] Summers, R. 'Environment and culture in Southern Rhodesia: a study in the personality of a land-locked country' (in *Proceedings of the American Philosophical Society*, v. 104, 1960, p. 266–292)

and other animals used to roam through these little-inhabited regions, but at the same time the dreaded tsetse fly abounded; 'fly' belts formed formidable barriers to cattle-owning invaders who probably travelled inland along definite routes which varied as the 'fly' areas tended to shift.

A modern scholar has described the whole of Southern Rhodesia as a kind of 'corridor', connecting the lower Zambezi valley to the upper Limpopo, the Zambezi *mopane* barrier effectively separating the two Rhodesias throughout much of prehistoric times. The country in some ways forms a 'landlocked' island, where local cultures often developed in comparative isolation. Beira, the nearest modern port on the Indian Ocean towards the east, lies only about 160 miles away from the picturesque Rhodesian border town of Umtali, but a traveller has to traverse difficult mountain country before he reaches the sea, and oceanic influences have always remained somewhat remote. Southern Rhodesia's mineral wealth, the agricultural possibilities of the better-watered central and eastern portions, as well as the lure of the grazing lands to the west, have nevertheless attracted many different immigrants, of whom the British and South African settlers of the nineteenth and twentieth centuries merely came as the last in a long succession. Today, the inhabitants of Southern Rhodesia comprise some 3,700,000 Africans, 223,000 Europeans, 7,500 Asians—most of them of Indian or Pakistani origin—and about 11,200 people of mixed blood. In referring to Rhodesians who themselves, or whose ancestors, came from Europe, the author has employed the words 'settlers', 'whites' or 'colonists'; he has used the words 'natives' or 'Africans' for the black-skinned Bantu-speaking races who inhabit the area, the term chosen depending on the usage customary at the time. Individual native communities are referred to in the manner current in everyday speech, so that the *Ndebele* become the Matabele and the *Lozi* the Barotse, though the two former terms would be linguistically more accurate. The geographical names used are normally those which a reader would find on a modern map.

L. H. GANN

Salisbury
Southern Rhodesia
1963

AUTHOR'S ACKNOWLEDGEMENTS

In writing this book I have received help, advice and encouragement from a great number of people of all races and from all walks of life, whose knowledge I have sometimes found a great deal more enlightening than written records. To mention them all would turn this into a catalogue of names, and might still—through a lapse of memory—exclude some who should have been mentioned. I owe, however, a special debt of gratitude to a number of Rhodesians who have read through individual chapters, or spent a long time in discussions, who have made private papers of their own available to me, or supplied me with written statements. These include Mr D. P. Abraham, Senior Research Fellow in Ethno-History at the University College of Rhodesia and Nyasaland, Mr J. Cowie, O.B.E., formerly Secretary for Education in Southern Rhodesia, Alderman L. B. Fereday, J.P., a one-time Cabinet Minister, Dr M. Gelfand, C.B.E., Professor of African Medicine at the University College of Rhodesia and Nyasaland, Colonel A. S. Hickman, M.B.E., formerly Commissioner of the British South Africa Police, Viscount Malvern, P.C., C.H., K.C.M.G., formerly Prime Minister of Southern Rhodesia and later of the Federation of Rhodesia and Nyasaland, Dr J. McHarg, Principal of Luveve Technical College, Major H. G. Mundy, C.B.E., once Secretary for Agriculture and Lands in Southern Rhodesia, Mr C. Mzingeli, formerly an African trade union leader in this Colony, Lieutenant-Colonel T. Nangle, a past Member of the Southern Rhodesia Legislative Assembly, Mr N. O. Paasche, farmer, now on the Southern Rhodesia Dairy Marketing Board, Father W. F. Rea, S.J., of St George's College, Salisbury, Mr J. V. V. Rukara from the Fort Victoria district, Mr R. Summers, Curator and Keeper of Antiquities at the National Museum of Southern Rhodesia at Bulawayo, and the late Mr H. Susman, merchant. I also owe a debt of gratitude to my colleagues on the staff of the National Archives, especially Mr T. W. Baxter, the Director, Mr E. E. Burke, the Principal Archives Officer, who has carefully checked and criticized my manuscript, and Mr J. A. Edwards, the Librarian, who has provided valuable aid with regard to the bibliography. Any errors which may nonetheless have crept into this work are of course purely my own.

Chapter One

Early Rhodesia

I

Bushmen and early Bantu south of the Zambezi

In August 1871 a lonely white explorer by the name of Carl Mauch found himself stranded somewhere near the present Fort Victoria in what is now Southern Rhodesia. Mauch, an adventurous German schoolmaster, made his way to the Limpopo after a lengthy journey through the Transvaal; but then his carriers deserted him and his condition became desperate. When he was almost at the point of death, he was found by some indigenous Makalaka people who kept him as 'guest and prisoner'. But Mauch at last heard of another European, Adam Renders (or Render), an American of German birth who had settled in the Zoutpansberg from where he used to trade and hunt beyond the Limpopo, and who was now living in an African village nearby. Mauch at first almost hesitated to avail himself of Renders' help, but had no choice and Renders assisted him to make his departure from an oppressive local chief, kindly receiving him in his own village. The American knew the country well, and had previously stumbled on the Great Zimbabwe ruins, imagining that he had found one of King Solomon's forts. Mauch, who was familiar with stories of a long-lost civilization in Central Africa, now heard marvellous tales of white people who were supposed to have lived in this part of the world a long time ago, of occult occurrences, and even a strange account of a mysterious piece of pottery which was supposedly hidden on a hill nearby. The young teacher, who a short time ago had been contemplating suicide, was delighted at hearing these theories confirmed. He decided to explore the hiding place of the magic pot with the help of local people, and became even more excited when an African pointed out to him yet another hill, about two and a half miles to the east where, Mauch was told, he would find ruins of ancient buildings constructed many centuries ago by white people. On 5 September 1871 Mauch finally managed to reach the now famous Zimbabwe, Rhodesia's most remarkable and best-known ancient monument, of which he provided the first eyewitness description in print.[1]

Mauch, echoing earlier views propounded by Portuguese writers some three centuries ago, never imagined that these ruins might be the work of black men. He thought that they were probably built under Hebrew inspiration, that the ancient building on the hill was copied from Solomon's temple, and that the constructions in the plain must have resembled the palace where the Queen of Sheba stayed during her visit to the Jewish monarch's court. According to him, Phoenician artisans most likely directed the original building operations, the German regarding the lands of Sofala as identical with the biblical Ophir, where Hiram, Israel's Phoenician ally, 'sent in the navy his servants, shipmen that had knowledge of the sea, with the servants of Solomon . . . and fetched from thence, gold four hundred and twenty talents, and brought it to King Solomon.'[2] These ideas appeared reasonable enough at the time, and made a tremendous appeal to a Bible-reading Victorian public, which was familiar with the Scriptures and captivated by the still undisclosed mysteries of the African continent. Most Victorians moreover looked upon the Bantu-speaking tribesmen as people who had not yet advanced beyond the lowest stage of human evolution, a nation without a tradition or a past, incapable of creating anything as imposing as Zimbabwe, and nineteenth-century Europeans were thus naturally inclined to accept an 'Asian' theory of Zimbabwe's origins which they placed in remote and romantic antiquity.

Modern archaeologists, however, have arrived at different conclusions. Their researches have extended Rhodesia's past over several hundred thousand years, over an infinitely longer period of time than Mauch envisaged; but Hiram, Solomon and the Queen of Sheba play no part in this story. The exact sequence of events cannot easily be traced with accuracy, and much work still remains to be done on the subject. Archaeologists have done detective work on a considerable scale in Southern Rhodesia and have made a major contribution in breaking through the barrier of time that separates us from the past. Archaeologists naturally concentrate on artifacts; but whereas ancient stone tools and weapons survive to be classified by scholars, ideas and social systems do not, so that no one will ever tell the full story. Archaeological researches can of course

---

[1] Mauch, C. 'Reisen im Inneren von Süd-Africa 1865–1872' (in *Petermann's Geographische Mitt-heilungen*, Ergänzungsheft no. 37, 1874, p. 28–52). This has been translated by Summers, R. 'Carl Mauch on Zimbabwe ruins' (in *NADA: the Southern Rhodesia Native Affairs Department annual*, no. 29, 1952, p. 9–17). Mauch's reports contain his version of Renders' life. A somewhat different version appears in Lansdown, G. N. 'Zimbabwe discoverer' (in *United empire: the journal of the Royal Empire Society*, v. 25, 1934, p. 598–599)

[2] I Kings, 9: 27–28

be supplemented to some extent by tribal traditions, but folklore is liable
to telescope important events in time, or perhaps omit them altogether,
while tradition frequently becomes modified in accordance with the
changing structure of society. Orthodox historians, working from written
sources, also have something to add to the story, but the earliest Portuguese documents concerning this part of the world unfortunately do not
go back further than the beginning of the sixteenth century, and there is
possibly a good deal of relevant Arab material still remaining unexplored.
Ethnographers and linguists can also help to illuminate the past, but even
so the full story of Rhodesia's prehistory still remains to be written, and
the following account can therefore only serve as a very general and
possibly somewhat inaccurate introduction.

The story of mankind almost certainly began with small bands of food
gatherers who made a precarious living by collecting roots and berries and
by slaying such animals as they were able to catch. Early Stone Age man
probably did not know the use of fire, and possessed no permanent
habitation, but sought shelter from animals behind simple windbreaks or
in pits in the ground.[1] But at some stage in their development these
primitive people achieved the greatest advance ever made in the history of
human endeavour: they began to fashion tools according to a set and
regular pattern. Archaeologists divide the Earlier Stone Age into several
periods, beginning with a little-known Pebble culture, which was succeeded by what is known as the Chelles-Acheul culture. Gradually
primaeval craftsmen improved their techniques, and finds related to the
so-called Sangoan cultures contain hand-axes, cleavers and scrapers of
various kinds; all these tools are roughly worked, but their makers may
have employed cylindrical batons in trimming axes and larger tools.
Gradually Stone Age hunters penetrated wider areas of grassland, and
during the Middle Stone Age, when Southern Rhodesia probably experienced more rainfall than it does now, prehistoric man developed what
became known as the Rhodesian Still Bay cultures. Roving bands hunted
with spears furnished with stone points; the forest country contained
plenty of game, and cave-dwellers fashioned a profusion of small scrapers,
backed blades and piercers which may have served for making up skins
into blankets and similar coverings. As people acquired growing skill in
making stone tools their implements became smaller and handier; some of
them also learned the difficult art of boring a hole through stone. As time
went on a drier period followed and a new culture, known as the Magosian,
developed, which centred on perennial streams where animals would come
to water.

[1] Clark, J. D. *The prehistory of Southern Africa*. Penguin Books ltd, 1959

These developments, which have been traced in such brief and summary fashion, in fact extended over an unimaginably long period. The Early Stone Age has been estimated by some to have lasted something like 400,000 years, whilst the Middle Stone Age may have begun about 35,000 or 40,000 years before the birth of Christ. Later on, however, early hunters made further advances in the technique of working stone, and by a long-drawn process of trial and error learned how to haft a number of small, highly finished stone blades or flakes into wood or bone. With this new method they could use stones of smaller size and higher quality which improved the performance of their tools. Hunters began to use arrows with barbed points which stuck in the flesh and which, if dipped in poison, made certain that the toxic substance would effectively disperse in the body of their prey. Arrows at the same time became lighter, giving nomadic archers a greater range, so that the huntsmen would be able to bring more meat to their women and children. However this may be, there is no doubt that typical stone finds of the Southern Rhodesian Wilton culture reveal an entirely new blade technique; in addition new types of tools made their appearance including ground stone 'axes'. Some scholars also believe that a migration of people may have taken place during the Magosian and Later Stone Age, the Zambezi serving as a great highway, with tributaries like the Mazoe and Gwaai providing easy access to the country.[1] The Wilton people also developed a splendid rock art which modern Rhodesians can still admire in rock shelters in the Lake McIlwaine National Park near Salisbury, at Diana's View, Rusape, in the Chibi Reserve near Fort Victoria, in the Matopos, and elsewhere. These pictures were painted in a very lifelike fashion and have been associated with the grassland and open bush country of Southern Rhodesia. The denser woodlands north of the Zambezi produced a different culture, named after the Nachikufu Caves. Racially the inhabitants of these more wooded regions may have been somewhat different from the Bush people in the south and may have been linked to other strains in East Africa. These people also produced painters, but these expressed themselves in a different style, making extensive use of a schematic, non-naturalistic rock-art, whilst they probably used wood to a much greater extent in their day-to-day lives.[2]

Towards the end of the Stone Age, Central Africa already formed a melting pot of different races, and scholars distinguish between several

---

[1] Summers, R. 'Environment and culture in Southern Rhodesia; a study in the "personality" of a land-locked country' (in *Proceedings of the American Philosophical Society*, v. 104, 1960, p. 266–292)

[2] These paintings have been splendidly reproduced in Goodall, E., and others. *Prehistoric rock art of the Federation of Rhodesia and Nyasaland*. Salisbury, National Publications Trust, 1959

physical types, including Bushmen with their characteristically small skulls, Boskop people and various hybrids between them, the mixture possibly having been enriched by other strains who came to the country from the north. But whatever their ancestry none of these early people learned to herd cattle or raise crops; they lived 'from hunt to mouth'; and their margin of survival accordingly remained precarious. But at some time towards the end of the Later Stone Age the nomads of the veld suddenly encountered strangers who lived in a very different fashion. Bushman painters in Mashonaland have recorded this invasion, and their rock paintings show how tall men came into the country, driving cattle or fat-tailed sheep. At Ruchera Cave, Mtoko, for instance, an aboriginal artist did a picture figuring two men and two women who lead a cow between them, perhaps one of the historically most important scenes ever to have been executed in this country.[1] No scholar is quite certain when this early *Völkerwanderung* took place, but some archaeologists believe that some time about the birth of Christ a people manufacturing a characteristic kind of 'stamped ware' pottery arrived in the Lake Nyasa region from the north, and subsequently divided into several streams. Some time, possibly during the first 500 years A.D., 'stamped ware' communities made their way to the south of the Zambezi, where they found plenty of land in which to spread out; they generally managed to live at peace with the indigenous hunting bands, who did not compete with the immigrants for their grazing ground but gradually retreated into the less accessible regions, with the result that the Bush groups in the Matopos became geographically separated from those of Mashonaland.

Some time before A.D. 300 this Stone Age culture was succeeded by one of considerably greater complexity, marked by a distinctive kind of pottery adorned with channelled patterns as well as the impressions of square-toothed stamps. At the same time the extraction of metal became an important industry in what is now Southern Rhodesia. The early miners possessed neither explosives, pumps, nor hard steel tools, and had to split ore bodies by alternately heating and cooling them. Nevertheless they were highly skilled prospectors and, despite their limited equipment, reached very considerable depths—sometimes over 100 feet—being stopped only by water or insufficient ventilation. Judging by the large number of female skeletons found in these old workings, it appears that much of the underground drudgery was done by girls, so that female mine labour was not peculiar to the early Industrial Revolution in England. Most of the mining was concerned with gold, payable ore being carried to the nearest stream, where it was crushed and concentrated in

[1] Goodall, E., and others; *op. cit*, p. 33, plate 14

running water.[1] The 'Ancients' also worked copper and tin; and it seems likely that by the ninth century a good deal of precious metal was channelled through Sofala, from where Arab merchants traded gold to the Near East.

The next step came with a new group of invaders who began to move into Southern Rhodesia some time in the first millenium, or perhaps somewhat later. These immigrants possibly spoke a Bantu tongue and were probably the ancestors of the present-day Karanga, who are said to have come from Lake Tanganyika via Nyasaland. Seeking new pastures for their vast herds of cattle the invaders made their way across the Zambezi, probably avoiding the more tsetse-ridden areas, and marching perhaps to somewhere near the present Sebungwe district, from where they fanned out southwards, settling in the great, grassy plains which border the Kalahari Desert. Here they encountered Bushmen and also various pastoral communities, familiar with the use of iron, who were already previously settled in the country, and now worked for the immigrants as herdsmen and smelters.[2] The 'proto-Karanga' prospered, and as their numbers increased, spread south and eastwards towards the Limpopo valley. These black settlers were technically more advanced than their predecessors and developed an elegant type of pottery. They also put up numerous stone constructions, including the buildings known today as the Dhlo-Dhlo and Khami ruins, which controlled important areas of gold production.[3] Mining continued to play an important part in the country's economy, the yellow metal being sold to Muslim merchants who made their way inland from the East Coast. In exchange, Mohammedan traders brought beads and cloth to the inland people who, under the impact of the new exchange economy, learned how to put up big stone walls without using mortar, and developed a highly aristocratic culture. Zimbabwe, the 'Great Stone House' on which Mauch later stumbled, was their most outstanding achievement. From early days scattered bands sought refuge on Zimbabwe Hill, and archaeologists now feel sure that by the end of the first millennium a visitor would have found clusters of huts with thin daga (daub) walls, spread over wooden wattle work. Local techniques of massive stone walling probably originated on Zimbabwe Hill, and by the

[1] Summers, R. 'The Southern Rhodesian iron age' (in *Journal of African history*, v. 2, 1961, p. 1–13)

[2] Based on the work of Abraham, D. P. 'The early political history of the Kingdom of Mwene Mutapa (850–1589)' (in *Historians in tropical Africa: proceedings of the Leverhulme inter-collegiate history conference held at the University College of Rhodesia and Nyasaland, September 1960*. Salisbury, The College, 1962, p. 61–91); and Abraham, D. P. 'The Monomotapa dynasty' (in *NADA*, no. 36, 1959, p. 59–84)

[3] Summers, R. 'Zimbabwe: capital of an ancient Rhodesian kingdom' (in *Africa south*, v. 2, no. 2, Jan–Mar 1958, p. 50–58)

middle of the fifteenth century the 'Acropolis' formed a safe retreat in wartime:[1] a naturally powerful position with huge boulders it was reinforced with a network of great walls whose construction must have required a very large labour force, and a well-organized commissariat to feed the builders. Lookout posts could keep the whole of the surrounding countryside under observation; the stronghold was almost impregnable to the assaults of native warriors armed with little more than arrows and shields, daggers and assegais. Further down in the valley, where aloes grow in fantastic shapes and kaffir-booms burst forth into magnificent red, stands the 'Temple'. This massive complex was probably the chief's palace, its general layout showing a remarkable resemblance to that of other Bantu royal headquarters such as that of the Barotse Paramount Chief on the Upper Zambezi. The king and his people lived in huts made of pole and daga, with floors of hardened earth which were partitioned off by walls, the 'Valley Ruins' probably also containing cattle kraals as well.

Having to hold their own against other black invaders from the north, the Rozwi, a dominant Karanga clan, developed a strong military monarchy, whose stability was further assured by their control of numerous gold mines, and by their wealth in cattle. The country was organized into a number of territorial fiefs under the control of great dignitaries whose rule was supported in the spiritual sphere by the priesthood of Mwari, the high-god of the Karanga. The Karanga traded in gold, and their commerce became even more important during the thirteenth and fourteenth centuries, by which time the town-dwelling communities along the East Coast may have become fully Islamized.[2] The port of Sofala became a major outlet for the gold trade of the interior. Arab merchants made their way inland, providing the Karanga with trade goods in return for gold, with the result that the precious metal acquired commercial value, and the Karanga monarch was able to pay his soldiers and followers with cloth and other commodities. In the fifteenth century the Karanga began to expand northwards, the new policy of conquest being influenced by many different political and economic factors which are now difficult to disentangle. Perhaps the Rozwi were urged on by Muslim traders, who now held a strong position inland, and who would have been likely to favour a strong kingdom, capable of making the country safe for the strangers' persons and purses;[3] perhaps Karanga political cohesion gave

---

[1] For the best summary of archaeological work see Summers, R. *Zimbabwe: a Rhodesian mystery.* Nelson, 1963

[2] Mathew, G. 'The east coast cultures' (in *Africa south*, v. 2, no. 2, Jan–Mar 1958, p. 59–62)

[3] See Abraham, D. P. 'Maramuca: an exercise in the combined use of Portuguese records and oral tradition' (in *Journal of African history*, v. 2, 1961, p. 211–225) which is also a most valuable contribution to methodology in the field of tribal history.

added confidence to the paramount; perhaps he wished to acquire new gold mines or more land for his growing population and their cattle. Another motive for expansion appears to have been the ever-present need for salt, a most precious commodity for an inland people—far removed from the coast—who laboriously recovered this essential substance from dung and reeds. The Shona people's own tradition has it that Mutota, one of the most outstanding Karanga monarchs of the fifteenth century, was greatly troubled with a shortage of salt. He sent out an ambassador who explored as far as the country south of the Zambezi and west of present-day Tete. The envoy returned, thoroughly satisfied with his intelligence mission, and brought Mutota a block of salt which he handed to his lord with the message 'Cease now from eating the droppings of goats', meaning that it would now no longer be necessary for the people of the Mambo, the Paramount Chief of the Rozwi, to extract salt from the ashes of goats' droppings. Mutota then led a great host northwards, which swept all resistance before it; the vanquished Tavara people of the north bestowed on their conqueror the title of 'Mwene Mutapa', meaning 'master of the ravaged land', which became a praise name, and later a hereditary title generally known as 'Monomotapa'.[1] According to native tradition Mutota shifted the focus of his kingdom to his new lands in the north, establishing his headquarters by the escarpment near the Chitako-Changonya Hill, east of Gota, and constructing a large solid stone fort down near the Utete river for the protection of his household.

Visitors possessed of enough patience to make their way down through the bush to the foot of the escarpment can still see the remains of his work, consisting of stone walls, all built of granite slabs, piled upon each other without mortar, the main stockade being scalloped, probably in order to accommodate round huts with their walls adjoining the stockade. Mutota had an excellent eye for country, and no one could have chosen a better site. A brown, friable *mopane* type of soil made things easy for the farmer; kaffir corn and similar crops would flourish, and there was no need for the women to hoe the soil before planting. Water was plentiful but the relatively sandy soil was reasonably well drained, preventing to some extent the formation of puddles and the consequent breeding of malarial mosquitoes on the same scale as would have been found further north. Good communications towards the Zambezi were assured, whilst in case of defeat the tribesmen always had the chance of retreating into the broken hill country to the south. The laminated granite slabs found in the area provided ideal building material.

Mutota wielded considerable power, and messengers from far-away

[1] Abraham, D. P. 'The Monomotapa dynasty' (in *NADA*, no. 36, 1959, p. 60–61)

districts would make their way down to his headquarters in the somewhat eerie escarpment country, where ghostly white 'fever trees' and grotesque baobabs grow amongst the *mopane*. Mutota, however, was troubled by plotting among his brothers whom he left in charge in the south, the size of his kingdom now probably outrunning the monarch's economic and administrative resources. In the end, force of circumstance reduced the southern areas of the kingdom to mere provincial status, the northern portion becoming the most important part of his dominions because of ease of access from the Zambezi tributaries, and it attracted numerous Arab merchants who set up trading posts along the Zambezi. Tradition has it that later on in the fifteenth century Matope, another strong monarch, initiated a vigorous policy of further conquest, which carried Karanga arms to the shores of the Indian Ocean, turning the kingdom of Monomotapa into an empire over many other tribes, who were allowed to keep their own chiefs but were obliged to forward tribute. In exchange the king's subjects received protection from their enemies, as well as gifts; the royal court perhaps acted as the centre of a vast system of tributary exchange which functioned without money.[1] A later Portuguese observer thus wrote that whenever the Monomotapa wanted gold he sent cattle to his people who divided the beasts amongst themselves according to the labour accomplished and the hours worked.

The Monomotapas in time managed to build up a great tribal confederacy. Hoe-cultivation and small-scale industries like weaving, gold mining, pottery and the production of ironware built up a surplus; trade in luxury goods enhanced the country's wealth. As time went on, powerful men could afford richer clothes, finer ornaments and better weapons than their followers, whilst warfare may have accentuated incipient social differences. The king himself used great nobles in his household which formed the nucleus of a rudimentary state organization. He also received assistance from a body of tribal intellectuals, part royal spirit mediums and part official historians, who were supposed to voice the will of ancestral kings, and maintain the traditions of their race. There was too a host of office bearers, described by a Portuguese chronicler of the sixteenth century as the governor of the kingdoms, the captain-general, the chief major-domo, the chief musician, the captain-general of the vanguard in wartime, the king's right hand, the chief wizard, the king's doorkeeper, 'and numerous other officers of lower rank whom it would be unending and tedious to enumerate.' All these dignitaries held land and vassals, but

---

[1] For what was perhaps a parallel situation see the works of M. Gluckman on the Barotse, especially his *Economy of the central Barotse plain* (Rhodes-Livingstone paper no. 7, 1941) and *Essays on Lozi and Lozi royal property* (Rhodes-Livingstone paper no. 10, 1943)

they resided at the King's court of which a vivid description survives from the sixteenth century:

'The dwelling in which the monomotapa resides is very large, and is composed of many houses surrounded by a great wooden fence, within which there are three dwellings, one for his own person, one for the queen, and another for his servants who wait upon him within doors. There are three doors opening upon a great court-yard, one for the service of the queen, beyond which no man may pass, but only women, another for his kitchen, only entered by his cooks, who are two young men from among the principal lords of his kingdom, his relations in whom he has most confidence, and the lads who serve in the kitchen, who are also nobles between fifteen and twenty years of age. These are also employed to lay the food when the king wishes to eat, which they spread upon the ground, upon a carpet or mat, with muslin extended above, and many different kinds of meat are set before him, all roasted or boiled, such as hens, pigeons, partridges, capons, sheep, venison, hares, rabbits, cows, rats, and other game, of which, after the king has eaten a portion is given to some of his servants who are always provided from his table.

'The third door leads to the king's apartments, which none may enter but the young nobles who serve him within doors, who are all from fifteen to twenty years of age and are called *massacoriras*, and are the sons of the nobles of his kingdoms and have their captain who looks after and commands them. When they are twenty years of age, and upwards, they are withdrawn from the service of the king within doors, and others are put in their place. The reason of this is that the king will not be served by those who know a woman, but only by these youths, who are enjoined to observe chastity as long as they serve the king, and if any one is found guilty of the opposite vice he is severely punished and expelled from the king's service. Thus when they reach the age of twenty they render out-door service, and live out of the palace; they are then called *maueiros,* and the king gives them lands from which to subsist. These have also their captain, and they continue in this service for several years. Afterwards they are called *chureiros*, and under this name they serve as ambassadors, and in such posts and offices as the king gives to their charge, until lands and large houses fall vacant, of which he makes them lords, either of such as belonged to their fathers or by virtue of new grants.'[1]

Local government remained in the hands of minor chiefs and headmen whose position probably depended on their ability to attract followers

[1] Bocarro, A. 'Extracts from the decade . . . of the performances of the Portuguese in the East' (in Theal, G. M., ed., *Records of south-eastern Africa.* . . . Cape Town, The Government of the Cape Colony, 1896–1905, v. 3, p. 356–357)

through gifts of food. As a contemporary Portuguese observer put it:

'The greater part of this Kaffraria is governed by fumos and petty rulers, and though it has powerful kings whom it obeys, it has nevertheless these fumos and headmen by whom the people are governed. The fumos near Sena are Kaffirs, natives of the country, and very often the lowest are elected to this dignity. Most of them are forced against their will to accept the office, for when one has cows, millet, or naqueny which he can give them and spend, they elect him fumo, and his dignity lasts as long as he has anything to spend. When they have eaten up his property, they cast him out of the office, and pre-eminence is the most that they give him.'[1]

The life of the ordinary people went on in much the same way as that of African communities in later days. Millet formed the nation's staple food as well as palm oil 'which is a penance to those who are not accustomed to its use', but the Africans also liked to eat fowls, capons and mutton, as well as game which was then plentiful.

African society developed a material culture of its own; builders and smiths, weavers and potters, acquired considerable skill; but the nation depended entirely on the spoken word to pass on its traditions and accumulated experience; writing remained unknown, and the African never learned how to translate his thoughts into symbols engraved on stone or penned on papyrus. At the same time the villagers relied entirely on human muscles which formed their sole source of power. The use of the wheel was not known. No draught animals were used, neither were ploughs or carts, with the result that indigenous cultivators had to rely on hoes, and could produce but a limited surplus of food. The tribesmen could only keep alive by a rigidly laid out system of village co-operation; and religion and custom alike upheld a society where communal cohesion stood out as the supreme good. The whole tenor of society accordingly remained extremely conservative and men looked askance at innovations. As Father Monclaro, a somewhat prejudiced Portuguese observer put it:

'Their only houses are small straw huts plastered with clay, resembling round dove-cotes. The land is sterile for the most part, but its sterility does not equal their sloth, for even on the well watered plains, which they call *antevaras*, they sow very little, and if there is one among them who is more diligent and a better husbandman, and therefore reaps a fresh crop of millet and has a larger store of provisions, they immediately falsely accuse him of all kinds of crimes, as an excuse to take it from him and eat it,

[1] Monclaro, Fr. 'Account of the journey made by the fathers of the company of Jesus with Francisco Barreto in the conquest of Monomotapa in the year 1569' (in Theal, G. M., ed. *Records of south-eastern Africa. . . .* Cape Town, The Government of the Cape Colony, 1896–1905, v. 3, p. 227)

saying why should he have more millet than another? Never attributing it to his greater industry and diligence; and very often they kill him and eat all his provisions. It is the same with cattle, and this is the cause of the scarcity. They are not provident, but quickly waste and consume the new crops in feasts and drinking.

'They do not make use of any kind of animal for labour, and therefore many came to Sena, where we were, and showed much surprise and laughed heartily when they saw the oxen at the plough or drawing carts full of stones for the fort. They dig the earth with small hoes, and in the furrows and little trenches they throw the millet or other seed they are to sow and cover it lightly with earth; and it yields a good crop.'[1]

African religion corresponded to this way of life. Bantu thinkers now recognized a supreme God; but there was no formalized theology, and tribal life was thought to be influenced rather by the ancestral spirits who might either help their descendants or punish them for their sins, and kept up a never-ending interest in the affairs of the village. There was a whole pantheon of regional or tribal deities; the Bantu considered that the ever-present dangers of the material world were duplicated by threats of a supernatural order which, like the material ones, could only be resisted by co-operative means. Misfortunes not otherwise explicable in rational terms were explained in terms of witchcraft or sorcery, and supposed offenders cruelly punished, so much so that when Monomotapa once fell sick it was said, probably with some exaggeration, that he put four hundred wives to death for casting spells on him.

Within these limits of thought and technology Bantu cultures showed considerable flexibility, and the various African communities skilfully adapted their way of life to the differing conditions which they encountered. The Zimbabwe builders were of course not the only black-skinned people to develop a fairly complex way of life, the Eastern Highlands (especially Inyanga) in time became too the scene of another culture, which is still being investigated by archaeologists today. Originally the country was inhabited by Stone Age hunters, but perhaps some time at the end of the Later Stone Age immigrants came into the area with a knowledge of how to use iron, and their pottery has become mixed up in the upper levels of several rock shelters with tools of Later Stone Age people. Not much is known about these newcomers, except that they made fine pottery and practised agriculture, peacefully intermarrying with the local Bushmen. According to one theory, the so-called Ziwa culture was probably fairly short-lived and may have come to an end as the result of drought and soil exhaustion which caused people to leave the district.

[1] Monclaro, Fr. 'Account of the journey . . .', *op. cit*, p. 231

Later on, perhaps towards the end of the fifteenth century, Bantu refugees from the north were driven on to the inhospitable mountains of Inyanga to seek safety from their enemies. The settlers probably lost their cattle, but appear to have kept sheep, pigs or goats, and patiently made a living by cultivating the harsh soil on the windswept uplands, taking refuge in their strongholds whenever an enemy approached. As the country became more peaceful these highlanders may have moved down to the western side of the Inyangani range where conditions were more pleasant, but they nevertheless still had to struggle hard, having to clear an immense number of stones from their fields. But by now the uplanders were expert stone builders who had learned, possibly under Arab influence, how to terrace the hillsides, construct anti-erosion works, put up stone fortifications and grain stores, and they had developed an extraordinary skill in making walls without mortar. They cultivated sorghum, millet and pulses, and kept animals which were driven overnight into stone pens, now fancifully described as 'slave pits'. Their culture possibly flourished some time between the fifteenth and the end of the seventeenth century; but much more work still remains to be done on the early history of these and other Bantu peoples of Southern Rhodesia.[1]

II

The Portuguese in East Africa from the sixteenth to the eighteenth centuries

Whilst the Monomotapa's state was becoming a power in South Central Africa, Portuguese seafarers were laying the foundations of one of the world's greatest maritime empires. In the middle of the thirteenth century Portugal freed herself from Moorish domination and developed a strong national state as well as a commercial bourgoisie. With the advent of the House of Aviz at the end of the fourteenth century the merchants gained powerful champions, and in 1415 Portugal launched a career of African conquest, when a Christian army captured Ceuta from the Moors, to gain a foothold on the northern shore of the Continent. Portugal's greatest figure in this early stage of expansion was Prince Henry the Navigator, who himself took a leading part in the conquest of Ceuta. During this campaign Henry's attention was probably drawn to the possibilities of trade and expansion in Africa, and he may also have gathered information

---

[1] See Summers, R. *Inyanga: prehistoric settlements in Southern Rhodesia.* Cambridge University Press, 1958

about the lucrative traffic in gold and slaves that Muslim merchants were carrying on between the ports of North Africa and the Niger region of Africa across the Sahara. Henry was also anxious to extend the boundaries of the Christian faith; and the Prince's residence at Sagres in time became the headquarters of Portuguese maritime enterprise and something of a great geographical research institution. Here the best charts were assembled, and expert navigators and map-makers advised on the task of exploration, the Iberian peoples taking over a rich scientific heritage previously accumulated by Italian, Jewish and Arab scholars.

Henry pushed exploration nearly as far as Sierra Leone in West Africa; and after his death in 1460 his enterprise was continued as a national undertaking under the Portuguese crown. The Portuguese were playing for high stakes. By sending their ships down the South Atlantic, they hoped to secure a direct share in the trans-Saharan gold trade and cut out their Muslim enemies. In addition they hoped to outflank the Moors by making alliances with non-Islamic rulers, including the Christian emperor of Abyssinia. The Portuguese moreover were determined to extend the boundaries of Catholicism and save the souls of unbelievers, their missionary and political ambitions going hand in hand. As a long-term objective, they hoped to find a sea route to India and gain direct access to the rich spice trade of the East, which meant that Christians would no longer have to deal through Muslim middlemen in the Near East.

Portuguese explorers succeeded brilliantly in this venture. In 1488 Bartolomeu Dias rounded the Cape into the Indian Ocean, and proved that Africa's southern extension did indeed possess a limit, instead of extending—as some feared—right to the Antarctic regions, forming one vast insurmountable barrier. Whilst Dias was unlocking the door to the Indian Ocean, another outstanding Portuguese explorer, Pedro da Covilhã, set out to the island of Rhodes, and from there to Egypt, to find out more about the northern route. Covilhã reached Calicut in India; between 1488 and 1496 he explored East Africa, getting as far as Sofala; later on he visited Abyssinia where he died. The voyages of these two travellers still left, however, a considerable gap, and after a lengthy delay, Vasco da Gama set out in 1497 with a fleet of four little vessels to complete their work. Da Gama successfully sailed round Africa, and on 20 May 1498, perhaps the most important date in the history of Portugal, he dropped anchor at Calicut, a centre of the Indian spice trade.

After da Gama's return, the Portuguese decided to consolidate their gains, and in 1505 a great fleet set out from the Tagus to make Lusitanian power supreme in the Indian Ocean. Trade with the Indies was of course the first objective; but the East African coast also played a part in these designs. The Indian Ocean formed a commercial unit, and merchants from as far afield as Arabia, Persia, India and China visited the eastern shores of Africa. The Portuguese also needed refreshment and refitting stations on their way to the east, whilst the gold trade of Sofala was supposed to be of fabulous value. In 1505 the Portuguese established themselves at Sofala, south of the modern port of Beira; a few years later the lonely little post contained a small community of 62 people, a microcosm of Portuguese colonial society, comprising soldiers and craftsmen as well as a chaplain, physician and 'infirmarian', eleven *degredados* (convicts) and thirteen slaves, some of whom served as interpreters and others as building workers. In time a massive fort went up to dominate the gateway to the east. The encroaching sea now covers the ruins of this stronghold, but when the tide goes out the remnants of powerful stone walls stand out in sodden sand and mud against a low shore, about half a mile away, where mangrove swamps and coconut palms still make the same sort of picture which Portuguese navigators saw four hundred years ago. Sofala became an important stepping stone and a centre of the gold trade to India, as well as a base for the exploration of the interior. In 1507 the Portuguese seized control of Mozambique and two years later gained a crushing victory over a Mohammedan fleet off Diu which assured the Portuguese of naval supremacy in the Indian Ocean; the rulers of Egypt and later of Turkey were gravely hampered in their efforts to build fleets for service against the infidels by the lack of timber on the shores of the Red Sea and the Persian Gulf. To make matters worse for the Mohammedans, the trading cities on the East Coast, largely inhabited by islamized East Africans of mixed Bantu and Arab, or, as in the case of Kilwa, of Shirazi descent, were at odds amongst themselves. Malindi and Mombasa especially carried on constant feuds and Malindi threw in its lot with the Portuguese. The coastal city-states by that time lacked political cohesion; and in addition they competed with each other commercially. The Swahili towns, which obtained slaves, ivory and gold from the Bantu of the interior in exchange for beads, cloth and other commodities, formed part of a 'triangle' of trade, which involved the Red Sea and Persian Gulf on the one side, and Gujerat, Malabar and Coromandel on the other side of the Indian Ocean. They were civilized communities, little inferior in the arts of peace to the Portuguese; but it seems likely that by the time Christian fleets were establishing their power in the Indian Ocean, Swahili prosperity was already in decline, partly as the result of internecine fighting, partly because of the disorders occasioned inland by Zimba and Galla invasions.[1]

[1] Based on Boxer, C. R., and Azevedo, C. de. *Fort Jesus and the Portuguese in Mombasa, 1593–1729*. London, Hollis and Carter, 1960

But the Portuguese also began to meet frustration. The garrison and fort at Sofala were expensive to maintain, and the port did not develop into a great centre of the gold trade, as the Portuguese hoped it would. Few Africans from inland made their way down to the port; the transit trade largely remained in the hands of Mohammedan merchants who were familiar with the bush paths, knew the ways of Bantu chieftains, and who probably—through the centuries—had developed a greater resistance to malaria and other tropical diseases than Portuguese immigrants. Mohammedan traders thus continued to run up the Zambezi with goods of non-Portuguese provenance, at the same time assuring the people of the interior that the Christians had raised the price of cloth and beads, a charge which was certainly true, though in all probability the Arabs passed on a disproportionately large share of the rise in prices to their African customers.[1]

To make matters worse the interior was shaken by disorder and by the time the Portuguese arrived the gold trade was already declining. The periphery of the Karanga empire was controlled by sons and other relatives of the king who conquered outlying areas, but would not willingly submit to the monarch's orders. The Monomotapa empire may also have suffered from the fact that the various provinces remained economically undifferentiated and therefore lacked any economic ties to hold them together, whilst the Portuguese occupation of the coast damaged the Mohammedans' elaborate commercial network. To make matters worse, most of Monomotapa Matope's sons appear to have been weak and unfitted to exercise the great responsibilities bequeathed to them by their father. However, a younger son, born of a lowly wife, inherited his father's ability. Under Matope this younger son, Changa, was first appointed to the key office of supervisor over the royal herds, and later placed in charge of the central and southern provinces. On his father's death, towards the end of the fifteenth century, Changa further extended his power and assumed the Arab title of Amir, the names 'Changa' and 'Amir' fusing into 'Changamire' which itself became a title. In the end Changamire proclaimed himself king of the southern and central provinces, styling his new state 'Urozwi' to accentuate its separation from the Monomotapa.[2] The Monomotapas for their part failed to re-establish their old authority in the south; and long-drawn out warfare weakened both parties.

The Portuguese decided to send out an emissary to establish direct contacts with the Monomotapa, and to find out more about the mineral and agricultural resources of the interior, hoping that they might purchase

[1] Axelson, E. *South-East Africa, 1488–1530.* London, Longmans, Green and co., 1940
[2] See Abraham, D. P. 'The early political history of the Kingdom of Mwene-Mutapa, 850–1589' (in *Historians in tropical Africa: proceedings of the Leverhulme inter-collegiate history conference held at the University College of Rhodesia and Nyasaland.* Salisbury, The College, 1962, p. 61–91)

directly the gold which was being diverted to Kilwa through the trading centres established by Moorish merchants along the Zambezi. The man chosen for this important task was Antonio Fernandes, Southern Rhodesia's first white explorer. Information about this valiant frontiersman is very scanty; but scholars believe that he may have been a ship's carpenter as well as a *degredado*, that is to say a felon, condemned to death, and given the alternative of service overseas, the sort of person whom the Portuguese were wont to employ on dangerous missions of this kind. Fernandes presumably could neither read nor write, but as an explorer showed himself a man of extraordinary courage and resource. He penetrated over five hundred miles as the crow flies into the unknown interior, covering a wide area, and supplied the Portuguese with accurate, firsthand information about conditions there. Fernandes started off from Sofala some time at the beginning of the second decade of the sixteenth century, and a report of his journey has come down to us; unfortunately it is confined to laconic notes of the kind that 'the king of Embya is distant from the king of Quytomgue a journey of four days, and he has nothing there except banditry.' The details of Fernandes' route are not quite certain, and modern scholars have worked out two versions which differ considerably from each other.[1] Both agree however that Fernandes made his way through the country where Penhalonga now stands, and that he reached 'Embire', which is 'a fortress of the king of Monomotapa, which he is now making of stone without mortar which is called Camhanhaya, and where he always is. . . . And from there onwards they enter into the kingdom of Monomotapa which is the source of the gold of all this land. And the latter is the chief king of all these. And all obey him from Monomotapa to Sofala'.[2]

Fernandes' expedition was an astonishing feat; and 'furunanda', the white-skinned stranger from the coast, appears to have made quite an impression on the Monomotapa's people. But all the same the Portuguese derived little benefit from the *degredado*'s enterprise. Sporadic fighting continued inland, and Nyamunda (Inhamunda), an indigenous chief in league with Changamire, stopped Portuguese caravans from reaching Monomotapa. The Portuguese for a time turned their attention to Madagascar, but later on in the sixteenth century a new attack was made on the

[1] See Tracey, H. *Antonio Fernandes: descobridor do Monomotapa, 1514–1515.* Lourenço Marques, Arquivo histórico de Moçambique, 1940. This version has been accepted by Axelson, E. in *South-East Africa, 1488–1530.* London, Longmans, Green and co., 1940. Another interpretation is that of Godlonton, W. A. 'The journeys of Antonio Fernandes . . .' (in Rhodesia Scientific Association. *Proceedings and transactions*, v. 40, April 1945, p. 71–103). Godlonton supplies a map showing both routes. The dates of these journeys are not quite clear, the most probable being the period 1509–1512

[2] Quoted from an undated report, translated by E. Axelson, in Godlonton, W. A. 'The journeys of Antonio Fernandes', *op. cit*, p. 72–75

far interior—this time with spiritual arms. The mission was entrusted to Father Gonçalo da Silveira, a Portuguese Jesuit of noble ancestry and outstanding personality, and a message was sent to the Monomotapa that a white *kasisi* (priest) wished to see the king, and sprinkle some special water on his head as a protective medicine. The message was passed on to the monarch by Antonio Caiado, a Portuguese living at the king's court near the west bank of the Utete; and Silveira was permitted to enter the country. He apparently made a great impression on Nogomo Mupunza-gutu, the young king, who was still unmarried and was assisted in the government by his mother, a Chiuyu.

The Monomotapa marvelled at the stranger who wanted neither gold, cattle nor servants, and received him in his private sanctum, an unheard-of honour. The king was further impressed by the picture of a fair European woman arrayed in splendid clothes, which the priest carried about with him, and asked to be allowed to meet this lady. Silveira then explained to the monarch that this was the Virgin Mary, the Mother of God, and presented her picture to the king. The story then goes that for four or five nights in succession the Monomotapa saw the beautiful lady with a halo round her head, speaking to him in a strange language with an expression of great sweetness. The king and his mother soon afterwards accepted baptism, their example being followed by several hundred of his lords who brought gifts of provisions, which Silveira distributed amongst the people. The priest's success, however, deeply alarmed the powerful Mohammedan party at the court whose leader came from Mozambique, for they feared Christian penetration both on commercial and religious grounds, and quickly got to work on the young king. The stranger, they argued, was sent by the Governor of India and the Captain of Sofala to spy out the land, so that they might later come in and seize the kingdom. The *kasisi*'s show of friendship was false, they said, and in reality he planned to destroy the nation by pouring water over the heads of its great men and uttering magical spells. These arguments proved only too convincing, and in 1561 Silveira was strangled, the first well-documented martyr to die for the Christian faith in South Central Africa.[1]

The death of Silveira provided the Portuguese with a perfect excuse for an expedition inland. The venture was entrusted to Francisco Barreto, a veteran who had previously gained wide experience as a general of galleys, a member of the King's Council, and as a Governor in India. The mission was accompanied by four Jesuits, including Father Monclaro who acted as

---

[1] The Silveira literature is considerable. The account given above is taken from the reconstruction in Abraham, D. P. 'The early political history of the Kingdom of Mwene Mutapa, 850–1589', *op. cit.*

its chronicler and explained that the Portuguese aimed at extending the Gospel's sway, increasing their revenue, and avenging the missionary's death. In 1569 a sizeable expedition set out from Lisbon amidst prayers and the warlike blare of trumpets, bound for East Africa. The little fleet first sailed to Brazil, following the customary route, and then rounded the Cape of Good Hope, casting anchor at Mozambique. Barreto's force was employed first of all in strengthening Portuguese influence on the East Coast itself, and later struck inland. The commander-in-chief, an experienced soldier, originally intended to go to Sofala and cross the Mashonaland plateau. But unfortunately Monclaro persuaded the Portuguese to take the unhealthy route up the Zambezi, the change of plan causing a major disaster. Slowly going upstream through the malaria-ridden river valley, the Portuguese reached Sena which was then ruled by a Moorish vassal of the Monomotapa; but the Christians suffered badly from sickness, and became convinced that the accursed infidels were secretly poisoning men and beasts alike. The Portuguese arrested several leading Mohammedans and put them to death under the most excruciating tortures; some were impaled, others were tied to the tops of trees and torn asunder, others were shot or hacked to pieces with hatchets. From Sena, Barreto sent an embassy to the Monomotapa who apparently welcomed the idea that the Portuguese would fight the Mongazes, a turbulent people living near the lower Zambezi who constantly warred against the Karanga. In 1572 Barreto set out from Sena on the long westward trek into the interior, accompanied by some 560 men on foot, 23 horsemen, and a few gunners with five or six pieces of artillery, his transport largely depending on donkeys. His army, however, was reduced by fever and the men were sweating in the tropical heat underneath the weight of their armour. Worse still, the unhealthy climate prevented the extensive employment of horses which played such an important part in giving victory to Spanish conquistadores over their Indian enemies in Central and South America, whilst the lack of draught animals made their supply problems difficult. Nevertheless the Portuguese gave an excellent account of themselves and utterly crushed a Mongaze army which tried to stop their advance.

Further negotiations then ensued with the Monomotapa. The Karanga monarch at the time still claimed suzerainty over the provinces of Butua and Manica, but realized that he would find great difficulties in controlling the turbulent tribes on the lower Zambezi. What was more, he had repented of his former anti-Christian policy, his country having been struck down by a terrible pestilence after Silveira's death. The Monomotapa's ambassadors promised extensive concessions; the Karanga would follow a policy of friendship towards the Portuguese; they would clear away all 'briars' or thorns in the way of trade, and surrender some of their gold-mines as well as part of their kingdom. Barreto, however, met with enormous logistical and health problems; worn out with care, he died of fever. Command of the expedition was taken over by Vasco Fernandes Homem, who not being influenced by Monclaro's ideas, refitted at Mozambique and went overland as far as Manica without, however, reaching Butua. Nevertheless the Portuguese gained a firm trading position inland where they prevented the further expansion of Mohammedan culture and commerce and established a tight hold over several main marketing centres. The nearest of these was Luanze, which lay south of the Mazoe on the Southern Rhodesian side of the border with Mozambique. A second was called Bocuto and was situated further up the Mazoe, beyond its junction with the Nyadiri. A third, Massapa, was close to the modern Mount Darwin, the Portuguese being forbidden to climb the hill itself. The Portuguese appointed a captain, who ruled over Massapa, the most important of them all, and exercised jurisdiction over all Africans visiting the settlement, as well as over all Portuguese traders travelling to the Monomotapa's country. No Portuguese was allowed to pass beyond Massapa without the permission of the Karanga monarch or of his 'Captain of the Gates', who collected on the Monomotapa's behalf one roll of cloth in twenty from all merchants who came to buy gold. The Portuguese traded with Chicoa, above the Kebrabasa Rapids, but there was little traffic northwards across the Zambezi, where fierce cannibal tribes, including the formidable Zimba, had established themselves. The Zambezi and its southern tributaries formed the main waterway inland, but in addition the Portuguese also used the route through Uteve, paying a transit duty of one roll of cloth in twenty in order to be allowed to make their way to the Manica, who lived around modern Macequece and Umtali, their chief being known as Chicanga. They also produced gold, but their miners met with many difficulties, having to sink shafts and drive galleries, which—in the absence of effective timbering—led to many difficulties, whilst their gold was inferior in quality to the alluvial variety.[1]

Despite their efforts the Portuguese met with little permanent success inland. They faced disease and distance, the two great obstacles confronting any invader of the interior of Africa. The Portuguese could not rival the Arabs as inland traders. Lacking the institution of polygamy, they could not so easily assimilate themselves to African ways, and they may also have insisted on a higher rate of profit from the gold trade than their Mohammedan competitors. Unlike the Arabs the Portuguese tried to

[1] See Axelson, E. *Portuguese in south-east Africa, 1600–1700.* Johannesburg, Witwatersrand University Press, 1960; especially the sketch map facing p. 22

become landowners, though their concept of private land ownership was at variance with Bantu custom; in addition they also seem to have misunderstood the political structure of the Karanga kingdom, which they regarded as a centralized feudal monarchy.

Further the Portuguese lacked men, for Portugal was only a small kingdom and the very vastness of her empire, stretching from India to Brazil, imposed an enormous strain on the small population of the motherland. To make matters worse, Portugal in 1580 came herself under Spanish rule, and only regained her independence sixty years later, after having been dragged into unprofitable warfare designed to further the aims of Hapsburg grand policy in Europe, whilst English and Dutch sailors began to challenge Portugal's position in the Indian Ocean. The country's East African possessions were controlled from far-away India, the senior officials having to report to headquarters at Goa. The local administration suffered further from an unsatisfactory system of making appointments, whereby captaincies were granted as favours to deserving noblemen who regarded their posts as financial investments for what they could make out of them. A good deal of money was of course made in the African trade, but very little reached the royal treasury, as senior civil servants evaded the royal monopoly of the gold trade, and some made fortunes on their own account.

The interior in any case was no Eldorado, even though imaginative writers would often exaggerate its riches and speak of Central Africa as King Solomon's long-lost Ophir. Some best-sellers of the day would depict the Monomotapa as a magnificent emperor, arrayed in gorgeous clothes, inhabiting splendid palaces and commanding enormous riches. But these were but fables, and João dos Santos, a Dominican who visited the inland regions towards the end of the sixteenth century, thus wrote with scorn of current stories about black Amazons and great wealth, and described the Monomotapa in more sober fashion as a Bantu Paramount Chief of moderate power, who could no longer control his outlying provinces.

The indigenous economy as a whole was largely self-sufficient; Africans would only buy a limited number of luxury goods and occasional supplies of food to carry them over a famine, which meant that the Bantu lacked incentives to produce gold steadily in predictable quantities. As a disgusted Portuguese put it, in language strongly reminiscent of the terms later used by Victorian writers, the natives were 'so lazy and given to an easy life that they will not exert themselves to seek gold unless they are constrained by necessity for want of clothes or provisions, which are not wanting in the land, for it abounds with them, namely millet, some rice,

c

many vegetables, large and small cattle, and many hens. The land abounds with rivers of good water, and the greater number of the Kaffirs are inclined to agricultural and pastoral pursuits, in which their riches consist'.[1]

From the military point of view, the Monomotapa faced serious problems; for his forces, armed with bows and arrows, spears and knobkerries, possessed no superiority of a technical or tactical kind over those of his opponents; and now that the empire was weakening, the monarch began to call on the Portuguese with their firearms to redress the balance. Thus in the beginning of the seventeenth century Gatsi Rusere, the reigning king, asked for Portuguese assistance against the chief of the Manyika, who lived near where Umtali now stands. The white man's arquebus proved invincible, but further serious troubles broke out, and in 1607 the Monomotapa promised to make over all the mines in his kingdom to the Portuguese in return for military aid. At the same time he agreed that several of his sons should be baptized and brought up as Christians. Further fighting followed; the Portuguese intervened again, and their help probably prevented the complete disintegration of the kingdom.

The Portuguese might have made more of these successes but they appointed a most incompetent man, D. Estevão de Ataide, who provoked a quarrel with the Monomotapa by refusing to pay him his accustomed share of the revenue from the silver mines exploited by the Portuguese. There was further bloodshed, and the Portuguese abandoned Massapa, leaving the whole country up in arms against them. Ataide then tried to restore the situation by force of arms, but stopped his first attempt when news was received of a Dutch expedition into the Indian Ocean. Later on he made preparations for a second venture inland, but this again came to naught, for in 1613 he received letters recalling him to Portugal in disgrace.

Ataide's successor, Diogo Simoes Madeira, first of all had to deal with Chombe, a local chief living near Sena who rebelled against Portuguese rule, and made history by equipping his men with European firearms, with which he successfully resisted the Portuguese for several months. Madeira then pushed on to Tete and in 1614 set off with about a hundred Portuguese and mulatto soldiers to reach the silver mines at Chicoa on the Zambezi, east of where Feira stands today. Gatsi Rusere, however, showed little willingness to surrender the mine. He became further incensed with the Portuguese when they refused to pay him his accustomed revenue, and aggravated their offence by receiving a rebellious son of his, and by executing the son of an important local chief. The Christians

---

[1] Bocarro, A. 'Extracts from the decade . . . of the performances of the Portuguese in the East' (in Theal, G. M., ed. *Records of south-eastern Africa.* . . . Cape Town, The Government of the Cape Colony, 1896–1905, v. 3, p. 355)

managed to defeat an attacking Karanga force, and in 1615 discovered a valuable silver deposit. But fever, lack of provisions and the hostility of local Africans played havoc with Madeira's plans; appeals to the Viceroy of India remained unanswered, and Madeira then decided to send a trusted nobleman by the name of Gaspar Bocarro by land to East Africa intending to by-pass Mozambique where the captain was hostile to Madeira's cause, with the intention that Bocarro should make his way to Lisbon through the Middle East. Bocarro left Tete in 1616, travelled through the Maravi country past Lake Nyasa, and finally made his way to Kilwa. Bocarro could not, however, complete his journey; and the Portuguese in East Africa suffered further from the presence of hostile Dutch and English vessels in the Indian Ocean. To make matters worse, the local Portuguese dignitaries quarrelled bitterly amongst themselves, and the Monomotapa once more took up arms, sending his men to raid as far as Tete.

In the meantime another emissary reached Lisbon from Africa bringing with him a sample of silver from Chicoa, and the Portuguese then decided on yet another expedition to replenish their impoverished treasury. D. Nuño Alvares Pereira was put in charge of the venture, and by 1619 the new commander was at Tete in communication with the Monomotapa. But Pereira too quarrelled with his subordinates as well as with the Karanga monarch. By this time a new Monomotapa, Nyambo Kaparavidze, had mounted the throne, and when the Portuguese failed to pay the expected revenue, the Makaranga decided on war and attacked the Portuguese marketing centres in the country. The local settlers, however, resisted bravely, and in 1629 a Portuguese force advanced inland, put the Karanga army to flight, and installed a new Monomotapa, by the name of Mavura Mhande, who promised to acknowledge Portuguese suzerainty, pay a regular tribute, allow the Portuguese to trade freely, and expel all Arabs from his kingdom.

The Portuguese followed up their success by building a church at the Monomotapa's court, close to the Kadzi river at the foot of the escarpment north of Sipolilo. Mavura accepted baptism; but the economic foundations of Portuguese power were cracked. Commerce languished in the interior where powerful Portuguese estate owners maintained their own private armies, exercised an independent jurisdiction, and waged wars against each other in the manner of independent little monarchs. The local administration found itself without funds; and money even had to be sent from Goa to Mozambique. Poor administration, the appointment of unsuitable officials and the absence of any effective central control all contributed to a major African rising. Portuguese traders and their followers were slaughtered, and even Quelimane itself came under siege.

Nyambo Kapararidze, the leader of the anti-Portuguese faction, effectively wiped out Lusitanian influence and captured two friars, who both suffered martyrdom; one of them, Luis do Espírito Santo, was tied to a tree and killed with assegais, whilst his wounded colleague, João da Trinidade, was hurled over a cliff. Some 300 to 400 Portuguese and some 6,000 Africans were killed, the Christians suffering the greatest military disaster that had as yet befallen them in South-East Africa.

News of the rising reached Mozambique in 1631. The position seemed desperate, for in the meantime Mombasa had also revolted; there was serious trouble in Ceylon, whilst the Portuguese found such difficulties in manning their eastern squadrons that they were forced to employ Canarin sailors. Nevertheless the Portuguese reacted vigorously and in 1632 Diego de Sousa de Meneses marched inland with 300 arquebusiers strengthened by local levies. Kapararidze's army suffered a crushing defeat; the trading centres were re-opened, and trade restored. The Portuguese authorities then seriously discussed a major European settlement scheme, whereby they hoped to exploit the country's mineral resources more effectively. The interior was described as healthy and fertile, and if only 2,000 colonists could be planted inland the country would be made safe, and neither Netherlander nor native would ever dare challenge Lusitanian power. Settlement, however, required a stable economic foundation which was lacking, as the reputed riches of the interior could not be found, and lack of manpower crippled Portuguese strength even in India itself, with the result that in 1637 the project had to be abandoned.

By this time the Portuguese colonists, both along the coast and in the interior, were becoming almost impossible to control. In the Monomotapa's country white traders built up their own private armies, supplied with imported firearms; and the king could maintain no kind of authority over these semi-independent dignitaries; the Karanga became even more disaffected with the result that mining declined further. After Mavura's death in 1652 the Dominicans in the country managed to get Mavura's son, Siti Kazurukumusapa, to accept the crown and become a Christian. News of the Monomotapa's conversion caused great joy in Lisbon. At Rome the Master-General of the Dominican Order caused a special service to be held and had an account of the baptism engraved on a bronze plate in the Latin tongue. One of the chief's sons adopted the name of Miguel, entered the Dominican order and in 1670 received the diploma of Master in Theology, subsequently renouncing his worldly position and dying as vicar of the convent of Santa Barbara in Goa. But the Portuguese proved incapable of following up these ecclesiastical successes, despite the efforts of a few forceful men like Francisco da Trinidade, a friar who brought five associates with him, one of whom was stationed with the Monomotapa himself, a second at Massapa and a third at Quiteve. Da Trinidade mainly resided at Tete and became an outstanding Bantu linguist, translating several sacred works into the local African tongue. The Dominicans continued to produce some able men, but the spirit of languor which paralysed so much of Portuguese society as a whole also affected the friars, many of whose inland stations were destroyed in the course of tribal fighting.

The political position of the Portuguese likewise remained bad. Earlier on in the seventeenth century the Portuguese had suffered a number of serious defeats at the hands of Muslim enemies in the Indian Ocean. In 1650 the Arabs of Oman captured Muscat from the Portuguese, and then almost at once responded to appeals from fellow Muslims on the East Coast to free them from Christian rule. The Portuguese were put on the defensive and in 1698 Mombasa fell to the Arabs, a major blow to Portuguese power in the region. Things went no better for the Portuguese in the Karanga country. From the 1680's onwards the Changamire dynasty began to expand its power northwards from Urowzwi and the Portuguese suffered one blow after another. In 1693 Changamire's forces attacked Dambarara; all Portuguese and Indian traders at the trading post were killed, the tribesmen disinterring the bones of the dead to grind them into a powerful medicine, as well as flaying several Portuguese corpses and displaying their skins at the head of their army. Portuguese and Indian refugees retreated to a fort near the Monomotapa's court, but soon had to abandon it, whilst Changamire's warriors overran the remainder of the Karanga country, raiding to the very gates of Tete. The Monomotapa was left with a sorry remnant of his empire, over which the Portuguese continued to wield some influence, but effective power remained with the Changamires, and Portuguese inland trade dwindled to very small proportions. Their political power in the interior remained largely confined to the lower Zambezi valley, where Sena remained the capital of the rivers, and merchants in Zumbo still occasionally despatched trading caravans. The whites still managed to exercise some control over the chiefs of Manica, but the 'fairs' in Karanga country remained closed, and Portuguese power inland could not be effectively restored. Gone was Portugal's precious commerce with the East Indies, where Dutch merchants now garnered the richest profits. The mother country was exhausted by a lengthy war with Spain. What energies were left turned to Brazil whose vast open frontier provided much better opportunities than fever-ridden East Africa, where few Portuguese would voluntarily settle, and a large percentage of the colonists consisted of *degredados*, Indians, half-castes and Arab traders. A little commerce continued with the interior where Zumbo and Manica marked the furthest points of Portuguese advance, and 'fairs' continued to be held at Luanze, south of Tete, where ivory, gold, honey, raw cotton, skins and cattle were exchanged with the Bantu people for arms, gunpowder, cloth and beads. Quelimane, Sena and Tete were still held, the country round each of these settlements being divided into great semi-baronial holdings. These grants were originally made as the reward for services, but later the estates were settled on Portuguese women, with succession through the female line for three generations, on condition that each holder should marry a white Portuguese. But this strange attempt to promote white settlement by introducing a system of matrilineal succession to a European people failed, and many estates passed into the hands of Indian or half-caste owners, who lived as semi-independent lords, often spending their time in Goa, Mozambique or Brazil, whilst their dependents showed little interest in developing the resources of the soil. Portuguese administration remained inefficient, for officials were desperately underpaid and forced to make money locally from trade, the traffic in human beings assuming ever greater importance, as Brazil became a profitable market for slaves.[1]

Amid this ever-darkening gloom the Portuguese would still occasionally produce some outstanding men, including a number of extremely able Jesuits who, at the beginning of the seventeenth century, set up a school at Sena, where white, brown and black scholars studied side by side. Nevertheless South Central Africa as a whole remained the scene of one of the world's greatest missionary failures which still remains unexplained. For over two hundred years Christian preachers tried to spread the Gospel inland; but the tribal communities of the interior remained almost completely impervious to ecclesiastical penetration. The Monomotapa's people and their neighbours maintained constant contacts with the Portuguese, but these seem to have exerted very little influence on native institutions, either in the spiritual or the material field. Scholars as yet can only speculate as to the causes of this extraordinary resilience; perhaps tribal beliefs still appeared perfectly well adjusted to a people who possessed land in abundance and felt no particular need to change their accustomed ways; perhaps the white man's Cartesian cast of mind, wont to categorize, and to separate the spiritual and material aspects of life into separate compartments, could make no headway amongst a people whose philosophy of life was as yet simpler and more unified. Perhaps the Karanga came to identify missionary with political penetration, and determined to reject both. Whatever the explanation, there seems little doubt that the Arabs,

[1] See Jackson, M. V. *European powers and south-east Africa.* . . . Longmans, Green and co., 1942

with their more flexible methods, were more successful than the Portuguese. The Lusitanian conquerors, with their top-heavy political superstructure, suffered from constant dissensions between the distant home government at Lisbon which wished for friendly relations with the Monomotapa, the local governors and their officials, and the white and half-caste frontiersmen who did the actual job of opening the interior. The Portuguese commonly despised the 'kaffirs', and often showed a good deal of racial prejudice, in which hatred of the unbeliever, and a sense of superiority curiously mingled with pride of rank, caste or colour.[1] Devoted friars found themselves unable to surmount these difficulties, and evangelization suffered accordingly. In the eighteenth century mission work took another crushing blow when between 1759 and 1761 the Marquis de Pombal, a reforming Portuguese minister, a man of the Enlightenment, and a bitter enemy of the order, expelled the Jesuits from Portugal and its dominions. In breaking the Jesuits, Pombal delivered a smashing defeat to mission work, not only in Africa, but also in Asia and America, depriving Portugal of its most effective instrument of cultural and religious penetration overseas. In Mozambique the ecclesiastical situation deteriorated further when in 1777 the last remaining Dominicans were ordered to Goa and replaced by a handful of secular clergy, whose efforts proved completely inadequate, with the result that Christianity died out amongst the Bantu, lack of staff and political commotions putting an end to the Gospel's assault on this part of pagan Africa.[2]

Right through this period the Portuguese political hold on the interior remained equally feeble, though again a few able men still managed to make their mark inland. The most outstanding of these was Dr. Francisco José Maria de Lacerda e Almeida, a Brazilian who had previously served as Astronomer Royal, done extensive survey work in Brazil, and helped to explore the Cunene in West Africa. When the British seized the Cape in 1795 during the Revolutionary Wars, Lacerda predicted with remarkable foresight that the new possessors of Table Bay would in time push northwards and gravely injure Portuguese trade inland, since the British could supply cloth more cheaply than the Portuguese. Both trade and strategy alike therefore demanded that the Portuguese should establish a permanent line of communications linking up their possessions in East and West Africa to cut off the English from future advances inland. Lacerda also bitterly criticized the general state of affairs in Mozambique itself, the Governor's lack of policy, the inhabitants' lack of energy, the lack of

[1] For a detailed discussion see Boxer, C. R. *Race relations in the Portuguese colonial empire 1415–1825.* Oxford, Clarendon Press, 1963

[2] Theal, G. M. *The Portuguese in south Africa.* ... T. Fisher Unwin, 1896, p. 244–248

craftsmen and other failings. The Brazilian scholar then set out on a journey into the interior, his expedition getting as far as Kazembe's country in what is now North-Eastern Rhodesia.[1] But Lacerda's career was cut short in 1798; worn out by fever and worry, he died in the bush; and though the Portuguese continued to clutch on to their possessions, their hold was now of the weakest, and remained largely confined to the coast.

III

The southern invasions

For untold centuries Bantu tribes drifted down into the southern part of Africa from the Congo and beyond, in one of the world's great migrations. In the early part of the last century this movement was suddenly reversed, and a 'backwash' of black hosts swept back into the interior of Africa. The story begins with the Nguni nation who grew their crops and herded their cattle in the vast area now comprising Swaziland, Natal and the Transkei. Originally the Nguni were divided into many small chieftainships. Most of the people lived in scattered settlements, run by the head of the household who held sway over his various wives and over kinsmen and friends who sought his protection. Larger homesteads consisted of the dwellings of chiefs and members of the ruling family, as well as of numerous dependants who might not be actually related to the king. The warriors were organized into divisions for fighting and hunting, each division being attached to a royal homestead, whilst the young men were gathered into 'age sets', composed of youths who were circumcized at the same time. At about the turn of the eighteenth century the age set system acquired greater significance, and royal homesteads began to play an ever more important part in tribal politics. Circumcision was discontinued, and age sets were welded together on a national basis into regiments, with the result that Nguni military power became far more formidable than of old. At the same time the Nguni states grew in size, and by about 1810 three kingdoms, the Mthethwa, the Ndandwe and the Quwabe, dominated the remainder. Bitter fighting broke out between the various leaders; and out of this turmoil arose Shaka, the Jenghiz Khan of Southern Africa, and one of history's great conquerors.[2]

Shaka first emerged when he established himself as the effective head of

[1] See Lacerda, F. M. J. *The lands of Cazembe: Lacerda's journey to Cazembe in 1798*; translated and annotated by R. F. Burton. John Murray, 1873

[2] See Barnes, J. A. *Politics in a changing society*. . . . Cape Town, Oxford University Press, 1954, for an excellent sociological and historical analysis of an Nguni people.

the Mthethwa kingdom and then defeated the Ndandwe, some of whom were absorbed into his expanding state, whilst others moved off to the north. Shaka, like other great military minds of the past, reformed both tactics and weapons, exploiting to its fullest possible extent the warlike potential of an Iron Age cattle-herding people, who lacked both horses and wagons and had perforce to rely solely on infantry. A redoubtable in-fighter himself, Shaka quickly realized that a warrior might do much greater execution by hurling himself on the enemy with a short jabbing weapon than by throwing spears from a distance in the customary fashion, and in developing his new methods he caused a novel type of weapon to be manufactured—a massive stabbing assegai. Shaka's forces were drilled into a highly efficient fighting machine, whose order in the warriors' imagination resembled the head, chest and horns of a bull; Shaka made effective use of tactics of envelopment; he was skilled in employing a reserve on the battlefield, and developed the mobility of his army to such an extent that he could break up the enemy in a series of brilliant strategic moves, crush him by massive assaults, and then ruthlessly pursue the beaten foe without leaving him time to rally. Shaka's black warriors wielded their stabbing spears with great effect, protecting themselves from the enemy with great ox-hide shields and moving with the precision of British guardsmen.[1] None could resist them, and by 1820 Shaka had laid waste most of the country between Delagoa Bay and Pondoland. Recalcitrant tribes were wiped out; their wives, their children and cattle being absorbed into Shaka's victorious host which grew like an avalanche.

The Zulu state, however, suffered from chronic internal instability which resulted in various secessions. Besides, Zulu campaigns of conquest in turn set in motion other groups of people living on the periphery of the state, which in time involved almost every Bantu people between the Orange and the Zambezi rivers in widespread bloodshed. There was a new 'migration of peoples' carried out by several great hosts, accompanied by their women and children, their captives and cattle, the warriors smashing their way across Africa, pillaging as they went along, and sweeping new peoples into their train. In the west the Makololo, a great host with a Basuto core, made their way across Bechuanaland, crossed the Zambezi, and finally conquered Barotseland where they found the malaria mosquito a more formidable enemy than the tribes encountered on the way.

Another migration was led by Umziligazi, one of Shaka's generals, whom the king accused of holding back some cattle which by custom should have been handed over to him; for his economic power largely

[1] See Ritter, E. A. *Shaka Zulu: the rise of the Zulu empire*. Longmans, Green and co., 1955

depended on controlling the nation's herds in the common interest. Umziligazi realized that Shaka would assuredly put him to death, and in order to escape this fate, he fled with his followers across the Drakensberg Mountains and embarked on a course of brigandage. By about 1830 his war-parties had laid waste most of the country between the Drakensberg range and the Witwatersrand. Umziligazi also followed Shaka's methods in other respects; he controlled the allocation of beasts captured in wartime and maintained in good order the accustomed regimental system, which strengthened his authority within the migrating warrior state. None of the young men could marry without the king's consent, which he would occasionally grant to a whole regiment at once as the reward for some unusual feat of arms.[1]

A third horde was led by Zwangendaba, who at one time was a sub-chief of the Ndandwe who were defeated by Shaka. About 1821 Zwangendaba led a party of refugees north-eastwards into the region west of Delagoa Bay. Here they met Soshangane, another Ndandwe refugee from Shaka's power who was at war with Nxaba, another minor chief from the south, all the three hosts themselves raiding the indigenous Tsonga people. Zwangendaba quarrelled with Shoshangane and moved further north, taking along with him his new Tsonga adherents as well as some small groups of Swazi who had fled independently from Shaka and now placed themselves under his rule. The people led by Zwangendaba called themselves Ngoni but as they made their way northwards they became known under a variety of other names.[2] The dreaded invaders hurled themselves against what was left of the Rozwi state. The Rozwi by this time had fallen into great straits. Their ruler, the Mambo, was engaged in constant local warfare, and native tradition has it that, disgusted at the amount of bloodshed involved, Mambo Mavina Mubaiwemazha refused to make any more of the traditional meat sacrifices. 'I don't want to waste my animals,' he said, but supernatural vengeance struck swiftly. 'Zwangendaba was sent and he fought for three days. Mambo Mubaiwemazha was caught and skinned alive. All his soldiers ran away.'[3] Rozwi historians add that Mutongi Tumbare, another local leader, subsequently managed to chase Zwangendaba's soldiers out of the country; but however this may be, Zwangendaba's host continued on their way to the north, probably crossing the Zambezi river in 1835, and it ultimately broke up into a number of separate communities. Shoshongane's people for their part clashed with the Portuguese, and in 1833 his warriors, now commonly

---

[1] Hole, H. M. *The passing of the black kings*. Philip Allan, 1932
[2] Such as Batuta, Landeens, Angoni, Mafiti, and Makwaranga.
[3] Information supplied by J. V. C. Rukara.

known as the Abagaza or Gaza, destroyed the fort at Delagoa Bay and massacred its garrison,[1] becoming a major power in their own right, and carrying out raids far into what is now the eastern portion of Southern Rhodesia.

In the meantime Umziligazi had dispossessed the Hurutsi people from the rich Marico valley and taken up his own quarters near where Zeerust now stands, finding abundant grazing grounds for the enormous herds of cattle he had collected during his raids. Shaka, his former master, was killed by his brother Dingaan, and Umziligazi—no longer in fear of the tyrant— was able to live a life of ease, visiting his military kraals, feasting his eyes on his stock and enjoying the society of his many wives and concubines. He lived in great state; wherever he moved he was preceded by heralds who shouted out his magnificent titles, and he was served by women carrying great calabashes of beer and bowls of steaming beef. Robert Moffat, of the London Missionary Society, visited the warrior-monarch in 1823 and was both impressed and horrified by the king's power. His word was law over his people, who became known as the Matabele; the black sovereign only had to lift his finger or give a frown, and the greatest nobles trembled in his presence; none dared to negative an opinion uttered by the sovereign; and tribesmen could only approach the royal person in a crouching position and muttering the accustomed praise names. But nevertheless the king's subjects remained utterly devoted to their master, who gave them such splendid victories, and maintained such ruthless military discipline, not hesitating to massacre a defeated band of his own warriors who returned home in defeat. In his person Umziligazi was below middle stature, rather corpulent, short-necked, with a soft and effeminate voice, but yet with the kind of mercilessness that would not pause in having a captive wife beheaded for daring to remonstrate with her lord.[2]

The king's iron rule was in fact extremely successful in his own tribes- men's view; the Makololo attempted to compete with Umziligazi's people in the deadly art of pillage, but lacking a settled base and finding them- selves inferior in organization, they were ousted and moved off towards the north. The Matabele suffered a reverse when an expedition of Griquas and Koranas, many of them mounted and armed with guns, made a sudden descent on them in 1831 and captured several thousand head of cattle, but a few days later the Matabele rallied, and inflicted a smashing defeat on their opponents during a surprise attack.

But even in the Far Interior the Matabele could no longer escape from

[1] Theal, G. M. *The Portuguese in South Africa.* ... T. Fisher Unwin, 1896, p. 279–280. Another name of the Gaza was the Ama-Shangana or Shangaans.

[2] Moffat, R. *Missionary labours and scenes in southern Africa.* John Snow, 1842

making contact with the white man. In 1835 Moffat and Dr Andrew Smith, a scientist of considerable reputation who was visiting the northern tribes in a semi-official capacity, came to the king. Smith informed Umziligazi that the Cape Government desired the Matabele to live at peace with the surrounding tribes and gave him a medal and chain. Umziligazi was most impressed by a display of rockets held for his benefit, and the king agreed to send an embassy to Cape Town, Umziligazi's main object apparently being to obtain guns in order to shoot elephants.[1] The Matabele mission charged with 'greeting the white man's chief' was deeply struck by the Englishmen's military strength, their public buildings, their houses and ships. A treaty was concluded pledging the Matabele king to an alliance with the Colony, to maintain peace with the British Government and to give his protection to Europeans visiting his country.

But these first diplomatic contacts between Britons and Matabele as yet meant little; the Redcoats were still far away, and the British had neither the wish nor the ability to make their power felt in the Far Interior. The Matabele for their part were much more concerned with another white nation, pastoralists like themselves, but far more dangerous on the battle-field than even the Zulu. These were the Afrikaners, who were destined to become rulers over the country in which the Matabele were then holding sway.

The history of Afrikanerdom began with a market garden! In 1652, when the Portuguese were trying to consolidate their influence in the Monomotapa's kingdom, the Dutch sent out an expedition led by Jan van Riebeck to establish a settlement at Table Bay, on the extreme southern tip of Africa, so that ships on their way to the East Indies might find a port of call which would furnish them with fresh water and provisions. A fort was built to protect Dutch market gardeners and cattle traders; but soon the governing Dutch East India Company realized that a permanent farming community was essential to assure the Colony's future. Europeans received grants of land so that they might supply the Cape garrison and crews of passing merchant ships with grain, beef and wine; but in time settlement expanded far beyond the Directors' original intentions. The colonists gradually pushed deeper and deeper inland; and as the road to Cape Town became longer, they took to pastoral rather than arable farming. The pressure of population increased, and the numerous sons of Boer families found difficulty in making a living in Cape Town where much of the skilled work was done by imported Malayan slaves. Sub-division of land, accompanied by more intensive cultivation, was not

---

[1] *The Matabele journals of Robert Moffat, 1829–1860*; edited by J. P. R. Wallis. Chatto and Windus, 1945, v. 1, p. 96

usually a feasible proposition, as long as capital was scarce and land plentiful. Often the best way for a poor man to get on in life was to make his way to the frontier. The Boers kept trekking in order to avoid competition with their neighbours for pasture land and to avoid boundary quarrels; the frontiersmen's extensive methods of cultivation moreover tended to exhaust the soil, 'the veld got tired'; and so they moved on, like the indigenous people whom they met inland. The white frontiersmen of course were never self-sufficient, and even on the extreme edge of settlement they depended on imported articles like guns, and gunpowder, wagons, tea, coffee and cloth which had to be paid for. The best way of making money was to drive cattle to the market, for the town was now a long way off; and herds possessed the great advantage that they could walk to the market on their own feet. In addition there were a few goods of small bulk and higher value, like soap, candles, beeswax and ivory that paid the expense of being transported to the coast on slow-moving ox wagons.[1]

First the trek-Boer supplied the Cape market; later the centre of economic gravity shifted more towards new ports that were opened on the east coast; Port Elizabeth, East London and Durban became the most advanced points of departure for inland expansion. By this time the trekkers themselves formed part of a new nation, no longer 'Dutch' in the European sense of the word, but Afrikaners, speaking a new language, an African derivate from the Hollands tongue. The Afrikaners moreover had become a very different type of person from the early Dutch farmers with their skill in intensive agriculture. The trek-Boers, steeped in the dour religion of Calvinism, and thoroughly familiar with the story of the ancient Hebrews, a warlike and religious nomad people like themselves, became some of the world's expert wilderness specialists, adjusted to frontier conditions that would have completely baffled their Hollands, German or Huguenot ancestors; they could handle a span of oxen in the roughest type of country, they were knowledgeable as 'soil prospectors', wise to the ways of finding the best land in the wilderness, and also crack shots, first-class horsemen and hunters. At the same time the trekkers developed a highly specialized system of military tactics, perfectly adjusted to their economic mode of production. The Boers learned to defend themselves behind closed circles of wagons, which served both as a means of transport and as mobile defences; the use of *laagers* was combined with the employment of mounted sharpshooters who proved excellent fighters

[1] For differing interpretations see Neumark, S. D. *Economic influences on the South African frontier, 1652–1836.* Stanford University Press, 1957; Van der Merwe, P. J. *Trek: studies oor die mobiliteit van die pioniersbevolking aan die Kaap.* Cape Town, Nasionale pers beperk, 1945; and Muller, C. F. J. *Die Britse owerheid en die Groot Trek.* Johannesburg, Simondium, 1963

on their own ground, superior alike to Bushman, Hottentot and Bantu warriors.

In the meantime the Union Jack was hoisted over the Cape. In 1795 British men-of-war anchored at Table Bay and established a military government representing the Prince of Orange who had remained faithful to the British alliance, whereas the Dutch Republic had formed an alliance with the revolutionary government of France, with which Britain was at war. In 1802 the Colony was restored to Holland, but four years later the British came back, and this time they stayed. The first of the regular British Governors, Lord Charles Somerset, clashed with the local Dutch inhabitants on various occasions; but an even more serious cause of friction between English and Dutch was found in the activities of the London Missionary Society, which campaigned in favour of a more liberal native policy. The Boers also objected to the emancipation of the Hottentots; many considered themselves to be insufficiently protected against the depredations of Bantu cattle raiders, the British authorities' constant call for administrative economy affecting local policy even more than humanitarian, missionary or commercial factors. Further trouble arose when the British freed the slaves throughout the British Empire in 1833, and much bitterness was caused by the inadequate way in which former slave owners were compensated for the loss of their property. Emancipation was a particularly serious matter for some of the wealthier farmers who found grave difficulties in working their holdings in the accustomed manner and now joined their poorer compatriots in search of a new life on the open frontier. Slavery of course was not the main issue. A pastoral frontier economy required only a limited number of hands, and thus greatly differed from, say, the cotton economy of the American South or the clove economy of Zanzibar. But in South Africa two wholly different sets of customs and beliefs came into conflict with each other; for egalitarian as the Afrikaners were amongst themselves, they would accept neither political nor ideological interference from overseas, nor equality with non-Europeans at home. Trekking was in their blood, and the Great Treks of 1835 and succeeding years formed the frontiersman's Declaration of Independence. Admittedly, their effects should not be exaggerated. A large number of Boers did not move; and the Western Cape especially, with its wealthy wine farmers, continued to follow a different tradition, partly because there were no warlike Bantu, whilst unskilled work was mainly done by Coloureds.

Nevertheless the Afrikaner people's centre of gravity gradually began to swing north; great, solid Boer wagons steadily lumbered inland, beyond the Orange and then across the Vaal rivers. At first the British Government took the line that the pioneers beyond the Cape Colony would continue to remain British subjects; but British sovereignty beyond the Orange river was not upheld for long, and in 1852 the Imperial Government, by the Sand River Convention, formally guaranteed the emigrant farmers beyond the Vaal the right to manage their own affairs, and to govern themselves according to their own laws without interference. Britons and Transvaalers furthermore agreed to facilitate trade; the Afrikaners promised to abstain from slavery, whilst the British assured them of access to gunpowder supplies and disclaimed any kind of alliance with the indigenous tribes inland. Two years later a similar convention at Bloemfontein admitted the full independence of the Orange Free State, and two white frontier states now held sway in the interior.

The Matabele developed raiding to a fine art; but their own magnificent herds of cattle in turn attracted experienced stock-lifters like the partly civilized Griquas and Koranas. Umziligazi successfully dealt with these bandits, but he found infinitely more dangerous opponents in the Boers, whose superior mobility and fire power proved more than a match for Matabele infantry dependent on shock tactics. The Afrikaners at the same time took an active interest in the Far North and in 1836 a reconnoitring party, led by Andries Hendrik Potgieter, crossed the Limpopo and travelled through the south-eastern portion of what is now Southern Rhodesia to investigate their hinterland.[1]

During the same period bitter fighting took place between Boer and Matabele. In 1836 Umziligazi's warriors massacred some elephant hunters, and later on in the year unsuccessfully assaulted a group of trekkers at Vegkop. In 1837 an Afrikaner force swooped down on Mosega, one of Umziligazi's kraals, and carried off all the cattle it could seize. In addition the Matabele had to cope with raids from Griqua and Bangwaketsi robbers and from Dingaan's men. Later on a further punitive expedition, led by Potgieter and Piet Uys, descended on the Matabele, and Umziligazi then decided that the position was becoming untenable and that his people must trek once more.

For a time he seems to have considered setting up a new kingdom north of the Zambezi, but found his route impeded by the dreaded tsetse fly. In the end he settled in what is now Matabeleland, which he reached some time about 1840, the exact date still being in some dispute. The immigrant warriors found a land where their cattle flourished; Umziligazi extended his sway from the Shashi river to the Zambezi, above the Victoria Falls, further expansion northwards being impeded by the difficulty of crossing

[1] See Van der Merwe, P. J. *Nog verder noord: die Potgieterkommissie se besoek aan die gebied van die teenswoordige Suid-Rhodesië*, 1836. Cape Town, Nasionale Boekhandel beperk 1962

the crocodile-infested Zambezi in the face of the Barotse,[1] who dominated the upper reaches of the river.

During the early 'forties the Matabele sphere of influence formed the home of a great congerie of small tribes which collectively proved incapable of offering concerted resistance. Vast areas in the south and south-west of what is now Southern Rhodesia were inhabited by a group of peoples whom ethnologists have conveniently grouped under the common designation of Makalanga. The Makalanga, once the mainstay of the Monomotapa dynasty, by now had lost all their cohesion, and they became the victims of all kinds of Matabele atrocities. But their cultural influence remained, and the bloodthirsty conquerors themselves to some extent fell under Makalanga religious sway. The native priests of Mwari, the Makalanga High God, continued to practise their rites in the Matopos, and received lavish gifts from Umziligazi, who would periodically summon them to his capital for advice on affairs of state.

The Rozwi, once a proud ruling tribe of farmers, smiths and artisans, likewise suffered heavy losses. Some sought safety in the tsetse country fringing the Zambezi; many were murdered; others again were incorporated into the Matabele tribe. Umziligazi's warriors of course did not always have it their own way. Rozwi tradition tells of a defeat which Zwitunya, a local chief, inflicted on the Matabele by using guns, thereby inheriting the proud praise-name of Usibamubamu 'because [the] guns said tu-tu or bam-bam'. By and large the Matabele prevailed over their less disciplined opponents, people who were disunited amongst themselves, and even tried to play off the Matabele against their own local enemies. Thus Washaya, a local pretender, called on Umziligazi to fight Chikore, his rival, and offered to guide the Matabele impi; Chikore then took refuge in a stronghold in the Ndanga district, but after a siege lasting for a whole month, the pangs of hunger and thirst forced the defenders to capitulate.[2] Umziligazi then ordered the captured chief to remove to another residence, presenting him with six beasts, thereby skilfully reinforcing his military might by economic means.

The Matabele likewise prevailed against the tribes living on the great plateau extending towards the north-east, and collectively known as the Mashona. The Mashona were mercilessly harried; Matabele war-parties periodically departed for the east to capture women and children, whilst captive Mashona blacksmiths were made to turn out blades for stabbing spears, hatchets and battle axes for their new rulers. Only the Makololo in

---

[1] For an excellent history see Becker, P. *Path of blood: the rise and conquests of Mzilikazi.* . . . Longmans, Green and co. ltd, 1962

[2] Information supplied by J. V. C. Rukara.

the north resisted successfully, and Umziligazi never managed to secure a permanent foothold beyond the Zambezi.

Matabele might thus rested on three main elements. The regimental system caused the Matabele army to remain at a high pitch of military efficiency, and the warriors were kept in good training by regular raids. At the same time the Matabele state tended to 'snowball'. 'The Matabele', wrote Moffat, 'take from the conquered tribes boys and girls. The boys of course acquire the language and the habits and customs of their captors and are reared for soldiers, so that by far the greatest majority of that people are composed of such tribes. At each town of any consequence of these people there is generally a Matabele officer and some soldiers to receive tribute, and to such natives Moselekatse [Umziligazi] in general gives over a number of cattle to be taken charge of. In conversing with such I have observed that there is nothing they deplore so much as their children being taken from them just at a time when they become useful to their parents. It is therefore quite common to see a soldier having a boy or youth, whom he calls his servant, whom he has taken in the above manner to rear up for war.'[1] The Matabele in other words constantly increased their manpower, thereby strengthening their war-making potential for carrying out yet further raids. Umziligazi at the same time strengthened his military and political position through skilful 'cattle diplomacy', which in turn was made possible by his complete control over the Matabele means of production. Umziligazi was a 'distributor-king', royal power facilitating a primitive system of inter-tribal exchange. The Matabele monarch moreover kept a particularly tight hold over the ivory trade which was steadily growing in importance. For 'Moselikatse is the only one with whom barter can be effected. Every tusk of ivory is his, and no one dare dispose of one but himself, and from what I have seen he is a hard merchant to deal with. He can ask what he likes, knowing that there is no one else in his extensive dominions that can undersell him'.[2]

This complex state did not of course form an immovable monolith. The Matabele were affected to some extent by the religious and cultural ideas of the people whom they conquered and absorbed: in addition there were social changes within the ruling race itself. After the occupation of Matabeleland the Sotho captives from the south, now considered as old members of the tribe, rose in status. The Sotho or *Abenhla*, the 'people from up-country', admittedly did not attain full equality with the *Abezansi*, the privileged Nguni aristocracy, the 'people from down-

[1] *The Matabele journals of Robert Moffat, 1829–1860*; edited by J. P. R. Wallis. Chatto and Windus, 1945, v. I, p. 319
[2] *The Matabele journals of Robert Moffat, 1829–1860 . . . , op. cit*, p. 325

D

country', who continued to hold the key positions within the state. But Sotho warriors too managed to rise to comparatively responsible military and administrative posts, whilst *Abenhla* and *Abezansi* alike looked down with undisguised contempt on the *Amaholi*, the Makalanga and Mashona captives, who formed the latest addition to the tribe, and the lowest social class.

Militarily and politically this hierarchically ordered warrior community proved more than a match for any of its African neighbours, but Umziligazi still had to cope with the Afrikaners now firmly established in the Transvaal. The Boers for their part at first still looked northwards as a field for further expansion, especially after the British annexed Natal in 1843, and many emigrants left the sea-board colony to find new homes beyond the Vaal. Andries Hendrik Potgieter, the great Boer commandant, was thinking in terms of a powerful trekker state which would stretch beyond the Limpopo river into 'Banyailand' where he previously carried out a reconnaissance. Potgieter also realized the need for an independent outlet to the East Coast and in 1844 travelled to Delagoa Bay where he amicably discussed the situation with the Portuguese and agreed on their respective spheres of influence. The trekkers at the same time faced the problem of preventing British expansion inland. They accordingly tried to close the missionary road through Bechuanaland, the evangelists' route to the interior, asserting with some justice that hunters and even missionaries were disregarding the rules which forbade the sale of arms and ammunition to the tribes of the interior. In 1852 an Afrikaner commando thus taught a sharp lesson to Sechele, a Bechuana chief, but the Boers in the end proved unable to dominate the country; short of revenue and internally divided as they were, they could not maintain a permanent occupation force in this strategically vital area, and decided to cut down their commitments.

In 1853 the Transvaalers signed a treaty with Umziligazi whereby the Matabele agreed to stop the traffic in firearms, and to hand over gunrunners to the nearest *landdrost* or local administrative officer. Umziligazi also promised to give full protection to hunters and travellers from the Transvaal. Admittedly, the trekkers could never effectively stop the gun trade in which some of their own folk took an active share. But the diplomatic advantage clearly remained with the Boers, and the year 1853 marked a turning point in Matabele history. Hitherto Umziligazi had pursued a policy of isolation, which was only occasionally broken. From now onwards approved foreign traders and hunters were allowed into the country, even though they still had to travel inland along a single well-guarded route. In 1853 three Transvaal brothers, Pieter Jacobus, Jan

Abraham, and Frans Gerhard Joubert, took advantage of the clause guaranteeing good treatment, and visited the king. A year later two young Englishmen, Samuel Howard Edwards and James Chapman, made their way inland via Kuruman; and as time went on the sight of white elephant hunters and traders became more familiar in the 'Far Interior'.[1]

[1] See Rademeyer, J. I. *Die land van die Limpopo in die ekspansiebeleid van die Suid-Afrikaanse republiek*. Cape Town, A. A. Balkema, 1949; and Tabler, E. C. *The far interior*. . . . Cape Town, A. A. Balkema, 1955

Chapter Two

The frontier moves north

I

Gospel and ivory north of the Limpopo

For several centuries Portuguese pioneers of the Gospel tried to carry Christianity into the interior; but their efforts proved unavailing and Catholic missionary ardour exhausted its impetus. Enlightenment and rationalism drove traditional Christianity on the defensive; the Bourbon Monarchy tottered; and then the French Revolutionary and Napoleonic Wars threw Europe into turmoil for some twenty years. When the nineteenth century began, few prophets would have dared to predict one of the greatest periods of Christian expansion in history. But this is what happened, and the ground was already prepared. The eighteenth century witnessed a religious revival, popular and emotional in character, which swept over many parts of Europe, affecting thought amongst people as different as poverty-stricken German peasants, disinherited Jewish hawkers, and English factory workers. In Eastern Europe the Chassidim protested against the Rabbis' aristocratic intellectualism, whilst the Moravian Brethren sought to bring about a more personal approach to religion, stressing the Scriptures as the only rule of Faith, and preaching the fundamental unity of all Christians. In 1732 the Brethren began a far-reaching missionary movement of profound consequence for the future. In England this great religious revival became closely linked with industrialization. Popular dissenting groups made ready to preach the Gospel, not only in the countryside, but also in the new factory towns which the older Churches usually neglected. Itinerant preachers in the Puritan tradition stressed the popular element in Church government, and their dramatic sermons and singing made a deep appeal to some of the peasants who were flocking into the grimy slums of Glasgow and Manchester. Poverty, the dissenters taught, was neither holy nor an inevitable state, but something that men should overcome by thrift, sobriety, hard work and individual effort, which in their turn would lead them to the Kingdom of Heaven. The Nonconformists would have nothing to do with political revolution, but thought that men should use the new opportunities which factories, workshops and counting houses were now creating in Britain, and that each should trust in his own initiative. At the same time the Dissenters, as well as those Anglicans who were influenced by their doctrines, argued that children and aged, sick people, and slaves—all those who could not look after themselves in the hurly-burly of free enterprise—should be helped by charitable ventures, a belief that also appealed to humanitarians of a more secular and rationalist cast of mind. In time the Dissenters' intense desire to convert and improve the masses at home spilled over into the foreign field, and in 1787 the Methodists set up a regular system of foreign missions. Eight years later the London Missionary Society was founded to carry the Gospel in Protestant form to the remoter parts of the world; and work began in India, China and other distant countries which were now becoming far more accessible through the steady expansion of British trade and improved communications. The Napoleonic Wars brought the Cape within the sphere of British influence, and at the turn of the century Dr Johannes Theodorus Vanderkemp, a Dutch missionary, began to work for the 'L.M.S.' in the Cape, which in time proved a convenient base for further expansion through Bechuanaland into the Far Interior.

One of the most outstanding of the Society's missionaries was Robert Moffat, a Scotsman who began life as a gardener, and whose subsequent career turned out to be a sort of religious success story of the kind which deeply impressed his contemporaries. Moffat came under the influence of revivalist preachers, and like so many others who became missionaries as a result, suddenly underwent a deep spiritual experience; testifying at a Methodist meeting he thought he could see the chains which bound him, and that the fetters of guilt were now rent in twain.[1] Driven forward by this evangelical impulse he studied for the ministry and in 1816, at the age of twenty-one, was ordained a missionary of the London Missionary Society. In the same year he sailed to Cape Town in a vessel prophetically called the *Alacrity* and a year later set out for Namaqualand. In 1825 Moffat laid out a new station at Kuruman on the Cape frontier, where he made a name for himself by his religious work and also as a linguist, and over many years he translated the Bible into Sechuana, thereby laying the foundations of Sechuana literature. The new faith made a considerable impact on the Bechuana people and Moffat's fame spread further until it reached Umziligazi. In 1829 the Matabele monarch sent an embassy to enquire into the doings of the strange preacher and Moffat showed the

[1] R. Moffat to his parents: 23 Nov 1814 (in MO 5/1/1 Nat Arch MS)

envoys every kindness. When difficulties arose as to their return through Bechuana country where the Matabele were hated and feared, Moffat escorted the party himself and took the opportunity of paying a visit to Umziligazi. The tall white stranger, with his shaggy hair and beard, his clear-cut features, piercing eyes and immensely strong convictions, made a great impression on the Matabele king, over whom the Scottish missionary established a quite astonishing personal ascendancy, even though Umziligazi would not permit his people to be converted. In 1835 Moffat made a further journey to Umziligazi's court, but the Matabele remained impervious to his teachings. Towards the end of the 'thirties Umziligazi finally made his way into the unknown interior across the Limpopo and Moffat for a time lost touch with him. In 1854, however, he embarked on yet another trip inland. Travelling together with Sam Edwards and James Chapman, Moffat journeyed by way of Sechele, chief of the Bakwena, and Shoshong, the residence of Sekhomi, head of the Bamangwato. The party then made its way by compass over an uninhabited and unknown country in a north-easterly direction for eighteen days, until they reached Umziligazi. The Matabele king again showed his friendship for Moffat, even though he would not permit him to preach Christianity because he feared that evangelization would destroy the social order of his tribe, whose god in the missionary's view, was one of 'war, rapine, beef-eating, beer-drinking and wickedness'.[1] Moffat could get no news of David Livingstone, his son-in-law, who was now exploring the interior, and contented himself with making certain that the Matabele would take charge of supplies for Livingstone, and deliver these to the Makololo country.

In the meantime the cause of Central African exploration was making swift progress. In Dr David Livingstone missionary Protestantism found a splendid pioneer who aimed at spreading the Gospel in Africa by indirect means. He believed that the geographical, scientific and medical exploration of Africa would in turn open the Continent to 'Commerce and Christianity', to Western economic enterprise and thought; these would eliminate the slave trade and erode paganism, thereby laying the foundations of a Christian continent. Earlier on, in 1852, Livingstone had departed from Kuruman for the north, and two years later he reached Loanda, having travelled all the way to the West Coast with the help of the Makololo who were themselves anxious to expand their trade with the outside world. Livingstone then turned back inland, discovered the Victoria Falls in 1855 and a year later arrived at Quelimane, the first Briton to have crossed Africa. When he returned to Britain at the end of 1856, the one-time cotton piecer found himself a celebrity. The strong-

[1] R. Moffat to Mary Moffat: Aug 1854 (in MO 5/1/1, Nat Arch MS)

minded and enthusiastic Scottish doctor made a first-class propagandist, and effectively used his power of drawing wide audiences to impress upon the public the need for the opening up of Africa. Livingstone's whole approach, with its implicit belief in the virtues of commerce and science, linked to a deep personal religion, proved profoundly congenial to the spirit of his time. His optimism, his conviction of the absolute superiority of Western civilization were attuned to the temper of his age, and for all his personal weaknesses he made a tremendous appeal. To working class people he was one of themselves, a one time factory hand who had made good; to wealthy industrialists he was a man who preached social peace at home and commercial expansion abroad; to the believers of all classes he stood out as a pace-maker of the Gospel; and however impractical he often proved as an organizer, his tremendous personality carried all before him. In 1858 the British Government sent the Scottish doctor to command an expedition for the purpose of exploring the Zambezi basin from its mouth to the interior to prepare the way for trade, navigation and white settlement; for Livingstone believed—like Rhodes after him—that British colonists would lift Central Africa out of its poverty. The London Missionary Society became equally enthusiastic, and resolved on a new offensive into the Far North.

One missionary party was to open Barotseland to the Gospel, Livingstone having brought some very enthusiastic reports about the Makololo who had so greatly assisted him in his work as an explorer. A second party was to go to Matabeleland where Umziligazi might be persuaded to abandon his traditional hostility to the Makololo. The Makololo might then be enabled to move from the unhealthy river valley to the more salubrious, though less defensible, highlands north of the Zambezi, where missionaries would be able to preach the Gospel to them in a healthier climate. Moffat, now in his sixties, returned to the Matabele country in 1857 and obtained the king's consent to set up a station there. At the same time the preachers had to overcome opposition from the Transvaalers who objected to penetration into what they regarded as their hinterland, and were convinced that the L.M.S. was stirring up the tribes against them, supplying them with arms in contravention of the Sand River Agreement, and poisoning British public opinion through a mischievous and inaccurate propaganda campaign. The British Government, however, backed the missionaries, and so did local opinion at the Cape, where many merchants feared that the Transvaalers might achieve a monopoly of the inland trade.

The whole campaign, however, was badly conceived. The Makololo party, consisting of Holloway Helmore and his wife and four children, and Roger Price with his wife and infant daughter, as well as two Christian

Bechuana teachers, met with disaster. White women and children should never have been allowed to go into the insalubrious interior, and most of the company perished of fever. Sekeletu, the Makololo Paramount Chief, stole their supplies, and the project of proselytizing north of the Zambezi broke down. The Matabele venture turned out to be a little more fortunate. The travellers on this, Moffat's third visit to Matabeleland, consisted of Moffat himself, his son John Smith, the latter's wife, Emily, and Thomas Morgan Thomas, a former farm labourer who, like Moffat, had worked his way up to the ministry, and Thomas's wife and little child. The missionaries met with many difficulties; the dreaded lungsickness struck their cattle, the usual wagon worries plagued the party as vehicles broke down in need of repair. Worse still were the Matabele political commotions, for Umziligazi's people had now arrived at a parting of the ways. A strong anti-European party argued that missionary penetration would do away with polygamy, that Christian teaching was incompatible with the country's warlike way of life, and that Boer commandos would follow in the wake of the Cross. Umziligazi moreover complained that the missionaries would not supply him with firearms and ammunition, and at first asked for impossibly high prices for grain and slaughter cattle. The party thus went through a period of uncertainty when tempers got frayed and bitter disputes broke out; but in the end fortune favoured the missionaries. The Matabele decided on a compromise. They would let the teachers live in their country, even though they did not accept their way of life; and at the end of 1859 Umziligazi allocated land at Inyati, a Matabele kraal of about 2,000 people. The soil seemed rich, water was plentiful and the missionaries at last found themselves in possession of a firm base, Inyati becoming the first permanent white settlement in what is now Southern Rhodesia. Robert Moffat stayed on until 1860, helping as smith, carpenter and wheelwright, once more playing his part in what proved to be as tough a piece of pioneering as any carried out in Central Africa.

The old-time missionary had to be a jack of all trades, farmer, artisan, preacher and linguist, forced to do heavy manual work under a blazing sun, whilst malaria might be coursing through his veins and his wife suffering from the after-effects of repeated child-bearing. Only men like Thomas, with the iron constitution of a Welsh farmhand, could master a life which in many ways resembled that of the *Swiss Family Robinson*, stranded on a lonely island, a story much beloved by Victorian readers, and realistic enough in its contemporary setting. Early on, the missionaries never saw enough food on their tables; during the first years the crops generally failed, the local Africans seldom producing an adequate surplus. Umziligazi travelled about much of the time, and could not be relied upon as a regular donor of meat and grain. Inyati moreover was an isolated settlement; few traders came up from the south; freight was irregular and expensive, costing as much as between £30 and £50 per ton from the Coast, so that imported goods like tea and coffee, sugar, medicine and clothes remained scarce. Labour was a similar problem, for the Matabele considered manual work beneath their dignity, and the whites had to rely for help on a few children supplied to them by the king.[1] Worse still were the psychological pressures on the missionary settlers. They were on their own, alone in the far interior, dependent on each other for company, and under these circumstances quarrels would flare up fiercely. For whereas a modern missionary or anthropologist seldom deals with warlike tribes and has the whole resources of civilization behind him in the bush, his old-time predecessor remained solely dependent on his own efforts; if the crops failed, if he got sick, his family might starve. Even more crushing to morale was their lack of success. Hardy, pious, 'inner-directed' Victorians, convinced of the absolute truth of the Bible, found themselves face to face with a warrior people, to whom the values of Western civilization meant nothing, who stuck to their accustomed traditions and regarded the white strangers at worst as spies, and at best as technical experts, skilled in repairing wagons and guns, and useful only as interpreters, doctors and advisers. Christianity, with its doctrine of peace and monogamy, could make no headway in a Black Sparta; and however much Umziligazi admired Moffat as a man, he did everything in his power to prevent the Europeans' creed from spreading. Children could not attend school, adults who became too interested in the new doctrine were surreptitiously banished, with the result that the mission made no headway until white frontiersmen conquered the country. In the meantime the missionaries vainly struggled on for a whole generation.

Whilst missionaries sought souls to save, traders came in search of profits and found that ivory formed the most desirable commodity which the interior could offer. North of the Zambezi the traffic in elephant tusks generally went hand in hand with the slave trade; but south of the river the commerce in human beings never made much headway. British power and influence stamped out slavery in South Africa, which in any case possessed no great tropical plantations like those of Brazil or the American South, requiring regiments of forced workers to grow export crops. Warlike tribes like the Matabele preferred to assimilate their captives rather than sell them; but if no money could be made from 'black ivory', white ivory was so profitable that for a short time it dominated the inland

[1] Tabler, E. C. *The far interior.* Cape Town, A. A. Balkema, 1955, p. 243–274; and *The Matabele journals of Robert Moffat, 1829–1860*, edited by J. P. R. Wallis. Chatto and Windus, 1945, 2v.

trade. Elephants' tusks always found buyers in London, the world's main distribution centre for this merchandise, where the demand went up steadily with the expansion of luxury industries. Ivory was fashioned into billiard balls and piano keys, cutlery handles and those atrocious knick-knacks with which Victorians used to cram their parlours. At the same time India, known to merchants as the backbone of the trade, purchased enormous quantities of rings, left over from the turning of billiard balls, which were sold in bazaars as women's bangles, whilst ivory was also used as a raw material for carving toys and models, craftsmen preferring African to Indian tusks. Hunters thus got good money for their wares and William Finaughty, one of the great Nimrods of the interior, later recalled that in 1868 he was able to sell his tusks at Sesheke's town for drafts on Port Elizabeth at an average of 6/10½d. per pound. Hunters and traders accordingly extended the sphere of their operations, with the result that during the 'sixties and 'seventies the tuskers inland were exterminated on a scale comparable only with the destruction of the bison on the Great Plains of the American West.

In the slaughter of Central Africa's big game both white and black hunters alike played their part, the expansion of the ivory industry in turn promoting the spread of firearms into the interior. Bantu tribesmen sought guns both for hunting and war, whilst the possession of a good musket or rifle bestowed considerable prestige on its fortunate owner. Guns were in great demand and from about the early 'sixties onwards white merchants began to supply arms to the Matabele. As the decade drew towards its close many of the king's subjects possessed muskets, rifles, or badly-made gas-pipe guns, unreliable blunderbusses which were specially manufactured for the African trade, and which sometimes proved as dangerous to their possessors as to the prey. The Matabele made no real attempt to adjust their military tactics to the new means of destruction which Western technology now provided; but as far as the subject tribes were concerned, Umziligazi pursued exactly the same policy as the Boers, and tried to prevent the sale of arms to the people on the periphery of his kingdom, so as to retain a military and hunting monopoly of these much-coveted weapons.

White traders also imported goods like cloth, blankets, jackets, hats, as well as iron hoes, knives, kitchen utensils, pots and pans, or consumption goods like salt. Africans acquired these in exchange for ivory, so that the trade in tusks gradually changed the indigenous economy which in time ceased to be self-sufficient and became tenuously linked to the world market. The gun trade received a further impetus when in the early 'seventies Africans from Matabeleland and beyond began to make their way to the Kimberley diamond mines to work, taking back firearms which enabled them to stalk elephants more effectively. White merchants purchased the newly-shot ivory; and an expert has calculated that between 1872 and 1874 the Matabele king sold as much as 30 tons of ivory, whilst white men and their servants accounted for another 20 tons, the spoils from about 2,500 animals.[1]

The European hunter was also a businessman of sorts who required a certain amount of capital before he could start, and who employed some African workers. Thus in the late 'sixties William Finaughty set out into the interior with two wagons, accompanied by a Hottentot hunter and forty-five African servants of whom forty-two each received a musket, powder, lead and caps to last them for three months. Finaughty, a magnificent horseman and an excellent shot, later gave a vivid description of his experiences, and of what it meant to carry all day in the blazing sun a heavy old muzzleloader, with gunpowder loose in one jacket pocket, a supply of caps in another, together with the bullets in a pouch. The gun used to 'kick' its owner's shoulder with almost as much force as the bullet struck the elephant; and Finaughty himself was several times knocked clean out of his saddle by the tremendous recoil. No one could survive under these conditions unless he had an excellent sense of direction, so as to avoid the dreaded fate of getting 'bushed' on the lonely veld; in addition a man had to be an expert tracker, and of course a skilful rider and a deadly shot.[2]

The fraternity of the veld were on the whole an extremely honest lot, very different from the stereotype of the 'low immoral trader' denounced with considerable heat by some well-meaning philanthropists who thundered forth their philippics from well-padded armchairs in London. The hunters depended on African goodwill for their living; they were bound together by the camaraderie of the bush; most of them managed to establish a sound reputation for honesty. 'A Kafir who is owed money by one Englishman, perhaps the wages for a year's work, will take a letter without a murmur, to another Englishman hundreds of miles away, if he is told by his master that, upon delivering the letter, he will receive his payment.'[3]

The frontiersman's social background varied considerably. There were many Boers, men like Marthinus Swartz, a pioneer hunter. Another outstanding pioneer was John Lee, the son of a British naval captain and of an Afrikaans girl, the niece of Paul Kruger. Despite his British name Lee

[1] Tabler, E. C., *op. cit*, p. 51
[2] Finaughty, W. *The recollections of William Finaughty, elephant hunter 1864–1875*. Philadelphia, J. B. Lippincott company, [*c.* 1916]
[3] Selous, F. C. *A hunter's wanderings in Africa*. . . . Richard Bentley and Son, 1881, p. 247

could only speak English imperfectly, but he was an expert at veld craft, having served in several native wars before making his way into the Far Interior. He shot elephants in Matabeleland from the early 'sixties and then received a grant of land in the Mangwe valley, making his living by raising cattle, hunting, trading with Africans and selling provisions to white people. A third was George Arthur Phillips, an Englishman of enormous physical strength and huge build who because of his size became known to the Matabele king as 'playful elephant'; Phillips had a good education though a Portuguese later wrote that the Englishman affected a coarseness of manner which strangely contrasted with his evidently gentle breeding.

The great age of elephant hunting, however, soon drew to a close. The beasts retreated into remote, tsetse-infected areas where hunting from horseback, the normal way of getting ivory, became impossible. Few of the older Nimrods adapted themselves to hunting on foot, which was even more toilsome and dangerous than shooting from the saddle; and stalking elephants in time became a sport more than an industry. When Frederick Courteney Selous, the best known of them all, came inland, the ivory hunter's occupation was already decaying, partly owing to the enormous destruction of game, and partly as the result of restrictions imposed by the British Government on the export of firearms into the interior. Selous, a Rugby man, whose father served as Chairman of the London Stock Exchange, came to be regarded as the very model of adventurous upper class Englishmen, and probably served as prototype for Allan Quatermain, the hero of Rider Haggard's famous novel *King Solomon's Mines*. But Selous came too late, and in 1877 disgustedly wrote home that the trade had largely collapsed, and that elephant hunting was nearly at an end, most of the animals having been either killed or driven away.[1] Selous perforce turned to providing specimens and trophies for museums, guiding prospectors, tourists and sportsmen, the characteristic expedient of all professional hunters in the days of a closing frontier; and by the beginning of the 'eighties the lands south of the Zambezi were generally 'worked out' of ivory.

[1] F. C. Selous to Mrs F. L. Selous: 15 Oct 1877 (in SE 1/1/1, Nat Arch MS). See also extract of letter of 5 Oct 1877 printed in Millais, J. G. *Life of Frederick Courtenay Selous, D.S.O.* Longmans, Green and co., 1918, p. 112

II

Prospectors and politicians in the 'sixties and 'seventies

Ivory hunters led the trail into the interior, and one of the most know-ledgeable of these frontier specialists was Henry Hartley. The *Oud Baas* was of English descent—he came to South Africa as a child, the son of an 1820 settler—but was later naturalized as a burgher of the Transvaal, with whose interests he identified himself. He tried his hand variously at being a blacksmith, a farmer and a hunter, later acquiring a property south of the Magaliesberg which served as a base for extended hunting trips beyond the Limpopo. Hartley became a good friend of Umziligazi's, who was impressed by the Englishman's skill and endurance; and Hartley was able to travel as far as the Victoria Falls, which from the 'sixties onwards began to attract sportsmen and tourists from various parts of the world.[1] Hartley also made his way into Mashonaland; and in the course of his extensive travels to the north of the Umfuli, he came across white quartz reefs surrounded by heaps of refuse quartz, and broken by ancient diggings about six to twelve feet deep.[2] The hunter questioned the local people who told him that their ancestors used to work the yellow metal here. By this time the existence of gold north of the Limpopo appears to have been a matter of fairly common knowledge.[3] But Hartley acquired much more detailed information and passed this on to Carl Mauch, a German schoolmaster of adventurous disposition, who wanted to find out more about the Far Interior, with its reputed mineral treasures and ancient ruins. Previously a German missionary, A. Merensky, had tried to reach these remnants of a lost civilization, which he confidently linked to the Ophir of the Jews, but in 1862 the pastor was forced to give up his attempt.[4] His countryman, however, met with better fortune. The son of a minor official in the then independent kingdom of Württemberg, Mauch managed to win a scholarship to a teachers' training college; but, fired by zeal for African exploration, he gave up schoolmastering and made his way to South Africa where he settled in the Transvaal. Mauch possessed

[1] See for instance Baldwin, W. C. *African hunting and adventure from Natal to the Zambesi*. . . . Richard Bentley, 1863; Chapman, J. *Travels in the interior of South Africa*. Bell, Daldy and Stanford, 1868, 2v; Mohr, E. *Nach den Victoriafällen des Zambesi*. Leipzig, Ferdinand Hirth und Sohn, 1875

[2] Baines, T. Undated note (in BA 7/1/2, f. 982, Nat Arch MS)

[3] Baines, T. *The northern goldfields diaries of Thomas Baines* . . . , edited by J. P. R. Wallis. Chatto and Windus, 1946, v. 3, p. 616

[4] A. Merensky to A. Petermann: 14 Nov 1871, printed in Ingram, J. F. *The land of gold, diamonds and ivory*. W. B. Whittingham, 1889, p. 97–98

no formal training as a geographer or geologist, but his reports made such an impression on Dr A. Petermann, an internationally known authority of the day, that a subscription was organized to finance his further work. In 1866 the German was lucky enough to meet Hartley, who, just back from a hunting trip north of the Limpopo, invited him to come on his next journey at his expense. Mauch thus travelled northwards in the *Oud Baas*'s party in 1866, and in the following year embarked on a second trip with Hartley. These travels took him as far as the Sebakwe and Umfuli rivers, and convinced him of the existence of vast gold deposits in the interior. Mauch was unable to take many specimens out of the country, for the Matabele wanted no truck with prospectors and he had to conceal his intentions, becoming known to the Matabele guides as a madman not interested in anything normal, who was best left alone. On his return in 1867 Mauch wrote an enthusiastic letter to the *Transvaal Argus* which gave Hartley credit for the discovery of two supposedly enormous auriferous deposits, which became known respectively as the Tati and the Northern Gold Fields, the latter being situated in the Hartley Hills area. Gripped by prospector's fever the unassuming teacher grew quite lyrical, and recorded 'how the vast extent and beauty of these goldfields are such that at a particular point I stood as it were transfixed, riveted to the place, struck with amazement and wonder at the sight and for a few minutes was unable to use the hammer'. These finds made a considerable impression on public opinion, not so much amongst Afrikaans-speaking farmers in the Transvaal who were not particularly interested in mining or prospecting, but amongst English-speaking people in Southern Africa. Mauch then evolved a startling plan to travel through Central Africa right up to Egypt. In 1868 he started on another trip to the interior which took him as far as the Bubi and the Nuanetsi rivers, but he was arrested by the Matabele who objected to the German's unauthorized entry into their sphere of influence. Three years later Mauch embarked on his last and greatest journey in Africa. He was soon reduced to desperate circumstances but was rescued by Adam Renders, an American hunter who at this time was living in an African village with a native chief. Renders knew about the Zimbabwe ruins, which Mauch visited in 1871, and of which he provided the first modern description in print. Later on Mauch struck north and discovered what he believed to be extensive auriferous deposits in what he called the 'Kaiser Wilhelm Goldfields', now the Makaha Fields, in the north-eastern portion of Southern Rhodesia, subsequently continuing his journey to the Zambezi river above Sena, and finally making his way down to Quelimane and back to Europe.

Mauch's discoveries brought him fame but not fortune. His explorations were completed at an extremely small cost, the schoolmaster having little in the way of funds or equipment at his disposal; but despite these remarkable achievements Mauch, who lacked paper qualifications, could not get any kind of a scientific or academic position in the newly unified *Reich*, and counted himself lucky to be given a job in a cement factory whose owners were impressed by his feats.[1]

Mauch's real impact was made in Southern Africa whose people were now beginning to become aware of the mineral wealth in the interior. In 1867 diamonds were discovered near the Orange, and prospectors of many nationalities flocked to the river diggings. Their finds were thrown into the shade when in 1870 stones were also found on the open veld. Kimberley soon developed into a tough border town, attracting pioneers from as far afield as Europe, America and Australia, whilst overseas capital began to move into an area hitherto dependent on a few agricultural exports. Adventure was in the air, and many South Africans now began to dream of a boom of the kind which had previously come to California and Australia. Moreover when Mauch returned from the interior in the late 'sixties South Africa was suffering from an economic depression; the finances of Natal were in a poor way; and many Natalians hoped that their country might one day become the gateway to a new land of Cockaigne. The *Port Elizabeth Telegraph* thus announced that an Eldorado had been found beyond the Limpopo, whilst the *Natal Witness* burst out into an article headed 'I speak of Africa and Golden Joys' and explained that the desire to prospect was perhaps part of a great plan for enforcing the first Commandment requiring man to replenish the earth. The enthusiastic journalist concluded that 'the power of the precious metal . . . has transcended the influence of all systems of morality, philosophy, jurisprudence, legislation or government ever known', and hoped that new cities would spring forth in the wilderness at the yellow metal's magic touch. The tales of Ophir and of ancient Hebrew ventures added a touch of romance to the desire for wealth, and some enthusiasts began to think of the Far Interior in terms as fantastic as those that filled the minds of Spanish conquistadores in sixteenth-century America. The news reached England in 1868 and caused almost as much of a stir as in South Africa, and the new deposits were now written up in newspapers, discussed by learned societies, and glowingly extolled by pamphleteers who used alluring titles like *To Ophir direct*[2]

[1] His discoveries were published in Mauch, C. *Reisen im Inneren von Süd Afrika 1865–1872.* Gotha, Justus Perthes, 1874 (in *Petermann's geographische Mittheilungen*, Ergänzungsheft no. 37, 1874, p. 28–52). For his biography see Mager, E. *Karl Mauch: Lebensbild eines Afrikareisenden.* Stuttgart, W. Kohlhammer, 1895

[2] 'Bamang-wato' (i.e. Broderick, M.) *To Ophir direct: or, the South African goldfields.* Edward Stanford, 1868

to describe the reputed riches of the interior. This of course was the time when South African diamond discoveries were being widely publicized and the whole sub-continent was becoming better known to the world of finance. Only six years before, the Standard Bank of South Africa had been founded in London, where capital was plentiful at the time; the Bank, one of the first financial institutions to be incorporated under the recent limited liability legislation, helped to channel capital to South Africa.

The first burst of prospecting activity did not, however, come to very much. A number of fortune-seekers came to the area between the Shashi and Ramaquabane rivers, now known as the Tati district, where Hartley and Mauch had reported gold. The most important of these enterprises was the London and Limpopo Mining Company, founded in 1868 by a prosperous group of investors. The Company at considerable expense equipped an expedition, furnished with machinery and a steam-driven traction engine. Sir John Swinburne, a baronet and a relative of the well-known poet, led the expedition, which arrived at Tati in 1869 after propitiating Macheng who had a doubtful claim to the area. Swinburne then went on to Lobengula's kraal to gain the consent of the Matabele who had a counter-claim to the region, and Swinburne's company was able to undertake a certain amount of development work at Tati.

Another venture was the South African Gold Fields Exploration Company which was floated in London in 1868, and later despatched an expedition under Thomas Baines. Baines, one of the most attractive of these old-time travellers, was the son of an English sea-captain who apprenticed the youngster to an 'ornamental painter'. Baines, however, soon got tired of life in England, and at the age of twenty-one left for South Africa where he travelled and made a name for himself as an unofficial war artist with the Colonial forces then engaged in one of the many native wars of the period in the eastern Cape. He subsequently found employment with an expedition in northern Australia where he did good work with his paint brush at a time when photography was still in its infancy, and geographers relied on the artist's skill to record their discoveries. While in England in 1857 he met Livingstone who invited him to join his Zambezi expedition, but owing to a misunderstanding he, a sick man, was unjustly dismissed by the dour Scots doctor who was as inept in handling Europeans as he was good in dealing with Africans. Between 1861 and 1863 he accompanied James Chapman, the great South African traveller, on a journey from Walvis Bay to the Victoria Falls, hoping to meet Livingstone again and claim redress from him, but the meeting never took place. Baines's artistic work still stands out as a valuable record, executed with considerable technical skill in a naturalistic style, and his paintings of the Falls are notable as the means by which the world first judged their magnitude.

These white concession seekers, however, picked an inconvenient time for themselves; for as it happened, Matabeleland was going through a severe political crisis. Umziligazi died in 1868, and the king's demise occasioned a bitter succession dispute. According to the Matabele law of inheritance, the heir to the chieftainship was the senior queen's eldest son; that is to say, if the king was married to several wives, each of whom could boast of being a chief's daughter, the daughter of the greatest of these rulers would be regarded as the chief wife and her eldest son would be the heir-apparent. Unfortunately for the Matabele there were, however, several possible claimants. Umziligazi, like other Bantu kings, engaged in a large number of politically advantageous marriage alliances. His wives played an important part in the kingdom's affairs, the queens being strategically placed in various major centres, where they would advise local dignitaries on matters of local policy, check on possible disloyalty, and entertain their sovereign on his extended tours through the kingdom. The king's greatest wife was Umoaka, the eldest daughter of Uxwiti, Umziligazi's former sovereign. According to Matabele custom, Umoaka's eldest son, a youngster by the name of Unkulamana (Nkulamene, Kuruman) was the legitimate heir. Umziligazi, however, could never forgive Uxwiti for slaying Umziligazi's father, and therefore determined not to allow the murderer's grandson to succeed. According to the 'official' Matabele version the unfortunate young prince was put to death at Umziligazi's command, but the Matabele king managed to keep the dark deed secret. When he died few Matabele dignitaries would believe that Unkulamana was in fact no longer alive, the Pretender being supposed to live in Natal. A short interregnum followed, national affairs being handled by a regent named Uncumbata (Nombate), an aged councillor and one of Umziligazi's confidants. Uncumbata, though generally pro-white in his sympathies, would not commit himself on questions of major policy, such as granting concessions to Europeans, and a final decision was left over until the succession question was settled.[1]

At long last, after protracted and complicated negotiations, Lobengula (Ulopengule), a royal prince by a lesser wife, agreed to accept the chieftainship, and in 1870, after splendid ceremonies, he was installed as sovereign of the Matabele nation, and the interregnum came to an end.

[1] For a more detailed examination of this problem see Brown, R. 'The Ndebele succession crisis 1868–1877' (in *Historians in tropical Africa: proceedings of the Leverhulme inter-collegiate history conference held at the University College of Rhodesia and Nyasaland, September 1960*. Salisbury, The College, 1962, p. 159–175)

The new king, though supported by the concession companies, found himself in a desperately difficult situation. Lobengula's mother could never claim a rank much higher than that of some of the other queens, so that Lobengula's position at first was not very strong. The house of Uxwiti remained unreconciled to the succession, whilst Lobengula—for all his imposing personal presence—lacked both administrative experience and prestige born of military success. The young ruler found himself surrounded by his father's aged councillors to whom he owed his position and whose advice he could not ignore. Stepping into the shoes of a great despotic ruler like Umziligazi, the founder of the nation and a soldier of outstanding ability, was a hazardous undertaking at best, and no one could blame Lobengula for dreading at first to pick up the sceptre.

In addition to his political difficulties Lobengula also appears to have faced major economic problems. His father seems to have exercised effective control over most of the cattle in the country and was able to play the part of a Bantu 'distributor king' on a vast scale. Umziligazi owned beasts in most of the towns of his country and could order these animals to be slaughtered at any time. He would give away cows and oxen to his favourites, entertain swarms of visitors at his court and supply newly-formed villages with herds. Contemporary accounts do not make it quite clear how the interregnum affected royal control over Matabele means of production, but apparently local magnates for a time managed to take over many of the king's privileges, and when Lobengula became king he found himself in dire straits. Thomas Morgan Thomas, the missionary, wrote that the new chief himself only owned a few thousand cattle consisting of beasts received during his father's lifetime, animals attached to the royal capital and transferred to the king on his succession, and beasts specially provided for the young chief's inauguration. The remainder of Umziligazi's cattle were scattered about in the various towns of the kingdom; Lobengula could no longer order them to be slaughtered at will, and at first depended to a much greater extent on other kinds of revenue—including gifts from his magnates for special occasions like wars and festivities, and on customary income like fines and confiscations incurred for various crimes.[1]

At the same time his people's Spartan discipline appears to have weakened to some extent—now that the Matabele were safely installed in a secure position, and were no longer a harried host on the move, whose very survival depended on cast-iron obedience. In the olden days Umziligazi was able to insist on Shaka's practice that only successful warriors might be allowed to marry. But even before the old king's death many

[1] See Thomas, T. M. *Eleven years in Central South Africa*. John Snow and co., 1873, p. 241–243

Matabele warriors would disregard the custom. The wearing of the special head-ring—once prized as a sign of a man's right to marry—became general; some Matabele youngsters still continued to ask for the king's permission, but many others would scarcely even consult their own parents before taking a wife.

Under these circumstances Lobengula showed considerable skill. He clearly grasped that missionaries might to some extent be played off against traders and concession seekers, and diplomatically promised favours designed to appeal to the evangelical conscience. His harem would be limited in size, witchcraft executions without trial would cease, whilst subject tribes would be released from slavery. At the same time Lobengula at the outset of his reign attended some religious services and offered sites for additional stations, promises which meant very little, but which created an extremely good impression on white clergymen. With his own people the young king was equally successful. Lobengula for one thing had the advantage of immense physical bulk, and was outwardly a far more commanding figure than Umziligazi. He soon received an opportunity for showing his mettle in combat. Umbigo (Mbigo), a powerful chief, raised the standard of revolt against Lobengula in support of another candidate who claimed to be Unkulamana and tried to get help from the Transvaal Boers. For the first time Matabele clashed with Matabele, but Umbigo was mortally wounded and the royalist forces won the day. The crack Zwangendaba regiment was smashed, its kraals burnt, the women carried away, and Lobengula's authority was at last assured at the price of a serious weakening of Matabele military strength.

The new government, however, still faced the problem of how best to deal with competing concession-seekers. Baines thought that the Matabele could in fact work gold for themselves with the aid of local Europeans. The tribesmen knew the value of the yellow metal as well as the whites, and even if they did not, traders would soon apprise them of the market price.[1] The Matabele, however, did not see things in this fashion. The Zulu possessed no tradition of gold mining, as did the Mashona people, and the Matabele never tried to change their accustomed way of life. They were warriors, trained to fight rather than do menial labour in the bowels of the earth. Even the employment of Mashona slaves would not have helped, for they would still have had to work as foremen and supervisors on jobs completely different to anything they knew. The Matabele therefore preferred to work with the whites and get a small, but regular, payment instead of mining metal themselves. No final decision could be made during the interregnum, but in 1870 Lobengula was able to act.

[1] T. Baines to A. T. Windus: 24 April 1874 (in BA 7/1/2, Nat Arch MS)

First of all he made a grant to the London and Limpopo Mining Company covering the country between the Shashi and Ramaquabane rivers, a decision which involved a difficult problem of foreign as well as of mining policy. The area in question, known as the Tati district, was in dispute with the Bamangwato, a powerful Bechuana tribe who adapted themselves much more readily to European ways than the Matabele. Bamangwato labour migrants brought back rifles from the south; some of them owned horses, and the tribe therefore managed to build up a fairly sizeable military force. The Bamangwato claimed that the gold-field formed part of their own territory, and at the same time tried to secure British backing against Boers and Matabele claimants alike. The issue became even more involved when the Transvaal Government also entered the fray, issuing a proclamation which annexed the Tati district. The Imperial Government for its part would neither recognize the Transvaal's claim nor assume responsibility for the district itself.

As it happened, Tati soon lost its importance, but not before facing Lobengula with a difficult problem. The London and Limpopo Mining Company sought the exercise of administrative power over the area, and Lobengula found himself unable to control the influx of Europeans. The Matabele of course never intended to sign away what they regarded as their sovereignty over the area in question, but they did not fully understand English legal language or European concepts of contract, and soon angry communications passed between Lobengula's court and the Company. For a time, however, serious disputes were avoided for Swinburne could not raise enough capital in England; only a limited amount of development could be undertaken, and the Company abandoned its venture when funds became exhausted. The only precious mineral in the country turned out to be reef gold, requiring expensive machinery to work it, and the attention of the small diggers soon turned to Kimberley where the sensational rich 'dry diggings' were distracting attention from the gold deposits of the north.[1]

Baines in the meantime secured some backing from the Natal Government, and in 1870 obtained a verbal grant from the king enabling the South African Gold Fields Exploration Company to dig for gold through-

[1] The London and Limpopo Mining Company for a time worked the Blue Jacket and New Zealand reefs, but the venture was not very profitable. In 1880 a new company, known as the Northern Light Gold Mining Company, obtained another concession. Its terms were made more comprehensive in 1887 when Lobengula appointed S. H. Edwards, one of the concessionaires, his deputy in the Tati district. In 1888 the rights in the Tati area passed to the Tati Concession Mining and Exploration Company, which was floated at Kimberley and controlled by Alfred Beit, as well as a group headed by Baron d'Erlanger and J. H. Schröder and co. The Tati area was specifically excluded from the Rudd Concession of 1888, by which Lobengula granted away his mining rights to Rhodes and his associates.

out the country between the Gwelo and Hunyani rivers, build houses, and take away precious minerals, though Lobengula firmly insisted that the concession entailed no property in land.[1] Baines's directors were not, however, satisfied with the mere word of a warrior chief, and asked instead for a grant in writing. Lobengula accordingly ratified the Company's claim in a formal document,[2] but Baines soon found himself in difficulties. The Company was drifting into debt, and investors would no longer put up money to keep the venture going. When Baines returned to Natal he learned that all attempts to float a mining company to work the concession had failed, and he was forced to take over a considerable burden of financial liabilities. Baines courageously toiled on, painting pictures for sale, making maps, lecturing, and participating in various expeditions, until at long last he had made enough money to try his luck once more in the Far North. In 1875 he ordered a battery and steam engine, making ready to go off on a third trip in order to work his concession. But success came too late. The veteran traveller was laid low by a terrible bout of dysentery, and within little more than a month Baines was dead.

Lobengula's policy towards the Christian missionaries resembled that of his father, though assuming perhaps a slightly more pro-European bias. When the new king moved his capital in 1870 the London Missionary Society received permission to set up a second station, which became known as Hope Fountain and was situated only a few miles from the capital at Bulawayo. But the chief would not allow any of his people to become Christians, fearing—quite correctly—that the Gospel would weaken the structure of his military monarchy. For years on end the white preachers, with incredible perseverance, continued to argue, teach and exhort, to tend the sick, school the children, and hold short services for visitors who might chance to come to their station. But all this work proved ineffective. When William Sykes, a former grocer's clerk turned missionary leader, and one of the outstanding pioneers of Inyati, died in 1887 after a lifetime of evangelical endeavour, his Society could not boast of a single convert in Matabeleland. As far as Lobengula was concerned, this was of course satisfactory enough. The white strangers' creed made no inroad in his kingdom, and yet an open break with the Europeans was avoided, whilst the immigrants' various technical skills were useful in all kinds of ways. But at the same time the Matabele derived no benefit from the literary arts which the whites might have taught them; and Lobengula failed to develop an indigenous intelligentsia, capable of reading and

[1] T. Baines to Mrs E. Elliott: 13 Dec 1870 (in BA 7/1/1, Nat Arch MS)
[2] There is a copy of this concession, dated 29 Aug 1871, in BA 8/3/1, Nat Arch MS.

writing letters, which would have been extremely useful in the king's subsequent dealings with the Europeans.

The missionaries' difficulties were further increased by internal divisions, the London Missionary Society, with its extremely loose system of Church discipline, finding itself particularly prone to disputes between its members. The most outstanding dissentient on the mission's staff was Thomas Morgan Thomas. Thomas, the son of a small tenant farmer, started off in life as a farm hand, with Welsh originally his only language. Later on he became a clergyman and came to Inyati as one of the original settlers, his skill as a hunter, bricklayer, blacksmith and carpenter proving as valuable as his linguistic and evangelical gifts. Thomas, however, disagreed with his colleagues on various issues, especially on the practice of exchanging gifts with the king, which his critics regarded as trading. In 1872 Thomas broke off his connexion with the Society, becoming a kind of missionary freelance. He published a most valuable and informative book called *Eleven Years in Central South Africa*, which came out in both English and Welsh, Thomas himself hawking copies from door to door, and preaching on missionary subjects. In time the new publication became popular, particularly in Wales, and with the help of profits accruing from sales Thomas was able to go back to Matabeleland. Here he set up a station of his own, known as Shiloh, where he combined mission work with trading and hunting. The self-taught labourer also undertook a great deal of linguistic work, including a translation of the New Testament. His knowledge of foreign tongues included an acquaintance with Sindebele, Hebrew, Greek, Latin, Dutch and Sechuana, missionaries of his kind standing out in many ways as the intellectual élite of the British lower middle and farm working class.

In the meantime the Roman Catholic Church turned its attention once more to its ancient mission fields on the Zambezi, the new challenge presented by the exploration of inner Africa being met in the Church's traditional manner, by forming new religious orders, and by re-deploying older ones. The Jesuits, tried and well-disciplined shock troops with missionary experience all over the world, were entrusted with the newly founded Zambezi Mission, whose geographical limits were fixed by a Rescript of the College of Propaganda in 1879. St Aidan's College at Grahamstown, an important Catholic institution of learning, formed the Jesuit's rallying point, the missionary venture as a whole being put in the charge of Father H. Depelchin, a Belgian who for eighteen years had been preaching the Gospel in India. Late in 1879 the Jesuit party, consisting of eleven priests and brothers, reached Bulawayo, where the king gave them a friendly reception, the brothers, with their manual skill, forming a

particularly welcome addition to the pool of foreign 'technicians' north
of the Limpopo. In the following year the party split up, the Jesuits
embarking on an over-ambitious scheme of evangelization which in the
end broke down completely. Five missionaries made their way northward
to the Zambezi. Four more received Lobengula's permission to go east
to Umzila's country, near the Sabi river, in the Shangaan kingdom with
which Lobengula maintained friendly diplomatic relations. Three more
remained at Bulawayo. Disease, however, took an exceptionally heavy toll
of the Jesuits, and after terrible sufferings the Zambezi and Umzila
missions had to be wound up. The Jesuits at Bulawayo fared a little better,
but met with no more success than the Protestants in teaching the Gospel,
and likewise failed to make a single convert.

Neither the London Missionary Society nor the Jesuits tried to counter
Lobengula's wishes by settling within his Mashona dependencies.
Lobengula's policy on this point was quite inflexible. White preachers
might reside in Matabeleland proper, where he could keep an eye on them;
but they had no business to set up stations within his Mashona sphere of
influence, a policy which the king probably regarded as on a par with his
practice of preventing the sale of firearms in the outlying regions. The
Paris Evangelical Missionary Society, a French Protestant body established in Basutoland, failed to understand this policy, and when it also
tried to penetrate beyond the Limpopo, the attempt resulted in complete
failure. The Paris Evangelical Society had established a vigorous and
active Church amongst the Basuto, ancient rivals of the Zulu, and in time
French missionaries and Basuto Christians alike looked towards the north
as a field for spiritual expansion. Hopes ran high in Basutoland when in
1875 three African emissaries returned from beyond the Limpopo, reporting that the local 'Banyai' chiefs would be only too pleased if missionaries came to their country. The Basuto were enthusiastic, and in 1877
a mixed European and African body was set up to manage the enterprise,
the expenditure for the mission's African agents falling entirely upon the
Native Churches of Basutoland.[1] In the same year a pioneer party
departed under the leadership of the Rev. François Coillard, a French
peasant's son, destined to become one of Central Africa's greatest missionary statesmen. The Society's high hopes, however, soon met with
disappointment. The original exploration party had probably justified the
advent of missionaries too exclusively in terms of temporal advantage,
and when local chiefs discovered that the strangers brought neither firearms nor gunpowder, they turned hostile. Coillard was blackmailed by
Masonda, a small local dignitary, and in the end the missionaries were

[1] F. Coillard to J. Smith: 15 May 1877 (in CO 5/1/1/1, Nat Arch MS)

taken to Bulawayo by a Matabele war party. Lobengula professed himself to be very angry that white men had entered his dominions without his permission, through the 'back door', and for a time detained the missionaries at Bulawayo where the mission's Basuto evangelists were treated with the utmost scorn. In the end Coillard was expelled from Matabeleland, and with a heavy heart turned southwards, reaching Shoshong in 1878. The attempt to preach the Gospel in Mashonaland having failed, the Frenchman now determined to avoid the Matabele and to push on to the Upper Zambezi; this decision was fraught with momentous consequences, and led ultimately to the successful evangelization of Barotseland, Matabeleland's northern rival.

The mission question, however, formed only a relatively small part of Lobengula's wider problem of foreign relations, which became increasingly complex as the South African mining frontier began to swing northwards. More and more diggers flocked to Kimberley, and even though this tented township lay more than 600 miles away from Bulawayo, the distant mines soon began to exert an indirect influence on the Far Interior. The diamond fields became a vast magnet for the inland tribes anxious to work for the white man in return for guns and other trade goods, whilst the Europeans for their part made active efforts to recruit more workers on short contracts. In 1876 the Griqualand West administration deputed Alexander Bailie, a land surveyor by profession, to visit the tribes to the north, gather more information about the Far Interior, and secure labour for the diamond fields where manpower was in short supply. Bailie got a good reception from Lobengula who agreed to supply men for the mines. Two strong Matabele patrols were sent out to collect labour and food, and after a few days a party returned with twenty-four men. The other patrol was overtaken by the rains in a sickly part of the country, and the king then gave fifty of his own attendants to Bailie.[1] Arrangements were made whereby the men would go down to the mines, to be replaced by another batch at the expiration of their time. In a small way the Matabele were for the first time drawn into a European-run migrant labour system, the king and his councillors quite naturally failing to foresee the ultimate incompatibility of a wage-working and a warrior economy.

Lobengula instead was far more concerned with the political aspects of British expansion. When Bailie came to the king's court, a body of some thirty white traders, including a remarkably high proportion of Scotsmen, presented an address of welcome, hailing the new official interest in the

---

[1] Draft despatch by A. Bailie to the Government of Griqualand West: 15 Mar 1877 and 31 Dec 1876 (in BA 10/2/1, Nat Arch MS), and the journal of T. M. Thomas: 9 Jan 1877 (TH 2/1/1, f. 25, Nat Arch MS). See also Agar-Hamilton, J. A. L. *The road to the north: South Africa, 1852-1886.* Longmans, Green and co., 1937, p. 142-143

affairs of Matabeleland, and asking for the appointment of a government representative in the country. Their views were very much in accord with those of Sir Bartle Frere, the British Governor at the Cape, who thought in terms of expanding British influence by appointing Residents amongst the northern tribes. For a time the policy of 'forward' seemed everywhere to be successful. In 1877 the British annexed the Transvaal, so that Imperial power at last touched the periphery of Matabele influence in southern Mashonaland. In the following year a small British force marched into southern Bechuanaland. At the same time the Zulu, the Matabele's kinsmen in Natal, were called upon to remodel their army system, the basis of their local military predominance. The Matabele therefore felt extremely wary, their apprehensions being increased by fear of possible British intervention in their succession disputes. Earlier on Sir Theophilus Shepstone, then Secretary for Native Affairs in Natal, had sent an ill-advised letter to Lobengula in which he made a good deal of Unkulamana's claims, even though not actually interfering in the question of the royal inheritance.[1] Later on more trouble arose when Richard Frewen, a wealthy Victorian globe-trotter of somewhat domineering temperament, came to Matabeleland to hunt big game, and felt himself aggrieved by various small disputes with the king. Frewen complained to Shepstone, and accused Lobengula of wrecking his expedition. Shepstone, who was now running the Transvaal from Pretoria in his new capacity as British Administrator, then arranged to send an embassy to Lobengula. This was headed by R. R. Patterson, a Scotsman who combined the mission with a private hunting trip inland. Patterson conveyed a letter from Shepstone to Lobengula, and discussed various outstanding trading matters with the king, without, however, making much headway. Lobengula feared that any kind of agreement might interfere with his unfettered powers, and distrusted Shepstone whom he suspected of challenging his right to the throne. The Matabele as a whole remained suspicious of the embassy, and rumours went round that the envoys formed the advance guard of a big army which would come and 'eat up' the country. Patterson failed to realize his own perilous position and asked Lobengula for permission to continue his trip to the Zambezi. Despite the king's reluctance, Patterson and his companion insisted on going, taking along with them Morgan Thomas, the Welsh missionary's son. In the end the whole party perished, all the available evidence pointing to their having been murdered by the Matabele.

The British, however, did nothing further in the matter, finding themselves occupied with more important issues. They now had to cope with various tribal outbreaks, the most important one being the Zulu War.

[1] T. Shepstone to Lobengula: 28 May 1871 (copy in BA 7/1/1, Nat Arch MS)

Early in 1879 the Queen's soldiers suffered a crushing disaster at Isand-hlwana, where the Zulu wiped out an entire force.The Redcoats re-established their military prestige at Ulundi; the Zulu military monarchy collapsed, and Lobengula was confirmed in a healthy respect for British arms. British policy towards southern Africa as a whole aimed at securing this strategically vital pivot of a great maritime empire by federating the several disunited white African states on Canadian lines. The new group-ing was expected to be strong enough to cope with its own frontier and internal native problems and save the Imperial Treasury from unwelcome expenditure, whilst the more populous, wealthy and loyal Cape Colony would dominate the northern trekkers and watch over Imperial interests. Carnarvon, the British Colonial Secretary, felt convinced that the 'balkanization' of southern Africa must end, but failed to take into account the strength of Afrikaner national feeling. Once the Transvaalers felt themselves free of the Zulu menace they took to arms, and in 1881 their mounted sharpshooters won the day at Majuba Hill. The insurgents met with considerable sympathy amongst their fellow-Boers in the Orange Free State and Cape Colony, so that rebellion seemed to strengthen the case for a conciliatory British policy. A pacifically-minded Imperial Government—now headed by Gladstone—was anxious not to spend British blood and treasure in a useless war, or to create another Ireland. The British therefore agreed to restore the Transvaal's independence.[1] 'Forward' policies fell from favour, and for reasons quite unknown to him Lobengula's British problem seemed to solve itself. Nothing more was heard of the Patterson murder, and when the 'eighties began the Matabele warrior state appeared as safely entrenched as ever in its bloodstained history.

III

Bechuanaland bottle-neck

In October 1871 an unknown immigrant from England left a pioneer farm in Natal to seek a fortune in Kimberley. Loading a few digger's tools and some classical volumes into a Scotch cart, the youngster set out on the four hundred mile trek to the fabulous diamond fields which, dis-covered only a year before, were already drawing flocks of adventurers from all over the world into the South African interior. His name was

[1] See Robinson, R., and Gallagher, J., with Denny, A. *Africa and the Victorians: the official mind of imperialism.* Macmillan and co. ltd, 1961, for an outstandingly good account of the whole political background.

Cecil John Rhodes, and his decision to go north was destined to make a country. Rhodes was born in 1853, in the same year that Livingstone set out on his journey to the Zambezi; he grew up in a large family in the vicarage at Bishop's Stortford where his father ministered to the local farmers. Herbert and Frank, Cecil's elder brothers, were sent to good public schools, but he had to be content with the local grammar school, where he showed no signs of special ability. At the age of sixteen the youngster was still wavering between becoming a barrister or a clergyman; but his health—like that of so many other Imperial pioneers—was weak, and at the age of eighteen the tall, lanky, anaemic-looking boy was packed off to South Africa where a sunnier climate was expected to put him right. Rhodes landed at Durban towards the latter part of 1870 to join his brother Herbert, and first of all tried his hand at farming. The two young men showed some aptitude for agriculture, but planting cotton seemed a much slower way of making money than digging for diamonds, and Rhodes decided on a mining career.

When Rhodes arrived at Kimberley in 1871 the fields still provided opportunities for men without money. Mining as yet required little capital, and from his tent door Rhodes could look out on to the Colesberg Kopje, or New Rush, where a huge tented city had sprung up, the whole kopje being divided into a large mass of small claims where some 10,000 people, white and black, were working every day on a piece of ground no larger than 180 by 220 yards. The diggers formed a turbulent, independent, largely English-speaking community, and though the Orange Free State at first tried to control their settlement, the Boer claims were soon pushed aside. In October 1871 the British High Commissioner proclaimed the whole of Griqualand West to be British territory, the Free State receiving a solatium of £90,000 for the loss of South Africa's new-found Eldorado.

Small-scale diggings at Kimberley soon, however, became out of date. Open workings were driven so deep that falling earth would bury the outer claims, while those in the middle of the huge pit filled with water. The smaller men were squeezed out and joint stock companies began to dominate the scene, diamond mining proving so profitable that the industry at first could largely pay for its own expansion without outside investment. Banks provided the balance by making loans, and a few enterprising men made great fortunes. The most outstanding of these financial magnates was Rhodes, who built up a great diamond empire, and in 1887 acquired complete control over the vital De Beers mine; then followed a hard-fought battle with Barney Barnato (formerly Barnett Isaacs), a Whitechapel boy who once used to knock around as a circus artist and prize fighter before becoming a brilliantly successful business man at Kimberley. But in the end Barnato could not stand up to his rival, and in 1888 Rhodes—with the help of Alfred Beit, his friend and associate, a financier of German Jewish origin—managed to acquire complete control over the whole of Kimberley's industry.

Rhodes, however, was far more than just a rich Colonial who managed to 'make good'. A strange mixture of schemer and dreamer, stock-pusher and statesman, he embodied all contemporary Britain's pride of race and confidence in her Imperial destiny. Money was to him no more than a means to an end, the expansion of British power to the ends of the world. He felt convinced, like most Britons of the Late Victorian Age, that Northern Europeans and especially Englishmen were best fitted to open up the backward parts of Africa. Rhodes also shared Livingstone's belief that white enterprise alone could save the Dark Continent from poverty and disease, and argued—like most British missionaries at the time—that the extension of British rule would itself prove an inestimable boon to the native peoples of Africa. As far as Britain herself was concerned—he concluded pessimistically—she could not afford to stand aloof from empire, for without her overseas possessions the little kingdom would be nothing—just an over-populated island somewhere off the coast of northern Europe. Britons therefore should go out into the world to found new English-speaking communities that would enhance the motherland's power and spread her ideals all over the globe. Imperial expansion would secure new markets and thus enable Britain to hold her own in the economic field at a time when foreign competitors were raising new tariff barriers against British goods. The existing British constitution was not, however, well suited to promote an active Imperial policy, and the Empire should therefore be re-modelled as a great oceanic federation.

Within this new imperial strategy Africa must play a vital part, for the Dark Continent held enormous wealth, riches that the natives could not exploit themselves, and which British enterprise should make available to world trade. South Africa in turn held the key to Britain's African policy, and the white states south of the Limpopo should be united into a new power under the Union Jack. Boer and Briton would then find a common task in opening up the Far Interior, whilst at the same time freeing themselves from meddlesome interference by the home authorities. Ultimately Rhodes hoped for a great new African Empire which would hinge on the Cape, his own adopted country, and one day rival the Indian Raj in all its splendour.[1]

---

[1] The Rhodes literature is enormous and was listed in Burke, E. E. *A bibliography of Cecil John Rhodes (1853–1902).* Salisbury, Central African Archives, 1952 (Bibliographical series, no. 1). A more recent work is Lockhart, J. G. and Woodhouse, C. M. *Rhodes,* Hodder and Stoughton, 1963

Rhodes's Imperial speculations possessed a peculiarly nebulous quality; one grandiose idea was apt to chase another, but Rhodes nearly always maintained a hard grasp of detail. He first began to take an active part in politics in 1880 when Griqualand, where the diamond fields lay, was incorporated into the Cape Colony and thereby became entitled to send representatives to the Cape Parliament. Rhodes bitterly disapproved of the clumsy efforts previously made by the Earl of Carnarvon, the British Colonial Secretary between 1874 and 1878, to impose a South African federation from above. He determined instead to conciliate the Afrikaners and therefore chose to stand for Barkly West, a rural constituency with a large Afrikaans-speaking community, getting himself successfully elected as their representative.

The South African frontier thus engendered its own expansionist drives, but these did not operate in isolation. Whilst adventurers from the south looked towards the interior for gold, gems or grazing lands, the European powers themselves became involved in the affairs of the Dark Continent. The 'Scramble for Africa' was triggered, oddly enough, by the declining fortunes of the Turkish Empire, which once held sway over a large part of Africa's northern shore. In the mid-Victorian era British policy aimed at shoring up the tottering Ottoman State on the grounds that Asia Minor formed Britain's first line of defence against any Russian threats to British naval and commercial interests in the Levant; the British therefore did all they could to strengthen the Sultan, whilst at the same time getting him to carry out reforms which would both benefit his underprivileged Christian subjects, and assist the cause of trade and sound finance in the Eastern Mediterranean. The British attained a strong position at the Sultan's Court, but from the Crimean War onwards the Turkish Empire showed increasing signs of strain. In 1876 the Sultan's Government went bankrupt, and when in the same year a Russo-Turkish War broke out the danger arose that the Ottoman Empire might be partitioned. In the end this peril was avoided, but at the Congress of Berlin in 1878 Turkey sustained serious losses in the Balkans; the British acquired Cyprus as a *place d'armes* to strengthen Turkey in Asia in case of a new Russian assault. France at the same time received a free hand in Tunisia which she occupied in 1881, thereby further upsetting the traditional order.

From the British point of view things were no better in Egypt, a semi-independent Turkish dominion; the country's strategic importance vastly increased with the completion of the Suez Canal in 1869; economically Egypt made considerable progress when cotton became a major export crop. But the weak and unstable Egyptian Government tried to do too much with too little, and steadily drifted into bankruptcy. In 1875 Disraeli bought for the British Government the shares which the Khedive, the Egyptian ruler, held in the Suez Canal Company, and a year later the Egyptians were forced to submit to Anglo-French financial control. Foreign interference produced a nationalist reaction led by discontented army officers, but the British intervened and in 1882 the Egyptians were crushed at Tel el Kebir. The British now stayed on in Egypt; and by the end of the 'eighties Imperial strategists regarded Cairo and Alexandria, rather than Constantinople, as the pivot of British policy in the Mediterranean, the British at the same time becoming entangled with the problems of Egypt's hinterland down the valley of the Nile.

Whilst the struggle for the northern portion of Africa was thus closely linked to the question of the Ottoman inheritance, colonial trade, philanthropy and the current interest in exploration caused a simultaneous irruption into West Africa. In Brussels King Leopold II of Belgium took advantage of the growing interest of European manufacturers in the potentialities of tropical Africa, and of strong Christian feelings against the slave trade, to set up an enormous private domain of his own. The whole Congo venture started—as it ultimately ended—with international intervention. In 1876 Leopold called a conference at Brussels which set up an 'International Association for the Exploration and Civilization of Africa' which proposed to crush the traffic in human beings, and open Central Africa to trade. In 1882 the committee was transformed into the 'International Association of the Congo', which explored the Congo and other Central African rivers, its sovereignty being recognized by all the powers in 1885. Leopold then received from the Belgian legislature authority to assume the role of ruler of the 'Independent State of the Congo', and the new state in fact became largely Belgian in character. Belgian enterprise in the Congo in turn whetted French ambition in Central Africa, and also gave a boost to Portuguese empire builders who maintained ancient pretensions to the Congo, and dreamed of establishing a great belt of territory right through Central Africa, stretching from Angola in the west to Mozambique in the east. At the same time Germany was drawn into the colonial race, diplomatic exigencies in Europe playing a major share in determining her new transmaritime policies. In 1884 the Germans proclaimed a protectorate over South-West Africa, and during the mid-'eighties they acquired colonies in Togoland and the Cameroons on the West Coast, and in what is now Tanganyika. Bismarck's coup completely transformed the political position in Southern Africa, where the British now had to reckon with another great power. The Transvaal was only a weak state by itself; but what if Germans and Transvaalers should succeed in linking up in the interior? Then there was the Portuguese problem. France and Germany settled their outstanding disputes in 1886, and for a time recognized Portuguese claims to a lateral belt stretching from coast to coast, so that Rhodes's plans of turning his Cape Colony into the gateway of a great African empire stretching to the north seemed in jeopardy.

Bechuanaland, containing the main road to the north, now became South Africa's most vital territory, 'the Suez Canal of the trade of this country [the Cape Colony], the key of its road to the interior.'[1] The Imperial Government first tried the 'soft' approach, and early in 1884 persuaded the Transvaal to sign the Convention of London, which kept the Republic's frontier to the east of the northern road; the Transvaalers likewise agreed not to make any treaties with the African tribes to the east and west of the Republic, save with British consent, though nothing was said with regard to dealings concerning the indigenous peoples living to the north. The London Convention, however, proved inadequate when Germany declared a Protectorate over South-West Africa later on in the year, the British position becoming further weakened by the need to conciliate the Germans over British policies in Egypt. Boer encroachments on the west of their two states continued, and at the same time the Transvaal granted a railway monopoly to a German-Dutch syndicate, designed to free the country of its economic dependence on the British. There were also ambitious designs of a railway from Pretoria to St Lucia Bay and Angra Pequeña, which would threaten the Cape merchants' hold over their trade with the interior. British prestige now stood at a low ebb, and the road to the North remained endangered by two small Boer communities, the Republics of Goshen and Stellaland, which emigrant trekkers set up in territory claimed by Bechuana tribesmen.

Negotiations achieved little, but at last British patience gave way. Towards the end of 1884 a strong expeditionary force, led by Sir Charles Warren, marched northwards, reaching the Vaal river early in 1885. Warren continued on his mission and broke up the Goshen and Stellaland republics without any trouble. On 30 September 1885 Bechuanaland was formally taken under British protection, and the sphere of British influence advanced northwards to 22° S and westwards to 20° E, the last mentioned line marking the eastern limits of German South-West Africa. The newly occupied country was divided into two portions. The country south of the Malope river became a Crown Colony under the name of British Bechuanaland, the remainder being declared a native Protectorate. Both British

[1] 'Vindex' (i.e. Verschoyle, J.) *Cecil Rhodes: his political life and speeches 1881–1900.* Chapman and Hall ltd, 1900, p. 62

Bechuanaland and the Bechuanaland Protectorate were administered by one man—Sir Sidney Shippard.[1]

The cause of British expansion thus gained a decisive victory. The Transvaal now found itself effectively hemmed in towards the west. More important still, the Bechuanaland Protectorate, a key position on the chequerboard of South African politics, was now governed by a man who fully sympathized with Rhodes's views regarding imperial growth. From the time the new Administrator assumed office, he made it his business to cultivate friendly relations with Lobengula whom he regarded as the most powerful native chief south of the Zambezi since the destruction of the Zulu state. Shippard, sober lawyer and civil servant though he might be, was full of the Californian kind of gold-fever which was aroused by South Africa's splendid mineral discoveries, and which envisaged the Far Interior as a mysterious kind of Eldorado. According to Shippard, the whole country between Khama's dominions, the Zambezi in the north and Gazaland in the east, was enormously fertile. Mashonaland moreover contained 'some of the richest deposits of alluvial gold in the world'— utter nonsense in fact, but credible enough in the light of explorers' reports which were reaching the Administrator. Shippard thus concluded that South Africa's future would hinge on the possession of Matabeleland, and that whoever could secure these fabulous lands as well as Delagoa Bay—characteristically described by Shippard as 'the future San Francisco of the Indian Ocean'—would hold the key to the sub-continent. The British therefore should annex both Mashonaland and Matabeleland; the new acquisition would pay for itself and not cost the Imperial Treasury a farthing. The cause of humanity would benefit from the extirpation of the African slave trade and the breaking of the Matabele stranglehold over the Mashona, as the more warlike portion of the Matabele tribe would ultimately be forced to emigrate beyond the Zambezi to try conclusions with the equally fierce Mashukulumbwe (the Ila in what is now Northern Rhodesia). Annexation finally would bring inestimable benefits to South Africa as a whole and help, by a single master stroke, to bring about the union of all its scattered colonies under the Union Jack.[2]

The British advance into Bechuanaland helped Lobengula in so far as it

---

[1] Sir Sidney Godolphin Alexander Shippard was called to the Bar at the Inner Temple in 1867, and subsequently followed a legal and administrative career in Griqualand West and the Cape. In 1885 he was appointed Administrator, Chief Magistrate and President of the Land Commission of British Bechuanaland, as well as Deputy Commissioner for Bechuanaland and the Kalahari. He retired in 1895 and then became Legal Adviser to the Consolidated Gold Fields of South Africa, Rhodes's concern.

[2] Shippard to High Commissioner: 21 May 1887 (Cape archives, Bech. 95/140); printed in Rademeyer, J. L. *Die land noord van die Limpopo in die ekspansie-beleid van die Suid-Afrikaanse Republiek.* Cape Town, A. A. Balkema, 1949

generally restrained Transvaal trekkers, who were forever trying to 'burst their kraals' in search of new pasture land. But at the same time Matabele power began to contract in the west. Khama, the chief of the Bamangwato, a reformer, a Christian, and a determined supporter of the British connexion, was now under imperial protection, and renewed his claims to the disputed territory between the Macloutsie and Shashi rivers, the Macloutsie being apparently regarded as the actual border line in practice.[1] Much worse from the Matabele point of view was, however, the gradual erosion of their military strength. Matabele supremacy in the north depended on the time-honoured tactics of the 'spear-crescent', which used to give victory to Shaka and Umziligazi, but were now beginning to yield diminishing military returns. The Bechuana, by working for, and trading with, the British, had by now acquired a large supply of firearms which the Matabele could not match; Khama's army of 2,000 men, though much smaller than Lobengula's, was better armed, and also contained 300 horsemen. The Matabele for their part possessed no cavalry of any kind; their guns largely consisted of ancient blunderbusses of old patterns and large bores, which the warriors would hand to gun-bearers when the fighting got really hot, in order better to get at close quarters with the assegai. The Matabele failed to adjust their military system to changing times, and in these circumstances their yearly raids became less successful. In 1883 a Matabele *impi* still managed to win a crushing victory over the Tawana by Lake Ngami, and returned in triumph, driving some 15,000 head of cattle before them, as well as many captive girls and children. In 1885 another expedition left for the Ngami country, but this time the invading army suffered an appalling disaster. The Tawana, now well apprised of the enemy's intentions, took up a strong tactical position beyond the Okovango river; when the Matabele tried to cross they were caught in devastating rifle-fire maintained from cover behind reeds, or from boats on the two flanks of the Matabele army. Only about 1,000 warriors—haggard and emaciated, without even their shields and assegais—returned to tell the tale, and Matabele military morale slumped in consequence. Many of the survivors of the Ngami disaster declared quite openly that if they were ordered out again they would feign sickness, whilst one of the king's brothers, an important chief in charge of a district, explained to a British envoy that his people were getting tired of war, that they wished to live in peace, and that they would be only too glad if the whole region became Government country.[2]

[1] Report by Lieut. C. E. Haynes: 5 Sep 1885 (Enclosure no. 9 in Sir C. Warren to Colonial Office: 26 Oct 1885; C. 4643 (1886), p. 121)

[2] Report by Major S. H. Edwards: 29 Aug 1885 (Enclosure no. 1 in Sir C. Warren to Colonial Office: 26 Oct 1885; C. 4643 (1886), p. 96)

F

The Matabele state was now drifting into dangerous waters. Northward expansion across the crocodile-infested Zambezi river remained a difficult undertaking in the face of Barotse canoe power. Boer and Briton blocked the way to the south. The western tribes were becoming too strong, with the result that the Matabele had largely to confine their raids to Mashonaland, where war parties ranged as far as Lomagundi and Mtoko, though some managed to get as far north as the Tonga country, in what is now Northern Rhodesia. The Mashona, the Matabele's main victims, were too disunited to maintain any effective resistance, their difficulties being increased by the fact that they lacked sufficient firearms. Some communities therefore tried to buy off the raiders by tribute, whilst others sought protection in the granite kopjes which, scattered profusely over the country, provide natural little fortresses in the bush. These periodic raids, however, formed no answer to the long range military problems of the Matabele. If they were going to maintain their supremacy they needed completely to reorganize their fighting services. But unfortunately, from their point of view, the required military revolution could not take place within the traditional framework of society. Weapons had to be paid for, and this Lobengula could not easily do. The country's ivory resources formed a wasting asset; by now the finest tuskers were largely shot out, so that the king could no longer trade elephants' tusks for breech loaders, at least not on any considerable scale. The Matabele of course controlled much valuable gold-bearing land, but lacked both will and skill to exploit it. An alternative was to send large batches of men to work in the mines at Kimberley, in exchange for firearms; some Matabele did indeed go down south but labour migration on a large scale would itself have tended to upset the traditional order.

Lobengula tried his best with the means available. He collected an armoury of six to eight hundred breech-loading weapons as well as ammunition, but his men lacked the technical skill to maintain them in good condition. Falling standards of recruitment caused a further deterioration in the army. The Matabele ranked their people according to the time of incorporation into the Matabele state, prestige increasing as lineage lengthened. The aristocracy were descended from the original horde that came up with Umziligazi. Next came the Bechuana who were taken prisoner on the way up, the lowliest position being occupied by the *Holi*, captives who were collected during periodic raiding expeditions against local tribes, who counted as slaves, though in practice living largely as their own masters. The recruits drawn from the latter two classes were inferior to those of the original Zulu stock, whose loss in battle was regarded as a much more serious calamity than that of men from the lower social classes. The dilution of the army with inferior troops in turn affected morale, and discipline grew lax. During the heyday of Matabele military might warriors only used to count the Zulus, Afrikaners and Griquas they killed; the Bechuana and others would be cut down, but not really considered worthy of Matabele steel. By 1885, however, Matabele fighting standards had dropped sharply, and returning warriors would even count old men, women and children, when boasting of the number of enemies whom they had slain. However imposing the Matabele army might still appear at the annual war dance, its real military strength was diminishing, and Lobengula's bargaining power was declining. In these circumstances the king could only play a waiting game. In 1885 he received a mission from Shippard, led by Major Samuel Howard Edwards, an officer of the Bechuanaland Field Force, who informed the king of the Bechuanaland annexation. Lobengula, whilst disputing Khama's boundary claims, showed himself at his most conciliatory, and promised to live in peace with Khama. The envoys returned, fully satisfied with their mission, and convinced that Matabele power was bound ultimately to disintegrate, a view which in turn strongly influenced Shippard's appreciation of the situation inland.

The British, however, were not the only ones interested in the Interior. By now the South African Republic was also consolidating its strength, and cast longing eyes to the Far North, the only open country still available to Boer trekkers. The British victory at Ulundi had rid the Transvaalers of the Zulu peril; the warlike Bapedi had ceased to give trouble, and the Transvaal was commencing a career of breath-taking economic advance. In 1886 gold was found on the Witwatersrand, and soon Johannesburg developed into a boom town where great fortunes were made. From being a forlorn backveld colony the Transvaal quickly grew rich, and mining revenues swelled its Treasury. The indigenous Transvaalers did not work the yellow metal themselves, leaving the exploitation of their precious minerals to English-speaking and foreign-born immigrants, but derived considerable financial and military benefit from their new source of income. President Kruger, the head of the state, was a far-sighted man, very different from the anachronistic seventeenth-century backveld Calvinist of British Imperial mythology. He fully appreciated the manifold advantages which his country might gain from its new wealth, provided only that political power was kept out of the immigrant diggers' hands, and restricted to the Afrikaner farming community. The gold mining industry made dramatic progress, but itself gave a new impetus for territorial expansion. Many farmers sold their land to mining concerns and decided to seek their fortunes in some other part of the country. The newcomers on the mines themselves needed food; agricultural markets expanded, so that farmers began to look for more pastures where they might graze their cattle.[1]

By now, however, the Republic could only expand to the north. The Bechuana bottle-neck was firmly under British control. St Lucia Bay, the only good harbour between Durban and Delagoa Bay, was in British hands, whilst the Portuguese in the east were acquiring a new interest in their colonies. Feeling worried about possible British designs on Matabeleland, the Transvaalers in 1887 despatched Pieter Daniel Cornelius Johannes Grobler, an experienced inland trader, to negotiate a treaty with the Matabele. Grobler at first met with considerable distrust, the Matabele having been warned by Shippard that the Transvaalers might attack them.[2] In the end the chief was pacified and Grobler brought home a document which purported to give extensive rights to the Transvaal in the country north of the Limpopo. The Grobler treaty, dated 30 July 1887, recognized Lobengula's independence, but stated Lobengula to be an ally of the South African Republic, and bound him to give military assistance to the Transvaal. Lobengula agreed to protect travellers, traders and hunters from the Transvaal who came to his country with a proper pass from the State President. Most important of all, the Matabele declared their willingness to admit a Consul from the South African Republic. The Consul would wield criminal and civil jurisdiction over all Transvaal subjects, and could also claim joint jurisdiction in civil cases between a Transvaaler and a Matebele.[3] Hugh Marshall Hole, a senior official of the British South Africa Company, who subsequently wrote the first standard history of Rhodesia,[4] later argued that the document bore 'the stamp of imposture from beginning to end'. The only European signatures were those of P. J. Grobler and his brother, F. A. Grobler. No resident missionary witnessed the document, neither did any other local European. The names of three out of the four chiefs who signed the treaty in addition to Lobengula bore no resemblance to Matabele words, whilst 'Omchaunien', the place where the treaty was signed, was supposedly not known in Matabeleland.

Hole's contention, however, carries little weight. Lobengula—determined to safeguard his sovereignty by playing off one lot of whites against another—was hardly likely to call on British missionaries in negotiating

[1] See Rademeyer, J. I. *Die land noord van die Limpopo*. . . . Cape Town, A. A. Balkema, 1949, ch. 4
[2] Shippard to Lobengula, draft: Mar 1886 (Enclosure no. 2 in Sir C. Shippard to Sir H. Robinson; 20 Mar 1886; C. 4839 (1886), p. 72–73)
[3] Printed in English in C. 5918 (1890), p. 5–6. The original is contained in State Secretary, In letters, R. 6535/87 in the Transvaal State Archives.
[4] Hole, H. M. *The making of Rhodesia*. Macmillan and co. ltd, 1926, p. 61–62

with Afrikaners; the Transvaalers found some difficulty in transcribing Matabele names, and 'Omchaunien' probably formed a Boer attempt to spell 'Umganin' (or Emganweni), one of the chief's residences. Grobler's own story sounded plausible enough. The Paramount Chief feared that the British might occupy the Transvaal because of its gold resources; emigrant Boers might then move into Lobengula's own domain, and rumours even went around in Matabeleland that a commando already stood to arms on the border. Grobler quietened the chief's fears, gave him a present of £140 in cash, as well as a rifle and some ammunition, and got Lobengula to sign the treaty. Lobengula then sent some ivory to the Transvaal, but firmly denied to the British ever having made any major concession to the Afrikaners, the exact truth being difficult to disentangle in the atmosphere of all-pervading suspicion that marked the Chief's foreign diplomacy.[1]

Later on, in 1887, two Matabele chiefs travelled down to Pretoria in Grobler's company, where they met Kruger who reassured them as to Transvaaler intentions regarding their country, and told them that the Boers would not seize any Matabele territory by force. Nothing much came of these negotiations. A year later Grobler lost his life in an affray treacherously provoked by the Bamangwato,[2] whilst the Transvaal proved incapable of asserting any claims north of the Limpopo. The Grobler mission, however, made a great impact on British imperialists in South Africa and thereby helped to set in motion the train of events that ended in the British occupation.

[1] For Grobler's side see Grobler to State President and Executive Council of the South African Republic: 13 Sep 1887, folios 113–115, R. 6537/87 in the Transvaal State Archives. For Lobengula's disclaimer see his statement of 25 Oct 1888 (Enclosure no. 2 in High Commissioner to Colonial Office: 19 Dec 1888; C. 5918 (1890), p. 149)

[2] See C. 5918 (1890), especially Lord Knutsford to Sir H. B. Loch: 16 Jan 1890

Chapter Three

Rhodes takes a hand

I

Treaties and Charter: 1887–1889

Transvaaler designs on the lands north of the Limpopo made a deep impression on imperially-minded men like Rhodes. For the Transvaal was now ceasing to be a poverty-stricken backveld state. When in 1886 gold was discovered on the Witwatersrand, the new deposits soon proved to be enormously valuable, making a most welcome contribution to the world economy, particularly at a time when most countries based their currencies on the gold standard, for a good many years had passed since the last great finds in California and Australia had given a much-needed stimulus to world trade.

In South Africa gold brought an economic revolution. The influential class of diamond merchants and entrepreneurs who made money in Kimberley soon interested themselves in these new deposits; the majority of the mining houses which opened at Johannesburg remained financially linked to the diamond industry. Rhodes also seized his chance and in 1887 founded Gold Fields of South Africa Ltd, though he missed the opportunity of establishing a quasi-monopoly. The gold mining industry on the Rand soon became a highly capitalized and organized affair, controlled by big concerns, whilst Rhodes's company—later renamed Consolidated Gold Fields of South Africa Ltd—developed into a huge share trust company, holding a stake in many important Rand mines, especially the deep-level ones.

Rhodes made great profits from his company. Many British immigrants now flocked to the Rand, and Johannesburg became a largely English-speaking community set within an Afrikaans-speaking hinterland. The southern colonies borrowed money in London to push their railways to the Rand in a determined bid to capture the interior trade. London investors sank a great deal of money into Johannesburg, and immigrants controlled most of the country's wealth. But the gold mines provided the

Transvaal with new revenue, and threatened to turn the most anti-British state in South Africa into the wealthiest. The Transvaalers—shrewd men despite their backveld upbringing—seized the opportunity with both hands; and as their country emerged from bankruptcy to solvency their ability to resist British schemes for a South African confederation enormously increased. President Kruger at last found the means of developing a separate political system, which one day might comprise the whole of the vast area between the Vaal and Zambezi rivers, and might achieve economic independence by a separate railway line to Delagoa Bay. Kruger's railway project also affected the southern colonies by threatening their railway investments; from 1886 onwards the old Imperial interest in strategy therefore became closely intertwined with a local struggle between the Cape Colony and the Transvaal, the Imperial authorities trying to back up the Cape, rather than become embroiled directly with Afrikaner nationalism.[1]

As for inland expansion, Sir Hercules Robinson (later Lord Rosmead), the British High Commissioner, at first took a cautious attitude; and late in 1887 Shippard still noted regretfully that the High Commissioner would not allow the pace to be forced, and discouraged appeals from Lobengula. Shippard concluded sadly that 'England appears to have no policy in South Africa' and seemed 'to be only anxious to shirk responsibility and expense',[2] whilst rumours were now circulating in Cape Town that the Transvaal might secure German protection, and that the Germans might try and get Mashonaland, Matabeleland and Umzila's country for themselves. There was in fact little truth in these stories. The Germans had their hands full with South-West Africa; but Rhodes thought that no risk should be taken. He therefore suggested to Robinson a kind of negative arrangement whereby Lobengula should undertake not to make any treaties without British consent, to which Robinson could see no objection.

The job of negotiating with Lobengula was entrusted to John Smith Moffat, a son of the famous missionary, and therefore *persona grata* with the Matabele. The choice was an excellent one in every respect. Moffat was well known to the Matabele; he possessed a wide knowledge of African languages and customs and had already gained local administrative experience as Assistant Commissioner for the Bechuanaland Protectorate. A firm believer in the concept of Imperial trusteeship for the native races, he felt honestly convinced that only the extension of British influence would solve the problems of the interior, and he was able to present a very

---

[1] See Robinson, R., and Gallagher, J. *Africa and the Victorians: the official mind of imperialism.* Macmillan and co. ltd, 1961, p. 210–253

[2] Shippard to J. S. Moffat: 19 Sep 1887 (in MO 1/1/4, Nat Arch MS)

convincing case to the Matabele. The Matabele for their part realized that they might require aid against the Transvaalers, or possibly even against the Portuguese who continued to claim Mashonaland; their boundary dispute with Khama remained unresolved, and nothing seemed more desirable than an understanding with Great Britain. On 11 February 1888 Lobengula therefore put his mark to a document of major importance. In the so-called 'Moffat Treaty' the paramount chief agreed that peace and amity should reign between Britons and Matabele, that he would not enter into any correspondence or treaty with any foreign state, or sell or cede any part of his dominions without the previous sanction of Her Majesty's High Commissioner for South Africa,[1] thereby signing away in practice the right to conduct an independent foreign policy.

In commercial language the British had secured an option on the interior, but these claims still had to be made effective. For one thing the Moffat Treaty led to protests both from Portugal and the Transvaal, but Lord Salisbury's government remained adamant, privately arguing that as Matabeleland and Mashonaland were bound to be opened up anyway by European enterprise, they had better be reserved to the Cape. The Imperial authorities, however, would at first go no further than diplomacy, fearing lest Parliament should jib at an outright protectorate over 'Southern Zambezia', with all the expenses which this would involve, whilst the Colonial Secretary ruled out any project for advancing British protection beyond the Zambezi.

As Rhodes saw it, the option still remained to be taken up, and matters were becoming all the more urgent, since he now had to deal not only with possible Matabele, but also local white opposition. Overseas two interlocking rival companies, the Bechuanaland Exploration Company and the Exploring Company were in process of formation. In Matabeleland some small traders were also trying to stake out claims, and a bitter struggle began, comparable in some ways to previous economic conflicts in Kimberley and Johannesburg, where the poor men were squeezed out and rival concerns merged into bigger and more powerful groups. Rhodes had the inestimable advantage of strong financial backing; behind him stood De Beers Consolidated Mines, his own diamond company, whose articles of association were framed in such a way that it could undertake almost any commercial or political task under the sun. In addition he ran the Gold Fields of South Africa Ltd, with its great stake in the Rand mines, and could thus afford to outbid the smaller groups.

He first of all tried to negotiate through John Larkin Fry and his son Ivon, but the older man became ill and returned to Kimberley where he

[1] Published in C. 5524 (1888), p. 13

died of cancer. Ivon was then superseded by a new embassy which contained the best men Rhodes was able to muster. The party was led by Charles Dunell Rudd, Rhodes's partner, who for sixteen years had shared in his financial ventures. Rudd, a Norfolk man, was a typical upper-middle-class empire builder of the Victorian period. Having distinguished himself at Harrow and Cambridge by a series of fine athletic performances, he suffered a breakdown as the result of over-training, and left for the Cape to restore his broken health. There he joined forces with Rhodes and the De Beers Group, and took part in the formation of the Gold Fields of South Africa Ltd. Rudd was accompanied by James Rochfort Maguire, a Fellow of All Souls, who later on, as a Director and then as President of the British South Africa Company, showed a financial acumen not usually associated with Oxford dons. The party's expert in African affairs was Francis Robert Thompson, who from the age of twelve onwards had been learning native languages and done valuable work in the Kimberley 'compounds'.

The party's task was a difficult one, but Rhodes enjoyed not only strong financial support, but also considerable 'pull' with the local Imperial authorities, as some of his rivals soon found out. In 1887 Joseph Garbett Wood, a sound and progressive farmer from the South who had served with distinction in various 'Kaffir Wars' and also represented Albany in the Cape Assembly, formed a syndicate with two other men to obtain a mining concession in Lobengula's country. After lengthy negotiations the wily king granted him a concession between the Shashi and Macloutsie rivers, in the area still in dispute between Khama and Lobengula, Khama having in turn granted a similar concession to the Bechuanaland Exploration Company. Baron d'Erlanger, a distinguished financier, offered to support Wood if he could establish Lobengula's title to the disputed region, and Wood set out once more for Matabeleland in 1888. On reaching Pretoria Wood learned that Sir Hercules Robinson had issued instructions forbidding Europeans to enter the disputed territory. Wood therefore decided to make for Bulawayo by a wide detour but the party was met by Major H. Goold-Adams, commanding the Bechuanaland Border Police, and Sir Sidney Shippard, who instructed Wood to return. On reaching Shoshong, Wood was arrested and charged with stirring up the Transvaal Government, and of inciting Lobengula to war. On Wood's agreeing not to enter the disputed territory the case was not proceeded with, but Wood was kept out of Matabeleland, and the field remained clear for Rhodes's emissaries.[1]

[1] For Wood's side of the story see *Case of the Wood, Chapman and Francis gold mining syndicate.* . . . Grahamstown, Josiah Slater, 1889. In 1891 the Bechuanaland Exploration Company, the Wood,

But Wood and his backers formed only one of Rudd's many problems. There were also smaller interests to be considered. These included, for instance, a syndicate set up by Thomas Leask, James Fairbairn, George Westbeech and George Phillips who in 1884 secured the mining rights between the Gwelo and Hunyani rivers, an extensive grant which was further extended four years later. Leask and his partners, however, widely realized the futility of trying to compete with Rhodes's immense resources and agreed to surrender their concession in return for a share in Rhodes's new company. Another small group, composed of John Cooper-Chadwick, a former trooper in the Bechuanaland Border Police, Benjamin ('Matabele') Wilson, and Alexander Boggie, similarly decided that discretion was the better part of valour, and threw in their hand with the 'Rhodes Party'.

Considerably more dangerous was the attitude of the Matabele war faction, including the crack Imbezi regiment and other units, which suggested that the Gordian knot should be cut once and for all by slaughtering all the whites in the country. Lobengula, however, would never countenance a war policy and sarcastically told the malcontents that if they wanted to fight, he would be only too pleased to 'give them the road to Kimberley' to try conclusions with the Europeans down south.[1] Rudd's hand was further strengthened by an official British embassy led in person by Shippard himself, and though the king tried to play for time, attempting to fob off his visitors by yet another partial grant, Rudd would not budge from his insistence that the document must comprise the whole country right up to the Zambezi, and including Mashonaland.[2] At last the Chief agreed, and on 30 October 1888 put his hand to the 'Rudd Concession'.

At first sight the document appeared extremely favourable to the Matabele. The grantees agreed to make a monthly payment of £100 to Lobengula and his heirs, which for the first time promised to provide the dynasty with a regular and guaranteed cash income. In addition the Matabele were to receive 1,000 Martini-Henry breech-loading rifles, with 100 rounds of ammunition for each, a most important concession from the military point of view, which—if properly exploited—would affect the whole balance of power in the interior. In return Lobengula agreed that the grantees should have 'complete and exclusive charge over all

Chapman and Francis Syndicate and the British South Africa Company agreed to amalgamate their interests in the creation of the Shashi and Macloutsie Exploration and Mining Company. This latter Company was not registered until 1894, permission for its formation having previously been withheld by the Colonial Office.

[1] Transcript of diary by 'Matabele' Wilson (WI 6/2/1, f. 51, Nat Arch MS)

[2] Hiller, V. W., ed. 'The concession journey of Charles Dunell Rudd' (in *Gold and the gospel in Mashonaland, 1888.* Chatto and Windus, 1949. Oppenheimer series no. 4), p. 202

metals and minerals situated and contained in my kingdoms, principalities and dominions', and that they should have 'full power to do all things that they may deem necessary to win and procure the same and to hold, collect and enjoy the profits and revenues, if any, derivable from the said metals and minerals'. More important still the Rhodes group received powers 'to take all necessary and lawful steps to exclude . . . all persons seeking land, metals, minerals or mining rights' in Lobengula's dominions, the king promising to give them all possible help in this respect, and not to grant any further concessions without the grantees' consent.

There is no doubt that the Matabele understood what they were signing; the matter was fully explained to them by the Rev. Charles Daniel Helm, a member of the London Missionary Society, who interpreted for the chief during the negotiations, and whose personal integrity was unassailable. The Matabele 'peace party' obviously assumed that mining could be carried out within the framework of a tribal economy, a view not shared by an old-timer like Benjamin Wilson who thought that the two systems were incompatible. But in assessing the situation, the Matabele may to some extent have been misinformed by Rhodes's emissaries; according to Helm the grantees explained that they would erect dwellings for their overseers, bring in and erect machinery, and use wood and water. They also promised that they would not bring more than ten white men to work in the country; that the newcomers would not dig anywhere near towns, and that they would abide by Matabele law and in fact 'be as his people'; these promises, however, did not form part of the concession itself.[1]

From Rhodes's point of view the concession was a considerable advance; the treaty represented an option, which kept out competitors in the economic field in the same way as the Moffat treaty excluded them in the political sphere. True enough, Lobengula's effective power extended over no more than a portion of Mashonaland, but the Matabele king now got a chance of making paper claims over a much vaster area, the chief's interest in exaggerating the extent of his territorial influence coinciding with Rhodes's design. The Matabele guarded themselves further; the document said nothing about land rights or jurisdiction, but Rhodes for his part now possessed a basis on which to raise his great financial edifice —the British South Africa Company—provided that Lobengula would stick to his promises.

Rhodes's plans involved a campaign on four fronts in the Imperial, the international, the financial and the local Matabele fields. In Britain Rhodes

---

[1] C. D. Helm to London Missionary Society: 29 Mar 1889 (in *Gold and the gospel in Mashonaland 1888*. Chatto and Windus, 1949. Oppenheimer series no. 4), p. 227–228

had to contend with various financial competitors, but much more serious from his point of view was the political opposition. Robinson was distrusted at the Colonial Office; and Lord Knutsford, the Colonial Secretary, then knew little about Rhodes, an 'Afrikander' who was widely suspected in England as an enemy of empire, as a man who sympathized with Boers and Irish Home Rulers and who competed with influential Unionist supporters for Matabeleland's mineral wealth. The South Africa Committee, led by Joseph Chamberlain and John Mackenzie, a well-known missionary, received support from a host of earnest humanitarians and clergymen, empire-minded politicians and retired colonial civil servants. This school of thought pressed for direct Imperial intervention, arguing that Britain as the paramount power should herself protect tribesmen against colonists, who were supposedly both enemies of empire and exploiters of the black. Experienced Imperial officials predicted that a chartered company would occasion a Matabele war, whilst philanthropists foretold that Rhodes's men would take the natives' land. Moreover, in the eyes of many British merchants, Rhodes stood for nothing more than an exclusive Cape mining group who might close Zambezia to British enterprise, and whose schemes were diametrically opposed to all British ideals of free trade.[1]

Rhodes, however, played his cards supremely well, and in fact the prevailing creed of keeping down state expenditure and public taxation even worked in his favour. Given the assumption that the interior must be kept out of foreign hands, Rhodes alone could 'deliver the goods'. With the riches of Kimberley and Johannesburg behind him, he wielded far greater financial power than any of his rivals; at a time when the Cabinet could not get money for the acquisition of Matabeleland he alone could provide the funds. Where the Imperial Government could only make paper claims Rhodes would plant a colony; where London shied away from responsibility he would take the risks. Rhodes also offered to build a railway through Bechuanaland—a tremendous undertaking at the time —and gradually the great amalgamator won over many of his most powerful opponents. In any case white frontiersmen were bound to make their way into the interior; they could no more be stopped than could the pioneers who opened the American West. If Rhodes was granted a charter, the Imperial policy might at least control the settlers who would flock to the Far North and thereby prevent the country from becoming a paradise for private filibusters. Company rights would be chained to responsibility; whilst the natives would be better safeguarded by Imperial

[1] See Robinson, R., and Gallagher, J. *Africa and the Victorians: the official mind of imperialism.* Macmillan and co. ltd, 1961, p. 224–253

supervision than by allowing private capitalists to act on their own. Rhodes moreover held a key position in Cape politics and must not be alienated. The Cape might be separatist; South Africa by itself might be separatist; but a South Africa reaching up to the Zambezi would lean upon Britain for safety against Portuguese and German interference. Lastly the interior would be settled by British colonists, whose influence would counteract that of the Transvaal, and a new English-speaking Zambezia would arise to redress the trembling balance of power in the sub-continent.

Ruling an under-developed country through a Chartered Company was moreover nothing new or untried; no Minister and no civil servant needed to take up the dreaded burden of creating a new precedent. During the 'eighties the Crown granted charters to the British North Borneo Company, the Royal Niger Company and the Imperial British East Africa Company; these differed from earlier concerns of that kind, established in the sixteenth and seventeenth centuries, in that they did not get officially recognized trade monopolies. They received instead specific privileges, such as the right to dispose of land, to promote mining, to tax the indigenous people, and to acquire concessions of various kinds, these rights being linked to well-defined administrative obligations. The British South Africa Company itself never tried to engage in trade; neither did it attempt to mine on its own account, or indeed compete in any other way with the colonists who in time made their way beyond the Limpopo. Instead the Directors hoped to encourage the flow of mining capital into the 'Far North', taking themselves a share of the profits in exchange for allowing others to work the yellow metal. The Company also became an important financial trust with shares in railways and other enterprises. Members of the Board likewise acquired shares or directoral appointments in other Rhodesian companies where their inside knowledge of local administrative and economic matters stood them in good stead.[1]

To the metropolitan government ventures such as the British South Africa Company offered many advantages. They supplied capital without making demands on the taxpayer; they took risks that the home government would not take; they built up pioneer administrations at a time when the British (and also German and Belgian) authorities lacked money and men to run some of these newly acquired possessions overseas. From the financial point of view chartered companies might in some ways be described as the 'forlorn hope' of investment capital, a kind of 'commando force' which would set up economic bridgeheads at the risk of being wiped

---

[1] For information on linked directorships in Rhodesia in the 'nineties see Wills, W. H., and Hall, J. *Bulawayo up to date*. Simpkin, Marshall, Hamilton, Kent and co. ltd, 1899

out itself. Contemporary financiers who put their money into such ventures of course did not see things in that light. Many investors wrongly imagined—like their subsequent critics in the Socialist camp— that profits would come in fast, that the barren veld only needed the investors' Midas touch to turn to gold. Imperialists and their enemies alike underestimated the enormous expenditure required to make African enterprise pay. The bulk of early 'Chartered' shareholders in fact never made any money from their share certificates; their funds in many cases simply paved the way for other investors whose enterprise only became profitable after the required foundations of transport and administrative services had been laid at the expense of the original pioneers.[1]

But this Rhodes and his friends could hardly realize at the time. With their experiences of Kimberley and the Rand they expected a golden torrent of wealth, and accordingly went ahead to deal with the remaining financial opposition. Minor claimants—including speculators with some very doubtful concessions—were bought out to prevent subsequent litigation. The rival Bechuanaland Exploration Company and the Exploring Company joined Rhodes, taking a hint from the Colonial Office that their objects would be more easily served if they combined their interests. Rhodes also made friends with W. T. Stead, an influential journalist, who at one time strongly supported Mackenzie against the 'Charter', but like so many others, was won over by the strength of Rhodes's personality. The Irish Party in Parliament—which might have wielded deadly powers of obstruction at Westminster—supported the 'Charter' by reason of Rhodes's very real sympathy for Irish Home Rule, which he regarded as part and parcel of Imperial federation. With similar persistence Rhodes overcame the forces of social prejudice against himself, a self-made mining magnate from the Colonies, and on 29 October 1889 the Queen at last signed the Letters Patent granting a Royal Charter of Incorporation to the British South Africa Company.

The terms of the Charter seemed sufficiently wide to satisfy even the most critical investor. The Company's 'principal sphere of operations' was deliberately vague; only the Tati district was specifically excluded; but otherwise the Charter comprised all Southern Africa north of British Bechuanaland, and to the north and west of the South African Republic, and to the west of the Portuguese possessions, no northern limit being assigned to the Company's field. The Charter thus kept the way open for further territorial extension at a time when the Company's own maps showed Lobengula's effective sphere of influence as going no further than

[1] The British South Africa Company only issued its first dividend in 1924 when it managed to pay 6d in the £, having by then been relieved of the burden of administering Rhodesia.

the Zambezi, and stopping well west of the Sabi. The Imperial authorities set the Charter to run for a quarter of a century. Rhodes thereby gained his object of allowing enough time for his company to get well established, and firmly to plant a new British community in the heart of the Continent, which he hoped would later hold the balance of power within a South African federation.

His Company was now confirmed in its existing concessions, subject to certain reservations, and it could also secure new ones, subject to the Secretary of State's approval. The Charter itself did not give political rights over Africans, but enabled the Company to acquire extensive powers by treaty, subject to Downing Street's consent; the Company could also engage in banking, mining, real estate deals and other economic activities. The Company was also given 'teeth' by being allowed to set up an armed police, thus supplying Rhodes with what in fact turned out to be a small private army. In return, the Secretary of State retained a few supervisory functions; he might veto ordinances; he might decide disputes between a tribe and the Company; he could interfere in the Company's dealings with foreign powers; he supervised its financial accounts. The new concern had to respect native civil law, subject to any British legislation which might be introduced from time to time; the Company was to maintain freedom of trade and religion; its administration was expected gradually to eliminate slavery and to protect Africans from the trade in liquor.

The capital for this vast undertaking was fixed at a million pounds in £1 shares, a large sum for the times, but in fact ridiculously inadequate for the purpose. The promoters, by a series of complicated transactions, took good care that their venture profited them; De Beers subscribed heavily; the Board boasted of splendid names, such as the Dukes of Fife and Abercorn, whose presence on the directorate symbolized an economic marriage between a great landed aristocracy and new financial men like Rhodes and Beit.[1]

In addition many small investors put up some money to take part in a venture which promised imperial glory as well as golden riches—an

---

[1] The great landowners included the Duke of Abercorn who owned 26,000 acres and Albert Henry George Grey who owned 17,600 acres. The Duke of Fife headed the banking house of Samuel Scott and co., of which Sir Horace Brand Farquhar was a partner. Alfred Beit was a member of Wernher, Beit and co. of Johannesburg and London, and also sat on the boards of other gold and diamond companies, as well as of the United Concessions and Exploring companies and, later, the Rhodesia Railways and Beira Railway companies. George Cawston was a leading member of the London Stock Exchange, Rochfort Maguire was a Fellow of All Souls and became a barrister, whilst Baron Gifford, V.C., supplied extensive military and administrative experience in the Empire. Politically the Board had an equally wide spread. Abercorn was a Conservative, Fife a Liberal Unionist, Maguire an Irish Nationalist, Rhodes what might be called a British South African 'nationalist'.

enterprise in which an elderly lady might own just a single share merely for the privilege of attending an annual meeting of shareholders and seeing the great empire builder in the flesh. Helped by a generally favourable Press, Rhodes built up considerable public support, and the great venture was thus launched in an atmosphere of all-pervading optimism.[1] Management within the concern turned out to be relatively efficient and highly centralized. The Company's Deed of Settlement vested control in the Board of Directors which was to number not less than seven persons— including three life members. The Board was also empowered to appoint up to three Managing Directors to act within defined areas; under this provision Rhodes was put in charge of affairs in South Africa, whilst Maguire—elected to Parliament in 1890 to represent North Donegal— became Rhodes's alternate in London. The newly issued Deed defined the powers of the Board in considerable detail. It could buy, sell or lease property rights and privileges for the Company; it could borrow money up to one-half of the Company's nominal capital; appoint and remove the Company's officers; institute, compound or abandon legal proceedings for the Company; invest Company money not immediately required or set aside for specific purposes; it could make by-laws for the running of the concern, and also wield many other powers. The shareholders of the Company, who by 1898 numbered almost 35,000, were entitled to attend the Annual General Meeting. Alternatively they might let themselves be represented by proxy, and in fact Annual General Meetings were always run in so expert a fashion that they never constituted a serious threat to directoral policy, whilst the Board maintained considerable continuity in its composition.

In the field of foreign policy matters went well for the Company. Diplomatic conflict continued with Portugal; but the little kingdom soon found itself almost isolated in the international sphere. In March 1890 Count Georg Leo von Caprivi, a German general, took over the Chancellorship at Berlin, and decided on a new course of restrained liberalism at home and friendship with Great Britain abroad. Caprivi dropped Bismarck's 'Reinsurance Treaty' with Russia, supported Austria in the Balkans, and pursued a more accommodating policy towards Britain, a relationship not as yet disturbed by German naval ambitions, and cemented by a common distrust of Russian plans in Turkey and the Middle East. The British were just as anxious to make a deal. They had to contend with French opposition in Africa and Russian designs in the Near East; they were anxious to secure their position in Egypt, and prevent foreigners from gaining access to the Sudan, a country which Britain at

[1] See Williams, B. *Cecil Rhodes*, 2nd ed. Constable and company ltd, 1938, p. 138–139

that time was not yet in a position to reconquer from the Mahdi. In July 1890 Anglo-German talks at last culminated in a major settlement of their African claims. The British secured most of the Nyasa-Tanganyika plateau; Germany was excluded from the Nile Valley and Uganda, and though the British forfeited the fulfilment of Rhodes's dream of a great belt of territory stretching from the Cape to Cairo, they secured something much more tangible, a firm hold on their position both in Egypt and in South Central Africa.

The Portuguese now found that they had played their diplomatic cards badly, and that by holding out too long the 'terms of trade' had gone against them. In 1888 Lord Salisbury, anxious not to press the Portuguese too hard, was still willing to leave the Portuguese in control north of the Zambezi, whilst Nyasaland should remain neutralized. But the colonists in the Cape protested, and Rhodes stepped in, promising to shoulder the cost of administering 'Northern Zambezia', and assisting financially in the cost of pacifying Nyasaland. Early in 1890 the British then dispatched an ultimatum, and the Portuguese accordingly gave orders for their small expeditionary force to withdraw. In August the Portuguese signed a convention, known as the 'modus vivendi', which was still relatively favourable to the Portuguese, leaving them with Manicaland, a decision which provoked Rhodes to boundless fury. The treaty nevertheless met with passionate hostility in Portugal where the Republicans used it as a stick to belabour not only the British, but also their royalist opponents at home. The Cortes assembled under great excitement and the Portuguese finally refused to ratify the document. But this proved bad tactics; the Portuguese were pressed further into the corner, and in the final agreement, signed on 11 June 1891, they came off even worse; Salisbury once more yielded to Rhodes who obtained all Barotseland and the Manica plateau, in exchange for a Portuguese salient north of the Zambezi and west of the Shire highlands.[1]

In the meantime there was a bitter struggle on the local front. Bishop George Wyndham Hamilton Knight-Bruce, at the time incumbent of the Anglican See of Bloemfontein, visited Mashonaland in 1888.[2] When he heard of the concession, he delivered a savage attack on Rhodes, arguing that the Mashona merited full protection against 'the diabolical horrors which mark the path of the Matabele impis', and that 'such a piece of devilry and brutality as a consignment of rifles to the Matabele cannot be

[1] For the Anglo-Portuguese treaties see C. 6212 (1890) and C. 6370 (1891). For the Anglo-German treaty see C. 6046 (1890). P. R. Warhurst has made a detailed study of the period in *Anglo-Portuguese relations in South-Central Africa, 1890–1900*. Longmans, Green and co. ltd, 1962 (Imperial studies no. 23)

[2] He resigned the See in January 1891, to become the first Bishop of Mashonaland.

G

surpassed'.[1] This 'brutal assault' caused Rhodes no little anxiety, but shortly afterwards Rhodes wrote to Rudd that the Bishop had 'repented'. What persuasion he used is not explained, but the Bishop's repentance came at an opportune moment, for his original remarks made a great impression on the High Commissioner, and awkward questions were asked in England. Shippard, however, defended the arms contract on the grounds that Matabele warriors would be more formidable with assegais than modern rifles, the kind of reasoning likely to convince the 'cold steel' school of warfare, though none other! Rhodes, however, stuck to his word, and made sure that the proposed firearms did reach the Matabele king.[2]

Strong opposition against the Rudd Concession lingered in Matabeleland among disappointed Europeans who resented Rhodes's monopoly or proposed to hold out until they were 'squared'. Lobengula, in order to play for time, sent an embassy to London, consisting of Umsheti and Babyaan, two senior chiefs accompanied by E. A. Maund, the guiding spirit in this political manœuvre, and Johannes Wilhelm Colenbrander, the latter a Natal trader with many interests in Matabeleland, and with a perfect knowledge of the Zulu tongue. At this time the Charter had not yet been settled; the Bechuanaland Exploring Company was negotiating with Khama, whilst the Exploring Company, headed by Lord Gifford, and represented at Lobengula's court by Maund, was still hoping for similar privileges. In March 1889 the Queen, advised by Lord Knutsford, therefore sent back a cautious letter, advising the king not to give away his whole herd of cattle and to keep some beasts in reserve for other deserving men. The royal despatch, as well as a communication from the Aborigines' Protection Society, was eagerly seized upon by the anti-Concession party in Matabeleland, the position being made more difficult by the fact that Lobengula received a copy of the *Cape Argus*, which provided him with details concerning the proposed Charter over his country.[3]

The worthy men who lived many thousands of miles away in England, and wrote about the country from the safety of their studies, had of course

---

[1] Extract from speech made at Vryburg on 8 December 1888, printed in Fripp, C. E., ed. 'The Mashonaland mission of Bishop Knight-Bruce, 1888' (in *Gold and the gospel in Mashonaland, 1888*. Chatto and Windus, 1949. Oppenheimer series no. 4), p. 137–138

[2] Later Rhodes wrote a letter to Knight-Bruce, stressing the danger that Lobengula might simply be driven into the hands of Kruger if he was alienated. As for the guns, he was bound to get them anyway. The great point was to encourage trade inland and to set up a British Resident who would use his influence to check raiding. See C. J. Rhodes to G. W. H. Knight-Bruce: 20 Feb 1889, in Fripp, C. E., ed. 'The Mashonaland mission of Bishop Knight-Bruce, 1888' (in *Gold and the gospel in Mashonaland, 1888*. Chatto and Windus, 1949. Oppenheimer series no. 4), p. 139

[3] Diary of B. 'Matabele' Wilson: 31 July 1889 (WI 6/2/1, Nat Arch MS)

not the slightest idea of the effect which their despatches would produce in Matabeleland; but as it happened their letters caused a furore. The white men at Bulawayo found themselves in considerable personal danger, though personal violence to Europeans was avoided. Nevertheless a scapegoat had to be found to assuage popular wrath. The chief victim was Lotjie, an elderly induna who headed the pro-Concession party, and had already previously incurred great unpopularity as a result of having led a disastrous expedition to Lake Ngami. Lotjie was liquidated with all his family and followers—victims of the time lag in British policy—for by the time he was done to death the Exploring Company and Gold Fields of South Africa interests had already merged and the Imperial authorities had accepted the idea of a Charter.

For the moment Lotjie's execution seemed a disaster for the Rhodes party. Thompson, who had remained in Matabeleland to represent Rhodes's cause, became sick with worry and hurriedly decamped, with the result that a 'political vacuum' appeared at Bulawayo, the very contingency which Rhodes feared more than any other. Rhodes moved quickly. In Leander Starr Jameson, a doctor from Kimberley, he found the perfect man for the job. Jameson, a Scotsman from Edinburgh, emigrated to Kimberley in 1878, after having taken a doctorate in medicine, and built up a good practice in what was becoming an important mining centre. Here he met Rhodes who was highly impressed by the young doctor's charm and ability. Jameson thus became involved in politics, the first of a run of medical men who—like Godfrey Martin Huggins and Hastings Kamuzu Banda—later took a prominent part in Central African public affairs. In February 1889 Rhodes sent Jameson to Bulawayo. The doctor, whose medical ability stood him in good stead with the ailing king, patiently pleaded the 'Charter's' case. He also received help from Moffat, and his diplomatic task was further aided by Portuguese designs in the north, which made it all the more desirable for Lobengula to get British rifles. The matter was clinched when late in 1889 Lord Knutsford despatched yet another letter to Lobengula, explaining that the Queen had approved of the Rudd Concession, that Lobengula should stick to his promises, and that the king would do well to hand over disputes between white men in his country to the Chartered Company's representatives. This time nothing was said about the undesirability of giving away a whole herd; and Lobengula must have realized that there was no going back. The Matabele had reached the 'point of no return', and their country's future lay with the white gold seekers.[1]

[1] For a detailed account see Hole, H. M. *The making of Rhodesia*. Macmillan and co. ltd, 1926 p. 104–126

II

The Pioneer Column: 1890

The Charter was signed, but Rhodes's hinterland as yet remained to be occupied. This on the face of it was a fantastically difficult task. The country beyond the Limpopo was devoid of railways, roads or staging posts—a happy hunting ground for frontiersmen and adventurers. Lobengula continued in command of a well-drilled army and was believed to be able to put something like 18,000 warriors in the field—a grim thought to South Africans who well remembered how, barely ten years before, a Zulu host had surprised and massacred a whole battalion of British regulars at Isandhlwana. Rhodes had no intention of permitting all his dreaming and scheming to end in one glorious 'Last Stand' in the frontier tradition, and at one time, as an insurance against this, thought of taking the Matabele by surprise. He found an able lieutenant in Frank William Frederick Johnson, a remarkable character, half soldier, half entrepreneur, the sort of man who would have gone far as a mercenary leader in the days of Wallenstein.

Johnson, born in Norfolk in 1866, came to South Africa at the age of sixteen, and soon afterwards enlisted in the Duke of Edinburgh's Own Rifles, subsequently serving with the Second Mounted Rifles in the Warren Expedition, and in the newly formed Bechuanaland Border Police. He sought discharge from the Police in 1887 and then went to seek his fortune further inland, obtaining a mining concession from Khama, and making an extended journey to Bulawayo and the Mazoe Valley. For a time Johnson acted as General Manager of the Bechuanaland Exploration Company, but his dreams of golden wealth vanished when he found himself the victim of what he regarded as an elaborate piece of financial trickery.[1] Johnson left the Company in disgust, bitterly incensed with Lord Gifford and George Cawston who became Directors of the British South Africa Company, and angry at having failed to get any of his claims squared before the signing of the Charter. Nevertheless he soon decided to throw in his lot with Rhodes and towards the end of 1889 the two arrived at a confidential agreement which foreshadowed in some ways the Jameson Raid of subsequent fame. The young adventurer cordially detested Lobengula who had, he thought, treated him badly during a visit

[1] For Johnson's side of the story see Report to the South African shareholders of the Bechuanaland Exploration Company: 20 Dec 1889 (in JO 3/1/1, Nat Arch MS)

to Bulawayo and accordingly was not averse to 'getting his own back'.
The proposed arrangement allowed him full scope. At this time prospectors were still busy in Khama's country, and the scheme was designed to
use them as a blind. Small and scattered parties would gradually be introduced into the Protectorate until they numbered about 500 men, all
trained frontier fighters. When the moon was right Rhodes's little private
army would quickly converge on a selected spot by the Shashi river, well
away to the north-west of Tati, in an uninhabited part of the country.
After a day's halt to take breath, the commando would make a rush by
night for Lobengula's kraals at Bulawayo. The coup would be made by
four hundred mounted men, travelling with spare horses and packloads of
ammunition, while another hundred coming behind would bring in
weapons and further supplies. Johnson's arrival at Bulawayo would come
as a shattering surprise, well in advance of any Matabele messengers
travelling on foot to bring news of the impending blow. Johnson himself
had, as he put it, 'an open mind' on what he would do subsequently.
Lobengula might perhaps be killed on the spot, and each military kraal
attacked in turn, in time to prevent Lobengula's army from mobilizing.
Alternatively the raiders might dig themselves in at Bulawayo and hold
the king as hostage in negotiating a peace treaty.[1]

Fortunately, however, he was never asked to put to the test his hare-
brained project, which might well have ruined Rhodes. Militarily the
scheme would have presented the utmost difficulties. The Matabele would
certainly have given a good account of themselves; they possessed firearms—like the Europeans—and enjoyed enormous numerical superiority.
In discussing his plans Johnson makes no mention of machine guns; to use
wagons would have meant forfeiting speed and the element of surprise,
but wagons had made an essential contribution to Boer victories in native
wars, and were in fact later adopted for the Pioneer Column. The commando would admittedly have enjoyed the advantage of greater mobility,
but if they lost the strategic initiative or allowed themselves to be shut up
in Bulawayo, cut off from future supplies of food and ammunition, their
position would have been desperate indeed. Apart from that their gamble
would have jeopardized the life of every white man in Matabeleland. From
the moral point of view the best that can be said about the plan is that it

---

[1] The details of this project are given in an unexpurgated version of *Great Days*, Johnson's autobiography, which was subsequently published with the offending passages left out. The manuscript
is kept in the National Archives (JO 3/6, Nat Arch MS). A copy of 'Memorandum of a confidential
agreement...' between Rhodes, Johnson and Heany, dated 7 December 1889, is at JO 3/2, Nat
Arch MS. The original of this agreement was seen by the Archivist of the then Government Archives
of Southern Rhodesia during a visit to Johnson, but it was apparently lost during the German
occupation of the Channel Islands in the Second World War.

differed in no wise from the kind of project hatched by the Matabele 'war-hawks', the swashbuckling young sub-chiefs who had not yet made their name within the tribal hierarchy and longed for a 'showdown' with the enemy quite as much as Johnson, their opposite, in the white camp.

Details of the scheme apparently began to 'leak', for an undertaking of such a kind could hardly be kept a secret—men talk in their cups. Rhodes moreover apparently received contrary advice from Selous. The hunter argued that Matabeleland could be circumvented by means of a wagon road which would lead into Mashonaland, avoiding the central core of Lobengula's dominions.[1] Rhodes and Johnson discussed the matter at great length and in the end arrived at an agreement which provided for colonization by contract. Fired by the magic of Rhodes's words, Johnson agreed to sign a document by which he would take over a country for the Company. Johnson engaged to construct a wagon road from Palapye to Mount Hampden, near where the city of Salisbury stands today, and to build a fort there. Johnson would recruit a corps of settlers, enlisted temporarily under semi-military discipline, who would, on disbandment, colonize the country. He also engaged to keep out white filibusters, the Company furnishing supplies and weapons, including four Maxims and two seven-pounder field guns. In return for these services he would be paid a total of £87,000 and receive 40,000 morgen as soon as the Company was in a position to make grants of waste and unoccupied land.[2] The strength of the projected Corps only amounted to about 200 men, a totally inadequate force if they should ever run into trouble.

Recruitment for the Pioneer Corps began immediately. Johnson recalls that on one occasion Rhodes stopped him from enlisting ordinary privates discharged from colonial military units, insisting that he should try and sign on sons of leading families in each district of the Cape. At first Johnson could not make out what Rhodes was after, but the great man's answer was in keeping with that odd mixture of cold realism and wild gambling that marked so many of his ventures. The expedition might be massacred; at least they might be surrounded and cut off. What could then save the Pioneers? Only Imperial intervention! How could this be secured? Only by agitation on the part of worried and influential fathers![3]

Johnson thus found himself with quite a task on his hands. The new

[1] F. C. Selous to Mrs F. L. Selous: 22 Dec 1889 and 26 Oct 1890 (in SE 1/1/1, Nat Arch MS). Selous claimed that the whole idea was his own. Johnson himself, much later, stated that he also worked out the idea.

[2] For Johnson's copy see 'Memorandum of an agreement . . . signed 14 January 1890' (in JO 3/2, Nat Arch MS), printed in Johnson, F. *Great days: the autobiography of an Empire pioneer.* G. Bell and sons ltd, 1940, p. 326–332

[3] Johnson, F. *Great days, op. cit,* p. 108–111

community was to contain a representative cross-section, butchers and bakers as well as lawyers and doctors with good social connexions—an aim which might well tax the abilities of the most ingenious selection board. Nevertheless Rhodes to some extent got what he wanted. There were Englishmen and Afrikaners, Germans and Frenchmen, usually men of fine physique, many of them with military experience—a fine force even though the officers lacked *esprit de corps*. Sons of peers served next to street arabs, prospectors mingled with soldiers; clerks jostled with cow-punchers, and one troop was known as the gentlemanly troop because the majority were brokers.[1] A large proportion of the men hailed from the Cape, from Cape Town, Kimberley or the Eastern Province, and the new white community in the Far North remained closely linked to the Cape throughout its formative years. Rhodes originally intended to rely on his Pioneers alone, but the British High Commissioner for South Africa decided that the undertaking would be too hazardous without an adequate armed escort, capable of protecting the settlers and securing their lines of communications. The Charter authorized the setting up of a Company police force, and the British Bechuanaland Police increased its strength, the extra troops thus raised becoming the nucleus of the British South Africa Company's Police. Acting under pressure from the Imperial authorities the Chartered Company increased its police to about 500 men, the new force attracting volunteers from as far afield as Cape Town, Kimberley and the Eastern Province of the Cape, as well as from Britain and other parts of South Africa. In the minds of many contemporaries an aura of romance surrounded the whole venture, Rhodes himself being influenced by this kind of feeling as much as the humblest trooper. Central Africa often appeared as a strange kind of dream land where the harsh everyday world ended and King Solomon's Ophir began, a land of mystery and unlimited opportunity. The police therefore never suffered from a shortage of recruits and attracted a great many youngsters from established families who were only too glad to serve in the ranks, even though they received much less pay than the Pioneer Corps which stood out as one of the best remunerated units in military history.[2] Typical of such police volunteers was a man like Sergeant Randolph Crosby Nesbitt, who later gained great local fame and a Victoria Cross in Mashonaland. Nesbitt was the son of an army paymaster and came from a family with a fine military record; he was educated at St Aidan's College, Kingwilliams-town, and at St Paul's School, London, the average pioneer or trooper often coming from a higher social background than was customary on

[1] Leonard, A. G. *How we made Rhodesia*. Kegan Paul, Trench, Trübner and co. ltd, 1896, p. 26
[2] A trooper in the Pioneers received 7/6d a day and a Sergeant-Major 11/6d.

most frontiers. In addition the Company recruited skilled and semi-skilled Africans from the Cape, cooks, drivers, general servants and so on, men who were attracted by the relatively good conditions of service offered, so that the enterprise right from the start bore something of a 'multi-racial' nature.[1]

The Column was fortunate in securing an excellent commanding officer, Lieutenant-Colonel Edward Graham Pennefather, who was seconded to take charge of the combined force of policemen and pioneers. Pennefather had seen much service in South Africa, where his regiment, the 6th (Inniskilling) Dragoons, took part in the Zulu campaign of 1879 and the Transvaal War. The Inniskilling Dragoons in fact, with their hard acquired knowledge of veld fighting, supplied some of early Rhodesia's ablest officers. Pennefather himself was both an excellent soldier and a sound leader. He certainly needed to be, for he soon found himself faced with a very difficult task. The enterprise involved delicate questions of Anglo-Portuguese and Anglo-Transvaal relations. There were the ordinary problems of man management, and those revolving round internal politics, the latter, as always, becoming inextricably entwined with personal conflicts. For whereas the military command was unified, civil control remained divided, an arrangement which gave rise to much heart-burning. The man in charge of civil affairs in the new territory was Archibald Ross Colquhoun, a former Imperial official in Burma, who at one time doubled as *Times* correspondent for the Far East, in which capacity he transgressed against the rules of his Service by criticizing his superiors in the Press. Having thereby fallen foul of the Indian Government, he looked round for another job, and with much pleasure in 1889 accepted an offer from Rhodes. But Rhodes at the same time insisted that Dr Jameson, his *alter ego*, should accompany the Column as his personal representative, with the result that the ill-assorted pair, the ex-Indian civil servant and the Kimberley doctor, soon began to disagree.[2]

Apart from the vexed question of administrative control, Pennefather also had to cope with a tricky military problem. The route chosen avoided the old 'Hunters' Road', and ran from Macloutsie to Tuli, to where Fort Victoria now stands, to Charter, and then on to the present site of Salisbury. The way proved just about passable for wagons, but the Pioneers had to traverse some unhealthy *mopane* country of the kind which tribal

---

[1] The pay and conditions of service are quoted in the 'Order book of A Troop, Pioneer Corps' 26 May–28 Sep 1890. (PI 2/6/2, Nat Arch MS). The daily rations laid down for Colonial natives amounted to 2 lb of meal, $1\frac{1}{2}$ lb of meat, 1 oz of coffee, 2 oz of sugar, $\frac{1}{2}$ oz of coarse salt. In addition they received 4 oz of tobacco per week.

[2] For his own story see Colquhoun, A. R. *Dan to Beersheba*. William Heinemann, 1908. The most exhaustive biography of Jameson is Colvin, I. *Life of Jameson*. Edward Arnold and co., 1922

invaders and white alike would avoid when they could; to this day the Pioneer Road remains marked by isolated groups of graves where police-men, transport-riders and mail carriers found their last resting place. The Column took a serious military risk. Had the Matabele decided to attack, they would have enjoyed three decided advantages; knowledge of the country, choice of tactical initiative and superior numbers; a big convoy of wagons, stretched out to an awkward length might have had a hard time defending itself, especially if caught on the march in the broken country of the low veld.[1] In addition there was the possibility of night attacks when the whites' superior fire-power would not have been as effective as in broad daylight.

But the Column on the other hand was well drilled and effectively combined the military technology of the back-veld with that of the later Industrial Revolution. The men had mastered the art of forming laagers; they also possessed light field pieces and Maxim guns, the kind of weapons which—unlike rifles—primitive warriors could neither acquire nor use, and which now began to tilt the balance of power against tribal levies all over the world. The British also had an electric searchlight for use in the event of a night attack, and a steam engine. In addition to mounted frontiersmen, the Column contained military technicians such as a small ex-naval detachment, commanded by Edward Carey Tyndale-Biscoe, a British officer, invalided out of the Royal Navy on account of a severe stammer, but admirably qualified to handle seven-pounders and war rockets.

In the face of this formidable threat Lobengula decided that caution was the only possible policy. In dealing with his own war party he played for time, staging a grand military review at Bulawayo and sending a vaguely-worded though somewhat threatening letter to the Column through Colenbrander. But he would not risk hostilities, sharing perhaps 'Mata-bele' Wilson's view that in the event of war the 'Maholi' would prove unreliable. Thus no large body of Matabele was ever allowed to get near the Column, who slowly toiled on through the almost tropical lowveld, sometimes cutting their way through timbered valleys, at others hauling their wagons by drag-rope across rivers infested with crocodiles and impassable for oxen unaided—never able to see more than a hundred yards or so, and constantly on the look-out for possible ambushes. The Column reached the Lundi river without incident, but the problem then was to gain the highveld from the lower river valley and there was no certainty of finding a road for the lumbering wagons. Selous, going ahead, found a way which the delighted Pioneers called 'Providential Pass'. The

[1] Leonard, A. G. *How we made Rhodesia.* Kegan Paul, Trench, Trübner and co. ltd, 1896, p. 56

Column thus safely reached the park-like, grassy savannah country of the highveld, and the main danger of being surprised and massacred by Matabele *impis* in the dense bush was over. The lines of communication were guarded by three small *points d'appui*, set up at Fort Tuli, Fort Victoria and Fort Charter, and at last the Pioneers drew near their destination.

At the same time the 'Charter' took steps to secure its eastern frontier against the Portuguese, and Jameson, Colquhoun and Selous struck across country from Fort Charter to Manicaland to establish British influence in the disputed border zone. Jameson was thrown off his horse and had to return to the Column with broken ribs, but the others pushed on with a small police escort to obtain a concession from Chief Umtasa, Colquhoun professing considerable anxiety over the presence of Portuguese agents west of the Sabi river.

Meanwhile the main body continued on its way, and on 10 September 1890 Pennefather himself, accompanied by two officers, rode ahead of the Column to look for a site for a fort near Mount Hampden. A day later the trio crossed the 'Makobisi river' and trotted ahead to the Gwebi, then down the river valley for about five miles towards Mount Hampden, and continued along the eastern edge of the plateau. Pennefather possessed a good eye for ground and decided that the water supply would not prove adequate for a future seat of government with a considerable population. He therefore returned to the Makabusi and selected another site where he found plenty of good water as well as possibilities for a future waterworks about two miles above the fort.[1]

On 12 September the Order Book of the Pioneer Column noted in sober and unromantic style that 'it is notified for general information that the Column having arrived at its destination will halt. The name of this place will be Fort Salisbury . . .', that all cattle should be kraaled to the south side of the river and that no shooting would be allowed within three miles of camp.[2]

On the following day the Column held a parade in full dress; the seven-pounders fired a royal salute, and the British flag was ceremonially hoisted over the new settlement. Two days later work began on a fort which was completed on 28 September, and the Pioneers' appointed task was done. The Company issued a mining law and the Pioneers were demobilized to take up the fifteen mining claims promised to each of them under the terms of their contracts, as well as a farm each which they might 'ride off' in Boer fashion, and to which title would be issued as soon as the Company

---

[1] E. G. Pennefather to B.S.A. Company: 11 Oct 1890 (in A 1/2/4, Nat Arch SR)
[2] Regimental order book of the Pioneer Corps, entry for 12 Sep 1890 (PI 2/6/1, Nat Arch MS)

could do so.[1] Each Pioneer received three months' rations; he was allowed to retain his rifle and a hundred rounds of ammunition, so that an efficient military reserve might remain in being, and then the men dispersed to look for Solomon's Ophir on the lonely veld.

III

Consolidation

Rhodes now possessed a great paper empire and a toe-hold in Mashonaland, but some of the best experts still predicted that the whole enterprise might crash. In 1891 the German Consul at Cape Town, a well-informed and intelligent man, likened Rhodes's Chartered state to a 'homunculus', a strange artificial man, who was still taking shape amidst surrounding chaos, but whose future existence remained precarious. Rhodes claimed an empire as large as the Hapsburg and Hohenzollern dominions put together, placed in the heart of tropical Africa, without roads, railways, or navigable rivers, cut off from the sea, surrounded by the Matabele in the west, the Portuguese in the east and the Boers in the south, and faced with supply problems of desperate difficulty. The German pointed out that regular customers might buy a ton of coal in Cape Town for about £2. In Kimberley purchasers paid between £8 and £9 a ton.[2] From Kimberley travellers still had to cover more than 800 miles to Mashonaland, a distance equal to that between Middlesex and Tuscany, most of the route forming no more than a track in the veld. The transport of food and fodder, tools and machinery all presented enormous problems; the cost of living rose steeply, and the arrival of each transport wagon became an event of considerable importance for the pioneers. Moreover neither Rhodes nor the pioneers realized that the gold resources of Mashonaland were highly overvalued; there was no second Rand and worse still for the pioneers Mashonaland contained only small quantities of alluvial gold, so that the man who lacked machinery and went to work with a pan did not have much of a chance. The pioneers also faced the problem of growing their own crops. Malaria still presented a serious danger on the veld, at a time when the connexion between the mosquito and the disease remained unknown. Worse still, the newcomers had the misfortune of encountering an exceptionally bad season; there were heavy rains; communications

[1] A. Rutherfoord Harris to A. R. Colquhoun: 20 Sep 1890 (in A 1/2/4, Nat Arch SR)
[2] Report by H. von Treskow, German Consul, Pretoria: 6 Mar 1891 (in GE 1/1/1, Nat Arch MS)

broke down, and many immigrants perished miserably of the dreaded blackwater fever.

The Company likewise found itself in serious straits; it was saddled with heavy financial obligations, having taken over vast commitments on a flimsy basis. In Mashonaland it possessed no land rights, yet the 'Charter' increased its sphere of operations when in 1891 the Imperial Government allowed it to extend its field beyond the Zambezi, into what is now Northern Rhodesia, whilst Rhodes took over additional financial burdens in Nyasaland. In addition the Board had to contend with possible threats from Portuguese and Boers, whilst its hold on Mashonaland remained precarious.

On the credit side the Company could rely on a strong sense of imperial sentiment at home; Britain's belief in her overseas mission remained unshaken, and few Britons objected to Rhodes's reliance on rifles. The Board managed to make good use of this national self-confidence, and many investors put their money into Chartered shares for Imperial reasons, even though they might have secured better returns for their capital in less risky enterprises.

Rhodes could also appeal to British pride for the purpose of keeping foreigners out of his country, and when it came to dealing with the Boers the Company found itself in a relatively strong position. In 1888 Louis P. Bowler, an English-speaking Transvaaler, got a concession from chief Mcheza in north-eastern Mashonaland, an area independent of Lobengula's influence. According to Bowler the indigenous Africans wanted settlers to come to their country to 'protect their hoes' against alien raiders.[1] He also approached Rhodes with a somewhat fantastic scheme for putting steam launches on the Zambezi, opening up properties in the Zambezi area, and combining this work with a settlement scheme which would enhance land values, the money expended in bringing colonists to Mashonaland being returned with interest by a rent charge. Bowler intended to recruit his settlers from the Transvaal, his project merging the time-honoured trekking tradition of the Boers with the more up-to-date technique of a modern estate company. Sir Henry Loch, however, put strong pressure on the Transvaal, and nothing more was heard of Bowler's design.

As for Transvaal policy as a whole, Kruger was more interested in securing an outlet to the sea via Swaziland than in promoting northwards expansion which might lead to trouble with Matabele and Briton alike; Kruger followed a cautious course, but all the same the Transvaalers found themselves steadily outmanoeuvred by Imperial diplomacy. In 1890 Britain and the Transvaal concluded a convention which affirmed the indepen-

[1] L. P. Bowler to Lord Knutsford: 20 Dec 1889 (in CT 1/6/5, Nat Arch SR)

dence of the Swazi, no inroad being allowed on their autonomy without the consent of both Her Majesty's Government and that of the South African Republic. At the same time the Transvaalers, still wanting an outlet through Delagoa Bay, bound themselves not to make any treaties with the tribes to the north or north-west of the Republic's existing boundary, and to assist the Company's administration in the Far North.[1]

The Transvaalers lost the diplomatic game, and when the last trial of strength came they were no longer in a position to put up a good case. Trouble arose when in 1890 a private committee of Transvaalers despatched an agent to Mashonaland, where he obtained promises from the 'Banyai' chiefs Chibi (Sebasha or Shebe) and Matini (Mozobe) to give land to a party of white trekkers. Louis Adendorff, secretary and shareholder of the concession, then went to work to advertise the project in the Press. He received applications from as far afield as the Cape, the Orange Free State, the South African Republic and Natal; many of the would-be immigrants appear to have been Boers of the old-fashioned kind, men who had begun to feel uncomfortable as the Zoutpansberg area became more and more densely settled, or who disliked the influx of gold seekers into the Transvaal, and resented the way game was being 'shot out'. But growing Afrikaner national sentiment also may have played its part, an assumption which would go far to explain the participation of colonists from the Cape.[2] The trekkers argued that the 'Banyai' people would be glad to receive Afrikaner help against the Matabele, that Afrikaans hunters were already well known north of the Limpopo, and that there was no reason why the concession should not be recognized. The British South Africa Company, however, took a very serious view of this project and the Board brought strong pressure to bear, both on Lord Salisbury and the Foreign Office, to put a stop to the trek.[3] By now the Transvaal could not but comply with Loch's requests, especially as the British insisted that they would not discuss the Swaziland question 'as long as a party of agitators are openly promoting and organizing an armed and hostile trek'. Kruger thus did his best to suppress the movement, and when the would-be emigrants finally reached the Limpopo they comprised less than a hundred white people instead of the projected number of 2,000. The trekkers found themselves face to face with a strong force of British South Africa Company's Police, supplied with light artillery and Maxims, guarding the drifts. Jameson told the leaders in unmistakable language that

[1] C. 6217 (1890), p. 8

[2] See Rademeyer, J. *Die land noord van die Limpopo.* . . . Cape Town, A. A. Balkema, 1949, p. 135–152

[3] B.S.A. Company, London, to B.S.A. Company, Cape Town: 24 Apr 1891 (in CT 1/11/3/8, Nat Arch SR)

no land concessions would be recognized, but that emigrants might settle in Company country as individuals provided they abided by the Company's laws. Colonel Ignatius Ferreira, the trek commander, himself accepted the offer and stayed in Mashonaland, where he became managing director of the Mashonaland Agricultural and Supply Syndicate, but most of his followers dispersed.

This was the end of the Adendorff trek and a milestone in Rhodesian history. Afrikaans-speaking immigrants continued to come into the country, Rhodes having assured the Afrikaner Bond in the Cape that settlers would be welcome from all parts of South Africa, provided they respected the Company's flag. But Afrikaner territorial expansion came to an end; the Transvaal lost its hinterland, and the Limpopo remained the extreme northward limit of Afrikaner political power in Africa.

The Portuguese question, however, still remained to be settled, for the Portuguese dominated the East Coast, controlling access to the Company's territory from that side, and at the same time attempting to make their influence over the inland chieftainships more effective. The most powerful of these African states was the kingdom of the Gaza, one of the remaining Zulu states which still continued their accustomed way of life in the interior. The Gaza, however, were falling on evil days. Gungunyana, their paramount chief, lacked the ability of his father Umzila; he was a confirmed drunkard, whilst many of his people appear to have become demoralized by cheap rum which was being sold through Delagoa Bay by Arab dealers. The Gaza faced internal dissensions; half-caste traders were now playing an important part in local politics, and an ill-fated rebellion broke out amongst the 'Chopies', a subject people. Aware of his weakness, Gungunyana in 1885 had placed himself under the overlordship of the King of Portugal, and now tried to play off the competing whites against each other. The Portuguese at the same time began to reinforce their garrisons in East Africa and the Company faced a possible trial of strength.

Rhodes had two possible choices before him. He might use his financial influence overseas, or he might try to get his way by action on the spot. For a time, it seems, a 'golden key' might have opened the door. Late in 1890 the Chartered Company's London Office informed the Cape Town branch, for Rhodes's private information, that the majority of shareholders in the Mozambique Company, a powerful concern in Portuguese East Africa possessed of extensive rights there, was willing to make a deal, provided the Chartered Company was willing to spend £200,000 for development purposes. If this project had succeeded Rhodes might have been able to control the Company, but the scheme came to naught, and early in 1891 negotiations between the two concerns were broken off.[1]

In addition Rhodes tried to make progress locally. The Company sent out Dr Aurel Schulz, a noted African traveller, to negotiate with the Gaza, and in 1890 the Chief agreed to grant full mining and commercial rights to the Company in exchange for an annual subsidy and a thousand rifles. The agreement involved an arms-running operation through Portuguese territory, and an international incident over the steamer *Countess of Carnarvon*, which carried guns for the Gaza; the Company at the same time urged the Imperial authorities to adopt a tough gunboat diplomacy which would secure the Limpopo and the adjacent coastline to the British flag, on the grounds that these territories properly belonged to Gungunyana who repudiated all Portuguese pretensions.[2] But these efforts all proved in vain. The Anglo-Portuguese treaty of 1891 settled the dispute in favour of the Portuguese; the Gaza were sacrificed, and three years later Gungunyana was defeated and captured, his 'spear-kingdom' sharing the fate of similar military communities in Zululand and Matabeleland.

A further dispute arose over Umtasa's (Mtasa's or Mutassa's) kingdom which was situated further north in Manicaland. The area was believed to contain gold, in addition it occupied an important strategic position on the route to the coast. When the Pioneer Column occupied Mashonaland, Archibald Ross Colquhoun, the Company's senior civil official, left in person for Umtasa's kraal to negotiate an agreement. Colquhoun secured a concession of mineral and other trading rights, and Umtasa put himself under British protection. The Portuguese, however, retaliated by seizing the chief's kraal, whilst Lomagundi, another African dignitary, whose headquarters were situated within a few miles of Hartley Hills, was likewise forced to accept the Portuguese flag.[3] But the Portuguese did not enjoy their success for long. Chartered police surprised and arrested the Portuguese emissaries at Umtasa's kraal, including Colonel Paiva d'Andrade and Manuel Antonio de Souza (alias Gouveia), a half-caste

[1] B.S.A. Company, London, to B.S.A. Company, Cape Town: 16 Dec 1890 and 16 Apr 1891, (in CT 1/11/3/3, Nat Arch SR). The Mozambique Company occupied a position similar to that of the Chartered Company in Rhodesia. In 1888 Count Penha Longa and Edmund Bartissol, a Frenchman, managed to raise some capital; the Company's agents used the Pungwe Bay for commercial purposes and laid the foundations of the modern port of Beira. In 1890 the new concern, its capital by now increased, applied for a Royal Charter, which was granted on 11 February 1891, the Company being allocated an area of some 60,000 square miles, with an obligation to build a railway from Beira to the British possessions. The railway obligation was later taken over by the Beira Railway Company, an English concern formed for the purpose. From 1892 the Mozambique Company assumed extensive administrative rights. It had considerable financial backing in France where Bartissol was Chairman of its Paris Committee. Colonel J. C. Paiva d'Andrade became the Company's Director in Africa.

[2] F. Rutherfoord Harris to Imperial Secretary, Cape Town: 2 Apr 1891 (in CT 1/7/5, Nat Arch SR)

[3] B.S.A. Company, London, to Foreign Office: 10 Dec 1890 and B.S.A. Company, Kimberley, to B.S.A. Company, London: 10 Nov 1890 (in CT 1/11/3/3, Nat Arch SR)

estate owner and trader, who maintained a large force of armed retainers as well as a well-stocked harem, and whose bands terrorized the indigenous people of the Gorongoza province. The two prisoners were sent off to Salisbury, and later on permitted to travel down to Cape Town.

The capture of d'Andrade, and even more so that of de Souza, made a considerable impression on the local African people, who became impressed by the way in which a handful of British policemen made short shrift of the Portuguese. But at the same time the incident deeply stirred Portuguese national pride. Students at Lisbon, Coimbra and Oporto enthusiastically demonstrated to form a patriotic battalion for the defence of Portuguese honour; more troops left for East Africa, whilst the Portuguese began to interfere with British navigation through the Pungwe, thereby putting themselves in the wrong under the existing *modus vivendi* between Britain and Portugal.

The inevitable clash occurred in 1891 and the Portuguese suffered a serious defeat, reminiscent in some ways of the Barreto disaster more than three centuries before. Portuguese officers displayed coolness and courage alike, but their troops were mostly raw; they suffered from lack of supplies and medical attention, as well as from the enervating heat and the malaria endemic in the Pungwe valley. The climate and tropical sickness also prevented the employment of either animal-drawn transport or cavalry, and in the end the mixed force of white and black foot soldiers proved no match for British mounted infantry from the highveld.

The collision between the British and Portuguese was laconically described in a field message which Herman Melville Heyman, the Company's local commander, hurriedly scribbled on a Portuguese visiting card when the fight was over:

'Portuguese force consisting of 50 Europeans and 9 officers, between 300 and 400 native troops and 9 guns in their fort at Massikessi (Macequece) attacked the English force posted in a temporary fort manned by 50 A troop BSACP and Pioneers and one 7 pr gun on May 11th Monday at 2 p.m. Action lasted two hours when the enemy retreated having apparently lost heart. In the same night they actually bolted en masse from their fort leaving all stores and 7 Hotchkiss and Nordenfelds machine guns. The English force entered Massikessi next morning and took possession, burning the fort. Casualties on the English side "nil".'[1]

The Portuguese version was somewhat different. The Portuguese commander later explained that he deployed a force of about 60 white and 50 black soldiers to occupy some tactically important kopjes and to reconnoitre the whereabouts of Umtasa's warriors. He had written

[1] Field message: 12 May 1891 (in HE 2/1/1, Nat Arch MS)

orders not to attack the British, and added that he would have taken his machine guns along, had he wished to launch an assault on the Company's forces. But he was stalking through the dense, six foot high grass when he suddenly heard the black troops on his left opening fire, and then nothing would stop the men. The Portuguese subsequently evacuated Massikessi, and having neither stores nor doctors, marched back.[1]

Whatever the exact details, the Portuguese position was now serious. In their attack against well-concealed and mobile sharpshooters, they seem to have committed all the tactical faults later made by the British in the Boer War, and suffered accordingly. The askaris' morale fell to zero; many of their white soldiers were stricken with disease, whilst the supply position remained deplorable. Had the British advanced to Beira they might have won, even though it would have been a hard battle in view of the Company's numerical inferiority and the local lack of horses. But Rhodes now came up against an unshakable obstacle. Lord Salisbury had little patience with what he called Portugal's 'archaeological' claims further inland. But the British Prime Minister recognized Portugal's claims to the coastline, firmly established by earlier Anglo-Portuguese treaties, and refused to give the Company *carte blanche* for a filibustering raid. The High Commissioner despatched Major Herbert Langton Sapte, his military secretary, with orders to instruct the Company's forces that Massikessi and its environs, in addition to the rest of Manica beyond the 33rd degree of east longitude lay outside the sphere of British influence. Loch later accepted the idea of setting up a temporary neutral zone, much to Rhodes's disgust, Rhodes urging that the Imperial Government should have seized Beira and opened the route.[2]

Sapte arrived in time to stop further fighting which, in any case, would not have affected the diplomatic position in Europe. The British were resolved to abide by their treaty obligations; moreover they feared to press Portugal too hard, lest perhaps the monarchy at Lisbon might crumble, upsetting the political and social equilibrium throughout the whole Iberian Peninsula. The Anglo-Portuguese Convention of 11 June 1891 finally settled the whole boundary question.[3] The British had won somewhat favourable terms, gaining most of the Manica plateau. They agreed, on the other hand, to make some considerable territorial concessions on the north side of the Zambezi above Tete, and, more important still, the entire coastline stayed in Portuguese hands. Rhodesia accordingly failed to secure that independent outlet to the sea, which a more forward

[1] H. L. Sapte; outline of conversation with commandant of Portuguese forces at Chimoio: 29 May 1891 (in SA 10/3/2, Nat Arch MS)
[2] Sir H. Loch to H. L. Sapte: 31 May 1891 (in SA 10/1/1, Nat Arch MS)
[3] C. 6375 (1891)

H

and less 'Euro-centric' policy might have assured, and the Chartered dominion—like the Transvaal—remained a landlocked country.

The Company's foreign relations were now settled, but the problem of how best to deal with the local African communities still remained to be solved. Colquhoun was at first only one 'chief' amongst many, more powerful than any single Mashona dignitary, but still quite unable to assert effective authority beyond the small area of white settlement. As far as the Mashona were concerned, they were content if the whites would keep out the Matabele, but they had no intention of submitting to the foreigners' law, of which indeed they knew nothing. The Company for its part found itself in a difficult position, in regard both to tribal diplomacy, and European law.

By the time the pioneers entered the country political cohesion between the local tribes had disappeared, and even though old men might still remember tales of Monomotapa's greatness the old Karanga suzerainty had gone. Each community ran its own affairs, and all that remained of the old political bonds appears to have been a common religious and cultural tradition—especially a great rain cult which centred on Chaminuka and other tribal spirits who each stood at the head of a heavenly hierarchy, with provincial deities below, who in turn were helped by ghostly district dignitaries; all these spirits spoke to their followers through mediums, men and women 'inspired' by a greater power than themselves, who were consulted on all matters affecting the people as a whole, such as rain, relations with foreigners and such like.[1]

But no Mashona chief wielded any great powers himself; no local leader could 'make rain' in the way Lobengula did in the highly centralized Matabele monarchy; there was now no powerful monarch with whom the Company might have negotiated, and whose traditional machinery of government could have been utilized for the purpose of administering a large area, as the Company later did north of the Zambezi, in Barotseland.

Law and order in the European sense of the words were, however, essential if the Company was to carry on mining and farming. To permit the continuance of inter-tribal warfare would have been incompatible with the Company's economic objectives; no settler could sink a mine or plough land if his labourers were to be called on to serve in local levies and end with an assegai through the chest; no postal service could work if the 'runners' were to be arrested by local chieftains, no colonists would come if they had to submit disputes with Africans to African village councils of

[1] See Gelfand, M. *Shona ritual with special reference to the Chaminuka cult.* Cape Town, Juta and co. ltd, 1959

small power. To permit local fighting would have been utterly opposed to the officials' own humanitarian convictions; outside critics of the Company would similarly have regarded non-intervention as a cynical betrayal of the white man's civilizing mission, a concept never challenged at the time, and one which the Company itself was obliged to maintain in terms of its Charter.[1]

The Company thus had to operate with a series of legal fictions. In 1890 Colquhoun received instructions to work on the assumption that Lobengula was supreme over the area, and that neither time nor money should be wasted on the 'so-called independent Mashona chiefs'. Colquhoun should only negotiate for trade and mineral rights with chiefs who were willing to make a deal.[2] A Matabele suzerainty which consisted of periodical raiding of the subjects or the levying of blackmail from small village communities proved, however, very difficult to uphold within a European legal framework, quite apart from the fact that Lobengula had never ceded any administrative rights to the Company. Besides even Lobengula's power never extended through the whole of Mashonaland. In 1891 Selous for instance visited Mtoko (Motoko), the 'paramount chief of the Mabudja'. Before he was allowed to come into the king's kraal, the tribesmen first consulted their *mondhoro* or 'lion god' who lived away in the mountains, and whose power exceeded the chief's. Each of the tribes in the Mazoe region, added Selous, possessed its own *mondhoro*, though only Mtoko's people maintained any kind of political cohesion. The Mabudja were greatly superior to all the other people in the area; they could mobilize several thousand warriors; they resisted de Souza's men and occasional raids from the Gaza, whilst 'the generality of them do not even know the name of Lo Bengoola'.[3] Jameson himself thought that the Matabele never raided beyond the 32nd degree of longitude and accordingly instructed a senior official to conclude treaties with chieftains between the 32nd and 33rd parallels.[4]

From the legal point of view the Company's administrators at first operated in a kind of twilight. The Charter permitted the Company to make ordinances for the maintenance of peace and order, subject to the consent of the Secretary of State. Two years later, on 9 May 1891, the Imperial authorities issued an Order in Council which gave additional powers to the High Commissioner who could now appoint magistrates and other officers for the Chartered territories and issue proclamations for

---

[1] For an excellent discussion of this question see Mason, P. *The birth of a dilemma: the conquest and settlement of Rhodesia.* Oxford university press, 1958, p. 152–162

[2] A Rutherfoord Harris to A. R. Colquhoun: 20 Sep 1890 (in A 1/2/4, Nat Arch SR)

[3] F. C. Selous to Administrator: 25 Jan 1891 (in SE 1/1/1, Nat Arch MS)

[4] E. C. Pennefather to B.S.A. Company: 11 Oct 1890 (in A 1/2/4, Nat Arch SR)

the administration of justice and the raising of revenue. The courts of British Bechuanaland assumed civil and criminal jurisdiction, though the Order insisted that laws and customs governing the 'civil relations' of the local tribes should be respected, in so far as these were compatible with Her Majesty's power and jurisdiction, a definition which would have been quite incomprehensible to any tribal councillor. Beyond this point the Imperial authorities refused to commit themselves. Knutsford argued that the Imperial Government should leave the burden of administering the country with the Company, and that he could not consent to the High Commissioner's suggestion of appointing an Imperial officer to supervise the Company's administration.[1]

In a newly occupied country the question of what properly speaking did or did not constitute the 'civil relations' of a tribe were difficult to settle; but whatever the legal phraseology, the Company soon began to intervene in the struggles of indigenous communities. Punitive expeditions were sent out to crush chiefs who refused to submit, despite criticism from the High Commissioner who thought that the Company was using too much force, a point of view which seemed to make some sense from the safety of a Cape Town office, but not to a handful of harried men in pole-and-daga huts on the highveld, charged with the unenviable task of actually enforcing British authority.[2]

The initial machinery employed in the country's administration was about as rudimentary as the primitive windlasses and dollies used for gold mining before more extensive gear was imported—it had to be adapted from material ready to hand.[3] The existing Roman-Dutch law of the Cape Colony was applied to Mashonaland and Resident Magistrates were appointed, whose powers, which were modelled on those of the Cape, gave them considerable administrative responsibilities. But none of the early Resident Magistrates possessed much legal experience beyond the sort they had acquired in the orderly room. Now a handful of young officers suddenly found themselves responsible for running the entire legal machinery, and, amongst other things, for 'paying careful regard to the customs and laws of the . . . tribe . . . especially with respect to the holding, possession, transfer and disposition of lands and goods and testate and intestate succession thereto and marriage, divorce and legitimacy . . .', to quote from the text of the Charter. Mistakes of course were made in plenty. Marshall Hole, the Company's historian and an early administrator, thus recorded how he once mistakenly married a man to the

[1] Lord Knutsford to Sir H. Loch: 26 Jun 1891 (in HC 3/5/17/7, Nat Arch SR)
[2] For a discussion of the Ngomo case which involved a bloody expedition against one of Mangwendi's sub-chiefs, see Mason, P. *The birth of a dilemma*. . . . Oxford University Press, 1958, p. 154–157
[3] See Hole, H. M. *Old Rhodesian days*. Macmillan and co. ltd, 1928

suitor's own niece; whilst the Public Prosecutor—to the universal amuse-
ment of the public—was called upon to try a company of gamblers in
whose game of baccarat he had himself taken part the night before. But
purely 'native' cases were at first left to the villagers, whilst the good
horse-sense of British officers made in practice for a reasonable degree of
equity. The Rhodesian police force moreover from the very beginnings
had the reputation of being one of the finest semi-military bodies in the
Empire, and competition to join was keen. The force contained a large
number of public school men, with a sprinkling of warrant and non-
commissioned officers from the regular army, some of whom later rose to
high military rank. What the force lacked in experience they made up in
zeal, and right from the start the country found itself relatively well policed,
whilst administrative corruption remained rare. But more important was
the social composition of the new community. Hannah Arendt, an American historian, once spoke of the Southern African frontier in terms of an
'alliance between mob and capital'. But the facts were different. The social
level of the English-speaking Rhodesian pioneers was relatively high,
there was no real criminal element, and the main foreign minority groups,
Boer trekkers and Yiddish-speaking Jews from Eastern Europe—Bible-
reading people both of them, presented no serious problems to policemen.
Whatever the reason, lynch law never ruled on the Rhodesian frontier;
nor did highwaymen or cattle rustlers ever make their appearance, as they
did in parts of the American West, where often an initial tradition of
lawlessness sprang up which was difficult to eradicate later.

The early settlers nevertheless had a great many worries on their
hands, nearly all of an economic nature. For one thing the colonists did
not at first receive adequate land titles, for Lobengula had never made over
any territorial rights to the Company. This difficulty was surmounted in
the end by the Lippert Concession. In 1891 Renny-Tailyour obtained a
grant from Lobengula who was still trying to play off the whites against
one another, and now gave away the sole right to issue titles to farms and
grazing lands. This passed into the hands of Lippert, and the Company at
first proposed to fight the case, Renny-Tailyour being excluded from the
Chartered dominions as one of those prohibited immigrants who were
kept out for what might be called 'concessionary' reasons. Later on
Lobengula confirmed the grant to Lippert who after some hard bargaining, in turn made it over to Rudd, who transferred it to the Chartered
Company. When Lobengula heard about this arrangement he was very
much put out, having thought that Lippert and Rhodes, the German and
the Englishman, were deadly enemies,[1] and imagining that he might play

[1] J. S. Moffat to Deputy High Commissioner: 27 May 1892 (in HC 3/5/17/7, Nat Arch SR)

the one against the other. But now there was nothing the Matabele could do, and for nearly two decades the Lippert Concession was regarded as one of the mainstays of Chartered land rights in Southern Rhodesia.[1]

Farming did not play an important part in the country's economic life at first, and as the Pioneers dispersed, the elaborate theories of planting a 'balanced' kind of community in the Far North were soon forgotten; the colonists settled down to prospecting as well as a little trading, transport riding and share-pushing, the average pioneer being ready to turn his hand to anything. Hardly any of them managed to make any money and most of them later left the country.[2] There were of course exceptions; Frank Johnson for instance earned quite a tidy sum from his Pioneer contract, and soon found himself in the fortunate position of heading the only firm in Rhodesia which possessed any sizeable amount of liquid cash. Johnson then began to buy numerous mining and land claims from ex-members of the Column who found themselves in urgent need of funds; he also attempted to do some serious development work, but even he quickly found that the capital at his disposal was inadequate for mining on a large scale, and in 1891 he threw in his lot with Rhodes's Gold Fields of South Africa Ltd, which acquired a controlling interest in Johnson's firm.[3]

Life under these early pioneering conditions was hard. Salisbury itself started off as a collection of huts, built in the native style from poles and grass cut on the commonage surrounding the camp, some of the streets later being laid out in such a fashion as to follow the irregular lines of scattered pioneer shanties. Food, like all other commodities, was extremely expensive and often of poor quality. The story thus goes of a pioneer lady who wrote a short note to her dairy, which still bears quoting in full:

'Dear Mrs So-and-so,

In future I will send you *two* bottles every day. Would you kindly put the milk in one and water in the other, and I will do the mixing myself.'[4]

---

[1] The revised Concession was signed on 17 November 1891. The details of the commercial transactions involved are to be found in CT 1/11/1/5, Nat Arch SR. Lippert received £30,000 together with a substantial block of shares. Later on, in 1918, the Judicial Committee of the Privy Council decided that the Lippert Concession was valueless as a title deed to the unalienated land, and that the Chartered Company could only dispose of unalienated land in its administrative capacity.

[2] Darter, A. *The pioneers of Mashonaland.* Simpkin, Marshall, Hamilton, Kent and co. ltd, 1914, p. 198–213, investigates the fortunes of 184 pioneers in 1914. Of these only 25 were still in Rhodesia, 24 were known to have been killed and 44 had died a natural death.

[3] Johnson's original partnership was known as Johnson, Heany and Borrow. In 1891 he came to an arrangement with Rhodes, the new firm becoming known as Frank Johnson and Company. Its papers are in the National Archives (JO 4, Nat Arch MS) and form interesting source material for early economic activity. Frank Johnson and Company at first engaged in a variety of ventures, including transport riding, trading and the purchase of mining claims, until it decided to specialize in mining.

[4] Hole, H. M. *Old Rhodesian days.* Macmillan and co. ltd, 1928, p. 80

Life nevertheless had its compensations; there were few social restraints; game was plentiful; whilst the ordinary colonist remained an incurable optimist, who firmly believed that mining claims and land were bound to rise in value soon, and that things could not help getting better. Rhodes, with his profound belief in the country, expressed in this respect only the pioneers' own sentiments. According to Frank Johnson's memoirs, the great man, when he first visited his Colony, somehow expected Salisbury to stand out as a splendid city. When actually he saw the town before his eyes, a little backveld *bidonville* of corrugated iron shacks and wattle and daub huts, he was bitterly disappointed. He crossed the Makabusi, feeling thoroughly dejected, but soon his spirits revived when Johnson pointed out to him the foundations of a Jewish synagogue. 'My country's all right,' he kept exclaiming, 'if the Jews come, my country's all right,'[1] and as the years went by, events justified his expectancy.

[1] Johnson, F. *Great days*. G. Bell and sons ltd, 1940, p. 207

Chapter Four

Clash of arms

I

The downfall of Lobengula

As more and more settlers drifted into Mashonaland Lobengula found
himself faced with a difficult problem. His armies could no longer raid
towards the west; he had now also to envisage the possible loss of his
raiding grounds in Mashonaland. If he continued to send his impis eastwards it might involve war with the whites, a contingency which the king
intended to avoid at almost any price.

The Matabele might of course have tried to escape from their dilemma
by crossing the Zambezi and migrating to the north—as Zwangendaba had
done some two generations ago—but such a move would have led to war
with the Barotse and presented the Matabele with the difficult military
problem of crossing the Zambezi in strength. But more to be feared even
than the Barotse was the dreaded 'fly' of the Zambezi valley; Matabele
cattle had no resistance towards tsetse-borne disease, and if Lobengula had
decided on a great northward exodus he would probably have lost his
nation's cherished herds.

Alternatively Lobengula might have tried to come to terms with the
white man's new economic dispensation by taking an active part in mining
enterprise. Lobengula actually tried this in a small way, and in 1891
Dawson, the trader, took a five stamp battery to the Umfuli river in the
Hartley district for the king; in addition Lobengula allowed some of his
men to work for the whites in Mashonaland.[1]

But the king dared not attempt any real reforms either in the Matabele
system of government or even in their fighting methods. Advice from the
'modernizers' was not entirely lacking. Mikca Nxobbe, a Christian

---

[1] A. H. F. Duncan to Lobengula: 10 Nov 1891 (in WI 6/1/2, Nat Arch MS). The mill survived
the Matabele War and in 1904 fetched £200 (M 3/11/16, Nat Arch SR). According to Johnson,
F. *Great Days*. G. Bell and sons Ltd, 1940, p. 209, the mill was a present from the Chartered
Company.

evangelist of Matabele descent, who had for many years been living in the Transvaal, wrote to the king and strongly advised against a war policy, arguing that Lobengula should follow the example set by the Basuto and place himself under British protection. In addition Lobengula must change his administrative system. 'Better for you must want a clark and put them in ann office to make your right', argued Nxobbe in halting English, but with the firm conviction that the future lay with European-educated men like himself. 'I am one of them. . . . Then you let the people build a big house for office and coming work. . . . If you got a high case with the nother [another] people, you send the case to England. . . . If you do not that you lose your country indeed.'[1] Nxobbe added that there were many Matabele Christians living in the Transvaal who would like to return. But he was after all nothing but an expatriate intellectual and no one took any notice of his views. Lobengula did not even take any effective steps to modernize his military system, beyond piling up rifles and enquiring as to the possibility of securing ponies from Basutoland.[2]

As far as the Chartered Company was concerned, the old talk of war was at an end for the moment. In 1891 Colquhoun, a conscientious ex-Indian civil servant, firmly wedded to the niceties of administrative procedure and not well adjusted to life in a South African frontier community, resigned from his office as Acting Resident Commissioner for Mashonaland and Dr Jameson took his place. Jameson, whose title was shortly altered to Chief Magistrate for Mashonaland, was under heavy pressure to cut down expenditure, for the Company was in low financial waters, and Rhodes saw no reason why his Pioneers—most of them healthy young men trained in the use of arms—should require a strong military police force to look after them in the bush. The Police accordingly were cut to the bone, and only a few small detachments were retained, the defence of the country being left to a volunteer corps, known as the Mashonaland Horse, which in emergencies might be supplemented by a burgher force of some 1,500 men who were liable for service in time of war. Jameson, born optimist that he was, felt convinced that financial confidence in the country was increasing, and expressed the hope that some of the white unemployeds from the Rand would come to Rhodesia,[3] and he at first believed that the Matabele might in time become peacefully absorbed into the country's labour force.[4] Peace was necessary for the

---

[1] Mikca Nxobbe to Lobengula: 3 Mar 1893 (in WI 6/1/1, Nat Arch MS)

[2] Chief Jonathan Malopo to Lobengula: 8 Feb 1893 (in WI 6/1/1, Nat Arch MS)

[3] L. S. Jameson to S. Jameson, his brother: 11 Oct 1892 (in JA 1/1/1, Nat Arch MS), partly printed in Colvin, I. D. *Life of Jameson*. Edward Arnold, 1922, v. 1, p. 232

[4] L. S. Jameson to S. Jameson: 4 Oct 1893 (in JA 1/1/1, Nat Arch MS); printed in Colvin, I. D. *op. cit*, v. 1, p. 266–267

shaky colony. Capital too was needed to develop a country which already had a fair-sized white pauper community.[1]

Jameson at first attempted to secure a *modus vivendi* with the Matabele on a basis of territorial segregation. The Chartered Company would be supreme in Mashonaland, the Matabele could continue to lord it in their own country, and he tried to establish an accepted boundary, following the River Tokwe to the north-west, then continuing north till it touched the Umniati, and so along that stream to its junction with the Umfuli.[2] He consistently tried to stop white men from straying west of this boundary, and he issued strict instructions to his people to leave Lobengula's country alone, while he refused to help compatriots who had got into trouble by disobeying his orders.[3] At the same time he sought to prevent Matabele from entering Mashonaland, except as workers on contract, though he refused at first to back this exclusion policy by force of arms, what they called 'bullying the weak and cringing to the powerful'— putting down Mashona dissidents with a strong hand, whilst trying to conciliate the Matabele monarch.

But whatever Jameson might think, the Matabele had not the slightest intention of losing Mashonaland. As far as they were concerned, the lands lying along the periphery of their warrior community formed their traditional raiding and hunting grounds, not a piece of real estate that could neatly be parcelled off and handed over to strangers. The whites might mine for gold; they were after all paying for the privilege with guns and cash; but the Europeans' labour problem was their own affair. If the whites found that their mining and farming operations became impossible because their Mashona workmen were murdered or abducted, this was no concern of Matabele warriors who generally despised the settlers and held the Mashona in sovereign contempt.

Initially all went well. The Matabele at first left the white area alone; their only incursion beyond the border occurred north-west of Salisbury where Lomagundi, a local chief, boldly refused to pay any further tribute to Lobengula. A Matabele company descended on the unfortunate chief, and threateningly enquired why Lomagundi had taken presents from the Portuguese and the English, shown the British where to dig for gold and supplied them with guides to the Zambezi. Lomagundi racked his brains

---

[1] L. S. Jameson to S. Jameson: 10 Apr 1893 (in JA 1/1/1, Nat Arch MS); partly printed in Colvin, I. D. *op. cit*, v. 1, p. 237

[2] See Glass, S. *The background of the Matabele war*, M.A. thesis submitted to the department of history at Natal University, 1959. Mr Glass's work is a notable reconstruction of the events leading to the outbreak of the Matabele War and has been used extensively for this portion of the chapter.

[3] L. S. Jameson to J. Colenbrander: 22 May 1893 (in CO 4/1/1, Nat Arch MS); also A 2/1/5, Nat Arch SR.

for an answer, but his diplomacy proved of no avail and on the next morning he was shot by the Matabele, together with three of his indunas. Jameson remonstrated with Lobengula, but Lobengula remained unimpressed, and from August 1892 onwards several raiding parties were despatched to areas north and south of Fort Victoria.

Jameson, anxious to avoid hostilities, continued to rely on diplomacy, but the settlers, especially those in the Fort Victoria region, strongly disagreed with what they regarded as a pusillanimous policy of appeasement, hatched in the comparative safety of a Salisbury office. Miners were sinking shafts to prove the country for gold; farmers with little or no capital behind them were trying to build up herds—but unless public order was upheld and confidence restored they might face ruin.

A serious incident arose in 1892 when the telegraph line from Cape Town was extended to Salisbury. Some Mashona cut the line, not as an act of military sabotage, but to get hold of the highly prized metal; the local Makalaka blamed the theft on the Matabele, and Captain Lendy, one of the Company's officers, left for Bulawayo to complain to the king. Lendy stressed that the Matabele should keep to their side of the border, and added that the Company would punish the culprits, having come to the conclusion that the true offenders were, in fact, 'Amaholi'. Lendy returned, but the general satisfaction over Lendy's interviews was short-lived. There was further trouble and Chartered police arrested several Africans and seized some cattle which—unknown to the white men—Lobengula had stationed amongst his subjects. Lobengula was greatly incensed, and Jameson agreed to send the beasts back to the king.

Lobengula, however, was determined to uphold his political authority, and in June 1893 a Matabele impi raided in the vicinity of Fort Victoria to punish the people of Bere, a small local dignitary who had stolen some of the king's cattle. Lendy warned the warriors that they must not interfere with the whites, but much to Bere's disgust went no further. Lobengula, now convinced that the Europeans would not dare to offer any real resistance, subsequently sent out a much larger impi, at the same time informing the whites that this raiding expedition had nothing to do with them, but was being despatched to retrieve stolen beasts. Later on Lobengula claimed that his men intended to punish the wire-thieves, an ingenious afterthought, which the Company's detractors in London used to establish their inaccurate theory that the Matabele had actually entered Mashonaland on the Company's invitation.

Lobengula did not plan a full-scale campaign, for a strong impi had gone off to the Zambezi, but a large body of young warriors still remained at Bulawayo, eager to garner the spoils of war, and the Victoria district made a splendid raiding ground. A strong force appeared at Fort Victoria on 9 July 1893, and the panic-stricken Mashona sought refuge in the settlement, with the Matabele hot on their heels. In addition to plundering in the environs the Matabele also insisted that the refugees in Fort Victoria should be handed over. Lendy refused—both for humanitarian reasons and to assure the Mashona that the white man's protection was really worth something to black men who agreed to work for Europeans. If Lendy had given way the Company's political problems overseas would of course have become even more serious than they actually were. A body pledged to secure 'law and order' by the terms of its own Charter could hardly have handed over a hapless mob of refugees in search of sanctuary. Had it done so the Board might well have had to face the full, unfettered fury of the Noncomformist Conscience in search of a cause. Men like Henry Labouchère, a Radical journalist and a bitter critic of Rhodes and of Imperialism, would have had an excellent case. Instead of blaming the Company for fomenting war—as they subsequently did—they would have condemned Rhodes, Beit and their friends for upholding an unholy alliance between a bloodstained feudalism and the forces of finance-capital —a charge that would have been hard to refute.

But whatever the rights and wrongs of this dispute many Mashona certainly lost their lives; their bodies were mutilated, their cattle plundered and their grain stores sacked. The survivors took refuge in the bush, and European enterprise came to a standstill. The whites themselves suffered no casualties, but fearing war, the colonists streamed into Fort Victoria. The settlement prepared for a siege; the 'Victoria Rangers' and the local burgher corps got ready to fight and—with 400 white men standing to arms—the settlers became convinced that war was inevitable, and the Matabele menace must be crushed.

The Europeans' case was simple. Fort Victoria, which in 1892 had been shifted to a new site away from the first pioneer camp, was now beginning to acquire some importance as a half-way house on the road from the south to Salisbury; and the settlement was developing into Mashonaland's main centre of mining activity. New residents had bought stands in the township, and peaceful conditions were imperative. The citizens therefore urged on the Administration that commercial confidence was waning, and that once capital was withdrawn a long period would elapse before money came back. Every section of society was being affected. Mine managers and prospectors were left stranded without labour as the workmen fled to their villages; transport-riders refused to forward mining equipment; shopkeepers found themselves without business; even though some £4,000 a month was being spent in wages and salaries no one would buy goods until the Matabele question was settled. People with capital were refusing to buy new properties; prospectors could no longer dispose of their claims. Farmers had lost their crops; much property was destroyed; and on every homestead native workers had been murdered—sometimes in their master's very presence. Lobengula's promises no longer deserved any trust, and decisive action was necessary, unless the whole local economy were to collapse.[1]

Jameson himself was no war-hawk. Had he wished to fight, he would not previously have disbanded his police; he would have struck earlier in 1893, when some 6,000 men, the major part of Lobengula's army, were on the war-path to the Zambezi, instead of waiting till the warriors had returned. Jameson came post haste to Fort Victoria and first of all he parleyed, as he had done so often in the past. The Victoria impi had to retire across the border and Lobengula must see to it that his warriors would no longer raid into Mashonaland. An indaba was held, and the Matabele were given an hour to commence to withdraw. At the end of the hour Captain Lendy was sent out with a patrol to see whether Jameson's instructions were being followed, but Manyao, the Matabele commanding officer, could no longer fully control his men, who were roused into opposition by Umgandan, a young and assertive induna. Lendy's small party of some forty-seven men encountered a Matabele detachment led by Umgandan which, instead of complying with Jameson's ultimatum, was attacking the kraal of a headman by the name of Mazabili. Lendy's troopers opened fire; the Matabele suffered considerable casualties and were scattered. When Lendy came back Jameson made up his mind. Lendy had shown what a small local force could do; the 'Imperial factor' would no longer have to be called on once the fighting started, and what was more, campaigning of this kind could be done on the cheap. From then onwards, from 18 June 1893 to be exact, Jameson decided on war. Come what may, the Matabele must be smashed, and the country pacified.[2]

Lobengula for his part still wanted to negotiate, though he refused to give up his claims to the Mashona raiding grounds. 'Are the Amaholis then yours?' he asked; the whites had never bought the country; they might only mine gold. War was being provoked by men like Captain Lendy who, said the Matabele king, 'is like some of my own young men; he has no holes in his ears and cannot or will not hear; he is young and all he thinks

[1] Petition by the citizens of Victoria to the Administrator: 22 July 1893 (in DV 13/6/1, Nat Arch SR)

[2] See C. 7171 (1893), C. 7190 (1893), C. 7196 (1893), C. 7290 (1894) and C. 7555 (1894) for published correspondence. For detailed research on all the primary sources in the National Archives, see Glass's account.

about is a row.'[1] The High Commissioner also insisted that raiding must
end, and that the whites who lost property should be compensated—a
demand which the Colonial Office, however, asked him not to press
further.[2] But the Company now made ready to fight, and on 14 August an
enlistment agreement was thrown open for signature whereby, in the
tradition of South African frontier warfare, the volunteers were to receive
land in return for their services. The so-called Victoria Agreement stated
that each man should be entitled to mark out a farm of 3,000 morgen in any
part of Matabeleland, and also receive fifteen reef and five alluvial claims.
The 'loot', that is to say Lobengula's cattle, would be equally divided
between the Company on the one hand and its forces on the other. The
Company's critics subsequently bitterly denounced what they called a
secret compact to despoil the Matabele. But there was nothing underhand
about this arrangement, whilst no one imagined that a Commando would
fight for nothing.[3]

In the meantime Lobengula's attitude stiffened. In reply to a message
from the High Commissioner he gave a defiant answer, stating that he
would neither return any cattle nor pay compensation until Rhodes
returned all the men, women and children, the cattle, goats and sheep who
were given protection by the people of Fort Victoria,[4] a communication
which destroyed any sympathy which Loch might still have felt for the
Matabele king. The Colonial Office agreed that Lobengula's reply was
unsatisfactory, but still insisted that the Chartered Company should not
take the offensive, limiting itself to defending its own territory.[5] But from
the Matabele point of view this contention itself begged the 'border
question', and an embassy sent by Lobengula to Cape Town refused to
discuss the question of a boundary, whilst trying to gain time.[6] Lobengula
by now was beginning to mass his impis; the Chartered Company started
to import horses, and on 21 September Loch informed the Colonial Office
that the Company would soon have enough mounts in the country; it
would then be anxious to bring the matter to a conclusion, since it could
not stand protracted expense or lengthened uncertainty.[7] The Colonial
Office still tried to maintain control over the situation, but this proved a
hopeless undertaking in a position where the Company held the purse-
strings and effectively commanded all the military forces in Mashonaland.

[1] J. W. Colenbrander to R. Harris: 27 July 1893 (in African (South) no. 454, p. 38)
[2] Sir H. B. Loch to Lord Ripon: 5 Aug 1893 (in African (South) no. 454, p. 12) and Ripon to Loch:
5 Aug 1893 (in African (South) no. 454, p. 13)
[3] See Mason, P. The birth of a dilemma. Oxford University Press, 1958, p. 173
[4] Sir H. B. Loch to Lord Ripon: 25 Aug 1893 (in HC 3/5/30/1, Nat Arch SR)
[5] Lord Ripon to Sir H. B. Loch: 26 Aug 1893 (in African (South) no. 454, p. 44)
[6] Sir H. B. Loch to Lord Ripon: 4 Sep 1893 (in HC 3/5/30/1, Nat Arch SR)
[7] Sir H. B. Loch to Lord Ripon: 29 Sep 1892 (in African (South) no. 454, p. 139)

Loch argued therefore that unless Her Majesty's Government would itself assist with men and money, the Colonial Office could hardly interfere with the Company's freedom of action, and that the final decision should be left to himself. Jameson accordingly received authority to force back the Matabele impis from the vicinity of Fort Victoria and also to take any other measures which he might consider necessary for the people in his charge.

In the meantime Lobengula had sent out yet another embassy who reached Tati on 14 October, after Jameson's forces had already taken the offensive. Colonel Goold-Adams, the Imperial officer-in-charge, did not realize that they were envoys, and anxious that they should not find out anything of military value, ordered them to be detained until he could find out why they had come. The indunas became alarmed, and one of them, seizing a bayonet from a trooper, stabbed two of the guards, with the result that two of the Matabele chiefs were shot.[1] Only Ingubugobo stayed motionless and survived. But in any case it was now too late. The Company's columns were already out of telegraphic reach, and Loch had decided that further negotiations were useless until events had taken a more definite shape.[2] The Europeans were on the march and the Matabele were fighting for their kingdom.

From the military point of view the Matabele War was not necessarily a foregone conclusion. Lobengula's warriors enjoyed great numerical superiority; they also had plenty of modern rifles, including all the Martini-Henrys which the Chartered Company had supplied under the terms of the Rudd Concession. Their best plan would have been to fight a long-drawn-out defensive campaign, avoid set-piece battles, and gradually wear down the whites until the Company's coffers were exhausted, and the burghers anxious to go home. Then a compromise peace of sorts might perhaps still have been negotiated.

But Matabele strategy was as out of date as the social system which had given it birth. Umziligazi's doctrine of warfare had been simple: victories were won by taking the offensive, an assumption that always used to work against the weaker Bantu communities whom the Matabele encountered. Where a straightforward assault proved impossible, as in war against the Voortrekkers or Shaka's famed regiments, the only answer was a large-scale strategic withdrawal.[3] Matabele military thought hinged on the assumption that attack would invariably prevail over the defence—an unsound doctrine which they shared with most contemporary European

---

[1] Sir H. B. Loch to Lord Ripon: 23 Oct 1893 (in African (South) no. 454, p. 138)
[2] Sir H. B. Loch to Lord Ripon: 20 Oct 1893 (in African (South) no. 454, p. 136)
[3] Summers, R. 'The Military doctrine of the Matabele' (in *NADA*, no. 32, 1955, p. 7–15)

planners overseas—and from the very outset of the war the Matabele high command seems to have envisaged the future course of events with much pessimism.

Matabele tactics only mirrored faulty strategy. The army was poorly trained in the use of rifles, and Matabele officers—like so many of their colleagues in European guards regiments overseas—had a blind faith in cold steel and what might be called the ceremonial aspects of warfare, a creed born perhaps from instinctive disgust at military developments of the day. Instead of breaking up their army into small, mobile units, trained to make full use of cover, relying on surprise and speed, and ready to wear down the white man in the bush, they continued to use the old 'chest-and-horn' or 'spear-crescent' formation which had already failed in the Ngamiland campaign against black fighting men equipped with firearms. Matabele warriors moreover never attacked at night, when the chances of a sudden *coup* were best; their out-of-date tactics were further vitiated by poor leadership, inadequate co-ordination of various regiments on the battlefield, and by the sharp decline in general discipline which has already been discussed in a previous chapter.

The Europeans on the other hand were mounted and possessed far greater mobility than Matabele infantry; their automatic weapons and light field pieces gave them a much heavier volume of fire-power, the Matabele War standing out in military history for the early employment of the Maxim gun, a weapon which conventional soldiers still tended to under-estimate. At the same time the tactical use of wagons provided mobile pivots, and what they lacked in numbers, they made up by superior morale and sound leadership.[1] The whites also received help from two Matabele guides whose relatives had been executed by Lobengula for political reasons, and who determined to avenge their kinsmen by helping the whites, whilst Matabele intelligence appears to have been quite inadequate.[2]

The Company's original plan of campaign provided that three separate units, the Tuli, Victoria and Salisbury Columns, should each set out from different points, unencumbered by wagons, and converge independently on Bulawayo. This project was later modified; the Victoria and Salisbury Columns each took wagons along, and joined forces at the Iron Hill Mine. The Tuli column was reinforced by the Bechuanaland Border Police,

[1] The Europeans engaged in the fighting numbered just over 1,100 men, including 225 Bechuanaland Border Police; there were also some 2,000 poorly armed and trained auxiliaries from Chief Khama, and about 400 Mashona auxiliaries as well as African drivers and other non-combatants. Lobengula was estimated to be able to mobilize about 18,000 men of varying degrees of morale, training and reliability.

[2] Journal of 'Matabele' Wilson: 1893 (in WI 6/2/1, Nat Arch MS)

under the command of Lieutenant-Colonel H. Goold-Adams, whose advance from the south managed to pin down some 8,000 Matabele without heavy fighting.

Major Patrick William Forbes, a courageous and capable officer of the Inniskilling Dragoons, and a Company servant, was given command over the Company's forces, and though some military experts regarded his scheme as rash, events soon proved him right. Forbes proved an able organizer; the Salisbury Column was quickly got ready; he also authorized the formation of a force of sixty 'Colonial natives', that is to say Africans from the Cape, and enlisted some Indians, who expressed a wish to take part in the fighting.[1]

The Matabele for their part played right into Forbes's hands. Instead of taking up a strong position in difficult bush country, and waiting for the rains, they decided to make a stand on the road to Bulawayo. Acting on the strategic defence, they tried to take the tactical initiative on ground of their own choice. Twice they attacked the invaders, at the Shangani and on the Bembesi, but suffered two crushing defeats and the decimation of the Ingubu, Imbezu and Insukamini regiments.[2]

Lobengula then burnt his capital and fled, though chivalrously insisting that the few remaining white residents in Bulawayo should be spared. Shortly afterwards, on 3 November 1893, a small advance guard entered the deserted kraals. On the following day the main body of volunteers entered the town, marching to the rousing sound of pipes. Little was left; everywhere smoke was pouring forth from the blackened ruins from whence the people had fled. The wagons outspanned amid the debris and the men paraded. The Union Jack with the British South Africa Company's lion badge was hoisted, and as the colours fluttered in the wind, a great cheer went up from the assembled ranks. Matabeleland had become British and a new chapter began in its history.

In the meantime the British Secretary of State had insisted that all negotiations with the enemy should be conducted through the High Commissioner, but Lobengula fled to the north, and the Company's forces set out in pursuit of the defeated king. The Matabele monarch, in one last tragic effort to gain time, sent a message to the Europeans, together with a bag containing about a thousand gold sovereigns. Two troopers of the Bechuanaland Border Police, James Wilson and William Charles Daniel, apparently took the money and kept it for themselves, without telling their commanding officer anything about Lobengula's

[1] Forbes, P. W. 'Organising the forces' (in Wills, W. A., and Collingridge, L. T. *The downfall of Lobengula*. The African review, 1894, p. 69)

[2] For sketch maps of these battles see Wills, W. A., and Collingridge, L. T., *op. cit*, facing p. 108 and 120

I

communication. An advance party under Major Allan Wilson pushed forward to find out Lobengula's whereabouts. Wilson disobeyed orders and failed to return when he should; instead he sent back word that the king had crossed the Shangani river, that he would continue the hunt, and asked for reinforcements.[1] Forbes, in charge of the operation, now faced the sort of indiscipline that any commander of irregular mounted troops must expect, and was left with a difficult decision. In the end he decided— perfectly correctly—not to break camp at night, at a time when his exhausted men might be attacked at any moment by strong enemy detachments in the neighbourhood, arguing that it would be dangerous to cross the flooded Shangani in darkness. Instead he despatched a small unit under Captain Borrow, too few to give Wilson a fighting chance, but sufficiently strong to encourage the Major in his headstrong ways. In the end Wilson and Borrow were forced to fall back; the Matabele cut off their retreat, and what happened then was later graphically described by Mhlahlo, a warrior in the Msukamini Regiment, who actually took part in the fighting.

'We then saw a number of white men riding along. There were about thirty. We surrounded them and started to fight. They got off their horses and fired at us over them. All the horses were killed, and then the white men, those that were left, all of whom were wounded, lay on their backs and held their rifles between their feet and fired. After a little the firing stopped, and we knew the cartridges were finished. We then rushed up and assegaied the remainder who covered their eyes with their hands. We lost many more than the number of white men killed, for they were men indeed and fought us for many hours. We never fought again after this fight and soon after we had peace. . . .'[2]

Legend later embellished the grim story which for white Rhodesians became a glorious memory, their own equivalent of the bloody Alamo massacre and Custer's Last Stand in the American West, a symbol of heroic courage and determination in fulfilling the frontiersman's Manifest Destiny. The conduct of the pursuit, like all these tragic incidents, later on produced a considerable amount of controversy. There was a Court of Enquiry where Forbes stated—quite correctly—that the blame for Wilson's remaining where he was with his fifteen men must rest entirely

---

[1] Wilson was born in Ross-shire in 1856, educated at the Grammar School at Kirkwall, Orkney, and at Milne's Institution, Fochabers, Morayshire. After working for three years in a bank he became tired of a sedentary life and joined the Cape Mounted Rifles, and was subsequently commissioned in the Basuto Police. He afterwards worked for the Bechuanaland Exploration Company, and when the Matabele War broke out he was appointed Major in charge of the Victoria Volunteer Force.

[2] Account by Mhlahlo, a member of Lobengula's Msukamini regiment (in Misc/MH 1, Nat Arch MS)

on the unfortunate Major, but that Forbes would take full responsibility for sending out Borrow with only twenty men.[1] Forbes, whose victory might in happier circumstances have secured him a knighthood, fell into unmerited disgrace, and was later rusticated to far-away North-Eastern Rhodesia where for a time he served as Deputy Administrator. But in actual fact the Wilson disaster in no wise affected the course of events. Matabele resistance collapsed; Lobengula perished on his flight—perhaps of smallpox, perhaps of self-administered poison—and his warrior kingdom became a matter of history.

The grim story had a strange sequel when the theft of Lobengula's golden sovereigns came to light. Wilson and Daniel, the two troopers thought responsible for the outrage, were put on trial. Public opinion was running high against the accused on the grounds that their cowardly act of embezzlement had prevented an armistice and thereby indirectly contributed to the loss of the Wilson patrol. A somewhat prejudiced local court sentenced each of the two men to fourteen years' hard labour. Two years later, when the public had forgotten all about the case, the conviction against Wilson was set aside, whilst Daniel got away with a sentence of no more than three months, the appeal court finding that the evidence against Wilson was insufficient, and that the local authorities had exceeded their jurisdiction.

Stanford Glass, an historian who has since authoritatively examined all the available evidence, has concluded that the two unprepossessing characters in all probability committed the theft, and got what they deserved.[2] The local court was not, however, correct in assuming that the troopers' turpitude caused the war to be prolonged. Jameson did in fact receive two further messages from Lobengula; but the British felt convinced that the king was merely trying to temporize before making good his escape to the north; this assumption was probably correct, as Lobengula may well have been hoping to make his way to the still unconquered Angoni kingdom in North-Eastern Rhodesia to seek sanctuary and sympathy from his kinsmen. Fate decided otherwise, and though the Chartered Company was not actually responsible for the affair, the incident cast a deep slur on the 'Charter's' reputation which its opponents remembered for many years to come.

---

[1] Statement at a Court of enquiry: 20 Dec 1893 (in CT 1/14/3, Nat Arch SR)

[2] I am indebted to Mr Glass for being allowed access to an as yet unpublished chapter on the trial incident. This is based on material in the High Commissioner's and other correspondence in the National Archives, the preliminary examination in the District Court, Bulawayo (in D 3/6/1) Nat Arch SR) and the records of the High Court of Matabeleland (C.R. case no. 275)

II

Smouldering embers

The Matabele War was fought to protect white settlement in the Fort Victoria area, but when it ended fate took an unexpected revenge on the struggling township. All interest was centred on the newly conquered province, where Jameson's men were rewarded with farms and gold claims, so that they had every temptation to stay in Matabeleland which was supposed to contain reefs far exceeding in richness anything to be found in Mashonaland. Emigrants from the south now made direct for Bulawayo; Fort Victoria was by-passed and fell into eclipse. All traffic was diverted, and when Matabeleland was officially thrown open in 1894 Bulawayo quickly developed into a main centre of settlement. Within two months some 400 gold-seekers acquired licences, 11,000 claims were registered, and the new settlement experienced a backveld boom. Bulawayo was easier to reach from the south than Tuli, the former gateway to the interior. Instead of travelling through thick bush and heavy sand, the wagons now rolled along the healthier plateau and reached their destination more quickly. Traders left their stores in Tuli, Fort Victoria or even Salisbury; and building plots in Bulawayo reached fabulous prices, as the settlement became the main distribution centre for a scattered population of white prospectors and cattle farmers.[1] First of all ramshackle little structures sprang up in what became known as the 'Old Camp', now covered by Bulawayo Cemetery, about a mile away from Lobengula's town. But early in 1894 Jameson decided on a better place and the whole settlement was removed to the New Township where Bulawayo now stands. A surveyor hastily got to work with a chain measure made up of various odds and ends of material, and wide, spacious streets were laid out, broad enough for a span of oxen to turn round without difficulty. Mail coaches brought new immigrants and buildings went up as fast as the bricklayers could work. Bulawayo was quickly through the 'pole-and-daga' stage which characterized Salisbury's early days and solid constructions soon appeared. Hotels with high sounding names like the 'Palace' or the 'Imperial' opened their doors; churches, clubs and stores sprang up as if by magic, and there was even a Stock Exchange where brisk business was done, much of it in anticipated or non-existent wealth. Newspapers

[1] For a good description see Hole, H. M. *Old Rhodesian days.* Macmillan and co. ltd, 1928, p. 96–101

followed and by 1895 advertisements in the *Buluwayo Chronicle* included announcements put in by grain millers, sawyers, attorneys, conveyancers, civil engineers, farriers, and a score of others. There was even a commercial lending library, whilst a naturalist was seeking customers for stuffed birds and prepared skins. These early Bulawayans were a cheerful and hard-drinking lot; they enjoyed 'pugilistic exhibitions' and concerts, the local art critic in the *Buluwayo Sketch* commenting favourably on one perfor-mance, noting that the artists were good and the audience orderly, a combination hardly ever found in Bulawayo together!

In addition to white immigrants, a handful of black settlers made their appearance. The Pioneer Column of 1890 was itself a multi-racial enterprise, containing 'Colonial natives' who were employed on transport work and as personal servants, receiving relatively high rates of pay, and 'Cape boys' continued to play an important part in the local economy. The African 'aristocracy of labour' consisted of drivers and leaders of oxen who received £6 and £4 per month respectively, including rations. Ordinary workmen were paid at rates going up to about 20/- per month, and the Chartered Company informed incoming settlers that natives should receive a pound of meal, a pound of meat, an ounce of coffee, two ounces of sugar and half an ounce of salt per day,[1] the country's black wage structure showing a considerable 'spread' right from the very beginning.

Africans again played their part in the Matabele War; the Victoria Column included 78 'Cape Boys' and 'Zambezia Boys' working with the wagons and at road-making. The Salisbury Column had 115 'Natives', probably 'Cape Boys' again, and the invading army also included a force of some 400 Mashona all armed with guns. Some of these volunteers obtained 100-acre lots in return for their services and the list of recipients included some Indians.[2] Most of these 100-acre properties seem to have changed hands quickly, for European purchasers bought the land at prices between £10 and £300, though the buyers also included a few Africans. An old register records the sale of two 'Umgusa lots' by one John Bepa, a former soldier, to H. Mangesana, another soldier, for £10 and £100 respectively. By 1899 Mangesana owned a 100-acre plot, having meanwhile disposed of two plots for a total of £200.[3]

Men like Mangesana, however, were quite exceptional; the Company's policy towards the ordinary man in the kraal was to convert tribesmen into wage workers. There were two ways of mobilizing this great potential

[1] British South Africa Company. *Report on the Company's proceedings . . . 1892–1894.* London, the Company, 1895, p. 9
[2] LB 4/1/1, Nat Arch SR.
[3] Transfer duty register, DB 5/8/1, Nat Arch SR.

labour army—by offering incentives and by open or disguised compulsion. The Europeans of course had a good deal to offer—pots and pans, blankets and beads—commodities which a village economy could not produce at all, or not as cheaply and efficiently. A Manyika historian, speaking of the Umtali area, thus records:

'When the Europeans arrived in this country, they began to hire African servants and rewarded them with clothes, soap and salt. . . . In the year 1895 when the Europeans were still living at Old Umtali, the Africans used to wear skins and those who were working under Europeans used to wrap themselves with pieces of cloth on the lower limbs only.'[1] There were however certain limits to this incentive. The market for consumption goods was small; in addition the introduction of the new kind of merchandise met with some resistance, for if Africans were given hats, shoes and trousers 'they could not put them on because their friends laughed at them. In those days it was funny to see an African in long trousers with a hat on and shoes. He appeared to them more or less like a ghost', whilst many Europeans at the same time made rude remarks about 'trouser niggers' who were supposed to display the worst characteristics of both races. Africans moreover had to look after their own land, where they continued to hold a stake, having no incentive permanently to abandon their tribal rights to work for white men. European employers found that Africans would only work for short periods, and that farm labour was generally short at the agricultural peak season when it was most required.

The Europeans for their part felt convinced that African men lived a life of blissful idleness in their villages, where the Bantu supposedly spent all their time drinking beer and watching their poor womenfolk work. Black men therefore ought to learn the 'dignity of labour' and improve their lot by earning wages. Victorian beliefs in 'self-help' and the virtues of thrift thus blended oddly with Western ideas of chivalry, whilst the European employers' own economic self-interest coincided with the missionaries' conviction that Africans should be prised out of their tribal environment to make them more responsive to the Word of God.

The Company of course could not help but regard the white employers' arguments with considerable sympathy. The Administration after all shared the farmers' and miners' economic interests—without the settlers' enterprise the Company would receive neither revenue from land sales nor mining royalties; in addition fiscal arguments played some part, for if Africans would pay tax they would make a contribution to the Administration's income. The Company's Secretary thus presented a strong case

[1] Machiwanyika, J. *History and customs of the Manyika people*, translated by W. S. Musewe in 1943 (an unpublished manuscript in MA 14/1/2, Nat Arch MS)

to the Colonial Office; as the result of white occupation the Mashona acquired a ready market for their labour and produce; the Company assured law and order, having done away with inter-tribal fighting; Africans should acquire habits of settled industry, and the necessity of making some small monetary contribution would furnish an incentive to labour.[1] The outbreak of the Matabele War caused the Colonial Office to postpone its decision but when the war was over, taxation—which after all formed an accepted means of native policy in every South African state—was sanctioned, and in 1894 a hut tax ordinance passed on to the Statute Book. This provided that every African man should pay ten shillings in respect of every hut which he occupied.[2] Native Commissioners were allowed to accept payment in kind where there was no other alternative, but the value of grain or stock was to be assessed on the current market price, whilst the taxpayer became responsible for 'the reasonable cost of carriage or driving as the case may be' to the nearest store. The Native Commissioners at first accepted mealies and kaffir corn,[3] but in 1895 the Chief Native Commissioner informed his officials that the profit realized from sales of stock or grain was not to be credited to the kraal from where it came, but to the department, the idea being to 'encourage Natives to earn their Tax by labour, as the Government are not anxious to take Stock for Tax'.[4]

This switch-over appeared as arbitrary to the governed as it seemed rational to the governors, and the feelings of ordinary Africans with regard to the new measure were probably best expressed by the Manyika historian quoted before, who recorded the story in his own tongue with some slight embellishments:

'The Europeans reached this country in 1897 and after having been in this country for three years, they gathered all the chiefs in the country and said to them "pay tax".

'The chiefs said "what are we to give you as tax?" The Europeans said to them "everything you own". The chiefs said "What do we own?" The Europeans said "Crops". So the chiefs and their subjects began paying tax with mealie meal.

'The second year the Europeans said "We do not want mealie meal for taxation, we want fowls". And they were given. The third year the Europeans said "We want to substitute fowls for goats and cattle for taxation".

---

[1] B.S.A. Company to Colonial Office: 7 July 1893 (in African (South) no. 454, p. 3)
[2] In Matabeleland the tax for the first year was 5/- and only became payable after a Land Commission, which was sitting at the time, had completed its settlement.
[3] Circular from Chief Native Commissioner: 19 Apr 1895 (in N 4/1/1, Nat Arch SR)
[4] Circular from Chief Native Commissioner: 12 Nov 1894 (in N 4/1/1, Nat Arch SR)

'The chiefs and their subjects were very unwilling to give out their cattle for taxation and gave them goats only. The fourth year they asked for ten shillings instead of goats and it was so. All this was happening while the Englishmen were at Old Umtali in 1897 and the Africans were suffering much because of taxation.'[1]

Taxation in other words began as tribute in kind, of a type not very different from the sort of impost which an African overlord would impose on his subjects. But with a money tax an African could only meet his obligations by entering the money economy, either by working for the whites or selling goods for coin; whilst the need to earn cash became a steady and predictable feature of life, not an occasional adventure which a man might face once or twice in the course of his career, in order to get a pot, a knife or a gun.

In addition to the indirect pressure of taxation the Chartered Company's administration also resorted to more direct means. Native Commissioners or Inspectors of Police called on the various chiefs and headmen, informing the villagers that a certain percentage must work for the white men in return for a minimum wage of 10/- per month as well as board and lodging; these orders were enforced by African policemen who often grossly exceeded their authority. The amount of pressure exerted seems to have varied considerably from district to district; the Resident Magistrate at Salisbury, for instance, denied that compulsory labour was ever enforced in his area; his opposite number at Bulawayo admitted that policemen would obtain workers in proportion to the African men at each kraal, though he added that the villagers soon got used to going out to work on their own, so that after July 1894 the need for obtaining men through the chiefs ceased altogether. Some individual settlers also complained, and a few angry letters even reached the Chief Native Commissioner's office after the country had been completely pacified. A European trader thus recorded that the Lower Umniati district was almost depopulated, the police having taken many of the local Africans away to work in Bulawayo, with the result that the others had moved further away to the north-west. The same trader had also heard of Matabele who preyed on Gorrodema's kraal where they took away tobacco and other goods in Dr Jameson's name, though he did not know whether these people were in fact policemen or just thieves.[2]

But whatever the extent of these depredations, and whatever the means employed, the Matabele now found themselves forced to participate in an

[1] Machiwanyika, J. *History and customs of the Manyika people* (MA 14/1/2, Nat Arch MS). The author appears to have made a slight mistake with regard to the dates.

[2] L. M. Wyllie to Chief Native Commissioner, Mashonaland: 28 Feb 1898 (in N 3/24/1/1, Nat Arch SR)

alien wage economy; this in turn appears to have exercised a levelling influence on existing tribal distinctions, despite bitter resistance from the one-time aristocracy. The Chief Native Commissioner, Bulawayo, thus explained during the course of an investigation that at first the chiefs forwarded *Holi*, that is to say lower-class people, whilst the *Zansi*, the one-time ruling class, considered work to be derogatory to their dignity and often appropriated the *Holi's* hard-earned wage packets when they returned. This caused a great deal of discontent, and as the demand for labour in the mining districts increased, *Zansi* men were also called up, Native Police being used in some cases to see that they turned out. The final result was considerable discontent, so much so that the bulk of the *Holi* made common cause with their erstwhile masters when the Matabele once more decided to appeal to arms.

Defeat also brought grave economic losses to the conquered. The whole Matabele way of life hinged on the ownership of cattle; herds supplied milk and meat; hides were used for clothing, bedding and the manufacture of shields. Horned beasts were also endowed with profound spiritual significance, and no man might marry without giving *lobolo*, a kind of dowry which passed from the bridegroom's relatives to those of his bride. During the great days of the Matabele kingdom most of the cattle belonged to the king; few people had beasts of their own, for a man who could boast of too much wealth always stood in danger of being 'smelt out'. Defeat, however, overthrew the whole network of Matabele property relations, and many tribesmen, including the once despised *Holi*, began to appropriate the king's cattle.[1] The Company failed to realize that Lobengula owned his cattle as a trustee for his people and regarded the late monarch's herds as legitimate booty for the victor. Estimates concerning the number of beasts taken varied greatly. According to the Company's records, 80,000 were seized, whilst the Matabele kept 40,000 for their own use. Others reckoned that about 200,000 animals were rounded up, of which 90,000 were returned to Africans to tend. In the end the Company kept no more than 30,000, but the Africans' sense of grievance and uncertainty continued to rankle, and united all classes against the conqueror.

Morally the Matabele could hardly complain, for they themselves used to raid their neighbours, but nevertheless the loss proved hard to bear. More disastrous still was the rinderpest which swept down from the north in the beginning of 1896, ravaging the white and black men's herds alike, and leaving the Matabele without cattle. The European settlers to some

[1] See statements by chiefs Umjaan, Inqubugubo, Langhali and Mazizi to the Land Commission in C. 8130 (1896).

extent managed to shield themselves against the worst effects of the epidemic by importing native stock from north of the Zambezi. The Matabele, however, had no cash to do likewise, and when European veterinary officers began to shoot beasts to prevent the infection from spreading, men began to mutter angrily that the whites, having imported the disease, were now going one worse, and killing the remainder out of pure spite.

To the Matabele the Company's land policy appeared equally harsh. In 1894 a Land Commission was appointed for the purpose of settling land claims. The Commissioners heard evidence from senior chiefs who told them that the Shangani region was splendid for cattle and that the country near the Gwaai river was well watered. Colenbrander explained that the total population of Matabeleland might amount to something like 100,000 people, that the majority of the Matabele lived to the west of the Gwaai and on both banks of the Nata river. The *Holi* dwelt on the Matopos and west of the Gwaai. The Matopo hills, however, should not be permitted to form part of a native reserve. European settlers had pegged out many farms in the district; besides, the country was so broken and inaccessible that it would be difficult to supervise the population adequately. The Commission therefore delimited two large areas, the Shangani Reserve which included about 3,500 square miles and the Gwaai Reserve comprising some 3,000 square miles. Most of this land, however, turned out to be quite unsuitable, and Africans preferred to stay where they were. When white farmers bought land from the Government they found kraals on their holdings. The new owner would tell the local Africans that they must regard him as their master, and that if they wanted to stay, they would have to help as herdsmen and farmhands. Unsatisfactory as these labour services turned out to be, they did not, however, provide the Matabele even with the security of feudal tenure, for farms changed hands quickly, and many African villagers were faced with a constant succession of new masters.

These land and labour grievances became even harder to bear because of local abuses; the administration remained understaffed and inefficient; the Chartered Company's native police was poorly supervised, and often used its privileged position to pay off old scores, or to loot. European ruffians preyed on the conquered, and a serving trooper recorded that 'the conduct of many of the whites towards their black sisters, married or virgin, in Matabeleland certainly contributed to the causes which have led up to this unfortunate rebellion',[1] thereby touching on a subject which Victorians did not like to mention, but which certainly played some part in fanning the embers.

[1] See Sykes, F. W. *With Plumer in Matabeleland*. Archibald Constable and co., 1897, p. 8–11

Whilst discontent was building up in Matabeleland and the more settled parts of Mashonaland, the 'Charter's' administrative machine remained small and weak. The Directors simply wished to save money; the settlers pooh-poohed the thought that the local Africans might still give trouble, whilst people such as Selous—who should have known better—had no idea of what was being hatched in the kraals. The Company's government had no intelligence service worth mentioning, and senior officials remained blissfully unaware of African discontent, or of the way Matabele warriors were hiding guns for another call to arms. In 1894 a new Order in Council reorganized the Company's government, vesting all real power in the hands of Jameson as Administrator,[1] whilst also providing for a Council of senior civil servants. A year later a proclamation divided the Chartered territory south of the Zambezi into two provinces which were again divided into native districts. On paper the scheme looked well, but in practice the Company's establishment remained extremely small; officials had to be posted from station to station without getting to know their areas, whilst the tribesmen would complain that hardly had they got to know their Native Commissioner when someone else would come in and take over.

Militarily the Company remained equally weak. The Company believed—probably wrongly—that the Matabele regimental system had been smashed beyond repair, and that the Mashona and even the *Holi* in Matabeleland were only too pleased with the white man's dispensation which did away with tribal raiding. Not expecting any serious native difficulties, the Company failed to provide for an adequate force and relied on nothing more than a small body of police and an unwieldy and ill-organized body of volunteers, the Rhodesia Horse.

The opportunity for a rising arose when Jameson embarked on his famous Raid into the Transvaal, determined to overthrow President Kruger's government there, and install a pro-British administration at Pretoria. Rhodes never took Johnson's sound advice of gradually infil-trating volunteers into the Golden City in the guise of mineworkers, and clandestinely arming them on the spot. Instead Chartered police were diverted to Bechuanaland and on the last day of 1895 a startled world heard the news that Jameson had made a raid into the Transvaal with some 600 horsemen, mostly police from north of the Limpopo. The Raid, a disastrous gamble from the start, ended in Jameson's capitulation at Doornkop, and for the time being Rhodes's political position in South Africa collapsed. To the Matabele the Boer victory seemed a portent. The invincible doctor had been beaten; Matabeleland was denuded of troops;

[1] The Matabeleland order in council, 1894

this was the time to strike and utterly to crush the white man and all his works.

The actual organization of the rebellion was a complex affair. The Matabele seem to have thought at first in terms of restoring their former state. The Rev. D. Carnegie, a knowledgeable missionary, thus reported that before Lobengula's death, the unfortunate monarch asked Umlugulu, his chief 'dance doctor', to restore the Great Dance and other ceremonies when this could be done once more with safety. Umlugulu later conferred with other important leaders, but the Great Dance never took place and the Matabele failed to restore their former ways. War decimated the *Zansi* aristocracy, and Rhodes took good care to take Lobengula's heirs out of the country and educate them at the Cape, so that no universally recognized successor remained in sight. The Matabele were divided; there was a peace party drawing much of its strength from the bush country of the north-west where the Europeans' impact was little felt; but a militant faction, centring on the Bulawayo area and the north-east, gained increasing influence, and black men once again talked of war.

The resistance groups used the surviving political machinery of the tribe as much as they could, white conquest probably having not proved as cataclysmic in its effects within the short space of three years as many Europeans later imagined. The vanquished also turned to their religious institutions which had not been directly affected by defeat—a common reaction amongst many different people, white or black, who find themselves under foreign sway, and seek consolation as well as a new assertion of their group identity by returning to their churches or more primitive equivalents. The Matabele drew strength from the ancient *Mlimo* cult which formed an important feature of the very Rozwi empire which Umzilikazi's host once dashed to pieces. The Matabele came as conquerors but from early days onwards fell under the religious influence of the people whom they subdued. According to one of the best-known experts, the Matabele, having settled north of the Limpopo, transferred their allegiance from *Nkulunkulu*, the Zulu high god, to *Mlimo*, the Karanga deity.[1] The reasons are not easy to explain, but apparently the Matabele recognized that the local tribes still maintained ties with the land, which the newcomers lacked, for the Matabele ancestral graves lay far away to the south, and the immigrants could not therefore boast of the same links with the earth and the dead possessed by the indigenous communities. Matabele warriors also captured wives from the local people, and their prisoners—as mothers, aunts and grandmothers—helped to pass on their traditions to the children of the tribe.

[1] See Bullock, C. *The Mashona and the Matabele*. Cape Town, Juta and co. ltd, 1950, p. 145–148

Lobengula of course carried out religious as well as secular functions, but his kingship, founded on military force, never enjoyed the divinely-ordained prestige that surrounded the ancient Mambos. The king took good care to conciliate the gods of the land, and after the disasters of 1893 the cult of *Mlimo* rapidly gained further strength, political discontent finding expression in what may perhaps have been a theological revolution. *Mlimo* originally appears to have been regarded as some remote *deus abscondidus*, the Ancient of Days, who took no notice of tribal affairs that remained the preserve of lesser deities. But when the Matabele fell on evil days the god gained increasing political importance, and his cult, centring on the Matopos, provided an effective machinery of revolt. Traditional African beliefs assume that the spirits speak to men through 'inspired' human interpreters, who correspond in some ways to the Pythia of the ancient Delphic Oracle, and possess greater insight than ordinary folk. In this time of trouble Mkwati, a former slave captured by the Matabele near the Zambezi, built up a great reputation for himself as the deity's mouthpiece and preached war to the death. Mkwati maintained close contacts with the influential spirit mediums of western Mashonaland; he also drew on the ancient reputation of the Rozwi by marrying the daughter of one of their surviving chiefs. The sacred shrines became the centres of revolt; specially appointed messengers, taking back prayers and presents from the chiefs, provided the insurgents with an efficient means of communication; the proud Matabele chieftains now agreed to operate under the supreme direction of an ex-serf whom they confidently identified with *Mlimo*. To the majority of Matabele war seemed the only way out, and black warriors once again took to gun and assegai.[1]

III

Dogs of war: 1896–1897

On 20 March 1896 a party of eight African policemen arrived at the native settlement of Umgorshwini in the hills by the Umzingwani river. They were sitting by their camp fire after the evening meal when a party of armed Matabele came up and began a fierce war dance in front of them. Suddenly one of the constables saw a man creeping steadily towards them round the back of the cattle kraal. At once suspecting mischief, he jumped

[1] For a most interesting account of the rising from the African point of view see Ranger, T. O. *The organization of the rebellion of 1896 and 1897, pts 1 and 2*, a paper read at the History of Central African Peoples' Conference, Rhodes-Livingstone Institute, Lusaka, 28 May–1 June 1963

up and shouted 'Look out, we're amongst enemies'. There was a scuffle and three people were killed.[1] Soon afterwards reports began to come in from various parts of the country that isolated settlers were being hunted down and murdered by Matabele war parties. From the rebels' point of view the campaign did not go quite according to plan; their high command apparently intended to strike on 28 March when the moon was full, but in spite of the error in their time-table the insurgents at first scored one success after another as unsuspecting whites and their families were shot, stoned, speared or bludgeoned to death.[2] White rule disintegrated over most of Matabeleland and for a time the Company's situation looked desperate. The bulk of the European police was out of the country, prisoners after the Jameson Raid; the native police could not be trusted and some in fact went over to the enemy where their training, knowledge and their arms and ammunition proved extremely welcome. There were of course many members of the Rhodesia Horse Volunteers at Bulawayo but rifles and horses were short, and a determined enemy might even have risked a sudden *coup de main* on the township itself.

But the local authorities acted swiftly; the available men were organized into the Bulawayo Field Force which consisted of about 850 volunteers, including an artillery and an engineer troop, Grey's Scouts, Dawson's Scouts, Gifford's Horse, an Afrikander Corps and about 125 'Colonial' natives commanded by Colenbrander. The township was hastily fortified; stores were hurriedly lodged in an eating house which was armoured with horizontally laid iron pipes; the garrison built a look-out post on top of a newspaper office from where they kept the surrounding countryside under observation. British miners and mechanics proved excellent engineers, and the laager, the focal strongpoint, protected by barbed wire, improvised dynamite mines, machine guns, and a few light guns, was soon impregnable to native attacks; although never put to the test, it would have been a hard nut to crack.

The Matabele were now much more formidable opponents than in the days of Lobengula. They had learnt the tactical lessons of the Bembesi and Shangani battles and avoided massed assaults in open country against automatic weapons and well-directed rifle fire. Instead they operated in smaller and more mobile bodies, fighting in skirmishing order, relying on guns more than assegais. The white men thus faced an enemy vastly superior in numbers, who chose to fight in broken country and dense bush, where machine guns could not do so much execution.

[1] Selous, F. C. *Sunshine and storm in Rhodesia.* Rowland Ward and co. ltd, 1896, p. 19–21
[2] According to calculations by H. M. Hole 122 white men, 5 women and 3 children were killed in March. During April there were 13 more murders, including 3 women and 5 children.

Matabele strategy, on the other hand, was badly conceived. The spirit mediums seem to have hoped that the whites would evacuate the country —if given an opportunity—and the Matabele therefore left open the main route through Mangwe and the western defiles of the Matopos, the white man's lifeline in the newly occupied country. The rising was inadequately co-ordinated, and some Matabele communities held aloof. The British managed to arrest Gambo, an important induna in the west who happened to be in Bulawayo at the time on business connected with the cattle plague. Gambo subsequently went over to the whites, becoming one of the richest and most influential chiefs in Matabeleland, his defection forming a considerable blow to the insurgents. The settlers, having set up a secure strong-point, were able to catch their breath, and small patrols sallied forth from Bulawayo to rescue isolated colonists. These parties did not do much fighting against the Matabele, but proved of some value in ascertaining the enemy's general strength and disposition, thus preparing the way for more concerted efforts.

At the same time the European colonists at Gwelo managed to go into laager and a sturdy little group of miners collected at Belingwe, some ninety miles east of Bulawayo, so that the insurgents now found themselves face to face with three strong-points which—remembering the experiences of the Matabele war—they did not dare to attack. A relief column of some 150 men was quickly organized from Salisbury, and the garrisons at Gwelo and Bulawayo were strengthened with much needed supplies.

Gradually the Europeans seized the initiative. On 28 April a force of 115 white volunteers and 70 'Colonial' natives managed to inflict a severe reverse on the Matabele, and Bulawayo, in the Administrator's exuberant words, 'now became as safe as London.' A further patrol from Bulawayo dispersed an impi at Tabas Induna and effected a junction with the column from Salisbury near the Shangani river, the combined force making a successful sweeping movement through Insiza and Filabusi before returning to Bulawayo.

In spite of these local successes the Company could not pacify the whole of Matabeleland with its existing forces and, reluctantly, asked for Imperial aid. It also took steps to reinforce the threatened colonists from the south, the task of raising the 'Matabeleland Relief Force' being entrusted to Lieutenant-Colonel Charles Onslow Plumer, who nineteen years later commanded the Second Army in France. Plumer managed to raise a well-paid irregular corps, recruited mainly in Kimberley and Mafeking, and containing many former soldiers, as well as a fair cross-section of South Africa's English-speaking miner's frontier, who shaped into an excellent fighting force.[1] In addition the Company employed a corps of some 200 'Cape Boys' from Johannesburg, led by Major R. Robertson, who gave a good account of themselves, and proved much more valuable than a contingent of some 240 Bechuanaland levies who soon had to be disbanded and sent home.

The supreme command was entrusted to an Imperial officer, Sir Frederick Carrington, an old campaigner from earlier Kaffir Wars, who now had some 2,000 whites and 600 black troops in hand, and was able to take vigorous action against the rebels. The country was scoured by mounted patrols which kept the rebels on the move; forts were built to interfere with their supplies and prevent their reforming in combat-worthy formations; in addition the whites exercised heavy economic pressure on the enemy by rounding up cattle, goats and sheep, and by seizing or burning crops, an essential feature in irregular operations designed to crush a popular rising. The British scored a major success by capturing Tabas Inyamba by a triple movement executed after a rapid night march. The rebel positions, though strongly held, were stormed after some hours of hard fighting. Carrington was then able to turn his attention to the Matopos where the enemy made their last stand. British mounted irregular troops gained a number of important successes, but nevertheless found themselves with a very difficult problem on their hands. The Matopos were too extensive to blockade, and difficult to storm, a jumble of precipitous kopjes, dotted with huge boulders which concealed the entrances of innumerable caves, from where unseen marksmen might fire with impunity on an advancing enemy, and which afforded easy retreats in case of defeat. There was only one way to break African resistance—to starve the rebels into surrender—and this would take time, and would throw an insupportable financial weight on the Company.

As it happened, Rhodes was on the spot. Early in 1896 he made a quick visit to London to consult with the Company's Board of Directors on the effects of Jameson's raid and to see Chamberlain at the Colonial Office. From London he sought refuge in Rhodesia, arriving at Salisbury in March. Rhodes, without knowing of course, merely jumped from one crisis into another, but the new emergency brought out his best qualities. A visitor who called on the great man some time before the Raid was shocked at the way in which he had morally deteriorated in the company

---

[1] According to Plumer the force contained some 100 miners and engineers, 50 employees of De Beers, 120 farmers, 100 clerks, and 50 old soldiers and veterans, 30 from colonial corps. The remaining 400 had previously served either in the Bechuanaland Border Police or the Company's police and included many former 'Jameson Raiders'. About 590 were English-born, 150 were English-speaking and 50 Afrikaans-speaking South Africans. The remainder came from the Dominions, the U.S.A. and various European countries.

of fawning admirers and lickspittles. With his country in ruins, his political influence gone in South Africa, Rhodes once more became an inspiring figure. He decided to negotiate, and in August 1896, at great personal risk, met the insurgent chiefs in the Matopos. Many white men thought that he would end with an assegai through his ribs, but Rhodes's magnetic personality, which could win over British barons and backveld Boers, cautious Treasury men from Whitehall and flashy financiers from Whitechapel, made an equally strong impression on despairing African warriors. The Matabele consented to further negotiations and in the end stopped the fighting. Rhodes agreed that each chief should have his own district and that chiefs should present their people's grievances to the Native Commissioner who would in turn communicate with the Administrator, so that the people would only have one head. Loyal chiefs would receive salaries, and their people might return to their kraals.[1] The work of disarming the Matabele began in October 1896 and by September of the following year the rebels had surrendered more than 2,500 guns and 13,000 assegais, so that the Matabele ceased to be a factor of military importance. Having made peace with the indunas, Rhodes gave them a prompt illustration of the way in which he meant to deal with them in future. The Matabele were starving, their lands unplanted, and the Administration distributed about 5,000,000 lb of grain to tide them over the most difficult months. At the same time Rhodes maintained an astonishing personal ascendancy over the defeated chieftains; his prestige remained unshaken as long as he lived, Rhodes taking care to settle a good many former rebel chiefs 'and half the dangerous characters in the land' on an experimental farm at Sauersdale, where some 4,000 Africans resided, so that they might be more securely watched and controlled.[2]

The political reputation of the discredited spirit mediums slumped. The prestige of Matabele kingship, not directly involved in the unsuccessful rebellion, revived; chiefs as well as schoolmasters and pastors now put their hopes in a revival of the Matabele monarchy and looked for a new king who would once more lead the nation to greatness.[3]

In the meantime, trouble had been brewing in Mashonaland. The British authorities denuded the area of troops to cope with the rising in Matabeleland and unwittingly reproduced a situation reminiscent of that in Matabeleland immediately after the Jameson Raid. Discontent was rife

[1] C. 8547 (1897), p. 68–82

[2] Diary of Sir Lewis Loyd Michell, then General Manager of the Standard Bank of South Africa and later a Director of the British South Africa Company (copy in MI 3/4/1, at Nat Arch MS)

[3] See the paper by Ranger, T. O. *Traditional authorities and the rise of modern politics in Southern Rhodesia 1898–1930*, read at the History of African Peoples' Conference, Rhodes-Livingstone Institute, Lusaka, 28 May–1 June 1963

amongst numerous communities, and soon many tribes burst out into open revolt, much to the surprise of the Europeans who thought that the 'cowardly' Mashona would never take to arms. But widespread murders began in June 1896, Africans objecting to the enforcement of labour services, taxation, and blaming the whites for locusts, rinderpest and the Europeans' resultant veterinary campaign. The indigenous people in the Salisbury area also had to contend with 'Colonial' natives, who settled amongst the local tribes, married girls from the villages nearby and often set themselves up as arbitrators in tribal disputes. There were additional outbreaks in the Salisbury, Mazoe, Marandellas and Lomagundi regions, the Zezuru taking a prominent part in the rising. Blood was shed in the Charter district which contained a relatively numerous white Afrikaans-speaking population of backveld farmers; risings also occurred in the Abercorn district and near Gwelo; in addition Makoni, a powerful chief in what is now known as the Eastern Districts, decided to go on the warpath.

The rising was, however, far from universal; the outer fringes of Mashonaland, including both the extreme north—the former centre of Monomotapa's power—and the extreme south were not affected. Mtoko's country, where there was apparently no forced labour, remained quiet; so did Melsetter where there was no rinderpest. The labour question more-over did not always necessarily make for war, for local politics were governed by a multiplicity of pressures which did not all work in the same way. The Makalaka in the south-west, for instance, would not fight the whites, even though supposedly ten per cent of their population was at work. One of the explanations given was that the villagers could get jobs in the Tati gold fields nearby, and were able to use the money earned abroad to buy stock, so that they had not so much reason to object to the new order of things.[1] The Fort Victoria district similarly remained quiet, possibly because the people there regarded the Matabele as a greater peril than the whites. In the east Umtasa cautiously decided to sit on the fence.[2] He was a former enemy of Makoni's; he was also well aware of the extent of British military strength for he had seen the Company throw out the Portuguese, and he finally decided, after Makoni's defeat, that the Administration was too powerful to be challenged.

The organization of the rising has for long remained an obscure subject. The rebels could not write, and there were thus no despatches to intercept;

---

[1] For details see the statements published by administrative officials in the various areas in C. 8547 (1897) and British South Africa Company. *Report on the native disturbances, 1896–1897*. The Company, 1898

[2] Alderson, E. A. M. *With the Mounted Infantry and the Mashonaland Field Force*. Methuen and co., 1898, p. 134

Africans maintained tight security, and the white men had no real inkling of what was happening before the rebellion started. During the fighting the British military authorities were more interested in details of military operations and supplies than in establishing causes; Sir Richard Martin, an Imperial officer who subsequently conducted an investigation into the rising, concentrated on the Company's real or alleged culpability, whilst the judicial enquiries, carried out when the war was over, concentrated on responsibility for individual murders. Nevertheless it seems fairly clear that the organization centred on two parallel and inter-connected systems of worship which the tribes inherited from their remoter ancestors.[1] The worship of *Mlimo*, or *Mwari*, still flourished in Western Mashonaland and the cult now acquired strong revolutionary overtones. The fires of resistance were fanned by Mkwati, a remarkable man who in 'normal' times would hardly have acquired much political influence. Mkwati, as we have seen, was taken by one of Lobengula's impis in a raid near the Zambezi. After the war of 1893 he set himself up in a cave on Taba za ki Mambo which rapidly became an important oracular shrine; Mkwati built up an astonishing moral ascendancy over his former masters and in time became known as the spokesman of *Mlimo* himself. In July of 1896, Plumer's forces, however, stormed the stronghold; the Matabele aristocracy decided to negotiate, and Mkwati took refuge in the north-east where he found many adherents. From here Mkwati maintained close contacts with the *mondoro* of Western Mashonaland. The *mondoro*, according to Mashona beliefs, are spirits who speak through human mediums, provide people with crops and send down plagues when angered; they are grouped into several hierarchies which may well reflect earlier political divisions. One of the best known of these spirit mediums was Kagubi, a native husbandman, who organized resistance in the Hartley district and ordered the local chiefs to attack the whites. An African witness giving evidence during the subsequent trial said that before the rising started Kagubi was just an ordinary person.[2] Later the tall, lean, cadaverous-looking man became a famous *mondoro*, imagined by the faithful to be the 'Son of God', and wielding tremendous political influence. Kagubi commanded a small band of faithful followers, known as the 'Hands of the *Mondoro*', who carried out killings. Little is known about these men, except that many of them appear to have been related to Kagubi, and that they included two 'native hut builders', an African wagon

[1] See Ranger, T. O. *The organization of the rebellion of 1896 and 1897, pts 1 and 2*, a paper read at the History of African Peoples' Conference, Rhodes-Livingstone Institute, Lusaka, 28 May–1 June 1963
[2] See High Court of Matabeleland Criminal sessions, Case no. 253, Regina v. Kargubi, Marimo, M'bobo, Chiganga and Makatsimi (National Archives)

leader and a native hunter, so that the rebels certainly included men who had been in touch with Europeans and picked up some of their skills. Kagubi, the 'Lion's Paw', effectively mobilized the *mondoro* in the Hartley area and Central Mashonaland, insisting that all white men must be killed without mercy, preaching war to the finish, the spirit mediums exercising tremendous influence upon the petty chiefs in the country. Kagubi closely co-operated with Nyanda, a short, stocky woman of about thirty-six and a long-established oracle who later accepted Kagubi's leadership; she organized the rising at Mazoe, where she inspired the local killings and maintained her followers at fighting pitch.[1]

For the moment victory seemed far away for the Europeans. White rule was only of recent origin; memories of the Mambo's long-departed glory were not yet dead. The spirit mediums preached war to the knife and the British found themselves with a desperate war on their hands. Most of the settlers at first took refuge in laagers at Salisbury, Charter, Enkeldoorn, Victoria and Umtali, only Melsetter and Tuli remaining unaffected. Many settlers were murdered in the backveld, though hurriedly improvised patrols managed to rescue a number of outlying families, and Rhodesian history became enriched with some exciting escape stories. One of the most colourful of these incidents concerned the defence of the Alice Mine at Mazoe. When the local tribesmen unexpectedly took to arms the local whites took refuge at the mine and the manager hurriedly asked Salisbury for help. The authorities in the capital at first failed to grasp the seriousness of the situation and sent out a small party which comprised John Lionel Leonard Blakiston and two other volunteers. Blakiston, an English clergyman's son, was in some ways rather the unsuccessful kind of intellectual; he emigrated from England and failed to make good in the Argentine and later went to the Cape. In 1895 he received an offer to work on the Transcontinental Telegraph Line in Mashonaland and accepted on being assured by all his friends that 'there is only a minimum of risk to a man who chooses to live carefully'[2] and that salaries, leave and pension conditions would be good. Blakiston, on the face of it, showed little aptitude for living in the Far Interior, and sadly wrote home that he liked neither the country nor its people, and that 'everyone in Mashonaland was either slave to Mammon or to Bacchus'.[3] But some ironic twist of fortune destined the shy young man, with his love for books and his interest in Macaulay, to become a martyr for the country's hard-riding, hard-

---

[1] See High Court of Matabeleland, Criminal sessions, Case no. 252, Regina v. Zindongu, Wata, Nianda, and Gutsa (National Archives). For a more detailed account see Ranger, *op. cit*, specially part 2

[2] J. L. Blakiston to H. E. D. Blakiston: 1 Mar and 7 Aug 1895 (in BL 1/1/1, Nat Arch MS)

[3] J. L. Blakiston to D. Y. Blakiston: 30 Aug 1895 (in BL 1/1/1, Nat Arch MS)

drinking, white frontier community. Blakiston found himself stuck at the Alice Mine, and for the moment the position of its little garrison seemed desperate. Blakiston, together with another volunteer, a telegraphist by the name of T. G. Routledge, succeeded in making his way to the empty telegraph office nearby and cabling for help; on his way back they were both cut down. The beleaguered party was eventually rescued by two patrols, commanded respectively by Lieutenant Dan Judson and Inspector Randolph Cosby Nesbitt, the latter receiving the V.C. for his daring coup.

The real military problem, however, centred on the far less romantic aspects of general morale, supplies and reinforcements. The Company never had occasion to worry about the white men's fighting spirit. The settlers lost something like ten per cent of their total number, a staggeringly high figure, infinitely greater than the proportion of casualties suffered by white colonists in the Algerian national rising or the Mau Mau war in Kenya in the twentieth century. The technological discrepancy between mounted white riflemen and irregular black infantry, with guns aplenty, was less than that which existed between a mid-twentieth-century 'colonialist' army, possessed of tracked vehicles, helicopters, fighter bombers and transport 'planes on the one hand, and modern partisans, with automatic weapons, hand grenades and light mortars, on the other. But the colonists' will to rule remained unbroken. They felt that history was on their side, that Europe stood behind them, and that they formed the vanguard of civilization in Darkest Africa. The European clergymen and missionaries in the country, the nearest thing to a local intelligentsia, were generally as full of fight as their fellow-whites; there was none to sympathize with the insurgents or call for concessions in the cause of peace. The settlers' estimate of themselves was shared by public opinion in Britain and America, so that the whites in Rhodesia never experienced that clammy sense of moral and political isolation, which weighed down their successors two generations later. Throughout the war the Europeans accordingly enjoyed complete moral ascendancy over their opponents whose resistance was born of despair rather than the certain belief in ultimate victory.

The purely physical problem of supply presented much greater difficulties. For the time being no post remained occupied on the main lines of communication to Umtali and the route to the coast stayed closed, whilst the road to Bulawayo could only be traversed by a strong force. The Salisbury garrison was fortunate in being able to draw on a large store of provisions which were at once commandeered, whilst patrols brought back some grain and cattle from the countryside. The rinderpest, however, had killed most of the draught oxen in the territory; the mules available barely sufficed for immediate military needs, whilst the remaining centres of Mashonaland soon found themselves in even worse plight than Salisbury. The Company's administration, however, took prompt and effective action. No private firm was able to cope with the pressing problem of supplying a population of some 2,000 whites under these conditions, and the Company therefore centralized the work of organizing a transport service and of purchasing and forwarding supplies under the Administrator's Department; Henry Wilson Fox, a young lawyer, who later became a Director of the Company and one of the most able people in its London Office, was placed in charge of operations, and did a brilliant job.

The British Imperial authorities sent reinforcements from Cape Town, and for once despatched a force entirely suitable for the kind of fighting anticipated, avoiding the mistakes that were subsequently committed on a large scale during the Boer War. The relieving unit—originally destined for use in Matabeleland—was commanded by Colonel Edwin Alfred Harvey Alderson (who was later knighted and became Inspector General of the Canadian Forces in the Great War). Alderson headed a force of Mounted Infantry who were specially selected by their battalions for this kind of work, and which 'skimmed' ordinary units of good men. Organization and tactics foreshadowed in a remarkable fashion those of the Commandos of the Second World War. The Mounted Infantry believed in decentralization, the men in each section of thirty being divided into permanent subsections of four who—remarkably for the times—selected their own leader, special stress being laid on the need to develop the individuality of each fighting man. Seven of these subsections formed a section under a subaltern who was entirely responsible for men, horses and equipment, four sections making up a company.[1] The Mounted Infantry moved into Mashonaland through Beira; the force engaged in several actions, the chief being the capture of Makoni's kraal in difficult mountain country, and arrived at Salisbury in August. Known as the 'Mashonaland Field Force', Alderson's Mounted Infantry was augmented by some additional regular troops and local volunteers, so that his command soon totalled about 1,500 Europeans.

The Colonel, however, still had a difficult task before him. The insurgents were well supplied with firearms and adopted skilful defensive tactics, their past military experience acquired in resisting Lobengula's impis standing them in good stead. On being attacked the gangs invariably took refuge in strongly fortified and stockaded kraals, or in caves in

[1] Alderson, E. A. H. *With the Mounted Infantry and the Mashonaland Field Force.* Methuen and co., 1898

broken hill country where they could only be dislodged after patient and difficult operations. Gradually, however, the Europeans made headway. Forts were built to secure their lines of communication; the enemy gangs were kept on the move, whilst the capture of enemy stock and grain caused hunger in rebel villages. In September 1896 a column from Salisbury stormed Simbanoota's kraal, which was strongly fortified, but successfully shelled, rushed and burnt; the defenders retreated into their caves which were blown up. In October 1896 a strong force captured Matshayangombi's kraal in the Hartley district, the spirit mediums' main headquarters. Later the Lomagundi district was pacified and in November Chiquaqua, an important chief thirty miles north-east of Salisbury, agreed to lay down his arms. Alderson had thus opened up all the main lines of communication and completely relieved the capital. But resistance still continued; there was no supreme political authority with whom the British could negotiate; Alderson found himself short of supplies, whilst the Company—which had to pay in full for all the Imperial assistance— objected to the way bills were mounting up. The authorities therefore decided that the work of final pacification should be left to the reorganized police, now known as the British South Africa Police, and by December Alderson's troops were out of the country. Partisan fighting, however, continued. Early in 1897 Kagubi and Mkwati sought refuge near Nyanda's kraal in the Mazoe valley. The spirit mediums apparently tried to revive the ancient Rozwi monarchy, but lacked the resources for such an enterprise. The Police proved better adapted to guerilla warfare than Imperial troops, and as the force increased the less efficient volunteers were gradually withdrawn. Mkwati was finally killed by the Mashona themselves; Kagubi surrendered; Nyanda was captured. Like many others the two were prosecuted for murder and condemned to death, Kagubi going to the gallows with the last consolations of the Roman Catholic Church, whilst Nyanda died screaming and yelling—defiant to the last.[1] Resistance petered out throughout the country. The Company confiscated most of the guns in native possession. The British South Africa Police instituted an efficient system of supervision, based on the sound theory that prevention was better than repression, and entailing extensive patrol work throughout the backveld. The 'war party' in Mashonaland disintegrated, and peace returned once more to a blood-soaked country.

[1] Richartz, F. 'The end of Kagubi and other condemned murderers' (in *Zambesi Mission Record.* v. 1, no. 1, Nov 1898, p. 53–55)

Chapter Five

A new society

I

Law and government

The war was over, but Southern Rhodesia remained in a parlous state. Casualties among the whites amounted to something like one-tenth of the population, a staggeringly high figure for such a young country, whilst Maxims, rifles and dynamite had taken a great toll of African lives.[1] But European self-confidence remained unbroken, and none doubted that colonization must continue. A few lonely critics overseas hysterically denounced the white frontiersmen as riff-raff, while Olive Schreiner, the well-known South African author, wrote a book called *Trooper Peter Halket of Mashonaland* which condemned the Company, made much of alleged white atrocities, and sometimes fell into a strange kind of African mysticism. Schreiner's novel in fact was not based on any first-hand knowledge of the events which she purported to describe, and William Henry Milton, the Chief Secretary in Rhodesia at the time, though himself a strong critic of early Company administration, disgustedly wrote back to his wife that the work was 'the most awful rubbish and quite libellous'.[2]

Milton, however, worried more than he need have done. Britain's belief in her African mission stood unshaken; the Boer War had not as yet tarnished the glamour of Empire, whilst even reforming bodies like the Aborigines' Protection Society only wished to end abuses, asking that Company government should be replaced by Colonial Office rule. The intellectual impact of writers like Schreiner or Labouchère, the prominent Radical and editor of *Truth*, remained small; even the missionaries in Southern Rhodesia mostly sided with Rhodes, for many of their converts, like Bernard Mitzeki, an African evangelist in the service of the Anglican Church, had been slain by the rebels. Popular writing during this period

[1] Hole, who investigated the question, found that of the settlers in the country at the time of the outbreak 372 lost their lives and 129 were wounded, or nearly ten per cent of the population were casualties. There are no reliable estimates of native losses, though the figure of 8,000 has been quoted.

[2] W. H. Milton to his wife: 5 Apr 1897 (in MI 1/1/2, Nat Arch MS)

rather tended to idealize the white settler as the representative of Imperial power and as a pioneer of middle-class virtues in the lonely bush; the public preferred to read the reminiscences of serving British soldiers in Rhodesia rather than the exploits of Trooper Halket, whilst even on the left of the British political spectrum the Fabians tended to favour a tough kind of imperialism, wedded to efficiency and military strength. As to popular opinion regarding Africans, Labouchère himself, the 'Truth-ful Member for Northampton', wrote a few years later that they were 'the laziest race in the world', spent their time boozing and brawling, and having knocked each other about in their cups would make up their feuds and drink again. 'For the rest they were perfectly content to eat their bananas and make their wives do a little hoeing.'[1]

Though the stock of the white colonist in Africa still stood high, the Chartered Company came under strong attack. Colonial Office opinion was never very favourable to the Chartered Company, and now the Company's prestige at Downing Street fell further; the 'Charter' had blotted its copybook by the disastrous Jameson Raid, and by its reputed record in Rhodesia, for most officials believed the Company responsible for provoking the rising by continued misgovernment. Rhodes, however, had a strong bargaining position for he was aware of Chamberlain's complicity in the intrigues against the Transvaal. Downing Street itself had not the slightest wish to brave both Treasury and Parliament by taking over Rhodesia. Caution mingled with parsimony, and the Imperial Government therefore agreed that Company rule should continue, whilst its powers for making mischief must be curbed. Reform entailed three essential brakes which were to be built into the state machinery. The Company ought no longer to control any military or armed police forces of its own and the Imperial Government should have a permanent 'watch-dog' in Rhodesia, an Imperial officer who would directly supervise the administration on the spot; in addition a Legislative Council should come into being where the settlers—whom even English Radicals regarded as victims of Company government—would be able to criticize abuses on their home ground.

The military question was the simplest to solve. In 1896, after the Jameson Raid, the Imperial Government appointed Sir Richard Martin to be Deputy Commissioner for Southern Rhodesia and Commandant-General. Shortly afterwards Sir Frederick Carrington was temporarily put in supreme command during the conduct of hostilities, and in October 1896 a proclamation placed control over the military and police forces in the hands of the High Commissioner for South Africa who also exercised

[1] *The Times*, 1 May 1900

extensive disciplinary powers. The position was further defined by the Southern Rhodesia Order in Council of 1898 which—with some subsequent modifications—formed the Magna Carta of Company government until its end in 1923.

Under the new enactment the Secretary of State appointed a Resident Commissioner in Southern Rhodesia, subordinate to the High Commissioner and paid by the Imperial Government. The Resident Commissioner was to be an *ex-officio* member of both the Executive Council and a newly instituted local legislature, where he might speak though he could not cast a vote. He was to report to the High Commissioner for South Africa on all proposed appointments and ordinances, as well as on any other developments. The High Commissioner had to sanction all administrative appointments, and approve all local ordinances before they could be submitted to the Secretary of State, no military operations being permissible without his 'say so'.

In addition the Colonial Office tried to strengthen its supervisory powers over the Chartered Company's London office. Initially the Company's nerve centre was at Kimberley, where Dr Frederick Rutherfoord Harris opened a local branch in 1889. In 1891 this establishment was transferred to Cape Town where it came under Rhodes's more immediate control. After the Jameson Raid, however, the importance of the Cape Town office greatly diminished, for Rhodes temporarily resigned from the Directorate, and Harris left the Company's service. In 1896, on the appointment of Martin as Deputy Commissioner in Southern Rhodesia, the Administrator advised that the Cape Town office should be abolished, on the grounds that the system of divided control was working badly. His advice was not accepted, but from 1896 the Company's senior officers began to correspond directly with London, and Cape Town became primarily concerned with commercial matters. The most important business was transacted in London, so that the Company's headquarters now became altogether much more 'English' than South African in complexion. The 'Charter' was ordered to communicate its minutes and resolutions relating to the administration to the Colonial Office, and the Secretary of State had the right to amend or cancel them. The Colonial Office was also given access to the Company's records and could remove any director or official who obstructed it, whilst the Company lost its right of making ordinances.

The effect of these changes should not be exaggerated; government by remote control never functioned well, and the vital work of day-to-day administration remained with the Company which carried out its task very efficiently. The Resident Commissioner was alone in Salisbury; he lacked any executive of his own, and much of his attention had to be devoted to military matters, especially later on, when the offices of the Resident Commissioner and Commandant-General were for a time combined in the same person.[1] In 1904 the Company assumed control over the 'civil constabulary' (subsequently absorbed into the British South Africa Police) and five years later the High Commissioner abandoned supervision over the police force as a whole, though his consent was still required before they could go on active service. In 1913, when the Jameson Raid was all but forgotten and Rhodesia no longer made headlines, the Commandant-General's functions passed to an officer appointed and paid by the Company, and divided military control came to an end at last. The High Commissioner could not do much himself, for he was overborne by the vast extent of his responsibilities south of the Limpopo, and hampered by the smallness of his staff.

In the same way Colonial Office access to Company correspondence meant less in reality than on paper, for important communications which the Company wished to keep out of Imperial hands simply found their way into private letters between Directors and the Administrator on the spot. Safeguards by remote control thus never worked well, and much more important than these outside 'watch-dogs' was the local Legislature. The colonists themselves desired representation and founded various associations to make their voice heard. A prominent part in these early politics was taken by the Bulawayo Literary and Debating Society, which comprised the township's best educated people, and in some ways foreshadowed some African associations which, having originally been formed for cultural or philanthropic purposes, later turned to politics. The Debating Society pitched its aim rather high, and in 1897 asked the Colonial Office to set up a Legislative Council where four Official members would be balanced by an equal number of Elected members with the Administrator as Chairman.[2] The rank and file of white colonists, however, were less ambitious. They wanted a chance to air grievances about the existing mining laws; they desired better educational and other services; some questioned the Company's land policy and mineral rights; others objected

---

[1] To avoid a confusion of names, it might be noted that the Resident Commissioner, appointed under the Order in Council of 1898 was solely a 'watch-dog', and not identical with a previous appointment of the same title. Earlier on, in 1891, a High Commissioner's proclamation had provided for the appointment of a Resident Commissioner who was to be the senior executive official in Mashonaland. In 1891 the Administrator of British Bechuanaland was gazetted Resident Commissioner for Mashonaland, but never exercised any actual administrative power. Instead Colquhoun currently assumed the title of Acting Resident Commissioner. Colquhoun, however, resigned shortly afterwards, and Jameson, his successor, took office as Chief Magistrate, Mashonaland, subsequently becoming Administrator.

[2] Bulawayo Literary and Debating Society to Colonial Office: 29 July 1897 (African (South) no. 552, p. 90)

to the quality of their own land titles. But, though some disappointed immigrants went back to England and wrote bitter letters to the newspapers, the 'Charter' was far from unpopular in the country; many colonists admitted that the Company would help them through difficult times or even waive rights to which it was entitled. The Company itself wanted a contented population and was prepared to make concessions, including four seats on the future legislature. The Directors at the same time insisted reasonably enough that the Administration should wield a majority in the Council as long as expenditure did not meet revenue, though admitting that Responsible Government should be considered when the country could meet its obligations from local income.[1]

The Southern Rhodesia Order in Council, 1898, established the first Legislative Council; this followed the normal British colonial pattern of containing both Elected and Official members, though it was unusual in combining representative institutions with Chartered Company Government. The Administrator acted as President and the Company had the right to appoint five additional members with the Secretary of State's approval. The Company always appointed its most able and senior officials to the Council, thereby forging a vital link between Executive and Legislature. In addition to the Officials and the Resident Commissioner, the Council contained four 'Unofficial' members who were elected on a 'colour-blind' franchise, which followed the Cape pattern in that the suffrage was linked to property. The franchise was given to literate British subjects, excluding lunatics or convicts; voters had to reside in the country, occupy premises worth at least £75, own a mining location or receive a wage of not less than £50 a year. The Administration's immediate object in imposing these financial qualifications was not so much to keep black men off the roll; there were as yet only a handful of English-speaking literate Africans with a reasonable cash income in the country, and all of these were 'Colonial' natives, most of them apparently Fingo, who took no interest in politics; the most imaginative Rhodesian could not envisage even loyal chiefs like Gambo or Umtasa taking part in the deliberations of a Western-style council. The Administration was much more anxious to prevent 'poor whites' from voting, especially poverty-stricken Afrikaners from the backwoods, whose rural radicalism and assumed disloyalty to the British cause in South Africa made them suspect to Chartered administrators and mining magnates alike.

The new Council was empowered to make ordinances though all these laws had to be submitted—together with the Resident Commissioner's report—for the High Commissioner's assent. The Secretary of State,

[1] B.S.A. Company to Colonial Office: 16 June 1897 (African (South) no. 552, p. 17–20)

however, might still disallow them. Following the normal British constitutional procedure, only the Administration could introduce a fiscal
measure into the House. Furthermore the Council was specifically forbidden to impose any restrictions or disabilities on Africans without the
Secretary of State's sanction, except where the supply of arms, ammunition
and liquor was concerned.

Despite these restrictions the new Council in some ways still formed a
stronghold of Company power. The Administration could rely on a
built-in majority; it commanded the best brains, and the majority of
ordinances were prepared by the Attorney-General and discussed first of
all in the Executive Council, an official deliberating body, solely composed
of senior civil servants. Little legislation was initiated by the Elected
Members, whilst outside interference was limited. The Crown, exercising
its authority through orders in council, only rarely intervened in the
process of law-making, confining itself to a few major points like
the country's constitutional law, neutrality in wartime, extradition, the
application of British laws in Rhodesia and so forth. The High Commissioner's share in legislation tended to diminish, whilst the Council itself
tackled an ever-widening range of subjects. But as the Council's stock
went up the importance of Elected Members increased; and in 1907 the
'Unofficials' were granted a majority on the Council and ceased to be mere
minority mouthpieces.

In addition the Company now began to reorganize its executive. In the
earliest pioneering days the administrative machine was small, highly
personal in character, unspecialized and mostly amateur. An 'army of
occupation' atmosphere hung over the country; and the records dating
from these days, poorly kept and generally small in numbers, reflect some
of this mood. But soon the influx of a larger white population anxious for
better administrative services, political pressure on the Company from
without, and the needs of a slowly expanding economy, all helped to make
the pioneer administration obsolete. As officials found themselves faced
with a steadily increasing number of tasks the old system no longer
worked. A Mining Commissioner could no longer continue in charge of
the general administration of a district; neither would a judicial scheme
suffice whereby a medical man might hold trials. Instead the Chartered
Company began to institute major reforms, and in William Henry Milton
(later knighted) the Board found just the right man. Milton was an
English parson's son who emigrated to the Cape where he joined the local
civil service and steadily rose to be permanent head of the Department of
the Prime Minister and Native Affairs. He enjoyed the complete confidence
of Rhodes, who had also been born in a parsonage. In 1896 Milton left for

Rhodesia to reorganize the administration, and in the same year was appointed Chief Secretary and Secretary for Native Affairs.

His initial task proved extremely difficult. Large areas of the country remained in a state of open revolt; finance stood out as an ever-present problem, but worse still was the amateurish incompetence which offended all Milton's instincts as a civil servant. 'Everything official here is in an absolutely rotten condition', Milton disgustedly wrote home to his wife; he was having constant trouble with 'titled understrappers', and things would remain in a mess 'until we can clear out the Honourable and military elements which are rampant everywhere, and are evidently expecting a reward with fat billets after the war'.[1] Milton moreover protested at the Board's initial policy of granting away vast areas of land and mining concessions to companies with well-connected directors; this policy looked well enough on paper, being designed to draw funds into an under-capitalized country, but in practice extensive assets were uselessly locked up, and the Administration's task thereby rendered much more difficult. 'Rinderpest and recalcitrant chiefs' remained to plague Milton, whilst he was struggling with incompetent colleagues and unreliable subordinates. Milton nevertheless went ahead and imported experienced men from the Cape who soon gave an entirely different tone to the Administration. In 1898 new regulations set up a regular civil service in the country.[2] These were modelled on those of the Cape, and a large proportion of civil servants were engaged locally or at the Cape, white men being used to fill even the lower ranks of the Administration as telegraphists, policemen and clerks. The Southern Rhodesian service therefore lacked the distinctive British upper middle class background which came to characterize the administrative machine in tropical de-pendencies like Nyasaland, and it became much more closely linked to the European colonists than were the 'birds of passage' employed further north.

The civil service was headed by the Administrator, who remained the king-pin of the Administration, corresponding to a colonial governor, but acquiring much greater continuity of office and closer ties with the country. In 1898 Milton was gazetted Administrator of Mashonaland and Senior Administrator for Southern Rhodesia, remaining in office until 1914. For the time being he had to deal with a separate Administrator in Matabeleland, who, under the stress of war, assumed in 1896 some limited administrative autonomy. In 1901, however, Sir Arthur Lawley, the last incumbent of this office at Bulawayo, resigned, and the entire executive

---

[1] W. H. Milton to his wife: 25 Sep 1896 (in MI 1/1/2, Nat Arch MS)
[2] Civil service regulations, Government notice no. 6 of 1898: 11 Jan 1898

machine was now unified in Milton's hands. Milton himself supervised the work of all departments, especially that of Native Affairs. In addition he presided over the Executive and Legislative councils, whilst at the same time retaining full control over the entire range of business.

Local administration was carried on by two separate hierarchies whose structure in some ways reflected the sharp social division within the country. Magistrates, whose powers were based on those of their colleagues in the Cape, primarily dealt with the Europeans in the country and performed a vast amount of judicial work, whilst also carrying out a wide range of administrative duties. Outside Bulawayo and Salisbury Magistrates normally acted as Civil Commissioners, and in this capacity they were responsible for matters like applications for land, and the bulk of the local revenue passed through their hands.

Side by side with Civil Commissioners and Magistrates there functioned a second hierarchy which dealt solely with African affairs, and soon began to perfect its methods. The Native Department quickly succeeded in attracting numerous recruits of high quality; many of these newcomers came from Natal, where the Administration was able to find white men who could speak Zulu and could therefore easily pick up Sindebele. The Administrator himself, standing at the head of the pyramid, acted as his own Secretary for Native Affairs. Below him came the Chief Native Commissioner who supervised Native Commissioners and Assistant Native Commissioners in the Districts.[1] As the country developed the work of the department steadily increased and Native Commissioners became burdened with many administrative duties of a more general kind. Between 1907 and 1908 the Company therefore began to appoint Superintendents of Natives who were placed in charge of 'divisions', later styled 'circles', the object of reform being to assure a greater degree of decentralization. Native Commissioners performed a multitude of functions, ranging from the collection of tax to the recruitment of labour, though this latter task came to an end when in 1903 the Rhodesia Native Labour Bureau came into existence for the purpose of getting African workers to sign up with white employers.[2]

The Native Commissioner's duties went beyond purely African work, as he often had to double up as Magistrate. His paper work grew, and he

[1] Originally there was a Chief Native Commissioner for Mashonaland at Salisbury and a Chief Native Commissioner for Matabeleland at Bulawayo. In 1913 the office of the Chief Native Commissioner for Matabeleland was abolished, and John Herbert Taylor (later Sir Herbert), previously Chief Native Commissioner for Matabeleland, became the first Chief Native Commissioner for Southern Rhodesia.

[2] For the history of the Bureau see British South Africa Company. *Memorandum by Mr Wilson Fox on constitutional, political and financial and other questions concerning Rhodesia.* Printed for the information of the Board, 1912, ch. 10

became more tied to his office. In 1909 an official Board of Enquiry thus considered that Native Commissioners were being regarded as nothing more than tax collectors, and that the Department was no longer in touch with the people.[1] The investigators added that the Native Department's prestige stood low, because Magistrates exercised all the main judicial functions. A new proclamation, issued in 1910, therefore enabled Native Commissioners to try all cases where Africans only were concerned.[2] They could also deal with criminal cases in which the accused was a black man; Native Commissioners now began to play a major part in the country's judicial system, as Africans dissatisfied with local decisions in their villages, or angry at being accused of witchcraft by their fellow-tribesmen, began to flock to the 'N.C.'s' courts to seek the white man's justice.

At the bottom of the administrative pyramid stood the native chiefs, who were left with only very limited powers by the law. Southern Rhodesia formed a northward extension of the Cape; the Colony also drew much on the experience of Natal, and 'Direct Rule' through European administrative officers seemed the obvious choice. In any case the Company in Southern Rhodesia did not have to deal with any comparatively strong native states such as Barotseland beyond the Zambezi; the Matabele military monarchy was smashed, and the Administration resisted any suggestions that the old Matabele hierarchy should be restored in any shape or form, or even that Njube, Lobengula's heir to the chieftainship, who was educated at Rhodes's expense, should return to Matabeleland. Taylor, the Chief Native Commissioner for Matabeleland, considered that the minor chiefs preferred being directly responsible to Government, that there was no cohesion amongst the Africans, each little community being opposed to the other. A certain amount of jealousy moreover had arisen between the indunas which had been fostered by Taylor, this being 'the most politic form of governing the natives'.[3] In Mashonaland the position was similar; the old Karanga supremacy was gone, and though faint memories of the vanished dominion continued there was no strong, centralized kingdom, which in any way could have assumed a role like that of the Barotse monarchy in North-Western Rhodesia.

Apart from that, Chartered Company theoreticians, for economic and ideological reasons, opposed the idea of building up or strengthening native institutions in any form. Henry Wilson Fox, by now the Company's General Manager, produced a confidential memorandum for his directors

[1] Southern Rhodesia. *Report of a board . . . to enquire into . . . the public service.* 1909
[2] High Commissioner's proclamation no. 55 of 1910: 3 Oct 1910
[3] H. M. Hole to C. J. Rhodes: 25 Mar 1901, and enclosed letter from H. J. Taylor to H. M. Hole of 14 Mar 1901 (in MI 1/1/1, Nat Arch MS)

in which he pointed out that the country's development would depend on black workmen who formed 'the privates of the industrial army in every department of work'. Fox shared the prevailing optimism of the time concerning the speed with which the country could be developed, and felt firmly convinced that prosperity would come much more quickly if only the tribal or communal system could speedily be liquidated. The Africans' main role would be that of wage labourers; their second as producers of foodstuffs, but both functions required more education, and neither object could be attained by segregating Africans in reserves. Fox was impressed by the way African agricultural production and native rural prosperity was increasing,[1] as European settlement in turn provided the Africans with a larger market. But nevertheless Fox believed that the most obvious way of employing African manpower was by using it on European farms and mines. The absorption of the native population into a wage economy was to be assured by a superior system of education, the settlement of Africans on private farms and company estates, the possible increase of native taxation, and the prohibition of timber cutting and burning, which Fox believed to be disastrous to sound husbandry. Fox therefore privately even criticized the Native Commissioners who talked of 'their' natives, and acquired a kind of vested interest in existing African institutions which stood in the way of general development.[2] The Native Commissioners, in Fox's view, were almost bound to become 'a retrograde factor in the corporate life of the country', representatives of 'a sleepy-hollow idea' of bolstering up outworn institutions, and this being the prevailing climate of opinion at headquarters, there was little chance of any 'Indirect Rule' concepts striking root in the country.

The law therefore gave few rights to the chiefs. The Administrator in Council was stated to wield all political power and authority over the natives. The Administrator in Council could remove chiefs subject to the consent of the High Commissioner, or even divide or amalgamate different tribes. The chiefs themselves had no recognized powers of jurisdiction. They were simply regarded as subordinate officials responsible for the good conduct of their tribes, for notifying crimes, deaths and epidemics to the Native Commissioners, for giving help with the collection of taxes and for the apprehension of criminals. District Headmen, appointed by the Secretary for Native Affairs on the recommendation of chiefs, were to assist them in this work. In their capacity as auxiliaries to

---

[1] According to his figures the number of cattle in native hands increased from 63,564 in 1902/3 to 204,000 in 1908; the estimated acreage under cultivation went up from 556,974 to 736,265 and the estimated probable yield of grain in bags of 200 lb from 1,273,027 to 2,175,367

[2] British South Africa Company. *Memorandum by Mr H. Wilson Fox on problems of development and policy*. Printed for the information of the Board, 1910, p. 16–29

L

the Native Administration the chiefs received subsidies, so that by 1911 there were 142 subsidized chiefs in Mashonaland and 129 in Matabeleland.

Militarily this administrative structure was supported by the British South Africa Police, an élite unit attracting many younger sons of upper middle class English families, or the descendants of professional officers who—for one reason or another—did not manage to get into Sandhurst.[1] The corps was therefore able to boast of a relatively high standard of education within its ranks; troopers could reach the highest appointments; turnout and efficiency made it the best force of its kind in Africa.

In the beginning military work received more emphasis than civilian duties; the Police was organized on the basis of two small cavalry regiments, one each in Mashonaland and Matabeleland, supported by an establishment of African auxiliaries, who in 1899 were effectively incorporated into the main body. Gradually the corps became more civilian in character and more specialized services were added.[2] Policemen became responsible for many other duties, including the enforcement of the pass laws, inspection of licences, maintenance of cattle and smallpox cordons, assistance in compiling statistics, prosecutions in magistrates' courts, and so forth. In the African areas they carried on a good deal of unofficial judicial work, acting as informal arbitrators, and thereby acquiring a very intimate knowledge of native life.

For some reason or other, perhaps because they did not wear such colourful dress uniforms, the British South Africa Police never quite acquired the glamour that surrounds the Canadian 'Mounties', but all the same the force ranked very high by all standards of training, military efficiency and even 'spit and polish'. What was even more important, the force—right from the start—appreciated the essential principle that policemen are paid to prevent and not to punish. Some early exceptions apart the British South Africa Police never developed the inefficient system of keeping order by punitive expeditions, the main stress being laid on the constant patrolling of districts whereby peace was effectively maintained without bloodshed. Policemen therefore spent a vast amount of time in the saddle in the open veld—the humble mule being found more serviceable for the purpose than the more picturesque horse, until later on in the century veterinary surgeons managed to cure horse-sickness. Rhodesian policemen acquired a thorough knowledge of the country and its people, and many volunteers from Britain later settled permanently in the country. In fact the recruitment of constables, and also of nurses, on

---

[1] For the background of one of these men see Bruce, *Sir* M. *Tramp royal*. Pan books, 1957

[2] For detailed administrative histories of all departments during the Chartered Company period see Central African Archives. *A guide to the public records of Southern Rhodesia under the regime of the British South Africa Company, 1890–1923.* Cape Town, Longmans, Green and co., 1956, p. 179–236.

short-term contracts in some ways acted like an assisted immigration scheme, providing a welcome addition to the country's scanty population, though entailing a high staff turnover in the services concerned.

II

Maxims, mines and railroads

Southern Rhodesia's government and people became subject to severe strain when in 1899 the South African War broke out. The Boers quickly established a firm grip on the country's vital rail link with the south, and a nervous London Board feared lest commandos from the Transvaal might cross the Limpopo and find support from local Boer sympathizers. Country and Company, however, responded to the challenge, and local Africans gave no trouble. The war remained a white man's conflict; neither party employed black troops, and Rhodesian Africans were not drawn into the bloodshed, though they suffered economically from the increased cost of merchandise and their temporary inability to seek employment in the Transvaal. There was, however, no serious political unrest, as the Africans apparently preferred a British to a Boer victory, and felt convinced that British rule was there to stay.

Practically all the British-born people in the country thoroughly believed in the war—just as, four years earlier, they had cheered the Jameson Raiders—though many Rhodesian fighting men seem to have shared the current misconception that the Boers would all 'run like hares the first time they are tackled'.[1] Reality turned out to be very different. The Afrikaners gave an excellent account of themselves, whilst the Rhodesians, lacking tents and many other items of equipment, suffered terrible hardships, malaria often proving a more deadly foe in unhealthy country than the enemy's shells and bullets. The Rhodesians nevertheless did extremely well; the country contained a very high proportion of young men, trained in the use of arms, familiar with horsemanship and veld-lore, with the result that by 1900 something like 1,700 men had gone to war, out of a total white population of little more than 11,000 people.

The details of the operations form more properly part of South African than of Rhodesian military history, but roughly speaking they can be divided into three main sections. Just before the outbreak of hostilities the British authorities formed the Rhodesia Regiment, one of many mounted

[1] Major W. A. Jarvis of the Rhodesia Regiment to his mother, Lady Jarvis: 27 Sep 1899 from Plumer's camp at the Umzingwani river (in JA 4/1/2, Nat Arch MS)

local units in Southern Africa which played an important part in the fighting. The Regiment was commanded by Plumer, and made its name in the relief of Mafeking, which partially broke the enemy's grip on the vital railway to the south. The British South Africa Police took a distinguished part in the fighting; policemen and local volunteers held the line of the Crocodile river, and disarmed suspected Boer sympathizers in the country, thereby preventing the possible despatch of Boer commandos into Rhodesia itself. Mafeking having been relieved in 1900, the Rhodesia Regiment no longer fought as a separate unit, some went off to the Transvaal; others returned home to be discharged; but the British South Africa Police maintained a contingent in the field until the end of the war and Rhodesians still continued to see action as members of various irregular units, including the Imperial Light Horse, Thorneycroft's Mounted Infantry and Kitchener's Fighting Scouts, who all helped to track down Boer guerillas on the veld. A Rhodesian contingent thus distinguished itself in a bloody engagement at Eland's river, and another at Pienaar's river in the Northern Transvaal, where Lieutenant-Colonel John Anthony Spreckley, one of Rhodesia's most gallant soldiers, fell in action.[1]

In addition to relying on local men, the Chartered Company came to an arrangement with the Imperial Government for the despatch of the so-called Rhodesia Field Force which reinforced the country through the Portuguese port of Beira. The Corps contained soldiers from many different parts of the world, including Imperial Yeomanry and attached sharpshooters, as well as substantial contingents from Australia and New Zealand. The Board took an important part in keeping this force supplied, making an excellent job of the organization tasks involved, the Company's efficiency in some ways comparing very favourably with that of the War Office.[2]

Finally Rhodesia made a minor though welcome contribution to the war through its rudimentary 'armament industry', the railway workshops at Bulawayo, which fitted out several armoured trains; these turned out to be remarkably effective specimens of the artificer's work, and did excellent service in Bechuanaland. A small engineer corps installed and maintained telephonic and telegraphic communications, operated heliographs, repaired damage to railways and bridges, the country turning up some

[1] The exact number of 'Rhodesian' casualties remains difficult to document, since many volunteers from Rhodesia who fought in other units did not figure on their muster rolls as 'Rhodesians'. Norris, F. *The Roll Call* ..., Bulawayo, 1902, p. 21, contains a list of 97 men killed between 1899 and the beginning of 1901, but the final total was higher.

[2] For greater details concerning all these various units see Amery, L. S., ed. *The Times history of the war in South Africa 1899–1902*. Sampson Low, Marston and co., 1900–1909. 7v.

unexpected resources of skill, of vital importance at a time when twentieth-century technology was already influencing the more traditional mounted warfare of the backveld.

The war not only formed a heavy drain on the Rhodesians' own resources, but also had serious effects on the economic stability of the Chartered Company. Expenses rose steeply; the Board had to issue further shares and yet was almost financially crippled through insufficiency of funds to carry out its work. The Directors therefore became all the more inclined to come to some political understanding with the European settlers—if only they could get over their financial difficulties. The settlers for their part stood out for their proven loyalty in the Imperial cause; they received much favourable publicity overseas at a time when warlike enthusiasm in England was reaching dizzy heights of near-madness, though fire-eaters in the Rhodesia Regiment like Major Weston Alexander Jarvis growled that the Londoners' war hysteria was really 'quite infra dig', and only calculated to give the Boers, 'these rotten skunks who are no good except behind a stone,' an undue sense of their own importance.[1] But this was a period when Imperial pride was bursting its bounds, when booklets like *Thrilling Experiences of the First British Woman relieved by Lord Roberts* caused patriotic heartbeats rather than tired smirks, and white Rhodesians benefited from a metropolitan climate of opinion which idealized British settlers in Africa as representative of all that was best in the nation. War placed a heavy strain on the country's economy, which suffered—like that of the whole of South Africa. But Southern Rhodesia also enjoyed a number of advantages. The territory, unlike the neighbouring Transvaal, did not suffer any devastation. In addition Rhodesians found themselves fortunate in that the Chartered Company supplied them with an adequate rail system which was largely completed south of the Zambezi just after the end of the century.

The country's development hinged on transport, and a flashback to the early 'nineties will make the story clearer. The construction of a northward railway and cable link to the Zambezi formed one of the original conditions of the Charter and Rhodes quickly got to work, a railway being built from Kimberley to Vryburg which was then taken over by the Cape Government. In 1893 the Chartered Company resolved on a further extension to Mafeking, and four years later the line at last reached Bulawayo, the building of the last 400 miles standing out as a record in railway history in quick construction and cheapness.

Rhodes usually had a knack for picking the right man for the job, and George Pauling, the contractor, displayed all the qualities needed to

[1] Jarvis to Lady Jarvis: 9 May 1900, from Kania (in JA 4/1/2, Nat Arch MS)

undertake a pioneering task of that nature. His father originally served as an engineer on the Indian Railways and intended that his son should join the Indian Civil Service. Pauling senior, however, suffered a dangerous sunstroke and the youngster's scholastic career came to a premature end. The fourteen-year-old boy was lucky to get employment in a drawing office in England, but later made a brilliant career for himself in Africa where he became responsible for building most of Southern Rhodesia's railways and served on the Council as Commissioner of Public Works and Mines; for a time he also looked after postal communications. Pauling was a man of tremendous physical strength—he once carried a 450 lb pony round a billiard table for a bet—and proved just the right sort of person for a tough frontier community like early Rhodesia.

Pauling's success in completing the line to Bulawayo made a tremendous difference to Matabeleland, still stricken by the rinderpest and deprived of most of its animal transport. But more money still had to be found for continuing the line to Salisbury. Gold-bearing reefs had been discovered, and the success of the Rand drove the gold fever to boiling point so that for a time Chartered shares commanded over three and a half times their nominal value. Gold and Empire formed the only lure which Rhodes could use to capture the imagination of investors. Having a way with his shareholders and skilfully bandying about the magic phrase 'the Cape to Cairo Railway', he succeeded in raising money in London, and after lengthy delays occasioned by the Boer War, Salisbury was eventually linked to the south in 1902.

In addition Rhodes sought to connect his new colony to the Indian Ocean, a more difficult undertaking, for the East Coast route passed through rough and fever-laden country which had already tested the endurance of Portuguese pioneers several centuries before. The Anglo-Portuguese Treaty of 1891 stipulated the building of a line from Beira to the eastern portion of Southern Rhodesia, and originally the railway builders hoped to use the Pungwe river as far as Fontesvilla as a means of access, but Fontesvilla proved quite unsuitable as a proper point of departure, the continually shifting sandbanks making navigation a hazardous matter. The floods in the area turned out to be disastrous, the men were plagued by mosquitoes and disease, and the planners realized that they would have to construct an extension from Fontesvilla to the coast at Beira, thereby turning this trading post into the terminus. Beira, a tiny, fever-ridden settlement was accordingly developed by British and foreign funds, becoming an integral part of the Rhodesian railway system and a vital point of access.

The new line met with considerable engineering difficulties and for economy's sake at first ran on a narrow gauge. The construction job proved so complex that the Chartered Company decided to move the frontier settlement of Umtali from an earlier to its present site on the route to the coast, finding it cheaper to make the town come to the railway than the railway to the town. In 1898 the first train steamed into Umtali from Beira, and a year later Salisbury was at last linked with the east coast— after a long and weary building job that took a heavy toll of life from malaria and blackwater fever.

The completion of the system owed a great deal to Rochfort Maguire, Rhodes's early companion, who dominated Rhodesian railway politics until his death in 1925. Maguire, a somewhat uncompromising and inflexible man, carried on a long and bitter struggle against Libert Oury, a financial magnate of Belgian origin, who acquired a leading interest in the Mozambique Company and the Beira railway, as well as in the port. Oury, a far-sighted and imaginative planner, tried, just before the First World War, to secure the right to construct a line from Sinoia to Kafue, hoping to shorten the trip from Beira to Broken Hill and Katanga, thereby increasing Beira's traffic and providing the 'Far North' with easy access to the Indian Ocean. Maguire, however, refused, fearing that the project might endanger existing lines, and in the end Oury gave in, the Chartered Company retaining a firm grip on the Rhodesian railway system.[1]

The construction of the main lines was followed by the building of a number of branch lines, and in this, as well as other sides of Rhodesian transport development, an important part was played by Alfred Beit, one of the most fascinating characters in Rhodesian history. Beit was born in Hamburg in 1853, the son of a Jewish businessman converted to Lutheranism.[2] The Beits were a well-connected family, belonging to that strongly Germanized section of the Jewish upper middle class which used to play such an important part in the economic life of Central Europe, the German equivalent in some ways of old-fashioned English nonconformists with their dour belief in hard work and saving, and their distrust of interference by the state. They were usually Anglophile, ready to look towards the West and ever-ready to try their luck abroad, as did Alfred Beit himself. Beit acquired a leading position in the South African gold and diamond business, and became Rhodes's most important financial ally.

[1] For the financial details see D'Erlanger, *Baron* Emile B. *The history of the construction and finance of the Rhodesian transport system.* Privately printed, 1939. D'Erlanger was himself intimately connected with the financing of the railway.

[2] See Beit, *Sir* A., and Lockhart, J. G. *The will and the way: being an account of Alfred Beit and the trust which he founded.* Longmans, Green and co., 1957, and also the author's own review article 'Rhodes's practical ally' in *Central African Examiner,* 22 Nov 1958

Up to this point his career might be looked upon as almost a textbook illustration of subsequent Socialist theories which explained how smaller enterprises were merged into great financial corporations. But then the parallel disappears. Free competition—according to men like J. A. Hobson and Lenin—would result in the creation of great financial trusts that would dominate their respective state machineries and lead their countries into wars for the division of the world, a theory supposedly borne out by the great Anglo-German conflict that broke out in 1914. Beit—who assuredly knew his own financial interest—remained however a convinced advocate of Anglo-German understanding. So for that matter did Rhodes—who in 1893 even went as far as to formulate a visionary project for an Anglo-German condominium in East and Central Africa, but it never came to anything.[1]

But more important still Beit's career foreshadowed the later development of 'welfare capitalism', which limited the free accumulation of capital by steep taxation and death duties, and which supplemented the investment of ordinary risk capital by extensive public investment, not designed to achieve immediate profits. There was indeed something prophetic in the way in which Beit disposed of his fortune. A large portion of his wealth, amounting originally to some £1,200,000, was bequeathed for public purposes through the creation of the Beit Trust. It was almost as if Beit had paid some huge voluntary death duty. But what was even more remarkable about the Trust was the way in which its funds were to be used. Other charitable trusts there had been before, but Beit was the only man who set up such a body for the specific purpose of assisting an underdeveloped country of the Empire, Beit's money being used to develop Rhodesia in a way that foreshadowed public assistance schemes for backward countries in later days. Firstly the Trust financed Rhodesian railway projects for feeder lines which could not hope to be paying propositions for a long time, but played a valuable part in development. Later the Trust turned to bridge building, and in addition a good deal of money was spent on education.

Looked upon in general economic terms Southern Rhodesia acquired its railways in a remarkably short time. The system formed in every sense a 'miner's railway', being built mainly with a view to serving the interests of the mining industry. The trains mostly traversed the highveld, and this later turned out to be an unexpected boon to white farmers, who now

---

[1] See Consul von Nordenflycht to Reichs Chancellor von Caprivi: 18 Mar 1893, printed in Holzhausen, R. 'Deutschland und die Gebiete nördlich des Limpopo . . .' (in *Afrikanischer Heimatskalender*, Windhoek, 1955, p. 58–70). As far as Anglo-German relations in general were concerned it is worth mentioning the fact that in 1914 no institution feared war more than the London Stock Exchange.

found the coolest and healthiest portion of the country served with transport. The railways of course represented a tremendous outlay; an enormous country, right in the middle of Africa, but inhabited only by a small population, had to be served with a vast system which had to be paid for. The builders therefore tried to avoid heavy engineering works, and where possible the line went along the watershed; earthworks were light, stations remained spaced at great intervals. But to make up for some of these disadvantages, Rhodesia managed to obtain her railway communications 'on the cheap', the Chartered Company and its associated interests with their unified financial control generally managing to raise capital at very favourable rates, so that Rhodesia spent much less per mile than South Africa or most other British countries in Africa.[1]

The Company at first put its economic hopes in mining, but development was slow. The Company expected that Rhodesia would prove to be a 'Second Rand' and framed its first mining laws so as to encourage prospectors, whilst reserving a large share of the expected profits to recoup itself for administrative expenditure. The Board at the same time granted extensive concessions to land and mining companies, hoping thereby to attract much-needed capital into the country, but things did not turn out quite as expected, and Rhodesia in the early days became a speculators' paradise.

Many gold-seekers made their way north of the Limpopo, hard-bitten men with few wants who would 'fossick' around the veld for weeks on end; they were accompanied by half a dozen or more African servants who carried a shotgun or rifle, a plentiful supply of ammunition, a pestle, mortar and pan, a hammer, a few picks and shovels and some provisions. They would live in the open air, shoot game for the pot, and look for ancient workings. When these 'blanket prospectors', who used to give blankets to Africans in exchange for information about old mines, found an indication of gold, they disposed of their claims to mining concerns, which exploited the new find either through contractors or their own staff. But little gold was produced. The initial transport costs were high and management usually inefficient. Much money was wasted by unskilled

---

[1] See *Southern Rhodesia: report by Brigadier General F. D. Hammond, C.B.E., D.S.O., on the railway system of Rhodesia.* Salisbury, Government Printer, 1925 (CSR 2–1926). Hammond calculated that the comparative cost per mile for different systems stood as follows:

System	Capital Expenditure £	Cost per mile £
Rhodesia	16,977,304	6,896
South Africa	114,769,666	10,327
Uganda	9,636,358	11,350
Gold Coast	6,469,742	16,279

contractors working with inadequate supervision, or in London where all too many promoters were only interested in buying worthless claims, dazzling their shareholders with wonderful tales of Rhodesian riches, whilst recouping their expenses by complicated, and sometimes dishonest, financial manipulations. The mining companies moreover had to surrender a considerable proportion of their vendor's scrip to the Chartered Company; they had to provide for the parent concern, for underwriters and promoters, so that initial flotations led to enormous over-capitalization, inadequate funds being left over for the actual working of the properties.

After the Boer War, however, conditions began to improve. The country now possessed an adequate transport system, more immigrants came in from the south to escape hard times in a war-stricken country, and in addition the Company introduced various legislative reforms, insisting that claims should be worked more efficiently than hitherto, and reducing its own share in vendor's scrip.[1] The reckless buying of mining claims from prospectors came to an end. The sounder companies reduced their overheads, and at a time when 'Southern Rhodesian stock stank in the noses of investors', the country at last managed to put its house in order. At the same time the Chartered Board began to court the 'Small-worker', the Territory's geological structure with its small and scattered deposits being much more favourable to men operating with little capital than the Rand. In 1904 the Administration allowed individual claim holders to work their properties without floating a company, payment being made on a system of graded royalties which minor entrepreneurs could afford more easily.[2]

The gold industry now began to pick up rapidly. Prospectors, knowing that they would reap greater benefit from fresh discoveries, set about their work—not with the idea of palming off some doubtful claim to a mining company, but with the genuine intention of finding and proving a gold

[1] The principal mining laws of this period were the Mashonaland mining regulations, 1890, which adopted the principle of 'one man—one licence', and introduced the principle of the American 'apex law', under which a miner might follow his reef in depth outside his surface claim. All reef claims had to be pegged on joint account with the Company on the basis of undivided half shares. The Mines and minerals ordinance, 1895, made continuous working of mine properties a condition of tenure, and conferred upon prospectors and miners various privileges in regard to access to wood and water, the law favouring the miner against the landowner. It also laid down the manner in which the Company's interest in mining properties might be commuted, generally on the basis of a share interest in flotation. The Mines and minerals amendment ordinance, 1898, forbade the sale of prospecting licences, but greatly relaxed the law relating to the compulsory working of claims. In theory the Company was entitled to a 50 per cent interest on flotation, but in practice this was always reduced, the Company agreeing, by the Mines and minerals amendment ordinance, 1903, to scale down its interest to 30 per cent, and at the same time granting various concessions to smallworkers.

[2] See the Mines and minerals amendment ordinance, 1903, and Government notice 212/1904: 18 Aug 1904

reef. Smallworkers set up in business on their own or pooled their resources to form syndicates with just enough capital to buy machinery. Mining of course still remained a chancy affair, and the names of many lesser mines read like *noms de plume* on today's Rhodesian lottery tickets: 'Cross Your Luck', 'Clean Up', and 'Broke'. The small entrepreneurs usually started off with inadequate funds and could rarely afford to employ more than one or two white men and perhaps sixty to eighty Africans. The men lived in mud huts thatched with grass, feeding in a common mess and dreaming of nothing but the work in hand.

'The partner who looks after the mine is his own miner, timberman, mine engineer, and blacksmith. On him the mill depends for a constant supply of ten tons of rock each day, which often has to be obtained when he has a shortage of natives. He also has to walk two miles into the bush to see that the gang of native woodcutters are not shirking their duty of supplying firewood for the boiler and cutting suitable timbers for the mine. He has a few head Kaffirs who help him in the skilled work, and superintend the other Kaffir labourers. He starts his work at six in the morning, and is busily engaged until six in the evening, except for a hurried breakfast and lunch. Then he has two hours for dinner and a pipe, and at eight o'clock at night he calls out the "night shift" (the natives who work the mine at night). He spends two hours in the mine, and leaves the head Kaffir to superintend the work for the rest of the night. The other partner takes a night or day shift from six to six at the mill, changing each week with their one white employé. When the partner who has charge of the mill has finished his twelve hours there, he has still all the secretarial work of the partnership to get through, and the mine books to make up, which keep him busy for another two hours. Such then is the typical life on a mine which has been started with insufficient capital, Sundays and weekdays continuing in unvarying monotony of strenuous work, month after month.'[1]

The white miner, himself a labour migrant as much as his black workmen, thus stood out as an individualist to the marrow, the sort of man who would try his hand at many jobs with the hope of ultimately becoming a capitalist on his own account. For the black worker—an inefficient commuter between kraal and compound—he usually felt nothing but undiluted contempt, borne of the daily worry and annoyance of toiling with unskilled men whose ways were strange and whose incompetence proved a constant irritant. Disease moreover was rife on the veld; mortality was high, amenities were few and conditions accordingly remained bitterly harsh for white and black alike.

[1] Hone, P. F. *Southern Rhodesia*. George Bell and son, 1909, p. 272

But with all his limitations the smallworker performed a major economic function. European miners could work at a greater depth than the ancients whose excavations seldom exceeded a hundred feet. The whites had pumps to deal with the seepage of water, and they could work ores too refractory for treatment by the primitive metallurgy known to the Bantu. European miners also had explosives and did not have to rely on the ancients' laborious method of heating the rock with open fires built against the face of the veins, and then pouring water over the heated rocks so as to make them crack. Smallworkers at the same time were still able to make a profit on deposits too small or too poor to interest the larger companies and thus dug up considerable quantities of gold which would otherwise have remained hidden below the veld. In some cases they also opened deposits big enough to attract larger concerns able to work on a more extensive scale. Nevertheless they always occupied a somewhat precarious position. Minor entrepreneurs could not easily cope with the problem of rising costs. Once the mine shafts reached a greater depth, more money had to be spent on equipment, pumping and other safety precautions, with the result that work could not continue unless more capital was found. A number of more important capitalists thus began to invest in the country and from about 1909 almost every important financial group on the Witwatersrand owned some sort of stake north of the Limpopo. The Globe and Phoenix mine, which first began work in 1900, already stood out as a successful example of enterprise on a larger scale; it was later followed by other concerns which took over properties like Shamva, Lonely, and Cam and Motor, from smallworkers for development on a bigger scale. By 1914 the Secretary for Mines reported that about 55 per cent of the country's gold production was controlled by fifteen producers, but at the same time the country's total output had leapt up in a way that surprised even the optimists, and mining completely dominated the country's economy.[1]

In addition to precious metals, mining men also began to interest themselves in the country's base mineral resources. The most important of these was coal of which the Territory possessed enormous wealth. The story started in 1893 when two chiefs of the Abananzwa tribe near Wankie came to Tati to establish friendly relations with the white miners there, hoping thereby to secure some protection against the Matabele. The *indunas* mentioned that there was 'combustible stone' in their country, and Albert Giese, a German-born prospector, went to look for what he assumed to be coal. The Matabele War for a time put a stop to his work, but in 1894 Giese came back and located Southern Rhodesia's first coal

---

[1] In 1900 Southern Rhodesia produced 54,981 oz of gold, in 1914 the output was 854,480 oz.

claim. A year later the German pegged a concession of four hundred square miles for the Mashonaland Agency,[1] an influential concern which counted amongst its directors men like Rudd and Edmund Davis, the latter being a mining man of Australian-Jewish descent and one of the ablest financiers to operate in the country.

The discovery of this vast deposit played an important part in getting Rhodes to redirect his proposed Cape–Cairo railway from the suggested route of Salisbury to Lake Tanganyika; instead the line now went via Wankie and the Victoria Falls, and completely changed the balance of economic power. Investors realized that there was ample fuel in the country to supply the mines and railways, and after several financial reorganizations Wankie Colliery Ltd came into being. The new concern was headed by Davis, now a financial power in the land, and was linked both to the Chartered Company and the Rhodesia Railways. Economic production of coal began in 1904, when the railway reached Wankie from the south, and thereafter quickly expanded, even though the new enterprise could hardly even 'scratch' the country's astronomical riches of 'combustible stone'. Prospectors also discovered a number of additional base metal deposits. These included copper, first turned out in 1906 at West Nicholson, whilst the Falcon Mine at Umvuma started production in 1914. Before the Great War a little chrome, tungsten, lead and asbestos also began to reach the market, so that Southern Rhodesia in a minor way began to enter the ranks of the world's base mineral producers.

III

The white farmer's frontier

Mining began as the Chartered Company's favoured child—farming was its neglected Cinderella. Rhodes's first object in developing the country was to attract capital to build up the fabled 'Second Rand', which would in turn generate new funds to finance further development, so that the farmer took a back seat in his planning. In any case the pioneers had to contend with enormous difficulties; communications were precarious, purchasers for agricultural produce few; newcomers faced the constant threat from plant pests and from disease which struck down men and beasts alike, whilst little was known about the country's resources. Farming thus started as a scratch affair, its main attraction being the low price of land. Southern Rhodesia had an area nearly twice that of Great

[1] Notice by Giese: 20 May 1895 (in GI 1/1/1, Nat Arch MS)

Britain; its native population numbered less than 1,000,000 and could therefore only effectively occupy a small portion of the available land.[1] The Administration thus believed that the country could absorb countless newcomers, and accordingly made grants to all and sundry, often without any regard for indigenous tenure.

Each member of the Pioneer Column for instance became entitled to a farm of 1,500 morgen (about 3,000 acres), to be held on 'military tenure' as soon as the Company found itself in a position to make such grants, whilst the beneficiaries of the Victoria Agreement each received a farm of 3,000 morgen, no occupation being required though the Company charged an annual quitrent of 10/-. In addition the Administration made various other kinds of grants to individuals, their common feature being low quitrents and large acreages. The Chartered Company's Board also ceded extensive areas to land and mining companies, whose directors were usually well connected with the Board,[2] Rhodes hoping thereby to attract investors to his country,[3] with the result that much of the best and most favourably situated land went to speculators mainly interested in the hope of making money from an anticipated rise in land values.

The newcomers accordingly did not put in much work; land changed hands rapidly and most immigrants at first preferred to seek a fabulous but elusive fortune by prospecting for gold. Some pioneers, however, accepted the hardships of farming, and built rude homesteads made of poles and mud, the roofs being thatched with dried gass. The better-provided broke the virgin soil with single-furrow ploughs, drawn by oxen; others followed the primitive Bantu method of using kaffir hoes, the settlers being helped by African labourers and drivers. In order to cultivate the most fertile soil, the pioneers had to do heavy stumping and clearing of indigenous trees. Maize was mostly planted by hand, the seed consisting of the multi-coloured kernels universally produced by Africans at that time. Some preferred to make a scanty living by cutting down timber and selling the logs as firewood, by using their oxen and wagons for transport riding or 'kaffir trading', whilst others eked out a livelihood

---

[1] Official sources estimate the native population in Southern Rhodesia at 500,000 in 1901. This estimate is almost certainly too low. The real population more likely stood at 750,000 or more. The total acreage of Southern Rhodesia amounts to 96,213,120; that of Great Britain is 56,200,000.

[2] In 1898 the largest individual grantee was Willoughby's Consolidated Company Ltd which counted amongst its directors A. Weston Jarvis, a soldier and director of numerous other companies, Major S. Wynne Finch, director of ten other companies, H. Wilson Fox, then General Manager of the British South Africa Company, J. J. Hamilton, director of four other gold mining companies, H. Partridge, director of ten other companies, Sir John Willoughby, one of Rhodes's most trusted agents in the Portuguese dispute and director of seven other companies, and Lieutenant-Colonel H. H. Heyman, formerly a soldier and administrative official in the Company's employment.

[3] By 1912 a total of 7,884,160 acres had been granted to 23 companies with a total working capital of £7,522,000

by market gardening. Very few of these early pioneers were in any way specialists; they included people from all walks of life, soldiers and policemen, civil servants with a taste for an outdoor existence, cattle traders who decided to raise their own beasts; but all had one thing in common; they were inveterate individualists and always willing to try something new.

In addition to these English-speaking farmers, Southern Rhodesia also attracted Afrikaans-speaking pioneers, many of whom made their way to the 'Far North' as members of organized treks, and played an important part in 'proving' the country's agricultural possibilities, and in bringing white families to the interior. Two of the most outstanding of these trekkers were George Dunbar Moodie and Thomas Moodie whose ancestors had originally come to the Cape from the Orkney Islands. Dunbar Moodie served in the Zulu War of 1879 and in Bechuanaland. In 1890 he was appointed to manage the property of the Sabi-Ophir Gold Mining Company in Mashonaland and subsequently he assisted Jameson on a concession trip to Gungunyana. This journey convinced him that the Eastern Districts would make splendid farming country, and Moodie sought an interview with Rhodes, who supported him, even though he could not provide direct financial help. From the Chartered Company's point of view there was much to be said for a farming community in Gazaland which would act as a buffer between Britons and Portuguese, as well as confirming the country's capacity for permanent agricultural settlement. Rhodes therefore sanctioned a scheme whereby a hundred families would emigrate from the Orange Free State, each head of family being entitled to a farm of 3,000 morgen at an annual quitrent of only £6; the allotment being made from vacant land near Umzila's kraal.[1] Dunbar got in touch with a cousin, Thomas Moodie, then farming in the Orange Free State, who listened to the scheme with keen interest. Thomas's sons were outgrowing their 'teens and each would soon require a farm; his own ventures had been doing badly, and he had lost heavily on angora goats and ostriches. Dunbar's kinsman, a splendid leader in every respect, volunteered to come, and so did many other Free State farmers who had also been hit by the agricultural depression. In 1892 the Moodie trek left Bethlehem in the Orange Free State, with 37 men, 31 women and children, and 16 wagons. The party encountered great hardships and there were quarrels, with the result that some broke away to seek their luck elsewhere. With incredible difficulties the Moodies and their followers, however, plodded on and with only 20 people and 7 wagons made their way to the high plateau near Chipinga, verdant, magnificent up-country where clear

[1] B.S.A. Company to Moodie: 30 Mar 1892 (in L 2/2/21, Nat Arch SR)

streams run down the slopes and the morning mists play strange tricks against the mountains. They named their settlement Melsetter, after the family's original home, and in time tamed the wild land.[1]

Despite their enterprise, the early settlers had a grim time; life became a harsh struggle for survival; hunger and disease hung heavily over the settlement, whilst markets and communications hardly existed. Thomas Moodie, *Groot Tom*, a splendid character endowed with almost legendary physical strength, died in 1894, and Dunbar seems to have abused his position as the Company's official representative and was accused of feathering his own nest at the expense of others.[2] The promised Eden became a vale of suffering, and many of the original trekkers left. Nevertheless the Moodies broke new ground, and several additional treks followed in their footsteps from the Free State. These pioneering parties included ventures like the Kruger-Bekker trek, run by a former transport rider who found that competition was getting too tough for him, and preferred to seek a new home in Gazaland. More important was an enterprise headed by Marthinus Jacobus Martin, a former member of the Free State Legislature and an excellent organizer, who led his wagons into the Chimanimani country.[3] Another was the Van der Byl trek which led to the creation of a small settlement at Lawrencedale. Rhodes favoured such ventures as part of his policy of uniting Boers and Britons from the Cape in the common task of colonizing the Far North. The 'Charter' subsidized Lawrencedale, and by 1892 had paid out £2,184, more than the original amount agreed upon. But like most early pioneers, the trekkers at first fared badly. Van der Byl died, and the settlement fell into something like chaos. By 1892 three out of the original twenty-five settlers from the Cape were dead; fifteen, including some office clerks and others ill-suited to farming, dispersed to other parts of the Colony, or went back to the Cape. Only seven remained, but these, after the painful process of weeding out, settled down, and found their feet as frontier farmers.[4]

Afrikaners—born 'soil-prospectors', with a knack for picking out good land in the bush, and making a living from a tiny margin of profit—also settled in other parts of the country, including the Enkeldoorn district,

[1] Diaries of George Dunbar Moodie for 1892, 1893, and 1894 (MO 11/2/3–5, Nat Arch MS). A detailed history of the Moodies is to be found in Burrows, E. H. *The Moodies of Melsetter*. Cape Town, Balkema, 1954. It should be noted that the modern Melsetter in Southern Rhodesia lies northeast from the original settlements.

[2] W. M. Longden, Magistrate at Melsetter, to the Administrator: 12 Apr 1896 (in L 2/2/95/22, Nat Arch SR)

[3] For a list of these early trekkers see appendixes in Olivier, C. P. *Many treks made Rhodesia.* Cape Town, H. B. Timmins, 1957

[4] Memo by H. M. Hole, Acting Secretary to the Chief Magistrate: 14 Oct 1892 (in CT 1/23/1 Nat Arch SR)

where in 1897 the Reverend A. J. Liebenberg selected a site for the present township. A trickle of Boer immigrants continued, even though the authorities took a less friendly view of Afrikaners after the Jameson Raid and the Boer War. 'Dutch' nationalism seemed a political danger; the early frontiersman's skills became less essential; many British-born Rhodesians feared that Boer immigrants would demand legal equality for their tongue. Expert observers nevertheless regarded the Afrikaners as good pioneers, however unprogressive in their methods, and in addition appreciated the fact that they came to settle for good, bringing their wives and families along to live in the new country.[1]

But no matter where a farmer came from, or what language he spoke, he had a desperately hard time in the early days. Rinderpest and native risings between them almost brought agriculture to a standstill, and as soon as pastoralists had re-stocked their herds, the dreaded African East Coast Fever made its appearance. The Chartered Company did all it could by calling in Robert Koch, a famous German bacteriologist, and also by providing assistance through Farming and Transport Aid Boards.[2] These bodies distributed donkeys to the needy, so that people later used to say that 'the jackass saved Rhodesia'. Farming nevertheless remained a gamble in a country where markets were so small, and where settlers could get so little accurate knowledge of the country's soil.

These difficulties all showed up very clearly when, in 1906, a wealthy Italian officer, Lieutenant Margherito Guidotti, tried to launch an early 'group settlement' in the Lomagundi District. About £7,000 was made available, a considerable sum for those days, and ten Italian settlers were brought out, all hard-working and intelligent men with some education. The newcomers did everything the text-books said they should have done; they worked hard; they farmed intensively by Rhodesian standards of the time; they had money to spend, and they settled sufficiently closely to each other to provide mutual help. Nevertheless Guidotti's project turned out to be a complete failure—a kind of 'Groundnut scheme' in miniature! There were personal quarrels and financial complications; there was also the perennial difficulty of the farms being situated too far from a market. Worse still was the fact that the land—even though bought at no more than 6/– a morgen—was still overvalued at that price, its real value

---

[1] Memorandum for the Board by Sir Lewis Michell, Director of the B.S.A. Company; 25 Aug 1909 (in A 1/5/9, Nat Arch SR). Michell pointed out that of recent arrivals 444 English-speaking immigrants had brought out 334 children to Southern Rhodesia, whereas 71 Dutchmen had brought 216. Afrikaner families contained girls of marriageable age at a time when the percentage of women to men was small, so that early statistics show a considerable number of marriages between Afrikaans-speaking girls and British or foreign-European men.

[2] Government notice no. 178 of 1902: 24 July 1902

M

never exceeding the paltry sum of 4/–. Official investigators later found
that the soil was chemically unsuitable. The Italian manager had apparently not understood these difficulties when selecting the land, and the
Chartered Company was not yet in a position to point out the deficiencies
of the soil. One farm was even short of water and would only have paid
its way as a cattle ranch, which in turn would have involved further
extensive investment of capital.[1] Boers or British frontier farmers from
the south, with their apparently inefficient methods, would not have made
these mistakes. But even they took plenty of risks, and the vagaries of the
season, frequent locust invasions, cattle disease, or blackwater fever
might easily cause them to lose their money or their lives.

After much trial and error the industry nevertheless found its feet, and
the first decade of the present century witnessed the beginnings of an
agricultural revolution. The growing mine compounds provided a small
but expanding market; goods trains carried the produce more cheaply;
African Coast Fever compelled farmers to turn from ranching to cultivation. In addition the Chartered Board, disappointed in its hopes of
making a quick fortune from gold, began to pay more attention to the
country's agricultural potential. The Company for one thing derived some
immediate economic gain from land sales in the shape of quitrents, lease
rents and other kinds of income; but more important still was the indirect
revenue which accrued from increased rail traffic, the administrative
revenue from customs, and the general benefits derived from a cheap and
regular supply of food for the mining industry in which 'St. Swithin's
Lane' held a major stake. The Directorate was much more familiar with
economic problems than the Imperial civil servants working in remote
London offices at a time when Downing Street officials never thought of
visiting the colonies; Directors kept in touch with Rhodesia by occasional
tours, and generally displayed far more enterprise and initiative in economic matters than most other South African governments or indeed the
Colonial Office itself, the Directors' alertness comparing very favourably
in this respect with the lethargic *laissez faire* creed that generally characterized early Imperial administration in Africa.[2]

A shift in Company policy began in 1907 when several prominent
Directors visited Rhodesia to discuss a broad range of political and
economic problems with settler representatives. The deputation, impressed by the colonists' case, agreed to make a considerable number of

[1] Files LB 2/1/8/4 and L 2/2/95/15–17 (Nat Arch SR). The farms involved were Oldlands, Kings-
wood and Pucklehill, each covering about 3,400 acres.
[2] For an interesting assessment of Company enterprise in Rhodesia see Thomas, O. *Agricultural
and pastoral prospects of South Africa*. A Constable, 1904, p. 302–6

concessions; the Company in future would issue simpler forms of land titles; it would ameliorate the position of farmers *vis à vis* the miners with regard to questions like timber and water rights. In addition commercial and economic matters were separated from the ordinary administration, and in 1908 an independent Estates Office opened its doors to deal with land applications and more actively to promote white settlement.[1] At the same time the Company agreed to reduce the minimum price of land to no more than 1/6 per morgen, privately arguing that land should be sold cheaply for the time being so as to encourage the growth of a white population, whilst the shareholders would ultimately benefit by the rise in real estate values which would later accrue from this policy.

The Company also introduced extensive reforms in its local Agricultural Department, and a promising start was made in 1908 when Dr Eric A. Nobbs, a trained scientist from the Cape, became Director of Agriculture, with a small staff of specialists and veterinary surgeons. Nobbs made numerous important changes, with the result that technical work greatly expanded. Insects and plant diseases were studied more scientifically; skilled investigators carried out research into local soils and products, and related subjects. The Department distributed various kinds of improved seeds and plants; it advised on the cultivation of tobacco; it carried out experiments in collaboration with individual growers; it opened an experimental station at Salisbury and a demonstration farm at Gwebi (now the Gwebi Agricultural College). The information was widely disseminated amongst the farming community through the *Rhodesian Agricultural Journal*, first issued in 1903, which made a promising start in the country's technical information service. The administration as a whole began to take steps to safeguard farmers by various legislative enactments, including laws to guard against the importation of plant and animal diseases, regulations for the proper grading of maize for export, and so on.

The new policy began to bear fruit in the years just before the Great War. More immigrants settled on the land, the great majority of them from south of the Limpopo, where the Chartered Company concentrated its settlement campaign, colonists from South Africa usually finding less difficulty in adjusting themselves to Rhodesian conditions than those from overseas.[2] Farming at the same time became somewhat more highly

---

[1] Government notice no. 22 of 1908: 23 Jan 1908. See also *Reports on the conferences between the Chartered Co. directors and the representatives of public bodies . . . October of 1907*. Bulawayo, Argus printing and publishing co., 1907

[2] See Rolin, H. *Les lois et l'administration de la Rhodésie*. Brussels, E. Bruylant, and Paris, A. Challamel, 1913, p. 396–7. Rolin, a Belgian jurist, who investigated conditions on the spot, estimated that some 95 per cent of Southern Rhodesian farmers came from South Africa, of whom

capitalized, as methods improved, and the Company insisted that applicants for land must possess a minimum of cash, varying between £500 and
£1,000, though some newcomers from South Africa managed to get past
the 'Charter's' screening with much less. As more settlers came in with
their families, many of the old pole-and-daga huts gave way to simple
little homesteads, built of brick, with mosquito-gauzed windows and
corrugated iron roofs, surrounded by broad verandas that kept the houses
cool and were often much better adjusted to conditions of the veld than
the more expensive city dwellings full of glass, put up by sun-starved
European immigrants of a later generation. As the settlers learned how to
protect themselves against malaria and blackwater fever, mortality
dropped, and with a more settled family life, with better schools and hospitals, the 'boom or bust' spirit of the early days began to evaporate.

But progress still remained slow. Farming continued to be impeded by
low prices, lack of overseas markets, and perhaps to some extent by
speculation in land; few of the original pioneers either managed to hold on
to their farms or to benefit from the gradual rise in land values. Cultivation
generally remained extensive in character, and even the Company's very
lenient terms of 'beneficial occupation' were often ignored since money
remained short.[1] Rhodesian farmers also found that, except for cheap,
unskilled labour, everything else—machinery, fertilizers, transport, credit
facilities and repair services—was more expensive than it would have
been for their American contemporaries, working within the framework
of a highly developed and integrated economy. Land swallowed up
capital at a higher rate than, say, the Canadian West, where farmers
secured their best crops from virgin country of prolonged fertility,
whereas the Rhodesian soil did not generally respond so well to cultivation in the first season; farmers had to wait longer for a return on their
outlay,[2] whilst sand and soil 'wore out' more quickly. Besides, the farmers
faced ecological problems of a more general kind. The railways, having
been built to connect the main mining districts with the towns, naturally
followed the bleaker, high-lying watershed, and avoided the low-lying,
sometimes richer but also more unhealthy low country. Many farmers

70 or 80 per cent were of British origin. The Chartered Company's offices in England, according to
him, were not able to give much help to immigrants, whereas the Company's agents at Cape Town,
East London, Durban, Pietermaritzburg, Bloemfontein and Johannesburg had the most up-to-date
information.

[1] Land could be purchased outright for cash, subject to certain occupation conditions, or might be
held under a 'Permit of Occupation' with an option to purchase after a specified period. In the latter
case farmers had to occupy their land personally or by a European substitute for five years. They
were also required to cultivate four acres of land for every 200 acres of the farm, or maintain two head
of cattle or ten head of small stock for every 200 acres, or make certain other specified improvements.

[2] Odlum, G. M. *Agricultural and pastoral Rhodesia*. British South Africa Company, 1909, p. 4

bought their land by the side of the railroad, in areas of uncertain rainfall, more suited to cattle than to cultivation; yields commonly remained small, and farming for long remained a speculative affair.

The early cultivators nevertheless played a vital role in the development of their country which, without their efforts, could not have fed its growing townships and mine compounds. For the first time in its history Rhodesia began to produce a marketable surplus of food, as white immigrants risked their capital and brought in new tools, new methods and improved crops. From the beginning of the present century, for instance, two-furrowed disc ploughs and cut-away disc harrows came into use. A few bold spirits even ventured their money on steam ploughs, though mechanization then rarely paid because of the broken type of country found on many farms, the high price of imported machinery and spare parts, the impossibility of employing these expensive engines for more than a short time in the year, and the inability of migrant African workmen to handle these monsters without damage.

White pioneers at the same time began to experiment with maize, the country's staple agricultural commodity. In the early days the settlers were inclined to depend on outside imports or African crops for the supply of this grain, but gradually the farmers found that they could produce it more cheaply than native growers with their small surplus, and production rapidly expanded, the country building up a little export industry of its own.[1] The Department of Agriculture experimented with varieties from America and Natal, and by crossing different strains produced new types, including improved Hickory King and 'Salisbury White', which yielded a high percentage of grain to cob, and had greater resistance to disease and higher yields on the more fertile red and chocolate soils.[2]

From the early 'nineties onwards European farmers also began to grow tobacco, small crops being produced for instance at Chishawasha Mission Farm, a Jesuit establishment, by Dr Sketchley in the Mazoe valley, and by Lionel Cripps, a well-known farmer in the Eastern Districts. From the turn of the century onwards tobacco 'caught on', and Rhodesian farmers discovered a crop that was relatively easy to transport, non-perishable when cured, and capable of giving quick returns on the capital invested. The growers also found themselves fortunate in receiving active and intelligent encouragement from the Chartered Company, which engaged some specialists from the United States to give advice with regard to soils and methods of cultivation. The

[1] Maize exports shot up from 27,308 lb in 1907 to 5,911,123 lb in 1910
[2] See Walters, A. T. 'Rhodesian maize: the principal types and their points' (in *Rhodesia agricultural journal.* v. 11, Oct 1913, p. 41–46)

Company leased warehouses to which tobacco was sent for handling, grading and subsequent sale.[1] G. M. Odlum, the Company's expert, went to America to study local methods, and later on, in 1907, made a trip to Turkey and Greece to learn more about Turkish tobacco. On this journey he engaged fourteen men for service in Southern Rhodesia, some of whom later settled in the country to take up tobacco-growing on their own account. Another important technical step forward was taken in 1903 when E. H. South, an enterprising farmer, produced the first flue-cured tobacco. The Chartered Company then sent some samples on to Salmon and Gluckstein, a big tobacco firm in England. The dealers reported in a lyrical strain normally absent from commercial communications, and with more perspicacity than is often displayed by top-heavy planning bodies, stated that if Rhodesia could turn out leaf of that quality the country had stumbled on an asset as precious as gold and diamonds, a crop that might ultimately drive American Virginia tobacco off the world market.[2] The Chartered Company decided to act on their advice. A big advertising campaign began to push Rhodesian tobacco; but the going proved hard, for the Company's own commercial staff on the spot lacked hustle and drive; farmers encountered many difficulties and supplies lagged behind, with the result that the Imperial Tobacco Company at Cape Town started making up so-called 'Rhodesian' tobacco, collected from all over the place and of wretched quality.[3] The Chartered Company, however, was not discouraged; experts organized 'Central Farms' where incoming settlers were taught how to produce flue-cured tobacco, the Chartered Board being anxious to expand the industry, and also to sell farms on sandy soil, hitherto largely neglected because of its lack of fertility, but extremely suitable for the new cash crop. By 1914 a sizeable number of white farmers were at work in the backveld, comprising some of the ablest and stablest elements in the population; the territory was turning out more than 3,000,000 lb of tobacco a year. But then prices suddenly slumped with terrifying rapidity. The limited South African market became overstocked; many farmers went bankrupt, and one grower was reduced to such straits that he coolly advertised his farm in exchange for 'a good strong bicycle, *must have* light'.[4]

Rhodesia also turned out to be suitable for all kinds of fruit; the Chartered Company itself made a valuable contribution with its Premier

[1] Department of Agriculture: *Southern Rhodesia handbook of tobacco culture.* . . . Salisbury, Argus printing and publishing co., 1913
[2] H. Wilson Fox, Manager of the B.S.A. Co., to Milton: 25 Nov 1904 (in A 1/5/6, Nat Arch SR)
[3] Wilson Fox to Milton: 28 Sep 1906 (in A 1/5/8, Nat Arch SR)
[4] See Brown, D. D. 'Pioneers of Rhodesian tobacco' (in *Rhodesian tobacco journal*, Aug 1953, p. 63–7; Oct 1953, p. 105–109; Nov 1953, p. 89–92; Dec 1953, p. 79–82; Jan 1954, p. 70–75)

and Mazoe orange estates, the Directors becoming convinced that they should develop the Company's own lands before concluding a final settlement regarding the country's political future.[1] Agricultural enterprise in turn brought about a slight rise in land prices, especially after 1910 when the Company somewhat belatedly realized that it had been selling farms much too cheaply, and determined that land should no longer be disposed of at 'prairie value'.[2]

In addition to arable farmers, white stock breeders helped to advance the country's infant economy; some colonists began to improve their stock by importing pedigree bulls, and by taking steps, with the help of government veterinary surgeons, to eliminate dangerous parasites. In 1911 an important ordinance passed on to the Statute Book allowing the Administrator to order the compulsory construction of cattle dips in affected areas for the control of ticks; two years later 'local option' was introduced to make the construction of dips obligatory in specified localities. Just before the Great War the Director of Agriculture could thus publicly remark on the relative sense of security that was now being felt against contagious cattle disease, a claim that would have appeared quite incredible to listeners just a decade earlier.

Farming also got further encouragement when some enterprising men began to lay the foundation of an agricultural processing industry. A creamery opened its doors at Gwelo, and in 1914 the Chartered Company's Commercial Branch set up a bacon factory at Salisbury which greatly increased the existing market for pigs.[3] In 1914 a Bulawayo enterprise began to produce cement so that farmers could put up more permanent buildings at less cost. In time the Rhodesian countryside began to change its appearance as immigrants altered the very landscape. The native woodland at first suffered considerable destruction through the operations of European miners in search of fuel, and also as the result of intensified African slash-and-burn agriculture, which involved the destruction of extensive areas of timber.[4] But Rhodes himself took considerable interest in the question, and his experts did good work at estates in the Matopos and at Inyanga, which Rhodes bequeathed to the nation in order to

---

[1] British South Africa Company. *Memorandum by H. Wilson Fox containing notes and information concerning land policy*. London, privately printed, 1912

[2] Wilson Fox to Milton: 27 May 1910 (in A 1/5/9, Nat Arch SR)

[3] Southern Rhodesia. *Report of the Director of agriculture ... 1914*. Salisbury, Government Printer, 1915

[4] R. Wallace, Professor of Agriculture at Edinburgh University, reported in 1908 that Nyungudya, a minor chief on the Victoria–Salisbury Road, showed him a vast plain, now cleared almost entirely of all timber by native methods of cultivation. The chief added that when he was a boy this plain was a huge forest full of game. Wallace concluded that the clearing of timber must have caused rainfall to diminish. Report by R. Wallace to B.S.A. Company: 19 Oct 1908 (in A 1/5/8, Nat Arch SR)

pioneer agricultural and forestry experiments. Ordinary immigrants and some municipalities tried various species, and in time the country's tree population became as cosmopolitan as its settlers. Different kinds of eucalyptus, capable of quick growth, made excellent wind-breaks, and also provided straight long poles. Wattle, a beautiful acacia, also of Australian origin, with a bark eminently suitable for making tan, flourished in the high-lying Eastern Districts, where the dark green foliage of the 'black' and 'golden' varieties now gives a characteristic touch to the hillsides. Various kinds of pine trees were tried, *pinus patula* and other varieties being planted as ornamental trees before spreading further afield. Other newcomers included the hardy *cedrela toona*, first introduced by Major H. G. Mundy, the beautiful jacaranda, a native of Brazil with gorgeous lilac-blue flowers, and the bougainvillea, another South American plant, which grew in profusion and added magnificent splashes of colour to the dusty, straggling townships and lonely homesteads on the veld, whilst the development of forestry as a whole in the long run also led to wider ecological changes.[1] In short, farmers and foresters found their feet and two decades after the Pioneer Corps wagons first rolled into the country, modern agriculture stood firmly entrenched.[2]

IV

In search of labour

Southern Rhodesia's multi-coloured society from the beginning resembled in some ways a slice of Neapolitan ice-cream! A small, tightly-knit white community was superimposed on a vastly larger black population which retained much of its social cohesion. On the edges, however, the layers slowly began to melt, as the immigrants tried to turn tribesmen into wage workers. Not only the colonists but also Imperial

---

[1] See Sim, T. R. *Tree-planting in South Africa*. Pietermaritzburg Natal Witness, 1927; Cmd. 865 of 1920; Hutchins, D. E. *Report for the Rhodes Trustees on the Matopo Park*. Cape Town, *Cape Times*, 1903, and early articles in the *Rhodesia agricultural journal*.

[2] The 1911 Census stated that 9·06 per cent of the white working population was engaged in agriculture—a total of 2,140 persons out of 23,606, as compared with only 1,029 persons in 1904. During the season 1914–1915 the acreage under crops owned by white farmers amounted to 183,407 acres (of which 142,950·5 acres were cultivated in Mashonaland and 40,456·5 in Matabeleland). Maize crops amounted to 914,926 bags (11 bags to the ton), 326,353 bags being exported, mainly to England and Australia. At the same time European and African farmers between them owned 748,058 horned cattle, an increase of 61 per cent since 1911. White farmers owned about half the cattle in the country. More accurate figures, and additional statistical details, are hard to obtain, for the Director of the 1911 Census found returns on agricultural matters so inadequate or unreliable that he did not bother to publish the full results.

statesmen and missionaries all felt convinced that Africans must be prised out of their tribal communities and integrated into the cash economy; in this respect there was little difference between South African administrators like Lord Milner, politicians like Chamberlain, the 'Charter's' own directors and local clergymen such as Father A. M. Daignault, a Jesuit, or the Rev. Isaac Shimmin, a Wesleyan who suggested that the discipline of steady work for a few months every year would be of the 'highest moral benefit' to the indigenous people.[1] The differences of opinion between the Europeans did not concern the strategic object to be gained, but only the means to be employed, the alternative methods suggested being those of the carrot and the stick. The settlers at first favoured compulsion, for the country's undercapitalized economy was still weak. Neither farmers nor miners could afford to pay good wages, whilst even European working conditions were deplorable. The Imperial Government, however, set its face against obligatory work in any shape or form, Chamberlain pointing out that he could not defend such methods in Parliament, and that he would prefer 'indirect inducements' to get Africans to leave their villages.[2] Any suspicion of force therefore had to be avoided, and when the Imperial authorities obtained details of the way chiefs were being put under pressure by Native Commissioners, the Colonial Office threatened to put the whole Native Department directly under Imperial control, and make the Company pay the bill. The 'Charter' came to heel at once and hurriedly cabled to the Administrator that Native Commissioners must at all costs remain neutral in the labour question, and that recruitment must be left to private agencies.[3]

The Administration now found itself in a difficult position. Admittedly recruiting workmen for short periods was no problem. Many villagers were only too glad to earn some cash in the dry season when there was no work to be done on the land. In addition to getting a small wage, the labourers received food and accommodation free of charge—like domestic servants in England. Wages of semi-skilled African mine hands in fact roughly resembled those of British domestic servants during those spacious Edwardian days—at the high tide of Imperialism—when *The Times* would carry such advertisements as: 'Plain cook wanted . . . four servants kept. Wages at £22.0.0. [per annum]. Apply by letter or in person. . . . The Vicarage, South Acton.'[4] More highly skilled African

[1] See letter by A. M. Daignault: 17 Nov 1897; and by I. Shimmins: 14 Nov 1897 (enclosures to no. 19 in African (South) no. 559)

[2] Chamberlain to Milner: 14 Jan 1898 (in African (South) no. 559)

[3] B.S.A. Company to Administrator: 7 Oct 1901 (Annex. 25 to B.S.A. Company minutes of 9 Oct 1901, in LO 1/2/12, Nat Arch SR)

[4] The advertisement is quoted from *The Times*: 3 July 1906

miners might indeed make more than a young house surgeon in a paid job in a London teaching hospital, whilst some unskilled workers in England, who relied only on their wage packets and got no 'perks' of any kind, may in certain respects have been even worse off than the better-paid African workers.[1]

Tribal cohesion, the existence of large land reserves and administrative paternalism, all combined to act as a kind of shock absorber, protecting Africans against the worst effects of incipient industrialization. Women and children never worked down the mine shafts during the Rhodesian pioneering days, as they did in the early stages of the industrial revolution in Britain. But Africans became used to regarding a money wage as nothing more than a supplement to their income from the land. On the other hand an African workman with all his traditional obligations to his kinsfolk had to carry a burden which was much heavier than that which a British labourer would be expected to carry on behalf of his relatives. Cash wages remained stabilized over long periods and yet employers kept grumbling. For mine owners and farmers alike not only had to contend with inefficient men who left their jobs as soon as they had picked up the rudiments, they also had to cope with the problem of never quite knowing how many people they could count on to work. Hence came the Europeans' insistent cry for a 'regular and non-spasmodic supply of labour', a commodity hard to get in existing circumstances, especially during the rainy season, when the tribesmen got busy on their own gardens.

The employers' position worsened when some African villagers started to sell part of their crops. The *Pax Britannica* and the growth of new townships and compounds had the unintended effect of creating a small market for African produce; mine-owners, prospectors and even white farmers all bought native grain and meat, thereby helping to 'spoil' their own local labour supplies. The weaker communities could now build up their herds without being raided; the people in the reserves could site their kraals and gardens where they were best located from an economic point of view, without having to pay heed to considerations of defence.

---

[1] According to *Palgrave's dictionary of political economy*, v. 3, Macmillan and co., 1926, p. 798–800, an agricultural labourer in Lincolnshire in 1902 received 15/– a week on an average, a Tyneside labourer 22/–. A woman in the silk industry in Britain received an average wage of 11/– a week in 1906. On these wages workmen had fully to support themselves. It might be added that even many English professionals received very low salaries at the start of their careers. Dr Godfrey Martin Huggins, later Prime Minister of Southern Rhodesia, during this period received £30 a year on his first paid job as a house surgeon in a London teaching hospital, where he also had board and lodging.

African cash wages during the first decade of the present century in Southern Rhodesia amounted to 5/– a month for a juvenile farm worker or a 'raw boy'. An ordinary farmhand got 15/– a month, and a skilled African driver 40/–. Wages on the mines varied from about 25/– to 60/– a month. Board and lodging of a kind were always provided, so that the problem of raising real wages at first hinged on the question of improving the quality of the payment in kind.

African wealth thus increased swiftly. According to the Company's own figures the estimated number of horned cattle in African hands leapt from just over 60,000 in 1902 to more than 200,000 in 1908; acreage under cultivation increased from some 550,000 to over 730,000, whilst the approximate yield of grain shot up from roughly 1,270,000 bags to above 2,175,000. Employers soon took note; Southern Rhodesian natives, sadly commented a local compound inspector, did not make good work-men, for the high price of grain was 'spoiling the local labour market, and a woman cultivating one or two acres could make as much money in a month as her husband in three'.[1]

After the Boer War the demand for native labour grew even more insistent. The economy at last got into its stride and needed more hired hands to cope with increasing work. The various employers thus com-peted amongst themselves for a limited number of local workmen. This state of affairs appeared quite unnatural to them, and led to angry out-cries about the 'shortage of labour'. The Administration now had three choices. It might raise taxes to force more tribesmen on to the labour market; it could import hired hands from outside, or it could make work-ing conditions more attractive, and improve systems of recruitment. The Europeans in fact tried all three methods, which to some extent followed upon each other in chronological order. The easiest way of all was to tighten the tax screw, which had the additional advantage of bringing more revenue into Government coffers. Early in 1903 the Chamber of Mines recommended that the Company should impose a uniform poll tax of £2, and shortly afterwards Milton wrote to his London office support-ing this suggestion. The Administrator considered that adult men should pay £2, and contribute an extra 10/– for each wife beyond the first. In putting his case to the High Commissioner, Milton pointed to the undoubted improvement in African living conditions, and added that Africans in fact were only contributing 4/4 per head to the expense of government, whilst administrative expenditure amounted to £1.6.8 per head of population. An increased tax would stimulate African agricultural production and at the same time turn out more labour.[2] Others argued that the new impost would also reduce polygamy, an institution to which most missionaries objected on moral grounds; the Administration itself believed that a levy on wives would act as a rough kind of graduated income tax, a concept which bore little relation to tribal realities. But now the 'Imperial Watchdog' stepped in. The Resident Commissioner was in

[1] Report by the Inspector of Native Compounds for the year ended 31 Mar 1903. (Annex. 19 to B.S.A. Company minutes of 22 July 1903, in LO 1/2/25, Nat Arch SR)

[2] Administrator to High Commissioner: 28 May 1903 (Annex. 13 to B.S.A. Company minutes of 1 July 1903, in LO 1/2/24. Nat Arch SR)

touch with Father R. P. Richartz, head of the Jesuit Mission at Chisha-washa, and Richartz came out strongly against the project. The Africans just could not afford to pay so much. In any case, he argued, if the Government increased the taxes native workmen would ask their employers for more money. Only the richer mines would be able to pay higher wages, and the poorer employers would suffer. Besides, if the Government were to proceed with the measure there would be more theft, many young men would have to pay their relatives' tax, and all kinds of undesirable practices would come into vogue.[1] The Resident Commissioner himself agreed with the Jesuit, pointing out that the new tax would throw more burdens on African women who would have to do extra labour in the fields, and that it would unsettle the natives, who had just been hit by a bad harvest. In any case, the Resident Commissioner added, local opinion was exaggerating the shortage of labour; the supply in fact exceeded the demand.[2] The Resident Commissioner had a good case, for the better kind of employer could usually find Africans to work for him; but the dispute continued, the settlers siding with the Company. In 1903 the Legislative Council accordingly passed an ordinance putting up the tax, but the Imperial Government refused to give its assent, fearing the consequences of possible unrest, and in the following year the impost was fixed at £1 over the whole country.[3]

In addition to raising taxes the Administration tried to recruit man-power from abroad. The countries north of the Zambezi, where European enterprise was as yet limited, formed the most easily accessible labour reservoirs; men also drifted in from Portuguese East Africa where again Africans could not easily get jobs. By 1903 some 3,000 to 4,000 Africans had found their way to Southern Rhodesia on their own. Immigrant workmen from the north could earn higher wages than at home and could now travel without danger of capture by slave raiders. Economic and tax pressures seem to have been reinforced by complex psychological factors, a kind of strange *wanderlust*, a deep-felt wish to get away from the

---

[1] Richartz to Resident Commissioner: 6 July 1903 (Annex. 90 to B.S.A. Company minutes of 17 and 19 Oct 1903, in LO 1/2/27b, Nat Arch SR)

[2] Resident Commissioner to High Commissioner: 29 May 1903 (Annex. 15 to B.S.A. Company minutes of 31 May 1904, in LO 1/2/36, Nat Arch SR)

[3] This still left the Southern Rhodesian native tax as one of the highest in South Africa. In the first decade of the present century the average contribution per head of the native population stood as follows in the different territories:

Southern Rhodesia (1908–9)	5/11d.
Natal and Zululand (1906)	5/1d.
Transvaal (after 1908)	6/0d. approx.
Cape (1904)	1/6d.
Bechuanaland (1904)	1/10d.
Basutoland (1904)	3/3d.

kraal for a spell and to see something of the white man's new world; besides, the migrants wanted to buy new kinds of goods—pots and pans, blankets and knives—commodities that white factories could turn out more cheaply and satisfactorily than Bantu craftsmen. Some labour recruiters tried to cash in on rising demands for new commodities by employing unscrupulous characters, white and black, who went round the villages and glibly told the most wonderful tales about high wages, their stories of a new Eldorado down south sometimes resembling perhaps the romantic myths that attracted white pioneers from beyond the Limpopo.

Southern Rhodesian employers much preferred workmen from afar to those from kraals nearby, for migrants from a distance could not desert so easily, and would sign on for longer periods. But even so, Bantu 'commuters' from whatever distance still turned out to be unsatisfactory employees, and the mine-owners agitated for a 'non-spasmodic' labour supply, for proletarians without a stake in tribal lands, men who would not wish to return to their villages after short spells of employment, but would depend entirely on their wage packets, and would therefore do more work. People of this kind could not be recruited in Central Africa where the traditional system of farming continued to afford some kind of social security to the villagers, and where only white artisans relied entirely on cash wages for their living.

The employers' demand for reliable unskilled labour set off a search for wage workers which, if successful, would have turned the country into a sociologist's paradise and a statesman's hell! In 1899 an enterprising doctor suggested that West Indians be recruited to Southern Rhodesia— intelligent people but not over-fussy about their food, already used to working as far afield as British Guiana and Central America, who would do a good day's work for 3/– or 4/–.[1] But Chamberlain, the British Colonial Secretary, would have nothing to do with the idea, and the project lapsed. The authorities then tried the resources of north-east Africa, and some Abyssinians and Somalis came to the country. But again the plan would not work. Many hired hands deserted, others rioted on board their steamer in Beira when rumours floated round that they were to be sold as slaves,[2] and the scheme came to naught. Additional labourers signed on at Aden, but then the local British Resident stepped in and objected to any kind of systematic emigration from Aden and southern Arabia; the Foreign Office supported him. In 1903 the Chamber of Mines suggested the importation of indentured Indian workmen, but again the

[1] Dr Calder to Colonial Office: 27 Dec 1899 (in African (South) no. 656)
[2] Milner to Chamberlain: 6 Feb 1901 (in African (South) no. 659)

plan misfired. There were already some Indians in Southern Rhodesia as traders, with a sprinkling of artisans and market gardeners, but local European merchants were resentful of the brown man's competition, and Indians were subject to various restrictions concerning conditions of entry to the country and the issue of trading licences. The Indian Government reacted very strongly to discrimination against their subjects; it insisted that Indians should be admitted to the country on the same terms as any other British citizens, and that Indian languages should be included in the literacy tests imposed by the immigration authorities. The Viceroy also argued that Indian mine-owners should have the first claim on labour, that compounding could not possibly be permitted, and that the Rhodesian labour laws were unsatisfactory.[1] Indeed the general tenor of despatches between the Indian and the various southern African authorities differed very little in the days of the British Raj from the tone customary in post-colonial days, the concept of a common Empire only concealing the deep-seated differences that already divided its various parts.

Finally Rhodesian mine-owners tried to import indentured labourers from China, and Colonel Raleigh Grey, the Chairman of the Salisbury Chamber of Mines, gave an excellent summary of their case to a special meeting of its Executive Council. Rhodesia lacked both labour and capital and was in a bad way economically. Worse still the Rhodesian gold industry would have to compete with the wealthier Witwatersrand which was itself about to import coolies. The Chinese workmen would all be repatriated at the expiration of their contracts, and unless something was done to supplement the inadequate supply of native labour, the country might face starvation. The mine-owners' demand led to a bitter campaign on the part of European contractors and skilled artisans who strongly opposed the idea of yellow people coming to the country, and 'taking bread out of the white men's mouths'. A sharp class cleavage began to open up within the European population itself, the Rhodesian anti-Chinese campaign running parallel with a similar movement in South Africa which opposed the employment of indentured Chinese workmen on the Witwatersrand. The Chartered Company naturally sympathized with the mine-owners, but the Resident Commissioner opposed the entry of coolies, arguing that conditions would improve as the railway pushed further beyond the Zambezi and Northern natives became used to mining. The mine-owners should instead make conditions more attractive, the scarcity of labour being much more marked at some mines than at

---

[1] Curzon to Milner: 21 Mar 1903 (enclosure in Colonial Office to B.S.A. Company: 22 June 1903, Annex. 12 to B.S.A. Company minutes of 1 July 1903, in LO 1/2/24, Nat Arch SR)

others.[1] The Colonial Office thus held back, and when the opponents of the scheme in the Transvaal succeeded in getting rid of Chinese labour, the Rhodesian project collapsed.

The labour problem remained so intractable that the authorities were willy-nilly forced into the way of reform; the shortage of manpower, pressure from the Imperial Government and humanitarian impulses from within the Chartered administration all helped to bring about a new climate of opinion. The first welfare campaign for Africans fell into two distinct phases—the improvement of recruiting conditions, and ameliora-tion of life on the mines. The Legislative Council passed several laws obliging labour agents to get proper licences, thereby spiking the guns of low-class 'touts'. In addition attempts were made to set up a proper recruiting organization which would supplement the scanty number of Africans seeking work on their own. In 1899 the Matabeleland Native Labour Bureau came into being in Bulawayo, and it was followed a year later by the Labour Board of Southern Rhodesia, designed to serve the country as a whole. The Board, however, had to compete with licensed recruiters from the Transvaal who could offer higher wages, and the organization soon ran into financial difficulties. After the Boer War, when the Witwatersrand gold industry revived, competition on the part of the wealthier Rand mines for Rhodesian labour became even fiercer, and the Rhodesian authorities then reorganized recruitment with the aid of government funds, the Rhodesian Native Labour Bureau being set up in 1903. Valdemar Gielgud, a keen and able man with considerable experience in native administration, was put in charge, and soon made a success of his new job. Recruitment was extended to Northern Rhodesia, and at the same time conditions en route were greatly improved.[2] The Bureau issued workmen in transit with food, blankets and jerseys; the men received proper medical examinations and an adequate diet; rest houses and other facilities were provided, whilst 'rejected' workmen got sufficient rations and some compensation. The Bureau mainly relied on labour from outside the country to fill its quota,[3] the constant influx of migrants from beyond

[1] Resident Commissioner to Colonial Office: 11 Dec 1903 (Annex. 7 to B.S.A. Company minutes of 16 Mar 1904, in LO 1/2/33, Nat Arch SR)

[2] See Gelfand, M. 'Migration of African Labourers in Rhodesia and Nyasaland (1890–1914)' (in *Central African journal of medicine*, v. 7, no. 8, Aug 1961, p. 293–300)

[3] In 1919 the Southern Rhodesia Native Labour Bureau obtained its recruits as follows:

Local	10,689
Portuguese territories	6,116
N.W. Rhodesia	4,436
N.E. Rhodesia	4,854
Nyasaland	5,074
Others	1,551
Total	32,720

its borders probably tending to keep wages down in Southern Rhodesia itself.

At the same time the Administration began to take steps to cope with mortality in the mines. In the early years of European enterprise compound managers imagined that African labourers living in pole-and-daga huts, eating the same kind of food as in the village—maize with some occasional meat—would keep as fit as in their kraals. But experience proved otherwise. The sudden influx of large numbers of men, working much harder than before, living under strange conditions without their wives' care, crammed together in overcrowded quarters with poor ventilation and inadequate washing facilities, resulted in death rates that shocked the most hard-bitten. Sanitary conditions remained inadequate, with the result that water supplies became infected, flies contaminated the food, and dysentery followed. Food might be adequate in quantity, but since the men had no one to collect the herbs which served as relish in the villages, it turned out to be deficient in vitamin content, and many men reported sick with scurvy. The biggest killer of all was pneumonia which accounted for well over a third of the deaths.[1] At one time the African miners' mortality rate amounted to over 7 per cent per annum, the casualty rate of many an army in wartime, and the Southern Rhodesian administration therefore came under heavy pressure both from the Chartered Company's head office in London and from the Imperial Government. Milton was anxious to take action, and at last something was done. The Administration appointed compound inspectors to look into health conditions and after exhaustive investigations the Government from 1907 onwards enforced the proper feeding and housing of African miners. The small companies, unable to spend as much money on social improvements as the larger concerns, put up some resistance, but could not reverse the trend. In 1911 the Administration introduced a further set of regulations which compelled employers to make additional improvements in the workers' diet, and three years later provided for one compulsory day of rest in seven. The small entrepreneurs growled angrily that all the Government wanted them to do was to 'feed, feed, feed', but the new reforms, added to the expansion of hospital facilities, soon proved their worth; mortality rates on the mines began to slump.[2] After an initial period of frontier friction in the 'nineties, the Chartered Com-

---

[1] In the year 1903 to 1904 282 Africans died on the Southern Rhodesian mines. Pneumonia accounted for 113, scurvy for 42, malaria for 24, malaria and scurvy together for 16, peritonitis 2, dysentery 24, dropsy 1, beriberi 3, measles 1, peripheral neuritis 4, senility 1, other causes 50.

[2] Mortality figures for Africans dropped from 75·94 per mille in 1906 to 21·68 per mille in 1917. The influenza epidemic after the Great War saw a sudden rise to 113·38 per mille in 1918, but thereafter the mortality swiftly went down again, reaching 15·39 in 1925.

pany established a better record in labour and health matters than
any British, French or Portuguese colony in Africa at the time.[1] Mine
work became more popular in the Rhodesian village, and native mine
workers generally became healthier and better-fed than their cousins in the
kraals.

   This improvement in conditions in the mines was only a part of a
much wider medical revolution which affected white and black men alike,
and which in some ways brought about a bigger change in the country
than almost any other European innovation. When the Pioneer Column
first entered Southern Rhodesia the causes of malaria and blackwater fever,
its deadly sequel, still remained unknown. The Far North was still a very
dangerous part of the world for white men to live in, for disease formed
an ever-present menace to immigrants and their families. Even if the
newcomers did not die, their energies were sapped when fever set in after
the rainy season. Having caught a dose of malaria, a farmer, miner or
prospector needed tremendous will power to attend to his work properly,
the farmers especially finding that malaria would strike them down just
when their crops were ready to be reaped.[2]

   Thus in the long run the anopheles mosquito represented a much more
perilous threat than any number of assegais or native blunderbusses.
Victory only came in sight when in the late 'nineties Ronald Ross, a famous
British medical man in India, first discovered how mosquitoes transmitted
malaria, a connexion that was once tentatively suggested by David
Livingstone on his Zambesi Expedition. Ross's lesson was soon learned in
Southern Rhodesia where, in 1899, a district surgeon in the Chartered
Company's employ established the presence of the dreaded anopheles.
Immediately afterwards Andrew Milroy Fleming, the Medical Director,
began to take vigorous counter-measures. Government, mission, private
and municipal doctors all joined the campaign, and gradually began to
make some inroads on sickness. The towns became cleaner and healthier
as the ragged-looking pole-and-daga huts or tin shanties gave way to
better buildings. At the same time the authorities began to clean up
stagnant pools of water, dangerous breeding places for mosquitoes, and to
provide better water supplies, thereby helping to do away with the once-
frequent outbreaks of typhoid fever. Improvements spread into the
countryside as farmers and miners learned how to protect themselves by
using mosquito nets, putting up better buildings and eliminating the
breeding areas of anopheles. The work of Fleming and his associates

---

[1] For a well-informed and balanced account of the Company's native and labour policy see
Duignan, P. J. *Native policy in Southern Rhodesia, 1890–1923.* Stanford University Ph.D. thesis, 1961
[2] See Gelfand, M. *Tropical victory: an account of the influence of medicine on the history of Southern
Rhodesia, 1890–1923.* Cape Town, Juta, 1953, which is the standard work on the subject.

N

in some ways proved even more remarkable than contemporary American successes in cleaning up the Panama Canal Zone, for Rhodesian doctors had to cover a vastly larger area, and cope with isolated settlers scattered all over the veld, and difficult to control. In time, however, sickness started to retreat, and medical treatment spread further afield, into the reserves, where the original pioneering was done by mission doctors. More hospitals were built, and from 1911 the Southern Rhodesian administration began to set up village dispensaries in native areas, Southern Rhodesia taking the lead in all medical improvements that white men brought to Central Africa. Success of course took a long time to achieve, but the country on the whole was fortunate in the quality of the doctors and nurses who came from overseas and from South Africa, and by the beginning of the 'twenties Southern Rhodesia had turned the corner. From being a stagnant pool of disease the Colony now stood out as one of the healthiest in the world, and future development could rest upon a firm base of medical achievement.[1]

V

Land and locations

White settlements in Central Africa formed but a chapter in a much bigger story. From the Middle Ages onwards Western Europeans began to push outwards against a multiplicity of tribal frontiers on the Celtic and Slavonic fringes of their society. Dutch and German settlers, to mention but one example, found new homes for themselves in tribal Prussia, where the newcomers not only wielded better weapons, but also brought along heavy ploughs with iron ploughshares which could break up difficult forest and bushland, unworkable by indigenous communities with their lighter scratch-ploughs. Later on, as European expansion continued, the story was repeated in different ways, and by the end of the last century the limits of white settlement had advanced into Central Africa. During the first three or four years after the occupation of Mashonaland a few farmers settled beyond the Limpopo, but their numbers were so small in relation to the size of the country that Africans at first suffered very little pressure from the newcomers.

---

[1] Between 1904 and 1922 the white death rate dropped from 18·8 per mille to 8·98 per mille. Accurate figures for overall African mortality for this period are less easy to provide, but after a time-lag there was also a sharp decline. For more modern African figures and comparative statistics for Southern Rhodesia and various other 'underdeveloped' countries see Gelfand, M. *Proud Record.* Salisbury, Federal information department, 1960, p. 50–53

After the conquest of Matabeleland, however, the picture began to change. Immigrants came to Matabeleland in larger numbers, receiving vast farms, 3,000 morgen in extent—double the size of those in Mashonaland—and in addition exploration and land companies received the right of selecting vast blocks for future development. Most of the early settlers selected their land on the heavy red and black loams which had been favoured by the Matabele. The Mashona tribes also sometimes worked red soils. On the whole, however, they stuck to light coloured granite country and sand soils, situated in rugged regions broken by kopjes, capable of affording natural defence in time of war. Women with hoes could scratch sand soils with less effort than heavy loams, but these soils were not coveted by European maize growers, and only acquired commercial value with the advent of tobacco farming. The Matabele thus suffered much more heavily, and by the middle of 1894 a large portion of the so-called 'gold belt areas' in Matabeleland, with their richer soils, had passed into European hands.

The whites at first occupied only a very small proportion of their farms, but the Imperial Government insisted that some additional land should be set apart for the Matabele where they might find homes, in case more settlers came in. In 1894 the Imperial authorities promulgated an Order in Council which provided for the setting up of a Land Commission. This new body designated two large blocks, the Shangani and Gwaai Reserves, whose areas were estimated at 3,500 and 3,000 square miles respectively, in addition to a small reserve for Lobengula's surviving relatives. The Matabele, however, preferred to stay where they were, rather than abandon their ancestral acres for the sake of dry, sandy granite country, whilst farmers encouraged the Matabele to remain and work for them.

Four years later the Imperial Government again considered the land problem when drafting the Southern Rhodesia Order in Council, 1898. Under the new law Africans retained their constitutional right of buying land anywhere in the Colony on the same terms as Europeans. But very few black people ever managed to make use of this provision. A small number of black settlers from South Africa—'alien natives' in the queer language of the day—managed to buy some land on individual tenure; these included some Fingoes at Bembesi, and a few Basutos and a Shangaan in the Victoria District.[1] Such people, however, remained quite exceptional, for the vast majority of Africans in the country possessed neither cash, knowledge nor inclination to buy land like white men, whilst

[1] For a more detailed discussion see Rolin, H. *Les lois et l'administration de la Rhodésie*. Bruxelles, Établissements Emile Bruylant, 1913, p. 242–275

neither white civil servants nor black chiefs would encourage them to abandon their traditional system of holding property.

Much more important therefore was the question of land held in tribal ownership. The Order accordingly placed a statutory obligation upon the Company to provide sufficient holdings, with an adequate number of springs and streams, for the Africans under their rule, and even before the new law passed on to the Statute Book, the Chief Native Commissioner submitted his proposals for demarcating reserves. In Mashonaland Native Commissioners usually allocated between 15 and 20 acres of arable land to each hut,[1] whereas the rule of thumb followed in Matabeleland only allowed some nine acres of arable land to each family, the average apparently being based on the allocation made under the Glen Grey Act in the Cape Colony.[2]

The Native Commissioners, however, worked in a very haphazard fashion. The resources of the country were little known; there were no proper maps and surveys; the Administration lacked a uniform policy, and local officials seem to have acted very much according to what seemed good in their own eyes. The size, quality and arrangement of the reserves thus varied widely. Some Native Commissioners tried to reserve all unoccupied land in their area—notably in Mrewa where the reserves covered practically the whole district. Others used the somewhat arbitrary boundaries of Native Districts as lines of demarcation, even though these did not necessarily correspond to tribal divisions. In general, the Native Commissioners attempted to leave the indigenous people as far as possible undisturbed; they also tried to make allowance for a fair increase in population, but in some regions could not find enough suitable land not already alienated. In other instances officials adopted a principle radically different from that of demarcating huge and little-known areas; they provided small reserves for every petty community wherever it happened to be settled, an arrangement which resulted in small patches being sandwiched amongst European farms.

The lack of system in this policy led to enormous disparities; some reserves, as for instance the Shitowa Reserve of 5,000 acres, had less land than a big farm. At the other end of the spectrum stood the Matibi Reserve of 3,475,170 acres, as big as a small principality. The quality of the soil available and the number of springs and streams showed immense variation, not only from reserve to reserve, but also in different localities within the reserves, so that generalizations are very difficult to make. In

[1] Chief Native Commissioner to Under Secretary, Administrator's Office: 18 Mar 1898 (in N 3/24/1/1, Nat Arch SR)
[2] Cd. 8674 (1917), p. 7

certain areas Africans got by far the worst of the bargain, finding themselves relegated to drier and more inhospitable country. In others they did extremely well; for instance, more than twenty years later the Native Commissioner at Mount Darwin reported that the Chiswiti Reserve contained some of the finest land in Southern Rhodesia. In this part of the country there was so much room to spare that every kraal might increase its population fourfold without overcrowding, the lowveld below the Mvura Dona mountains being capable of immense development,[1] whilst the Chief Native Commissioner concluded that there was so much land in the area that Africans from Nyasaland might safely be allowed to settle there.[2] Again pressure on individual communities in white settlement areas varied considerably. In some regions like the Bushu Reserve in Mazoe, the local Africans were left with their own part of the country. In other portions of the same district tribesmen had to shift to make room for white farmers, the people living in the Chiweshe-Negomo Reserve being the main sufferers in this respect.[3]

As time went on the demand for reserves became more insistent. In the old days, when European methods themselves were backward, the presence of African villages on a farmer's land or nearby did not matter. But once white farmers began to cultivate their fields somewhat more intensively, their methods began to clash with those of African 'slash and burn' cultivators, who would move about as they exhausted the soil, and also caused uncontrolled veld fires. In addition native-owned cattle began to compete with white-owned beasts for grazing. Just before the Great War the authorities estimated that between 1902 and 1913 the number of native-owned cattle had gone up from 55,155 to 377,000, whilst the corresponding figures for sheep and goats amounted to 257,000 and 893,000 respectively. The rate of increase appears to have been even more rapid in Matabeleland than in Mashonaland, the Matabele with their Zulu traditions, showing greater reluctance to kill or trade animals than any other tribe in the territory. The presence of native scrub stock near a white man's cattle kraal became all the more irksome, as European breeders began to improve their beasts. European agriculturists in fact soon acquired as keen a dislike of their more backward neighbours, as did 'improving' English landlords in the eighteenth century, who wanted to do away with the village common and thought that only enclosures would stop the 'vicious and idle poor' from allowing their inferior stock to

---

[1] Native Commissioner, Mount Darwin (memorandum): 30 May 1923 (in N 3/24/1/4, Nat Arch SR)

[2] Chief Native Commissioner to Administrator: 11 July 1923 (in N 3/24/1/4, Nat Arch SR)

[3] Native Commissioner, Mazoe, to Superintendent of Natives, Salisbury: 7 May 1914 (in N 3/24/13, Nat Arch SR)

mingle and mate with the gentleman's pedigreed animals. White farmers also blamed Africans for breaking down fences, for stealing cows and implements and for abusing their roads with sledges. In addition more intangible factors began to make themselves felt. European families, living lonely lives on the veld, wanted their neighbours to be white people, folk who spoke the same language—both literally and figuratively—people who could be relied on to help in cases of emergency, an important consideration at a time when serious sickness on a farm was a disaster, entailing a long and nerve-racking trip on a creaking ox wagon. European landowners soon found therefore that the presence of Africans on land nearby depreciated the value of their investment in real estate and of their savings, and they usually became keen advocates of territorial segregation.

Native Commissioners, even those most anxious to improve the lot of their charges, also tended to support the idea of separate development. The Native Commissioner at Mazoe, a man who stoutly fought for 'his' people, and took their part against the Chartered Company's land office in a dispute over a section of the Chiwaridza Reserve, thus ultimately came to the conclusion that it would be better if the whole of that area was given up; in his view the whole region was too close to mines and white settlements. Africans were only learning all kinds of vices in the compounds, and would be better off if further removed from their baneful influence, an idea with which the local chiefs fully concurred.[1] The Native Commissioner at Marandellas likewise staunchly held out for 'his' Africans; he argued that even though they were not yet in a position to use the whole of their reserves they would nevertheless be able to cultivate their spare land later on when ploughs would come into wider use, and that their territory should not therefore be reduced. But he too agreed that white should be segregated from black lands, and that small reserves surrounded by farms would prove a nuisance.[2]

Missionaries usually took a similar line. Archdeacon Etheridge, a prominent Anglican clergyman, explained to a Commission that large reserves provided a better opportunity for developing native life and carrying out experiments, both from an evangelical and administrative point of view, whilst small reserves, interspersed with farms, always led to friction over matters like straying stock, right of way, and so forth.[3] Expatriate clergymen also wished to protect African villagers from the baneful influences which supposedly emanated from the towns, where

[1] Native Commissioner, Mazoe, to Superintendent of Natives, Salisbury: 7 May 1914 (in N 3/24/1/3, Nat Arch SR)
[2] Native Commissioner, Marandellas, to Superintendent of Natives, Salisbury: 4 May 1914 (in N 3/24/1/3, Nat Arch SR)
[3] Cd 8674 (1917), p. 65

black men picked up evil ways from low whites, and where local employers would seduce mission teachers from church employment with promises of higher wages as clerks and storemen.

The Chartered Company's own point of view was more complex. Henry Wilson Fox, the Company's General Manager, explained to his Directors in a confidential memorandum that tribalism must be liquidated, and that prosperity would only come if the communal system of tenure went by the board. Fox in fact resented the way Native Commissioners talked of 'their' Africans and acquired a kind of professional vested interest in their 'retrograde' ways of life. Fox's criticism gained all the more substance by the fact that the Native Commissioners often stayed in the same district for years on end, until they came completely to identify themselves with their charges. The Chartered Company moreover wished to have a free hand in selling land to white men and Fox privately explained to Milton that 'the great point is . . . not to agree to any final settlement which will for all time to come prevent European settlement in areas which are suitable for white occupation'.[1] The Company also wanted some idea of how much land it could sell; the local Estates Office usually pressed the case for white settlement, whilst the Native Department stood up for the black man's right. In addition the Company came under pressure from the Colonial Office which suggested in 1913 that a Commission be set up to investigate the reserves question. The 'Charter' agreed to its appointment on the understanding that the delimitation of the reserves thus arrived at would be final, and in 1914 the Commissioners took up their work.

The investigators included two Imperial nominees, Robert Thorne Coryndon, a former Chartered Company official who was then serving as Resident Commissioner of Swaziland, and Major Edward Charles Frederick Carraway, later Resident Commissioner of Basutoland. The Chartered Company appointed its Treasurer, Francis James Newton, with William John Atherstone, the Surveyor-General, acting as Newton's alternate. The Commissioners travelled all over the country, and made their final report at the end of 1915. They concluded that some native areas needed enlarging, but that others could actually be diminished, far more land having been set aside for Africans than was necessary. The size of the Sabi Reserve for instance had been originally fixed at 400,000 acres, but was subsequently found to contain over 1,500,000. The Commissioners therefore recommended that the area should be cut down to just over 1,261,000 acres, a decision which engendered bitter disputes afterwards. Looking on the land position as a whole, the Commissioners felt

[1] H. W. Fox to Sir H. W. Milton: 29 Apr 1910 (in A 1/5/8, Nat Arch SR)

convinced that Southern Rhodesian Africans had in fact come off rather well, and that they had far more land at their disposal than the natives of any other part of South Africa—except drought-ridden Bechuanaland.[1] The investigators therefore argued that the total area of reserves should be slightly reduced, from 20,491,151 to 19,428,691 acres, about one-fifth of the country's total extent, an area equivalent to more than four times the acreage of Wales. Their recommendations were influenced to a considerable extent by pressure from the Company's own Lands Department.

In making their proposals the Commissioners held that European immigration was inevitable, and that the impact of a progressive white community was bound to dislocate the normal process of tribal development. People like Newton and Coryndon were as yet quite unaffected by cultural relativism or romantic dreams of 'unspoilt savages' or 'preliterate societies in a state of balanced social equilibrium'. They were not afraid to make what a later generation has called ethnocentric value judgements, and did not beat about the bush. 'Tribal barbarism' was doomed; the presence of a European industrial community, the example of white farmers and native education between them were bound to break down the old ways; the only problem was to make the process of transition easier. The natives could not at once become assimilated into the new society, and the reserves should form a kind of buffer for the backward. But the amount of land in the country was limited—an idea hard to swallow for African tribesmen who assumed that the soil should be as free and plentiful as air. The native population would go on increasing; but no one could expect that every African as yet unborn must retain 'an indefeasable right' to land sufficient for all his traditional needs. If once this idea was accepted the whole of Southern Rhodesia would ultimately have to be turned into one

---

[1] The comparative figures quoted stood as follows (Cd. 8674 (1917), p. 66)

Territory	Acreage per head of population then on reserves
Pondoland and Transkei	10·2
Bechuanaland and remaining Cape Province	14·4
Zululand and remainder of Natal	13·8
Transvaal	5·1
Orange Free State	2·1
Basutoland (practically all reserve)	16·5
Swaziland	19·1
Bechuanaland Protectorate	476
Southern Rhodesia	50·55

Rolin, writing in 1913 as an independent observer, similarly thought that the reserves were far from being overpopulated. (Rolin, H. *Les lois et l'administration de la Rhodésie*, Bruxelles, Établissements Emil Bruylant, 1913, p. 250–251)

gigantic reserve. There was only one way to deal with the problem: Africans must improve their methods of cultivation; the yield of reserves should be increased by the provision of boreholes and other facilities; tenants ejected from European farms should occupy more distant blocks where there was still much good land available, though the Commissioners did not go into the question of how convenient these areas were with regard to trade and communications.

In 1917 the Colonial Office finally accepted the report which—from the European point of view—seemed convincing enough. Men like Newton and Coryndon spoke for an individualistic kind of society—enquiring, experimental and acquisitive. They were people convinced that man must master nature and use her for his own betterment—folk for whom, in the words of a local African, 'the whole, wide world was a farm.' In Coryndon's universe there was no place for sacred shrines and groves; spirits did not speak through mediums, neither did they keep guard over specific clans or specially allocated regions of the country. Land had an economic but no spiritual value; cattle were raised for the abattoir, not for the sacral act of giving bride-wealth for a wife. Economic progress was desirable in itself, for it increased the number of choices open to a society; change was praiseworthy if it added honestly-earned money to a man's bank balance, and if a person could not get on, he should get out.

The colonizers believed in development, but only had three ways open before them. They might pour vast funds into technical and training establishments and employ an army of experts to turn tribesmen into producers. Some kind-hearted British theorists later thought that this was indeed the way, but even had the Board agreed with these views, they would have lacked the men, the means and the money. Alternatively the Company could rely on forced labour and build up an initial surplus by brute force in the manner later tried by Chinese Communists. But the Imperial Government would never have stood for such a course, even had the Company been willing to try. The third method was to attract white colonists, used to a market economy, to endow them with a limited number of privileges and rely on their enterprise to give the country its initial economic 'take-off'. This was done, and results on the whole justified the Company's expectations. Rhodesia had a low population density; its indigenous people possessed little physical or social capital. White farmers had more cash and skill than tribal Africans; many immigrants gradually began to improve their holdings with dips and dams and boreholes; they put up windbreaks, gradually got used to the practice of green manuring their land and thereby improved its fertility. Farmers of that kind stood a better chance of unlocking the country's wealth than slash-and-burn cultivators who changed their ways slowly, and for long thought in terms of group rather than individual achievement. The Commissioners were also right in assuming that the tribes as a whole still had enough land, even though local shortages were already beginning to appear and the whole system of land allocation was designed to favour immigrant farmers.

Nevertheless the Chartered Company might perhaps have done more to hasten change amongst the indigenous people. Africans could and did learn. In the late 'nineties, for instance, the authorities imported improved bulls for distribution to black men at cost price. Native purchasers bought the lot, but then East Coast Fever stopped further importation, and the constant cry for economy prevented further experiments. A few years later Valdemar Gielgud, then in charge of the Sebungwe-Mafungabusi district, reported that the people in his area were growing Nyoka (Inyoka) tobacco. If only the Government would train a few intelligent youngsters to prepare leaf for sale, the natives might find a ready-made cash crop. The Chief Secretary, however, showed no interest. The Government could not provide tuition, and the best way for Africans to improve their knowledge was to take service with European tobacco growers[1]—a proposal which, like some 'liberal' suggestions of a later vintage, confused the purpose of a farm with that of a training school for the backward! The Company's own Director of Agriculture complained that the Administration lacked a policy with regard to African farming,[2] whilst lack of funds and staff proved an ever-present obstacle.

This of course did not mean that there was no change. Some intelligent chiefs like Gambo—himself an important cattle owner—had boreholes sunk at his own expense in the Nata Reserve. African cultivators in certain parts of the country began to use the white man's plough, a revolutionary innovation that relieved women of their age-old drudgery in the fields by putting men on the job. The plough allowed Africans to bring much more land under cultivation than before, even though its indiscriminate use might also cause far more damage to the soil than the old-fashioned hoe. Some Africans also began to buy carts; the villagers got more used to selling their surplus crops, and to the idea that better qualities of grain would command higher prices. But change was slow; by and large the tribesmen preferred the old accustomed ways; whilst the very shifts and changes in reserve policy helped to discourage innovation.

At the same time the reserves gradually had to accommodate more

---

[1] Chief Secretary to Chief Native Commissioner, Bulawayo: 27 Nov 1906 (in NGB 2/3/1, Nat Arch SR)

[2] E. Nobbs (memorandum): 5 Nov 1914 (in G 1/1/1, Nat Arch SR)

people. The more progressive white landowners began to look askance at those of their neighbours who went in for 'kaffir-farming', that is to say who allowed Africans to live on their land in exchange for rents—a system profitable for absentee landlords or estate companies. Tenant farming led to some bitter disputes between farmers and their African retainers who complained at having to pay too much. The native tenant found himself in a difficult position, for the reserves were not centrally placed and in many cases quite unsuitable for the purpose of accommodating more Africans, who—in any case—preferred to stay where they were. 'The root of the whole matter of the natives moving from one part of the district to another continually, and from one district to another is this question of land rents,' commented the Native Commissioner for Inyati, and since the Government could not interfere with the citizens' liberty of contract, there was only one solution. The number of huts on any one farm should be limited, the Government should provide unalienated land for Africans, whilst landowners not complying with their occupation clauses should not be allowed to charge rent.[1] The Chief Native Commissioner also agreed that some landlords were taking advantage of their tenants' ignorance to extort rackrents, and suggested that agreements should be made in writing before the Native Commissioners so as to prevent injustice. The Government passed an ordinance which did away with the worst abuses. 'Private locations' from now on required the Administrator's approval; landlords had to conclude their agreements with tenants in writing, in the Native Commissioner's presence, and Native Commissioners acquired the right to inspect locations. The law likewise limited the number of tenants who might live on any one farm, and in addition the ordinance imposed a kind of differential tax upon 'kaffir farmers', that is to say landlords who did not actually work their own land.[2]

The law did not, however, attempt to set a 'ceiling' on rents; nor was kaffir-farming abolished. The pressure on rural Africans to some extent even increased, for the Chartered Company itself began to charge rent for natives living on unalienated land. To the Directors this was simply another way of legitimately raising revenue. Wilson Fox privately wrote to Milton that the new impost had nothing to do with the labour question; it did not aim at driving the natives to work. In fact, thought Fox, it would be much more likely to make Africans grow more crops for sale, thereby promoting native agricultural production.[3] But villagers in the

---

[1] Native Commissioner, Inyati, to Chief Native Commissioner, Bulawayo: 25 Sep 1906 (in A 3/21/53, Nat Arch SR)

[2] Private locations ordinance, 1908

[3] H. W. Fox to Sir W. H. Milton: 9 Mar 1906 (in A 1/5/7, Nat Arch SR)

backveld could hardly be expected to grasp this subtle distinction; rates varying from 10/- to £1 per hut appeared to them as another kind of tax —one which they might only escape by moving into the reserves.

The settlement of the urban 'native problem' was similar to the solution proposed for the countryside. In the early days, when life was hard and the European townships themselves little more than slovenly collections of rough huts, nobody cared very much about how Africans lived in these settlements, or where they put up their flimsy shelters. The white men themselves were experiencing the toughest possible conditions; typhoid fever and malaria were common; sanitary facilities remained primitive; and many people would simply empty their slop water out on to their own stands, or litter the sanitary lanes with refuse. Salisbury, the capital, was itself but a big, sprawling 'dorp' in the backveld; most of the streets were covered in dust that blew across the settlement in summertime, causing hay fever and throat troubles; whilst heavy, slushy, red mud would cling to the boots of passers-by when the rains started pouring down.

As the country became a little more prosperous conditions slowly began to improve. In 1905 the Salisbury City Council adopted bye-laws to minimize overcrowding; four years the Mayor reported that:

'. . . Second Street, from the Northern Commonage to the Railway Station, a distance of one and a quarter miles, has been built and made a good hard road, and a culvert near Livingstone Avenue has been constructed to carry off the storm water. All the material for the construction of Manica Road has been transported to convenient situations along this road which is now in course of construction. It is then the intention to complete the portion of Moffat Street, from Jameson Avenue to Manica Road, and then when Moffat Street and Second Street have been linked up there will be one good hard road right round the town.'

Towards the end of the decade the municipalities began to view the typhoid question from a more realistic angle and took steps to provide pure piped water. In 1913 Lady Milton opened the first of Salisbury's dams, an event which the *Rhodesia Herald* of the day described quite rightly as 'one of the most important and interesting' events of the period, and as time went on Salisbury developed into a quiet, pleasant, country town with tree-lined streets, and a well laid out public garden.

As urban conditions improved, the white public became more conscious of the 'native problem', and demanded that Africans living in towns should be better supervised, either by their employers if in white domestic service, or by the municipality. The legal machinery was there, for as early as 1894 a Towns Management Ordinance conferred powers on Sanitary Boards to set up and control locations. At first, however, many local authorities remained lax in doing their job, and practice varied widely throughout the country. In 1905 the Administration finally decided to act, and brought in an Urban Locations Ordinance, modelled on Cape lines. In drafting the law the Administration did not think in terms of any segregational theories; they did not argue that Africans should develop on their own lines, but simply viewed the question as a public health matter. The Ordinance—the Administrator explained—really aimed at dealing with the Salisbury municipal location, over which the municipality exercised no legal powers, since the compound was not situated within its boundaries. The Government proposed therefore to transfer control of locations to municipalities, where they existed, and provide these with adequate powers, whilst at the same time making practice throughout the country more uniform. The Imperial Government quite agreed with these provisions, though it delayed assenting to the bill until the appointment of location inspectors was made subject to the Secretary of State's approval.[1] The new ordinance empowered the Administrator to define the limits of locations and make rules for the way in which they should be run. 'No native . . .', added the law, 'may reside within the municipal or other prescribed area, within or near which he may labour or reside, save and except within the area of the location established . . . by such notice.' Africans living beyond the limits of such locations could be removed from their dwellings; the only exceptions were domestic and other servants living on their employers' premises, or Africans who received a special exemption. Persons not entitled to live within the location could be thrown out, the entire legislation being based on the assumption that Africans would continue to remain what they were —migrant labourers with no permanent stake in the township.

Within its limits the locations legislation succeeded in its object. Municipal inspectors performed a good job; infectious disease in the townships—a standing threat to white and black men alike—was reduced. At the same time, however, the new law also led to friction, as Africans living in the locations began to feel irked by municipal government. Some complained at the quality of the 'kaffir beer' provided in their canteens; others objected to municipal measures against illicit beer-brewing or demanded that beer should also be supplied on Sundays. Many Africans protested at the amount of rent they were being charged. The cost-of-living problem became more serious, as the workers' wants increased and as locations became larger, with the result that free 'perks', like dead wood from the commonage, became more difficult to get.

---

[1] Southern Rhodesia. *Legislative Council debates*, 27 Apr 1905, p. 4–5; 28 Apr 1905, p. 10–11; 15 May 1906, p. 6. The Native urban locations ordinance, 1906, was promulgated in the same year.

Urbanization also involved African townsmen in more complex social conflicts of which the Administration hardly seems to have been aware. For instance the spirits of the dead cannot, according to Mashona belief, be successfully contacted without ritual beer, which could no longer be brewed in town. Neither could a Zezuru labourer sacrifice a bull or goat in his location, for such an offering would offend against municipal bye-laws and quickly land the faithful in gaol. In addition of course black townsfolk faced the same personal problems which worried Europeans; there were few women in the township, and harlots began to prey on white men and black. But whereas Europeans at any rate could bring in their wives freely, black newcomers required special permission; besides, the tribal elders objected to the exodus of village girls to the town; the traditional place of a Bantu woman was on the land, where she had an accepted status which she lacked in the city.

Friction accordingly seems to have developed from a fairly early date. In 1913 the Administration authorized a Native Department official to inspect the Salisbury Native Location and enquire into local complaints. But agitation did not diminish; local grievances culminated in a demand, advanced by Salisbury Africans in 1919, that they should be allowed to scrutinize draft bye-laws affecting black people, and protest if necessary to the Government.[1] Urbanization with its losses and gains had come to stay.

VI

An expanding mission field

In the history of religion the nineteenth century stands out as an age of paradox. On the one hand the era saw a concentric assault on all established religious creeds, more thorough-going and better conceived than any launched in the past. On the extreme left of the political spectrum stood Karl Marx, who taught that the light of religion was but a pale reflection of a given system of economic production and social relationships. The working classes did not need God, and once the revolutionary proletariat had established their dictatorship, the toiling masses would hurl the Almighty Himself from His throne. On the extreme right stood Friedrich Nietzsche who denounced the morality of the herd and the creed of slaves

---

[1] Chief Native Commissioner to Salisbury Municipality: 4 Jan 1919 (in N 3/20/2, Nat Arch SR). Salisbury Municipality for its part argued that much of the trouble arose from people who illicitly brewed or sold beer, and that illicit brewing must be repressed. The Council had no objection to Africans being informed of contemplated amendments of bye-laws, but could not undertake always to accept their point of view.

and exalted the Superman, joyous in his unfettered strength, ready to bend the weak to his will. But he too believed, like the Communists, that God was dead and man must find a substitute to take His place. Between these two extremes were moderate men like Thomas Henry Huxley who questioned traditional religion from the standpoint of experimental scientific method and an empiricist philosophy, which played an even greater part in weakening traditional systems of faith. Scepticism or out-right unbelief became an accepted part of the ideological scene. At the same time many secular thinkers proclaimed the optimistic creed that either the whole of mankind, or a particular section of it—the proletarians, the Nordics, or some other élite—were fundamentally good, and did not therefore need the creaking crutches of religion. Gradually these views seeped through to a wider public, and as they became popular the churches lost much of their hold.

Yet at a time in history when so many prophets foresaw that religion was on its way out, Christianity gained an almost unparalleled access of new strength. Theologians of various schools tried to reformulate their creeds in the light of current intellectual challenges. Simultaneously the Churches embarked on a world-wide crusade which promised to make up for their losses in Europe by new conquests overseas; European and American evangelists became fired by a profound enthusiasm that found an echo amongst their supporters, whilst the missionaries' determination and often their heroism revealed untapped resources of spiritual strength which sceptics often failed to grasp. The age that sent white explorers and prospectors, traders and soldiers of fortune, miners and civil servants to the remotest corners of the world, also witnessed a similar outburst of ecclesiastical pioneering, and at the time the Union Jack went up over Fort Salisbury, this great wave of missionary endeavour was still rolling ahead.

Rhodes shared the missionaries' outlook in some ways. A Darwinian rather than a Christian, he acted on the creed that a good business man like himself might safely gamble on a fifty-fifty chance of God's existence, and that in any case the missions had a major part to play in opening up the Dark Continent. Rhodes likewise thought in terms of 'Commerce and Christianity'; he too claimed Livingstone's heritage, and backed his belief with generous land grants to various societies. Southern Rhodesia there-fore became one of the last great new mission fields in Southern Africa, where older and newer bodies alike moved in to stake out competing claims.

Catholic priests again played an important part in the country's early pioneering history. Andrew Hartmann and Peter Prestage, two Jesuit

Fathers, accompanied the Pioneer Column, and until 1896 Catholic organization in Southern Rhodesia came under the Society of Jesus, subsequently falling to the charge of a Prefect Apostolic. Dominican sisters, led by Mother Patrick (Mary Patrick Cosgrave), an outstanding Irishwoman who took the veil at the age of seventeen, put up the first hospital in Salisbury in 1891. A year later Jesuit Fathers set up a mission at Chishawasha, on a large unoccupied tract near Salisbury. Lacking financial resources, the Jesuits tried to make each one of their houses self-sufficient, and they developed a great 14,000-acre farm there. The Fathers concentrated on agricultural and industrial rather than literary training, everyone, white or black alike, doing his share of physical labour. 'They work like clockwork . . .' later wrote an agricultural expert, and 'the result is that the whole farm of Chishawasha is a garden'. There were bananas, apples, oranges, mealies, potatoes and wheat, and, the writer concluded enthusiastically, 'as pioneers of civilization in savage countries, the sons of St Inigo Lopez de Recalde have no equal.'[1] Chishawasha in fact resembled in some ways a kind of Paraguayan 'reduction' in miniature; the Fathers governed with a firm hand and successfully resisted an attack during the Rebellion. In Bulawayo a second mission came into existence in 1894 after the Matabele War, when the collapse of the Matabele military state at last permitted effective religious penetration.

The London Missionary Society had rather similar experiences. It continued its work in Matabeleland, commenced in 1859, and shared the vicissitudes of white pioneering there. Helm in the early days thought that 'we shall never do much good in Matabeleland until the Matabele have had a lesson', though he hoped that the British would enter such a war with clean hands.[2] He believed that war was inevitable, and when it had happened he doubted allegations that the Company had forced the fighting on the Matabele at a time convenient to the 'Charter', which in fact had not wanted a collision with Lobengula for another two or three years.[3] The mission suffered heavily in the Rebellion, but once armed conflict was over the white evangelists' chances improved dramatically. Interference from the Matabele tribal authorities came to an end, and the missionaries felt jubilant at the breakdown of what they regarded as a bloodthirsty tyranny. 'For the first time,' reported the Society, 'the natives are having a taste of real freedom. They are free to wear European clothing instead of skins, free to work and hold the proceeds of their labour, free to attend

---

[1] Thomas, O. *Agricultural and pastoral prospects of South Africa*. Archibald Constable and co. ltd, 1904, p. 250–251
[2] C. D. Helm to R. W. Thompson: 9 Oct 1893 (in LO 6/1/5, Nat Arch MS)
[3] C. D. Helm to R. W. Thompson:12 Jan 1894 (in LO 6/1/5, Nat Arch MS)

worship and to send their children to school.' Admittedly many of the white newcomers were nothing but unprincipled adventurers who set a bad example, but no one could complain about the Chartered Company's treatment of the native people. The natives were adapting themselves to the new conditions, and as soon as they realized the old days would not come back, many bought ploughs and some bought wagons.[1]

The Society received various farms as part of the Company's general land policy. The missions at Hope Fountain and Inyati each obtained about 4,000 morgen, whilst Bulalima station became the centre of a vast mission tract, nine miles long from north to south and about three miles across from east to west. The L.M.S. clergyman on his station became a new kind of chief; he alone now had the right to say who might live on the land, with the right to eject any person or village whose 'disorderly conduct or persistent carelessness in cultivation, or refusal to send their children to school, made him feel that they are not desirable tenants'.[2]

The emissaries of the Gospel thus received enormous physical powers over their flock, though they scrupulously abstained from forcing un-believers to attend church services, and allowed their tenants to run their own village affairs—subject always, of course, to European Christian ideas of orderly behaviour and sobriety. At the same time, however, the missionaries had a check on their own freedom of action, brought about by the new concept of private property in land which they themselves helped to bring into the country. In the olden days they could roam as they pleased on their preaching tours. Now freedom of movement de-pended on the goodwill of neighbouring white farmers. Later on the movement of Africans into the reserves forced them to extend their field of evangelization into out-of-the-way regions like the Shangani Reserve where work began in 1913. Some stations had to be abandoned, and new ones set up, the problem of readjustment sometimes being made more difficult by internal disputes within the Society.

The Anglican Church had also tried to spread the Gospel in 'Zambezia' before the Company's arrival, and as early as 1876 the Rev. W. Green-stock, a clergyman from Port Elizabeth, made his way to Lobengula's capital. But trouble in the Transvaal brought this project to naught, and the Anglicans did not resume their efforts until 1888 when George Wyndham Hamilton Knight-Bruce made an adventurous journey to the Zambezi. Knight-Bruce, an Eton and Oxford man, first of all worked in the London East End, one of those many idealistic clergymen who in

[1] L.M.S. Report of 1895, quoted in Lovett, R. The history of the London Missionary Society, 1795–1895. Henry Frowde, 1899, v. 1, p. 631
[2] London Missionary Society. Report of the deputation to South Africa, January to March, 1898. Printed by Alexander and Shepheard, 1898, p. 25

o

certain ways tended to equate service to the 'internal proletariat' and the 'external proletariat' of Western society. Later on he accepted the almost bankrupt episcopal See of Bloemfontein, in the heart of a Dutch Republic, for which no applicants could be found, but his heart still remained in mission work in the Far Interior. In 1891 Knight-Bruce took over the newly founded missionary bishopric of Mashonaland, and in the same year work began at St Augustine's mission, Penhalonga, in the Eastern Districts. Knight-Bruce believed in a policy of taking over as much land as he could, arguing that the mission blocks could later serve as native areas if the Mashona ever got crowded out by white men, but his ideas were rather grandiose. He did not prove an easy man to work with, and also made the common error of dispersing his Church's efforts over too many small and undermanned stations.[1] In addition the Anglican clergymen had to carry out a considerable amount of European pastoral work, not an easy job in a tough pioneering community, where the whole of Umtali on one occasion was shut up lock, stock and barrel, because it had collectively gone 'on a binge' and was too drunk to carry on business.[2] Knight-Bruce retired in 1894 and died four years later, worn out by fever and hardships, but under his successors the mission gradually consolidated its position. In William Thomas Gaul, Edmund Nathaniel Powell and Frederick Hicks Beaven the Anglicans had fine bishops. Work expanded greatly; new stations opened their doors, and the Anglican Church, though never the Established Church as in England, became a powerful community, wielding considerable influence on Government, and probably enjoying a higher social status than any of the other mission bodies in the country.

The wave of missionary enthusiasm that sent so many British clergymen to convert the heathen overseas also affected most countries in Western and Central Europe. In Prussia evangelically-minded people in 1824 founded the Berlin Missionary Society (properly the 'Gesellschaft zur Beförderung der Evangelischen Missionen unter den Heiden') which began work in South Africa in 1834, pushing forward its sphere of influence to the Transvaal in 1860. During the course of the 'eighties the Society promoted a number of missionary journeys to Mashonaland and, after the Chartered Company had taken over the territory, the Germans decided to carry out permanent evangelical work beyond the Limpopo. In 1892 the Rev. C. Beuster, together with two other Europeans, set out for the north to start a station at Gutu's. Sickness, however, prevented further expansion and partly for financial, partly for administrative reasons, the Society in 1907 decided to abandon its sphere of work in

---

[1] D. R. Pelly to Canon and Mrs R. P. Pelly: 14 July 1892 (in PE 3/1/1, Nat Arch MS)
[2] D. R. Pelly to Canon and Mrs R. P. Pelly: 20 Nov 1892 (in PE 3/1/1, Nat Arch MS)

Mashonaland, and made over its interests to the Dutch Reformed Church. The Afrikaners in the meantime had also done their share of ecclesiastical pioneering in the country. Earlier in the nineteenth century the fire of evangelical enthusiasm burnt low on the backveld, for the Afrikaans-speaking farmers who made up the overwhelming majority of the Dutch Reformed Church did not feel much enthusiasm for the idea of converting their native servants and neighbours. Besides there were few ordained ministers. The Boer states were still academically too undeveloped to afford adequate training facilities, and Presbyterian clergymen even had to be brought in from abroad, from Holland and Scotland, to work for the Dutch Reformed Church in the lonely dorps inland. Gradually, however, missionary enthusiasm waxed stronger, especially after the first Transvaal War, when the Afrikaners became more conscious of their language and nationality. The main impulse initially came from the *predikants* who, though many of them might be of non-South African origin, like the Rev. Andrew Murray, a great missionary pioneer, completely identified themselves with their flock and its culture. Dutch Reformed clergymen in 1886 formed a Predikant Mission Union. Its members, though poorly paid themselves, agreed to contribute a fixed sum to the good work. The movement gradually gained support amongst the laity and further backing came after the great spiritual and national upsurge that emerged from the misery of the Boer War and its aftermath.[1]

Dutch Reformed missionaries in the Zoutpansberg had for long been interested in carrying the Gospel to the Far North. But Lobengula did not like the idea of European missionaries teaching in the 'Banyai' country, within his sphere of influence, and expansion only became possible after the Chartered occupation. Helm inspected the country on behalf of the Dutch, and in 1891 a religious trek set out for Mashonaland, led by the Rev. A. A. Louw. Nine ox-wagons rolled inland; after two months the party reached the Zimbabwe Ruins, in whose vicinity Louw set up Morgenster, the 'Morning Star' mission.

In addition to the followers of Calvin, the disciples of John Wesley made an important contribution to the evangelization of Southern Rhodesia. The earliest Methodists in Southern Africa were plain British dragoons who went out to the Cape during the Napoleonic Wars. As time went on the Wesleyans expanded their influence, a great impact being made by the Rev. William Shaw who accompanied the 1820 Settlers, the

---

[1] See Cronjé, J. M. *En daar was lig: die sending van die Ned. Geref. Kerk in die O.V.S. na Noord-en Suid-Rhodesië, gedurende die jare 1899–1947.* Bloemfontein, Algemene sendingskommissie van die N. G. Kerk in die O.V.S., 1948; Du Plessis, J. *The life of Andrew Murray of South Africa.* Marshall brothers limited, 1920; and Du Plessis, J. *A history of Christian missions in South Africa.* Longmans, Green and co., 1911

first large body of British emigrants to go to the Cape. Later on in the century the Methodists gained a foothold in the Transvaal which soon became a base for further northward penetration. Rhodes thought highly of the Methodists and offered them a small grant, if only they would come to work within the Chartered Company's sphere of influence. In 1891 Owen Watkins and Isaac Shimmin, two Methodist clergymen, left Good Hope in the Transvaal, and a year later the first Methodist Church opened its doors at Salisbury. In addition Wesleyans began to work amongst local Africans, making extensive use of black teachers recruited from the south who were posted to outstations. Two teachers took up residence at Hartleyton in the Lomagundi area, another couple at Epworth, on a farm presented to the Methodists by the Company, and after the Matabele War the Society pushed forward its work into Matabeleland.[1] Very soon the Rev. John White became the dominant figure of Rhodesian Methodism. An excellent linguist and administrator, White made himself extremely unpopular amongst members of his own race for his outspokenness, becoming the most influential of Rhodesian 'Negrophilists'. A contemporary cartoon indeed once showed him with a smile on his face and a pot of paint and a brush in his hands, daubing an African all over, and promising the man: 'However black you are, my friend, I'll whitewash you!' White, however, made a very considerable impact on the mission scene, and having been appointed head of the local organization in 1901, exerted great influence on mission work for the next quarter of a century.

Another important body was the Methodist Episcopal Church, an American denomination which adopted the more conservative principles of episcopal government. Towards the end of the last century the Church began to embark on an aggressive missionary policy under the guidance of Bishop William Taylor who planned to take Africa by storm in a great crusade which he hoped to base on a system of self-sufficient missions. Taylor, however, did not prove a good staff officer, and the mission did not prosper until his successor, Joseph C. Hartzell, reorganized the system, abandoning the principle of self-support. Hartzell began work in Portuguese East Africa, and subsequently founded an important new mission field in the Eastern Districts of Southern Rhodesia. When the Chartered Company decided to move the township of Umtali to the railway line, Hartzell quickly stepped in, asking to take over the abandoned site of Old Umtali, together with 6,000 morgen of ground. The Chartered Company consented and from 1898 Old Umtali became an important centre of evangelization.

[1] Whiteside, J. *History of the Wesleyan Methodist church of South Africa.* Elliot Stock, 1906, p. 461–474

In the meantime some of Hartzell's compatriots had already started work in Mashonaland under the auspices of the American Board of Commissioners for Foreign Missions, the oldest foreign missionary society in the United States. In 1893 the American Board received an offer from Rhodes to provide land for missionary work and in the same year a mission party settled down at Mount Selinda among the Ndau people, close to the Mozambique border. The missionaries for a time met with counterclaims for land from other European settlers, but the Americans held their own and in 1895 Chikore, a second station, was opened west of Mount Selinda. Other ecclesiastical pioneers included the Salvation Army, who in 1892 began to work amongst Africans in the Mazoe valley, and the Seventh Day Adventists who set up a station at Solusi near Bulawayo in 1894.

The end of the Rebellion saw the end of the heroic period in the country's missionary history. Life became safer; work slowly assumed a more routine character, and the administrator's skill became more important. At the same time evangelization vastly increased in scope, as more volunteers came in, and additional societies, ranging from as far afield as Britain, Sweden and South Africa, set up new centres. Some of the remoter areas, Nyamandhlovu, Wankie and Sebungwe—as large as Scotland in the aggregate—remained little touched by evangelical work, but elsewhere a network of stations and outstations, dispensaries, central teaching institutions and bush schools spread through the country, completely transforming the rural scene. The missions emerged as a major force, whilst Chartered generosity assured them of great areas of land, whose extent found few parallels in other parts of Africa.[1]

The missionaries' first task was to preach the Gospel, and this immediately raised the question of what evangelical strategy they should adopt. 'No man putteth a piece of new cloth unto an old garment,' taught Jesus, 'for that which is put in to fill it up taketh from the garment, and the rent is made worse. Neither do men put new wine into old bottles; else the bottles break, and the wine runneth out, and the bottles perish: but they put new wine into new bottles, and both are preserved.'[2] Late Victorian and Edwardian missionaries took this injunction very seriously, and interpreted their Saviour's words in such a fashion as to try and bring about a complete change in the old Africa. The tribesmen's ways must change in root and branch, and what the white preachers aimed for was not 'reformism', but a complete ideological revolution.

But this proved a tremendously difficult job, much harder than they

[1] By 1925 the missions between them owned a total of 325,815 acres. See Smith, E. W. *The way of the white fields in Rhodesia. . . .* World dominion press, 1928. In appendices 3 and 4 Smith gives detailed tables illustrating the missionary occupation of the country.

[2] St Matthew, ch. 9, v. 16–17

imagined. Christians like Prestage and White alike conceived of the universe as a place both divinely and rationally ordered, guided by a God both immanent in and transcending the world. Before God all souls were equal; all men could reach Him through prayer; all had to stand before His judgement seat. God wanted a pure heart—not the traditional burnt offerings made by the Children of Israel; he punished a man for his own transgressions—not for the sins of his kinsmen. Moral law flowed from the Deity who revealed himself in history—at Mount Sinai and Golgotha. The Christian concept of the world entailed some kind of progress, even if only from the Old Covenant to the New, though of course most Victorian missionaries took this belief in progress a great deal further than their ancestors, tending to link their creed in the step-by-step revelation of God with a more down-to-earth faith in what they regarded as the inevitability of human progress. The missionaries' world at the same time was one of spiritual battles and prayers, of mental strife—a world where man went forward or slipped back—a universe of intense individual endeavour.

The Mashona universe was a very different place. Tribal or tutelary spirits governed particular areas and spoke through specially designated mediums. The spirits made particular demands on the members of their group, and if transgressors offended through loathsome crimes like incest or murder, the whole group must accept supernatural punishment. Lower down the hierarchy, ancestral spirits would watch over their children and grandchildren in the villages, both tribal and ancestral spirits standing for a traditional order of society that resisted change, and extolled the accepted norms of the community. The Mashona admired neither sinners nor saints; they just wished to follow in their parents' footsteps. The man who diverged from normality was liable to be called a wizard and killed. All misfortunes, inexplicable in terms of ordinary natural causation, were regarded as the result of witchcraft. In this kind of world there was no room for giants like Jacob who would dare to wrestle with the Angel, or like Faust, challenge the Devil to gain perfect and everlasting happiness. Africans of course also believed in a supreme God, but the Deity was so remote that there was no point in praying to Him directly, and He could only be reached through the good offices of his ghostly intermediaries.

Missionaries and their fellow whites—whether Christians or sceptics—threw down the gauntlet to spirits and spirit mediums, as well as to the whole social order which hinged upon this ancient faith. The spirits for their part fought back savagely. Mediums played a decisive role in organizing the Rebellion—a battle waged by tribalism against Western enterprise and an individualist concept of life. The Europeans in turn also looked upon the war as a religious conflict. 'The witch-doctors', white men would grimly say over the camp fire, 'are at the bottom of it all,' regarding native medicinemen as creatures unspeakably vile and depraved, whose baneful influence must be utterly destroyed before the country could have peace once more. Spirit mediums remained suspect to Native Commissioners and missionaries alike, the *mondoro* being regarded as possible leaders of new subversive outbreaks. The spirit mediums' cult, nevertheless, continued to flourish underground, its survival being made easier by spiritual decentralization whereby the head *mondoro* of each totem clan ruled his region with little regard to what was happening in neighbouring areas.[1]

The white preachers took up the battle and tried to spread the Faith through example and sermons, and also by employing black intermediaries; these comprised teachers and evangelists who lived apart from their own communities, but knew how to spread the word of God in a language and terminology which other black men could understand. The extent to which pioneer missionaries utilized these 'middlemen' differed considerably; the South African Methodists brought in a fair number from the start, whereas the Jesuits, unmarried men sworn to poverty and obedience, an unpaid though highly efficient ecclesiastical labour force, relied initially on their own efforts alone.

Nevertheless these African evangelists played an important part in the country's religious life right from the start; more trained preachers, in the same way as skilled drivers and drill-men, came in from the south to help in the white man's work. Perhaps the best known of them all was Bernard Mitzeki, a native of southern Mozambique. Mitzeki made his first acquaintance with white men through itinerant traders and in the early 1880's went to Cape Town to find work. He gained acceptance as a scholar in St Philip's mission, an Anglican institution in Cape Town, and then graduated to Zonnebloem Native College for further training. When Knight-Bruce decided to work in Mashonaland in 1891, Mitzeki volunteered to accompany the Bishop and settled down as catechist in the territory of chief Mangwendi, near Rusape, also giving valuable aid in producing a local translation of parts of the Prayer Book and New Testament. Mitzeki wedded a grand-daughter of Mangwendi's, but his marriage did not save him when Mangwendi's people took to arms in 1896. His wife was spared, but he himself was cut down by Mangwendi's sons, one of the first African martyrs to die in Southern Rhodesia. In addition to Mitzeki several other Africans also gave their lives for the new

[1] See Gelfand, M. *Shona religion*. . . . Cape Town, Juta and company, 1962

religion. A Methodist teacher at Nungubo by the name of Molele, hearing that a farmer in the vicinity had been attacked by rebels, inspanned two oxen to his wagon, and set out to rescue the Englishman. He managed to lift the badly wounded man to his cart, but having got to within two hundred yards of his own house, was attacked by a party of hostiles, who killed them both; the rebels then shot two of Molele's children, leaving his wife battered and senseless on the ground. Anta, a Methodist teacher at Hartleyton, the son of a chief in Cape Colony, and once a well-known hunter, was also slain, and with him all the men on his station who bravely refused to give him up.[1]

Once the fighting ended spiritual resistance collapsed like its military equivalent; traditional institutions tended to fall into some disrepute amongst Africans, especially in Mashonaland where so many chiefs and spirit mediums were compromised by the Rebellion. Tribal creeds could not so easily adjust themselves to conditions in cities or mines; the *mondoro* did not rule in Salisbury as in out-of-the-way villages, whilst the Christian God could be worshipped anywhere, under any sky. Paganism moreover lacked flexibility. A great Jewish teacher like Rabbi Gershom ben Jehuda of Mainz could decree in the early Middle Ages that polygamy must henceforth cease amongst his people exiled in Europe; but no sage and no synedrion of spirit mediums could ever make similar changes for their own society. The Christians, moreover, brought organized knowledge, the very thing which Africans now began to want. 'The natives who have been taught reading and writing in mission stations pass their knowledge on to others of their tribe, and these again spread it further,' wrote a Chartered official just over ten years after the end of the Rebellion. 'Pass by the huts of a mining camp at night, and from many sides you may hear words of two or three letters spelt out from an English spelling book. On a Sunday boys may be seen basking in the sunshine outside their huts, learning words from the same books; and where a few years ago there was but a single spelling book in a camp, today there are a dozen or more.'[2]

The churches almost right from the start turned to teaching, a prominent missionary estimating that 'probably ninety per cent of the Christians have come into the Church by way of the school',[3] the missions in other words pioneered the country's educational system for Africans and, until 1920, it remained entirely in their hands. The Administration supported the missions in a small way. The country's first Education Ordinance in 1899 provided for limited grants to mission

[1] Whiteside, J. *History of the Wesleyan Methodist church of South Africa.* Elliot Stock, 1906, p. 469–470
[2] Hone, P. *Southern Rhodesia.* George Bell and son, 1909, p. 80–81
[3] Smith, E. W. *The way of the white fields in Rhodesia.* World dominion press, 1928, p. 153

schools, on condition that industrial training would form part of their work. In 1906 the missionary societies held their first general conference, and as the result of their recommendations a new ordinance in 1907 divided schools into three classes for the purpose of making grants according to the work accomplished. The Administration at first did not exercise any legal control over 'non-grant earning schools'. But soon the authorities began to get worried about the setting up of 'independent' African schools; in 1912 the Chartered Company tried to halt the formation of little bodies with odd religious teachings, low academic standards and social revolutionary sentiments by prohibiting the setting up of new schools without permission from the Director of Education, whose staff could inspect educational establishments, and if necessary, close them altogether.

At the same time the African schoolmaster became an important personage throughout many native areas. As early as 1898 the Wesleyans paid one or two of their teachers as much as £5 a month, a princely salary for those days, which placed its recipient well above the aristocracy of native labour.[1] But the normal thing was to provide teachers, except those of the most advanced class, with gardens in addition to their salaries, so that they might grow sufficient food for their families, an arrangement which still left black schoolmasters in the dual position of being half academic workers and half peasants.

Evangelical work in turn entailed linguistic pioneering. The Christians, whatever their denominational differences, came as the 'people of the Book'; they brought literacy to communities that had never evolved the art of writing. The Christians moreover attached supreme importance to the word of God, as written down in the Bible; their hymns and prayers were passed on through books rather than by word of mouth. Missionaries therefore began to compile grammars and dictionaries; they translated the Scriptures, hymn books and devotional works into native tongues.[2] There were various vicissitudes; the Rev. T. M. Thomas, for instance, produced a translation of the New Testament into Sindebele, but most copies fell into the hands of Lobengula's warriors during the Matabele War, and ended up as head-dresses! In addition some of the translators committed errors, whilst the range of the reading material provided remained small. But missionaries nevertheless were the first to reduce the local languages to writing, thereby laying the earliest foundations of an indigenous literature, whilst Bible stories and biblical names became part of the popular African heritage.

[1] London Missionary Society. *Report of the deputation to South Africa, January to March, 1898.* Printed by Alexander and Shepheard, 1898, p. 28

[2] See Doke, C. M. *Report on the unification of the Shona dialects.* (CSR. 25–1930), p. 119–135, for lists of linguistic work produced in Southern Rhodesia up to 1929.

The end effect of all this work is not easy to gauge. The first decade of the present century onwards saw a rise in the number of conversions, and Christians became quite a substantial element of the African population.[1] God alone of course knows how many of these people were sincere; many were but 'rice Christians' eager to learn the white man's intellectual techniques, but not interested in his creed. Western ideas of sexual morality made only slow progress and mission literature of the time is full of outbursts even against schoolmasters and catechists, trusted men who fell into 'sinning' and 'backsliding'. Many European colonists—some of them anti-clerical at heart—spoke out a good deal more frankly, and complaints about lying, thieving 'mission boys' became common in the press. Some converts—wanderers between two worlds, and at home in neither—may indeed have justly deserved censure. But the missions also produced people like Mitzeki, whose personal courage stood unsurpassed, and who presumably could have saved his own life by apostasy.

Critics of a more modern vintage have blamed the early missionaries for failing to understand their flock's religious heritage, and for refusing to graft Christianity on existing concepts of African spirituality. Christians as well as pagans agree that the souls of a man's ancestors survive; the idea that the spirits of the dead still take an active interest in the doings of the living is not in itself opposed to the Gospel. The Jesuits in China faced a similar problem and at one time attempted to integrate ancestor worship within a system of Christian beliefs—yet no ecclesiastical pioneer attempted a similar synthesis in Rhodesia. But it would have been asking for the impossible at this period of Rhodesian history. Frontier clergymen at first lacked the requisite knowledge. As time went on, and a better understanding of African life became possible, some missionaries, like Father Prestage in Matabeleland, did try to get to grips with indigenous thought, though Prestage himself concluded that fear of the ancestors and the attendant mystique of the spirit-mediums was so strong that Christians could not build on these foundations. Besides, the clerical climate of opinion differed greatly from that of today. An analytical frame of mind and a permissive outlook do not flourish on the frontier; they are the products of affluent cities. Early evangelists—black or white—took their lives into their hands by going out to the Far North; they did not go to analyse, synthesize or apologize, they went to fight Satan and all his works; they took risks because they believed they were fighting evil, and evil brooked no compromise. To some extent they may have been mis-

[1] Exact figures are hard to obtain, as the mission societies used differing statistical standards, and often found themselves under an obligation to paint a somewhat rosy picture. Smith, E. W. *The way of the white fields in Rhodesia, op. cit,* a reliable work, estimates that there were 86,000 Christian Africans in the country by 1928.

taken, but modern critics, working under very different conditions, should at least seek the same kind of unbiased understanding for the concepts of the Moffats and Moleles which anthropologists adopt for those of Mashona spirit mediums!

The missionaries' educational work has since come in for similar criticism. Standards varied vastly from station to station, and much of the teaching remained inferior. Black schoolmasters—in out-of-the-way bush schools—barely advanced beyond literacy themselves and did not possess much knowledge to pass on. The mission societies always found themselves short of industrial and agricultural instructors, and backward African communities could absorb only a limited amount of training. Victorian and Edwardian Christendom did not produce many religious-minded technicians willing to pass on their knowledge to underdeveloped countries for the love of God alone—though a historian should add that modern secular working-class movements are even less successful in turning out such people. Lack of good tuition meant that native artisans usually left their courses badly trained, and generally required white supervision on the job.

Educational standards for white children were not, however, much better. In Fort Victoria in 1902, for instance, there was no school and out of the 40 white children of school age, eight were attending Morgenster mission, where they were rubbing shoulders with black youngsters. Southern Rhodesia was vast and thinly settled; communications were poor and money short, so that state education for Europeans did not begin until 1903. Many settlers lacked money to pay school fees; the population in the mining townships for long remained a floating one, so that pupils often left their classes as soon as they had settled down to work. Many state schools, as well as religious societies like the Jesuits and the Dominican sisters of course did excellent work, but by 1911 experts considered that about one-fifth of the white youngsters in the country were still not going to school. Even those Europeans who did get education often fared badly. 'School C. Country School. 24 present,' later wrote a disillusioned inspector during a tour much later, in the 'twenties, '21 were in Stds I–V. Fourteen professed never to have heard the name of Jesus nor could they recall to mind, even when told, any incident of his birth, life or death.'[1] These comments of course were not all typical, but illustrate better than anything else the general kind of milieu in which missionaries had to work.

[1] S. de J. Lenfestey, Inspector of Schools, to Director of Education: 24 Jan 1920 (in E 2/5/1, Nat Arch SR). Lenfestey also found that, at a primary school in a large town, only one child in a class of children from seven to thirteen had ever heard the story of the Good Samaritan.

Chapter Six

The birth of modern politics

I

European politics before the Great War

Early Rhodesia was almost a monarchy, and Cecil John Rhodes its uncrowned king. In spite of the country's constitutional trappings 'the Old Man's' word was almost law, and however much Rhodesians may have disliked the Chartered Board they trusted 'Mr Rhodes' and enthusiastically stood by him when his star seemed to wane. Rhodes sincerely reciprocated these feelings. Rhodesia was 'his' country; Rhodesians were 'his' people; he would always try to help a needy petitioner or rectify some local grievance. Rhodes at the same time also appreciated the political advantages of conciliating local whites. He thought that the introduction of Elected Members into the Legislature would strengthen his position in the country, for British ministers were less likely to meddle with a Chamber containing European popular representatives.

In 1902, however, the great Empire-builder died. His body found a hallowed resting place in the Matopos; his name lived on as an inspiration and a myth, but once he was gone there was no one left on the Chartered Board to take his place, and when, later in 1902, Beit and Jameson visited Rhodesia, they found an embittered country. The aftermath of war hung heavily over the territory and trade languished. 'Businesses are being closed down,' wrote a mine-owner in a depressed mood, 'houses vacated, and many people, particularly mechanics and small tradesmen, leaving the country.'[1] Tempers accordingly ran high and white Rhodesians put forward many grievances. The most serious ones concerned the extent of the mineral royalties payable to the Company, the high cost of living, the expense of sending goods by rail and, most important of all, the question of whether the Company owned the unalienated land in its commercial or merely in an administrative capacity. Apart from that, of course, white Rhodesians were also a disputatious lot, a people who would not let

---

[1] M. Heany, quoted by H. W. Fox to Lord Grey: 26 Oct 1903 (in A 1/5/5, Nat Arch SR)

themselves be intimidated by the 'Establishment'. A poverty-stricken country like theirs naturally produced a harsh sort of radicalism that easily turned 'agin the Government' without always understanding very clearly what the disputes were about. Rhodesia moreover had only home-made amusements. There were no permanent cinemas, theatres, opera-houses, organized lotteries or professional football teams. People occupied their spare time with sports, social occasions or amateur theatricals, and when the newspapers announced a public meeting almost the whole citizenry in any one township might turn up to hear the Company's directors denounced amid popular glee as 'Chartered libertines'.

Things being as they were, the Board wisely decided to make a gesture of good will—as Sir Lewis Michell, one of the Resident Directors in South Africa, put it—and give some politic concessions that would help to tide the country over the slump.[1] The mining levy was cut; small-workers received much improved terms, and railway rates went down a little. In the political sphere the Rhodesian colonists likewise managed to make some progress. In 1903 Milton pointed out to the High Commissioner the advisability of raising the number of Elected Members from four to seven, thereby giving them equality of representation with the Officials. As long as the existing state of affairs continued, wrote the Administrator, the Government majority could always steamroller any proposal through the Chamber; this meant that the Legislature did not carry sufficient influence in the country, and many of the most substantial people would not bother to take any part in politics. Moreover, said Milton, the country should rearrange its constituencies. The existing system rested on the Provinces of Matabeleland and Mashonaland which also served as electoral districts, each returning two members, thereby greatly favouring Salisbury and Bulawayo. This arrangement was arbitrary, and the arrival of the railways made the division obsolete. Instead Milton put forward a new scheme whereby the smaller mining and farming communities would get a greater say in electing members, whilst the number of 'Unofficials' would increase.[2]

Chamberlain did not feel entirely happy about an increase in Elected Members. The Colonial Office anxiously pointed out to the Company that as long as the latter bore the expense of governing the country, there must be no chance of the Official Members being outvoted by Elected Members,[3] but the final arrangements sufficiently satisfied the Imperial authorities to become law. In 1903 a new Order in Council provided for

[1] J. A. Stevens, B.S.A. Company representative at Cape Town, to B.S.A. Company, London: 21 Oct 1903 (in A 1/5/5, Nat Arch SR)

[2] W. H. Milton to High Commissioner:—Dec 1902 (in A 3/20/4, Nat Arch SR)

[3] Colonial Office to B.S.A. Company: 3 Dec 1902 (copy in A 3/20/4, Nat Arch SR)

equality of representation between Official and Unofficial members, the Administrator being left with a casting vote in the event of a deadlock.[1] The Elected Members thus emerged from the dispute with a stronger position, and the Company fully determined to make the amended constitution work. Fox advised Milton to keep on the best of terms with the Unofficials, because good relations with them were essential, and because they must be educated to the realities of Government; he should give them full latitude in debate to discuss and criticize the administrative estimates; they should feel that their interest was welcome, for 'we do need their assistance and want it to be given ungrudgingly'.[2]

But this advice was easier to give than to carry out. Public opinion in Southern Rhodesia continued to challenge the Company's mine and land titles; white Rhodesians also argued that even though the country's administration was still being run at a loss, the administrative deficits accumulated in the past should not be looked upon as a charge against the future of a self-governing state. The Company for its part did not like raising more funds without an understanding on how this money would be repaid to the Company's shareholders. The settlers were admittedly making a large contribution, but they forgot that of the country's total revenue of £435,000 in 1903/04 some £130,000 was being raised from Africans through taxes and customs, whilst the London shareholders were putting up some of the remainder through stamp and transfer duties.[3] In order to get an agreement, the Company sent out Sir George Dashwood Taubman Goldie to report on the terms under which Rhodesia might assume self-government whilst at the same time safeguarding the investors. Goldie, a great empire builder in his own right, who had formerly played a major share in establishing British influence in Nigeria, sympathized with the Company, and put forward a complicated scheme whereby it would retain the unalienated land and mineral rights free of taxation. Goldie at the same time estimated the public debt at something over £8,000,000 not including the large sums advanced in the course of developing the railways. He suggested funding this debt, the Charter retaining only £5,000,000 and the remainder being reserved as a trust fund to promote economic development. Rhodesians, however, refused to accept the underlying principle that they should shoulder the Company's past administrative deficits. The Board then came forward with a new proposal: if Rhodesians admitted the debt, the Charter would sell them a portion of its land and

[1] Southern Rhodesia order in council, 1903. The separate Administratorship for Matabeleland had been abolished two years earlier, in 1901

[2] H. W. Fox to Sir W. H. Milton: 14 Apr 1904 (in A 1/5/6, Nat Arch SR)

[3] For a full statement of the Company's case, see letter to *The Times*, by 'P.L.G.' [P. Lyttleton Gell]: 29 Aug 1904

mineral rights at a fixed price, for future delivery. But again Rhodesians proved unresponsive and further negotiations broke down.[1]

The Rhodesian colonists remained in an unenviable position. An Imperial doctrine of *laissez faire* had caused their country to start its career under Company government, with the result that the 'Charter' now claimed the colony's main assets, whilst leaving the settlers with a crushing burden against the future. To make matters worse, Rhodesia was short of both money and men. The white population stayed small, for conditions were harsh, the cost of living high, and malaria and blackwater fever would yet be an ever-present threat to health in the outlying districts for more than a generation to come.

Funds moreover remained tight. A large proportion of the cash spent in Rhodesia derived either from the 'Charter' directly, or from the railways which again depended on Chartered credit. No loans could be raised for Rhodesia outside London, so that the British South Africa Company could not consider shifting its headquarters away from there. The Rhodesian mining industry was beginning to expand, but even the bigger companies were only small fry when compared with the giants of the Rand. The Johannesburg gold industry, Wilson Fox explained to Lord Grey, started off with the immense initial advantage that much of its early capital was self-generating; the influx of money from London to the Rand only came later, by which time management was in the hands of local people of proven efficiency, and foreign capitalists modified rather than changed existing arrangements. But Rhodesia, with its more limited resources, in Fox's view only attracted what might be called the 'second team' of the mining industry. This included people like Dr Hans Sauer, R. (later Sir Robert) Williams, Colonel H. M. (later Sir Herman Melville) Heyman, J. H. Hirschler, and P. B. S. (later Sir Bourchier) Wrey—men who had failed to make their fortunes on the Rand—or aristocratic newcomers to South Africa like the Hon. Maurice Gifford, Captain the Hon. Charles J. White and Sir John Willoughby, who were tempted to the Far North by love of adventure. But few investments went from the Rand to Rhodesia as funds once flowed from Kimberley to Johannesburg; the country remained largely dependent on the Charter, which kept a tight grip over the local mining industry, with access to the papers of more than fifty companies. The Rhodesians moreover faced serious economic manpower problems; Rhodesian businessmen, thought Fox, had collectively less brain power than their opposite numbers in Johannesburg;

---

[1] For details see file A 11/2/18/28 (Nat Arch SR) and Fox, H. W. *Memorandum . . . on constitutional, political, financial and other questions concerning Rhodesia.* British South Africa Company, 1912. (Printed for the information of the Board.)

local managers of mining companies admittedly could boast of pluck, honesty and loyalty, but needed tight financial control to stop them going off the rails. As long as conditions remained in this state, London investors would not be content to hand over control to local people of whose standing and ability they had no means of forming a judgement.[1] The 'Imperial' view of settlers in fact bore some resemblance to that taken towards African political aspirations forty years later!

The Rhodesians did not even form a united bloc. The bigger mining companies could not always see eye to eye with the smallworkers;[2] the mining industry as a whole would sometimes clash with the farmers over matters like labour, timber and water rights, whilst the producers between them would in turn blame the merchants for the high cost of living. The Rhodesian settlers remained weak, and though they managed to acquire influence and extort concessions decisive power remained beyond their grasp.

In order to expand more rapidly the country urgently needed credit. Both Company and colonists wished to borrow more money; the Legislative Council in 1905 passed a Loans Ordinance which would have enabled the territory to set up a public debt, allowing the Administration to give more assistance to farmers. The Company strongly supported the measure. The Board pointed out to the Colonial Office that any funds raised under the new law would only be lent on adequate security, and that various other British colonies had already introduced similar measures. But these were the days of pre-Keynesian economics: financial orthodoxy ruled supreme, and the Colonial Office gave a crushing answer. 'Lord Elgin,' reads the magisterial reply, 'regrets that the explanations . . . do not lessen the strong objection which His Majesty's Government entertains to the principle of creating a public debt of Rhodesia, and placing a charge of that nature on the revenues of the territory, as distinguished from those of the British South Africa Company, which has been placed in possession of all the assets of the country.'[3] As long as Company rule continued Southern Rhodesia could not borrow money, thereby providing another strong argument for all those who wished the existing system to end.

Bitter controversy on the questions of past administrative deficits, the mineral and land rights thus continued, all these issues becoming inextricably interwoven with Rhodesia's political future. In 1907 another Directoral Deputation visited the country to calm the colonists, and again

[1] H. W. Fox to Lord Grey: 26 Oct 1903 (in A 1/5/5, Nat Arch SR)

[2] The increasing influence of the larger concerns was for instance expressed by the voting arrangements within the Chambers of Mines. The Articles of Association adopted by the Salisbury Chamber of Mines already sharply differentiated between the voting power of bigger and smaller companies.

[3] Colonial Office to B.S.A. Company: 13 Mar 1906 (in African (South) no. 802, p. 65)

made a number of concessions. The Company agreed to promote land settlement more effectively, introduce reforms in the civil service, revise mineral royalties, issue simpler forms of land titles, and make various other changes of a minor nature. More important, the Directors promised to reduce the number of Nominated Members on the Legislative Council to five, thereby for the first time giving the Elected Members a majority.[1]

The Directors' promise seemed of sufficient importance to Charles Coghlan, now a well-known Bulawayo lawyer, to make him stand as a candidate for the Legislature. Coghlan, a Cape-born Irishman and a practising Roman Catholic, had already made a name for himself by his unyielding opposition to Chartered claims, and by the way in which he had helped many small mining men to find a path through the country's tangled legislation. A burly, determined man, whose bristling moustache made him look rather like a Rhodesian Clemenceau, Coghlan took his seat on the Legislature in 1908, and his legal knowledge and public standing soon made him the most influential man on the Unofficial side.[2]

But from the colonists' point of view the grant of an Elected majority was but a paper victory. The Directors, though anxious enough to secure Rhodesian good will for a final settlement, firmly stuck to their guns. The Visiting Directors stated quite unequivocally that, subject to existing arrangements, 'the lands and minerals throughout Rhodesia remain as commercial assets of the Company', and Rhodesians remained economically hamstrung. The Colonial Office preferred to leave well alone, allowing matters to slide in a way that later provoked a Chartered Director privately to castigate their methods as smacking of 'perfidious Albion'. The British Government was, however, determined to safeguard the Company's financial position as long as it ran Rhodesia; a further Order in Council, promulgated in 1911 after a mass of controversy and correspondence, gave the Company all the protection shareholders could possibly desire against white backveld radicals. The Legislative Council of course remained unable to consider any votes or ordinances for appropriating revenue or raising taxes without the Administrator's approval. More important still, no 'ordinances interfering with the land and other rights of the Company' might be discussed without the Administrator's consent, a provision that largely nullified the Unofficial majority.[3]

---

[1] 'Declaration of policy published at Bulawayo by Committee of Directors, on 19th October, 1907' (in Fox, H. W. *Memorandum . . . on constitutional, political, financial and other questions concerning Rhodesia, op. cit*, p. 324–327)

[2] For a biography that very much takes Coghlan's side, see Wallis, J. P. R. *One man's hand: the story of Sir Charles Coghlan and the liberation of Southern Rhodesia.* Longmans, Green and co., 1950

[3] Southern Rhodesia order in council, 1911. The preceding correspondence is in file A 3/30/6 (Nat Arch SR)

P

Rhodesia's general weakness was also apparent in its external relations. Rhodes originally hoped to build a new British state in the Interior which one day would redress the balance of power against the Transvaal as part of a federated South Africa, thereby helping to keep the sub-continent within the Imperial orbit. But Rhodes misjudged the Dutch. His own policy helped to bring about war for supremacy between Briton and Boer south of the Limpopo, a bloody clash combining an Imperial campaign of the old kind with civil war between the two white races of South Africa, a conflict reminiscent in some ways of other struggles for national unification waged in the nineteenth century. The British won a barren victory in the field, but then their policy began to waver. Later on a Liberal Government assumed office in London, and in 1906 granted self government to the Transvaal in a bold bid to secure the conquered Boers' loyalty. The Orange River Colony received a similar constitution, with the result that power once more slipped out of British hands. The Cape, like Rhodesia, retained a 'colour-blind' property franchise. But in the Transvaal every European man over 21 was allowed to vote, which meant that 'poor whites' and *by-woners* received a considerable say in the country's politics. The spoils of office accordingly passed into Afrikaner hands. In 1907 General Louis Botha became Premier in the Transvaal and Abraham Fischer in the Orange River Colony. Early in 1908 a Bond-Moderate Ministry, headed by John Xavier Merriman, took over from Dr Jameson's administration in the Cape, and only Natal continued to adhere to the old British Imperial tradition.

The British 'High Mining School', represented by men like Francis Percy Drummond (later Sir Drummond) Chaplin, Joint Manager at Johannesburg for the Consolidated Gold Fields of South Africa, very much *persona grata* with the Chartered Company, and later their Administrator in Southern Rhodesia, viewed the situation with the grimmest forebodings. The mining houses, backed by many English-speaking shopkeepers on the Rand, supported the Progressive Association which stood for the British monied interest and the Imperial connexion. The 'Rand Lords' dreaded radicalism, both of the rural and urban variety, fearing alike the influence of poverty-stricken Afrikaans-speaking backvelders and of British artisans in the towns. They also criticized the new Transvaal Government's financial measures and its policy of pushing Afrikaners into the civil service, quite a number of embittered Englishmen leaving the Transvaal and accepting government jobs in Southern Rhodesia.

The Progressives could not change the course of events. Economic reasons, as well as pressure from ardent idealists who hoped that a South

African Union would overcome inter-white conflicts, all pulled the various South African states towards unification, and preparations began for a National Convention. Southern Rhodesia received an invitation to participate, though her delegates could not vote. The Company at first wanted to send only its own men, but Coghlan complained to Botha, whose good offices helped to secure Unofficial representation in the Rhodesian party.

The Unofficials nominated Coghlan to speak on their behalf, and when on a hot and sweltering October day in 1908 the Convention assembled at Durban, Southern Rhodesia also had a say. But soon the Boers' strong position became apparent. In the vital struggle over the allocation of seats in the projected Assembly, the Cape clashed with the Transvaal, which gained an important advantage. The Transvaal, where non-Europeans had no votes, insisted that the number of white electors should be taken as basis for representation. The Cape, with its very much larger electorate, demanded seats in proportion to the *total* white population. In the end the delegates agreed to accept the adult white male population, an arrangement which tilted the scales against the Cape, but even more so against Rhodesia.

White Rhodesians had therefore no incentive to throw in their fortunes with the new state. Coghlan of course felt convinced that the country's 'absolute and inevitable destiny' was to join the Union. But this was for the future. Better wait until Rhodesia had attracted more British settlers and could negotiate from a position of greater strength.[1] The Transvaal Progressives were even more outspoken. The country's position would be hopeless in a future union where political power rested on a population basis; even the local Provincial Council, to be set up under Union, would fall under the domination of Boer immigrants with big families, and thereby cease to be British.

The Company concurred, and strenuously denied that it was negotiating behind the Rhodesians' backs to get rid of their Rhodesian commitments to the south, whilst the Administrator assured his Legislature that the country's present position must remain 'one of detachment'.[2] Ultimately the country should 'take its rightful place as a member of the Union', but the times were not yet ripe. In addition to political complications, Fox wrote later on, Rhodesians would also have to face economic difficulties. The interests of Rhodesia might be subordinated to those of the Rand as far as labour was concerned; the territory might be inundated by Dutch younger sons and *by-woners*; railway facilities would certainly not be

[1] See Wallis, J. P. R. *One man's hand . . .* , *op cit*, p. 100–109
[2] Southern Rhodesia. *Legislative Council debates*, 15 June 1908, p. 1

extended, and the country's general development might even be deliberately retarded for political motives.[1]

Union with South Africa therefore fell into abeyance. The final arrangements made for South Africa's new constitution did make provision for the Rhodesias to come in at some later time.[2] So, when in 1910, amidst high optimism and splendid pageantry, the four southern states linked up into a new Dominion, the lands north of the Limpopo stood aloof, and as time went on Rhodesians found less reason than ever to be tempted into partnership with their southern neighbours.

White Rhodesians therefore felt inclined to make the best of Company rule; though quarrels continued, people could not see a workable alternative. Tempers ran high over individual issues. In 1910 for instance a drunken African assaulted a white woman lately confined—an unusual crime in a law-abiding country like Rhodesia. A local court sentenced the man to hang, but the High Commissioner insisted on a reprieve, his decision causing fierce anger to blaze up amongst Europeans who felt that their womenfolk were not getting adequate protection. But for them the culprit was now the Imperial Government—not the Chartered Company, which judiciously stood aloof.

The political temperature again rose sharply when in 1912 the Legislative Council passed an Ordinance reorganizing the Native Labour Bureau in the form of a limited liability company.[3] In order to finance the scheme the authorities imposed a special levy, but landowners and farmers refused to pay the impost and for a short time resorted to passive resistance. Coghlan himself supported the measure with the result that his political stock began to slump in the backveld. In the end the Administration rescinded the Ordinance, but the conflict symbolized not so much a struggle between Company and colonists as one amongst white Rhodesians themselves, a dispute that aligned farmers against miners and mining concerns.

Anti-Company men thus spoke in rather muted tones, and opposition to the Charter—though deeply felt—remained somewhat sporadic. In 1913 a more radical body, the Rhodesian League, came into existence drawing most of its support from farmers and small urban employers. The League demanded that the Imperial Government should take over the executive, settle with the Company, and give the country a constitution in conformity with the settlers' views. A popular referendum should decide

[1] Fox, H. W. *Memorandum . . . on constitutional, political, financial and other questions concerning Rhodesia, op. cit,* p. 83
[2] For a full account of the whole union movement, see Thompson, L. M. *The unification of South Africa, 1902–1910.* Oxford, At the Clarendon Press, 1960
[3] Rhodesian native labour bureau ordinance, 1911

on whether Rhodesia should join South Africa.[1] The League's programme, however, went too far for the electorate. Coghlan preferred to wait, whilst the Company again agreed to make a number of concessions. In 1914 nearly all the candidates who supported the League's platform were defeated at the elections. Only John McChlery, a retired builder and radical of the old school, a 'Home Ruler', teetotaller and sworn enemy of all monopolies, managed to get himself returned. But McChlery stood alone, and Coghlan prevailed with his view that only full Responsible Government would mark an advance on the existing state of affairs, that the country still needed the Company as a partner, and that the London Directors—for all their failings—were better people to deal with than Colonial officialdom.

The Imperial Government for its part had not the slightest intention of picking up the unwanted Rhodesian burden and for the time being no one could therefore offer a real alternative to Chartered rule. The Elected Members, for all their quarrels with the Company, now had no intention of 'rocking the boat'. They were after all a solidly respectable group of people, honest, law-abiding, with none of the colourful rogues amongst them who used to find their way into, say, Australian State Legislatures. The Unofficials, for one thing, always contained a solid bloc of mining directors and managers—people who could afford to spend some of their time deliberating in Salisbury; the remainder consisted of solid farmers and contractors, with a solitary lawyer, Coghlan himself, who now had a knighthood.[2] People of this kind were not men to upset law and order, and caution remained the key-note of politics.

This of course did not mean that the colonists were satisfied with things as they stood. In 1914 the Elected Members reaffirmed an earlier vote, taken in 1908, asking for an immediate settlement of the land question, and asserted that the Chartered Company did not own the unalienated land in its private capacity.[3] The Imperial Government, which had failed to make up its mind for the last twenty years, then introduced another element of delay by resolving to submit the question to the Privy

[1] Circular letter from R. A. Fletcher, chairman of the Provisional Central Committee of the Rhodesian League: 16 June 1913, and enclosed outline of the proposed scheme (in MA 15/1/1, Nat Arch MS)

[2] In 1914 the House contained Milton, the Administrator, as President, Colonel R. Burns-Begg, the Resident Commissioner without a vote, and six other officials. The Unofficials included Milton E. Cleveland and John McChlery, contractors or ex-contractors; Sir Charles Coghlan, lawyer; Burton I. Collings, mining engineer; Gordon S. D. Forbes, C.M.G., D.S.O.; Colonel Raleigh Grey, C.V.O., C.M.G.; Lieutenant-Colonel Herman M. Heyman; George Mitchell and Captain (later Lieutenant-Colonel) William B. Bucknall, company directors and managers; Lionel Cripps and John A. Edmonds, farmers; the profession at the time of Ernest A. Begbie, representative of Victoria, is not clear.

[3] Southern Rhodesia. *Legislative Council debates*, 17 Apr 1914, p. 42–56

Council which meant that the whole issue would again drag on. But as far as the country's political future was concerned the Imperial authorities proved more accommodating. A second Supplemental Charter provided that, if at any time after 29 October 1914 a majority of the Legislative Council should pass a resolution in favour of Responsible Government, and could show that the country was able to pay for it, the Sovereign might comply with the Council's request, and set up a new political order.[1] The immediate course however remained unchanged, and when in 1914 the guns began to boom all over Europe, Company rule in Rhodesia stood rooted as solid as before.

II

The First World War

When the fighting broke out in Europe, Southern Rhodesia was ill prepared. The Chartered Company's Government, like all other British colonial administrations, relied on only a minimum of armed force, and the British South Africa Police was not in a position to take the field as a unit. Well trained and disciplined though it was, the corps numbered no more than 550 Europeans and 600 Africans, and this small force was now charged with the impossibly difficult tasks of external defence and the maintenance of internal security. In addition the Company could rely on the services of white Volunteers, an enthusiastic but ill-equipped body of splendid fighting men, too poorly trained to fight as an organized regiment. The Germans fortunately were no better prepared. German territory, the Caprivi Strip, ran from South-West Africa to within a few miles of the railway where it crossed the Zambezi by the bridge immediately below the Victoria Falls. Had the Germans built up the 'Zipfel' as a military spring-board, they could have destroyed the vital bridge and cut the lifeline to the North. But the British struck first and a detachment of the British South Africa Police, acting in conjunction with the Northern Rhodesia Police, swiftly occupied the German station at Schuckmannsburg.

The Rhodesian authorities then quickly expanded the country's military potential. Two British South Africa Police Special Service Companies were recruited. In addition European volunteers flocked to the colours of the 1st Rhodesia Regiment. The Union Government were only too anxious to borrow the new unit to assist in suppressing a rising of Afrikaner nationalists who would not be reconciled with the British, and who hoped instead for a German victory. The Rhodesians fortunately

[1] B.S.A. Company. Second supplemental charter: 13 Mar 1914

were not required to shed South African blood, their activities being confined to garrison duties, until the insurrection collapsed. Then the regiment left for Cape Town and from there by boat to Walvis Bay, subsequently taking part in a general advance which terminated with the swift occupation of South-West Africa and the collapse of all enemy resistance. The Rhodesians on this occasion saw little fighting, though the campaign proved arduous in other respects, involving much fatigue-work in the building of fortifications and long marches across parched and thirsty desert country where rations were short and water hard to get. On disbandment many Rhodesians left for England and offered their services to the War Office, whilst others enrolled in new formations which were being formed in Rhodesia for service in German East Africa. The most important of these was the 2nd Rhodesia Regiment which, in 1915, embarked at Beira. The new campaign proved a grim and bloody affair. The British had to fight a well-led and well-disciplined enemy who operated in appalling country. Thick bush impeded visibility and held up movement; disease was rife; supplies often ran out when needed most; and the British and their Allies found incredible difficulties in pinning down an elusive enemy who usually managed to break off an engagement when the fighting turned against him. The soldiers at first did not quite realize what the war would hold in store for them. The Rhodesians cheerfully disembarked at Mombasa and then moved up to Kajiado, an up-country station, then used as a base for the advanced post of Longido which itself served to defend the main Uganda railroad and to cover Nairobi. The long British line of outposts, however, entailed the dispersal of troops to such an extent that the authorities decided to evacuate Longido, a decision which invited much criticism at the time. The regiment was then ordered further east and down the main line to Maktau and Tsavo. Fighting developed into a series of actions between small mobile columns and patrols, the Rhodesians proving their mettle against enemy askari who, in the early stages of the war, would sometimes torture and mutilate wounded prisoners. The rains began to pour down; malaria and dysentery decimated the troops; whilst the dense thorn bush required veld craft of the highest order. The Rhodesians later on took part in an abortive attack on the German advance post of Mbuyuni; and the regiment became so depleted by sickness that it had to be sent to the higher veld. In 1916 the enemy was at last turned out of Mbuyuni, and the Rhodesians subsequently took part in an unsuccessful attack on the Salaita position. By this time, Lieutenant-General Smuts, the new Commander in East Africa, had arrived, and South Africans and Rhodesians started a concerted move on Salaita and Taveta. There was further stiff fighting and the Rhodesians once more suffered serious casualties, operations in general being impeded by poor staff work at the centre, and by the general inadequacy of food, clothing and medical stores.

The Germans for their part held a strong hand. Paul Emil von Lettow-Vorbeck, their commander-in-chief and one of the best colonial generals ever to fight in Africa, determined to pin down as many Allied soldiers as possible in his East African 'side show', so as to prevent reinforcements from reaching the vital theatres of war in Europe. In doing so he was aided by the vast expanse of German East Africa, the difficult nature of the country, and the high morale of his troops, who operated in small but well co-ordinated and highly mobile formations. Lettow-Vorbeck moreover commanded the internal lines, the Allies advancing in several main bodies from the periphery of German East Africa to pin down and crush their elusive opponent. The Allies consisted of a polyglot army of Indians, East Africans, West Africans, Belgians, Rhodesians, West Indians, British and South Africans; they did not know the country in the same way as the Germans, who remained free to concentrate in the healthier regions whilst their adversaries had to traverse vast tracts of fly-ridden bush where disease inflicted terrible casualties on men and animals alike. Lettow's men acquired a considerable immunity to fever and needed no animals for transport, relying on native porters to bear their supplies on their backs. The Germans moreover made a first class job of improvising *Ersatz* production which—together with some windfalls accruing from blockade runners—helped to make up to some extent for the Allies' superiority of weapons.[1] The Germans also took good care to prevent supplies from falling to their opponents, for whom provisions were an ever-present problem. Under these conditions the Rhodesians showed incredible physical resilience; they marched till their uniforms were in tatters; many of them caught fever; rations ran low, and soon the medical authorities reported that some 65 per cent of the regiment were unfit for further fighting. The troops then retired to Nairobi for a rest, but soon 'bush-bashing' began again; the men returned to Taveta and worked their way down the left bank of the Pangani river, the regiment again becoming sadly depleted. But the Rhodesians managed to capture the German bridge across the Pangani, and this important success allowed of further advances.

The regiment, together with South African troops, subsequently helped to lever the Germans out of the Nguru Mountains and later participated in further action in terrible terrain. The country between the Morogoro and Mgeta proved one of the worst patches in the campaign; the men had to

[1] See Hancock, W. K. *Smuts: the sanguine years, 1870–1919.* Cambridge University Press, 1962, p. 409–423, for a brilliant discussion of these problems.

fight their way through low-lying forest and miles and miles of swamp, where the tsetse fly held complete control, and local supplies proved impossible to get. Myriads of flies filled the air, the roadside was littered with the stinking carcasses of draught animals; the heat was torture; the troops went down with fever and dysentery, until in October the whole regiment numbered only 126 men. In the end the Germans abandoned the Mgeta position, later clearing away from the Rufiji river, but in spite of hard knocks they managed to escape utter defeat by splitting up into small portions and melting away. By now torrential rains were coming down; further operations were held up, and the exhausted regiment at last received orders to return to Rhodesia. On 18 April 1917 the men reached Beira after one of the toughest tropical campaigns of military history. Back in Rhodesia the soldiers received a magnificent welcome, but the authorities decided that the regiment could no longer take the field as a unit, for the country simply had not got enough men left to keep it going. A contingent then left for Europe where they were largely absorbed in the South African infantry; many received commissions in other units, or joined the Royal Flying Corps or the Tank Corps.

In the meantime the British South Africa Police had also distinguished itself in action. At the beginning of the war some light artillery reinforced the troops defending the 'N.B.', the northern border separating British territory from German East Africa. Later on, in 1915, Southern Rhodesia sent further reinforcements to the area; the men were organized into two Special Service Companies of the British South Africa Police which consisted of a sprinkling of serving policemen, with a much larger proportion of Volunteers and some ex-members of the 1st Rhodesia Regiment. These Companies formed part of an all-white Rhodesian unit, called 'Murray's Column', after its commander, Lieutenant-Colonel Ronald Ernest Murray. The column rendered excellent service in East Africa under conditions very much like those encountered by the 2nd Rhodesia Regiment, receiving praise from Brigadier-General Edward Northey, Commander of the Nyasa-Rhodesian Field Force, for its work, especially on the Rhudji river and the Malangali. Early in 1918 Murray's health at last gave way, and he returned to Rhodesia. The column, depleted by sickness and casualties in action, could no longer be kept up to strength owing to the impossibility of finding reinforcements, and broke up. Its members formed machine-gun sections in Rhodesian native units and saw service till the end of the campaign.

The Europeans' military effort reflected the social conditions of a still relatively unspecialized backveld economy. The country mainly lived by small-scale mining and farming; there were few manufactures, bar some agricultural processing industries and railway workshops; Southern Rhodesia could not produce a bullet, much less a bomb. The country as yet contained but a limited number of more highly specialized technicians, and most white Rhodesians served as infantry, the most undifferentiated though the most harshly-tested form of military 'labour' in existence. There were of course a number of exceptions. Rhodesian doctors rendered excellent service. The motor car was beginning to make its appearance in the bush, and a small Southern Rhodesian motor transport corps did fine work in bringing up supplies. The call on Rhodesia's slender white manpower, however, became increasingly heavy. There was no longer any fear of native risings of the kind that shook Nyasaland and Portuguese East Africa during the war, and the authorities decided to enlist African front line troops, a policy which sharply diverged from the accustomed South African pattern. A new 1st Rhodesia Native Regiment, like similar Imperial units, was led by European officers and a core of white N.C.O.s. The regiment left Salisbury in 1916 and went via Beira and Nyasaland to New Langenburg, where they completed their training. The troops gave a good account of themselves, especially at Kitanda where Rhodesian askaris were besieged for a time, and at St Moritz, where they were surrounded, but relieved by other Rhodesian troops. So well did the black soldiers acquit themselves that in 1917 the Army Council asked Rhodesia to furnish another native regiment for service in German East Africa. More volunteers flocked to the colours, and in 1917 the 2nd Rhodesia Native Regiment left for service in Nyasaland. As the war went on the two units, however, proved difficult to maintain at full strength, with the result that early in 1918 they were merged into one complete battalion.

Rhodesia's contribution to the war effort was very considerable in relation to its slender resources: 1,720 whites, a high proportion of Rhodesian fighting men, received commissions, the self-reliance and ability to command acquired on lonely farms and isolated mines and workshops standing them in excellent stead; 5,577 Europeans as well as 2,752 natives and 22 Coloureds rendered direct military aid. More than 700 Europeans died in action or perished of wounds or disease.[1] The African casualties included 31 men killed and 142 who died from other causes. Rhodesians also won an impressive array of decorations, including two Victoria Crosses, and many whites returned with a military title and a string of letters behind their names.

The war stripped Southern Rhodesia of her European manpower, but

---

[1] See Lucas, Sir C. P. (ed.) *The Empire at war.* v. 4 [Africa]. Oxford University Press, 1925, especially p. 315–345. For the 2nd Rhodesia Regiment, see Capell, E. A. *The 2nd Rhodesia Regiment in East Africa.* Simson and co. ltd, 1923

Africans nevertheless kept quiet. Some rumours floated around of supposed British defeat, but few Africans seem to have wanted a German victory, and none now thought of fighting the British. Memories of the disastrous Rebellion still remained alive and, in any case, the conditions for an insurrection no longer existed. British security was extremely well organized and the Chartered administrators and policemen now knew the country inside out. For Company officials, unlike those in Imperial service, stayed in the same districts year after year; from the Administrator down to the lowest ranks there was continuity of tenure unparalleled under the Colonial Office. In any case the local African farmers were now doing relatively well. The country was never invaded and, unlike Northern Rhodesia and Nyasaland, Southern Rhodesia did not have to supply huge gangs of carriers to provide transport for the armies in the field. The blood-toll, in the shape of African soldiers wounded or killed, remained tiny in proportion to the country's total black population. The war caused a general rise in prices, and though black farmers might now have to pay more for merchandise in the stores, they received better prices for their meat and grain.

Southern Rhodesia lacked an unemployed African white-collar proletariat. The few educated black people in the country mostly came from the Union and looked towards the South, where Africans still put their trust in the Imperial connexion. The Union Africans' loyalist mood also found expression in Southern Rhodesia where—soon after the outbreak of fighting—the Union Native Vigilance Organization, a small body composed of expatriate black South Africans, sent a declaration of loyalty to the Administration. Apart from this, Africans made hardly any attempts to play a part in central politics and received no encouragement to do so. Before the war a few dozen Africans successfully claimed their vote under the country's 'colour blind', Cape-type franchise, and Rhodesians, with their inherited tradition of legality, never made any attempt to keep them out of the voting booths with the methods employed in the American 'Deep South'. Nevertheless most Europeans feared an increase of black voters, and in this respect the Chartered Company thoroughly sympathized with the colonists. In 1906 the Administration drafted an ordinance which would have prevented more natives from going on to the common roll. The measure might well have been put before the Legislature, but Selborne, the High Commissioner, thought that the Secretary of State would veto any such law.[1] Selborne did not, however, object to an alternative suggestion that the property qualification should be raised, a measure which would have the additional advantage of

[1] Lord Selborne to Sir W. H. Milton: 3 May 1906 (in A 11/2/12/3, Nat Arch SR)

keeping poor Afrikaners and semi-destitute European foreigners with British naturalization certificates out of politics. The Administration of course had to tread warily. If the bill's real object was to check the growth of the native franchise, Selborne privately wrote to Milton, 'This cannot very well be stated. The ostensible object therefore must be something quite different, but at the same time plausible.' 'There must not be', continued Selborne, 'anything either in the official correspondence or in the Council debates, any hint of a disability on natives if you want to avoid bringing Exeter Hall on your backs.'[1] A Liberal Secretary of State proved sympathetic. He saw nothing wrong in the raising of franchise qualifications as such, and agreed that the local Council was fully empowered to regulate such measures. The South African Federation issue then intervened, but in 1912 a new ordinance doubled existing income and property qualifications, thereby going a long way to satisfy white opinion.[2] Africans for their part took little interest in the question. This, of course, did not mean that political issues left them cold. Ten years before the outbreak of war, the Chief Native Commissioner had already reported that educated natives had an intelligent concern with public matters, especially those affecting black people; he added that the European newspapers were being read, and lettered Africans were passing on their knowledge to the less educated.[3] But there was little thought of active organization; political interest outside tribal affairs largely found refuge in the formation of independent churches, though even these never proliferated to anything like the same extent as south of the Limpopo. Southern Rhodesia thus remained politically quiescent and unaffected by rumblings of revolt in neighbouring Portuguese East Africa and in Nyasaland. In the lakeside protectorate, John Chilembwe, an African teacher influenced by American ideas, made an abortive attempt to set up a revolutionary theocracy. But Chilembwe lacked mass support in his own country, and his rising appears to have made no impression on Nyasa labour migrants south of the Limpopo. Some African informants told the local police that Chilembwe promised people in Nyasaland that he would make himself Sultan, drive out the whites, and receive money, clothes and military aid from the Germans. Chilembwe got some Anguru to help him, but did not call on the Yao, and his rising did not get far. The Government now were opening all the mail from Nyasaland and if they found anything about the rising they destroyed the correspondence, with the result that

---

[1] Lord Selborne to Sir W. H. Milton: 22 Feb 1907 (in A 11/2/12/3, Nat Arch SR)

[2] Existing qualifications embraced an annual salary of £50 *per annum* or ownership of land and buildings worth at least £75. The Voters qualification and registration amendment ordinance, 1912, increased qualifications to an income of £100 or occupational qualifications of £150.

[3] H. J. Taylor (memorandum): 11 Feb 1904 (in A 1/5/6, Nat Arch SR)

Nyasaland natives in Southern Rhodesia were not getting letters.[1] This, of course, did not mean that there was no discontent. In Matabeleland, for instance, the war awakened some hopes in the minds of a few Matabele chiefs who became impressed by rumours of supposed British reverses, the demand for African recruits being interpreted to mean that the British were getting into dire straits. Stories went around that the whites intended wholesale conscription, and one member of the Mlimo priesthood supposedly prophesied that the Germans would shortly enter the country and bring back a long-lost son of Lobengula to be king.[2] But the majority of chiefs stood aloof and refused to discuss the matter, whilst many young Matabele seem to have regarded service in the army as a desirable form of employment. Africans therefore remained quiet; many even rallied to support the war effort by donations, and the Chartered authorities never had any serious cause to worry about local security.

European society in the meantime was being affected much more profoundly. War for one thing gave a tremendous fillip to the economy, and the hard days prevailing just before the outbreak of war gave way to modest prosperity. The Allies now needed base minerals on a vast scale to make munitions, and bought Rhodesian metal ores of all kinds, including chrome, copper, tungsten and antimony, as well as asbestos, the latter now for the first time being produced on a large scale in the country. Wankie coal found many customers, both in the Rhodesias and the Belgian Congo. Gold production likewise went up, reaching an all-time high in 1916, though afterwards the industry ran into some difficulties because of lack of shipping and the rising price of equipment. The farmers similarly managed to make a good living, and pastoralists in Matabeleland found a growing outlet for their cattle on the Rand.

The needs of war and the growing demands of the economy in turn caused a general scarcity of white labour, which profoundly affected the structure of European society. More girls went to work, and even in the staid Government offices 'lady typists' started to hammer away on their machines. Women also did excellent work in looking after troops, serving on 'Comforts Committees' and suchlike bodies, the women's growing prominence in public life—linked to changing wartime attitudes—leading to their being enfranchised after the end of hostilities.[3]

The current shortage of labour also benefited European workmen who now, for the first time, found themselves in a strong bargaining position.

---

[1] Detective Sergeant F. G. Garton to Superintendent, C.I.D., Bulawayo: 23 Feb 1915 (copy in N 3/32/1, Nat Arch SR)

[2] Superintendent of Natives, Bulawayo, to Chief Native Commissioner: 12 June 1916 (in N 3/32/1, Nat Arch SR)

[3] Women's enfranchisement ordinance, 1919

Before the war jobs were scarce, and men working on the railways—the country's biggest employer—had to put up with all kinds of hardships. There was no overtime; men might work up to twelve hours a day and could be dismissed on the spot for refusing to obey even unreasonable orders. People who complained might simply be told that 'if you have a grievance, get out; we don't want people with grievances'![1] In any case the white labour force was hard to organize. Many workers employed by the railways were tradesmen who hoped that one day they would be their own masters. In addition there were migrants from other countries— Italian gangers who would slog away for £12 a month and finally go back to Italy with their accumulated savings—or Afrikaners from the south, *by-woners* and other folk in financial straits, who found working for the railways a welcome improvement.

The war, however, gave the men a chance and in 1916 a successful strike broke out which, in the same year led to the formation of the Rhodesia Railways Workers' Union. The stoppage spread to all stations, and for a short while life almost came to a standstill, since the country as yet possessed few motor vehicles and largely depended on rail communications. The social struggle of course did not lead to any serious flare-ups. Africans did not join the fray, the vast majority remaining but unskilled 'temporaries'. The Europeans, for their part, remained a tightly-knit body of people, almost one big family, where everybody talked to everybody else and knew all about his neighbour's troubles, a friendly community where the Administrator and his clerks would all ride around on bicycles and where a well-off surgeon and a poorly-paid working man might all be members of the same fraternal lodge. There were no great barriers of wealth to divide men from each other, and even the snobbery traditionally associated with the civil service never got the better of frontier equality.

More disastrous to Southern Rhodesia, in some ways, was the great influenza epidemic which hit the country, just as the Kaiser's armies were tottering to defeat. People found this new kind of plague much more terrifying in many respects than the war itself. 'Spanish Influenza' affected most of the world, but the virus may somehow have become more virulent on its passage through Africa, and for a time Southern Rhodesia was struck numb. Shops closed, transport firms stopped doing business, and life stood still, as the 'flu' claimed victim after victim. Africans suffered even more severely than white men, especially in crowded locations and

---

[1] For early union history, see Keller, J. W. 'The truth about the Rhodesian railwayman' (in *Rhodesian railway review*, no. 3, Nov 1921, p. 1–9) and Hall, H. J. 'The reminiscences of a Rhodesian railwayman' (in *Rhodesian railway review*, no. 21, May 1923, p. 4–5; no. 23, July 1923, p. 10–11; no. 24, Aug 1923, p. 4–5; no. 25, Sep 1923, p. 12–13). I am also indebted to personal information from F. Squair of Salisbury. Before 1916, guards got 11/– a day. Firemen started at £14 a month.

mining compounds, whilst doctors lacked any effective remedy with which to fight back. Stricken people would collapse in the streets, and experts estimated the total death rate in the countryside at about 2 to 3 per cent. Native Commissioners organized African teachers, messengers and policemen into groups to help; at Inyati, for instance, the Native Commissioner tried to treat afflicted white and black people at his station, helped by an African woman convict raw from the kraal.

In the towns there was a momentary feeling of panic, but the municipal authorities acted with commendable initiative and many volunteers came forward to act as nurses. The Salisbury Drill Hall was hurriedly turned into an emergency hospital, and Boy Scouts and young girls hardly out of school tried to cope with patients in their death throes. Many doctors were struck low, but others, including Andrew Milroy Fleming, the Medical Director, and Godfrey Martin Huggins, a young English surgeon straight back from the war, remained on their feet day and night, in some cases signing death certificates without even getting time to inspect the victims. When news of the Armistice came from Europe none felt like celebrating for death was still stalking the streets. In mid-November, 1918, however, the pestilence, after about five weeks, at last showed signs of abating and life began to return to normal. The crisis also did some good. In Bulawayo, the most flourishing and progressive settlement in the country, the plague resulted in more effective measures to prevent African overcrowding and ensure better supervision of native eating houses. Salisbury for its part began to agitate for better hospital facilities and more effective public health laws. The epidemic left many children without parents, and some time afterwards the Rhodesia Children's Home opened its doors to care for homeless white children, who—unlike African orphans—could not call on the assistance of extended family groups.[1]

The Civil Service in the meantime continued to hold the country on an even keel, relatively untroubled by political squalls. In 1914 Francis Drummond Percy (later Sir Drummond) Chaplin took over from Milton, continuing in office until the end of Chartered rule. The new Administrator had had rather an unusual kind of career. Born of Gloucestershire gentry parents, he received the accepted kind of upper middle class education at Harrow and Oxford, subsequently becoming a barrister. In 1897 he left for Rhodesia, hoping to set up in practice in a new and promising colony,

---

[1] See Gelfand, M. *Tropical victory: an account of the influence of medicine on the history of Southern Rhodesia, 1890–1923.* Cape Town, Juta and co., ltd, 1953, p. 204–207. I am also indebted to personal information from Lord Malvern, formerly Dr G. M. Huggins. During the epidemic 514 Europeans died of influenza. In Salisbury, out of 320 white admissions to the Drill Hall and General Hospital 49 people died, whilst 160 Africans perished out of 1,067 people treated at the Native Lazaretto.

but found the country's prospects so depressing that he preferred to accept an appointment as *The Times* correspondent on the Rand, then the hub of Imperial politics. Two years later he went to Russia to work for the *Morning Post*, but having made a most favourable impression on Rhodes, the thirty-four-year-old journalist, in 1900, received an offer to become Joint Manager at Johannesburg for the Consolidated Gold Fields of South Africa Ltd. Rhodes's hunch proved right, and Chaplin made an outstanding name in the industry and acquired numerous directorships in subsidiary companies of the Gold Fields and Wernher-Beit groups. In politics he stood out as an uncompromising imperialist of the Milner school, and as such, in 1907, took his seat in the Transvaal Legislature to represent Germiston for the Progressive Association. Later on the Transvaal Progressives fused with their Cape sister party into the Unionist Party, and in 1910 Chaplin was elected to the Union legislature where again he spoke for the mining interest.

An experienced politician, administrator and businessman, he seemed just the right sort of person to take over when Milton went on pension and the new Administrator soon justified the Chartered Company's choice. Chaplin, with his neatly clipped moustache, lined face and distinguished bearing, stood out very much as an aloof *pukkah sahib* of the old school, but quickly gained the Rhodesians' respect, and turned out to be one of the most able people ever to hold office at Salisbury. High-and-dry Conservative though he might be, Chaplin pushed a considerable amount of reform legislation through the Council, including laws to protect children and compensate white and black workmen. In 1918 his Administration also brought in a War Taxation and Excessive Profits Duty Ordinance which, for the first time, entailed the setting up of an Income Tax Department.

The new Administrator could make little headway with the vexed problems of inter-territorial relations. Neither Chaplin nor the Company liked the way things were going in South Africa, where the Unionists remained a minority party, and were losing many British working class votes on the Rand. Under these conditions the 'Charter' argued that Rhodesia should continue to stand aloof from the South, until the country became stronger and the political climate improved south of the Limpopo. It was better to strengthen the Company's hand in Rhodesia by unifying the separate territories north and south of the Zambezi. Fusion, for one thing, might result in some administrative economies, an important consideration at a time when the Imperial authorities rather meanly insisted that the 'Charter' should bear the whole weight of local war expenditure arising from hostilities with Germany. Amalgamation might somewhat reduce administrative costs, even though the local experts did not think that the savings would amount to much. The project would also, it seemed to the Company, have the additional advantage of leading to the gradual elimination of the older type of Southern Rhodesian officials by their better educated brethren from the north. But much more important were the expected political advantages. The Company would acquire a much stronger hand in its dealings both with South Africa and the Imperial Government. Amalgamation would improve the white Northern Rhodesians' constitutional position. The Europeans south of the Zambezi had representation in the Legislative Council; this body—strengthened by representatives from the north—must become the Parliament for the amalgamated territory, for a purely administrative fusion would not work. Chaplin, of course, by no means regarded this increase of European political power as an unmixed blessing; in fact he privately asserted that the local whites were no more fit to govern the natives than the Bolsheviks were fit to rule Russians! But unification was the best possible solution, and the final scheme therefore provided for the absorption of Northern Rhodesia; the country as a whole should be run by a single Administrator and a common Legislature would be able to make laws for the entire territory whilst Roman-Dutch law would extend beyond the Zambezi.[1]

The Company fought hard for its scheme which at one stroke might have eliminated the whole of the subsequent 'closer union' issue. But the majority of settlers would not have the project at any price. The Northerners put up all kinds of parochial arguments—ranging from expressed fears about their Katanga markets to the threatened status of Livingstone, or the likelihood of their being 'swamped' within the joint Legislature. White Southern Rhodesians believed that amalgamation would saddle them with a vast territory of little known potentialities whose acquisition would prove a constant drain on Southern Rhodesia's slender resources, and which might delay the achievement of Responsible Government. Worse still, the whites would have a vast native problem on their hands. He did not like colour bars, Coghlan argued in the House, but Rhodesians had to live side by side with a mass of black people and under these circumstances there was much to be said for excluding even educated Africans from the franchise. If a traveller went to Broken Hill or Fort Jameson, he would see the place full of native clerks, mechanics and

---

[1] For a more detailed treatment, see Gann, L. H. *A history of Northern Rhodesia.* Chatto and Windus, 1964. The Company's draft Order in council (in A 3/28/3, Nat Arch SR) provided for a constitution very much like the existing one in Southern Rhodesia. The Legislative Council was to contain an official bloc amounting to at least one-third of the total. For the time being the officials would have 8 seats, Southern Rhodesian elected members 12 and Northern Rhodesia 3.

typists, and under such conditions Southern Rhodesia could not afford to go in with the 'Black North'.[1]

Coghlan was in fact rather exaggerating the position. European skills were sufficiently scarce to command a relatively high market value in wartime, and, outside a few 'fringe groups', white men as yet did not have to worry about lower-paid African competitors. But his arguments nevertheless made a considerable appeal, and the speakers on the Company's side could make no headway. The Officials, and a minority of Elected Members who took their side, pointed to the expected economic advantages of the scheme. They spoke of the Zambezi as a great potential source of electrical power, and drew attractive pictures of great new agricultural schemes in the north. In any case, argued Lionel Cripps, himself a farming Member in the House, even Southern Rhodesia itself could not be truly said to be a white man's country; Rhodesians would have to live for all time with the native peoples of their country, and would have to fashion their policies accordingly. Amalgamation would improve the country's bargaining position vis à vis South Africa. If she did not absorb the North, Southern Rhodesia might one day find herself wedged precariously between a northern federation and a southern union, with the result that later on she would inevitably drift into the arms of her stronger southern neighbour under conditions she might not like.

The Company—backed by many local mining concerns—in the end managed to steamroller its proposals through the Legislative Council with the aid of a minority of Unofficials, but the Imperial authorities would not co-operate. When the Company first came up with its scheme the Colonial Office was in the charge of Andrew Bonar Law, a sound Unionist, and a vastly better man, from the Company's point of view, than Sir Lewis Harcourt, his predecessor, a Liberal and a critic of the Charter. But Law's tenure of office soon ended, and Colonel Walter Hume Long, his successor, proved less sympathetic to the Company. Long personally liked and respected Chaplin, but was much influenced by his Permanent Officials who, by this time, often tended to think of the Company as a bunch of rapacious capitalists, the old pro-Charter sentiments of the early 'nineties having almost completely evaporated. Long would do nothing, and rather apologetically wrote to Chaplin that he could not act against a majority of Elected Members, for once a country was allowed to choose its representatives His Majesty's Government could not go into direct opposition to an elected majority.

The Company of course did not think much of this argument. The

[1] For the main arguments for and against, see Southern Rhodesia. *Legislative council debates*, 25–26 April 1917

trouble was, wrote Wilson Fox, that white Southern Rhodesian politicians could always make a great deal of noise in the Imperial Parliament through left-wing Members, and Long was attaching an exaggerated importance to their views, simply because they could always become vocal through the 'Radical gang' in Britain's 'deplorable House of Commons'. The problem of African representation never came up in these debates. British 'progressive' opinion at home tended to side with the settlers, who were often looked upon in much the same way as Africans forty years later, oppressed people ground down by a ruthless financial monopoly. The main bugbear of Imperial reformers in those days was the British South Africa Company, whose reputation was steadily slumping in much the same fashion as that of European colonists in the 'fifties and 'sixties.

White Rhodesians thus missed their chance of uniting the two Rhodesias at a time when African opinion as yet played no part in politics, though to do justice to Coghlan and his colleagues, the projected scheme might in fact have made the ultimate achievement of full Responsible Government for Southern Rhodesia more difficult.

The Company suffered a galling defeat, made all the more bitter by the fact that 'the Charter' could never manage to secure any post-war territorial gains for its country. In 1917 Chaplin wrote to Long, suggesting a scheme whereby the victorious powers would dispose of German East Africa. The Portuguese would receive the bulk of the conquered country and, in exchange, yield Beira to Rhodesia and Lourenço Marques to South Africa.[1] But the scheme never got anywhere. The Portuguese, Fox concluded, would not surrender any territory, and the 'Charter' therefore preferred a working partnership with the Mozambique Company, especially since the Portuguese feared the Union and would sooner work on friendly terms with the British South Africa Company.

III

Responsible Government

Land always formed the life-blood of Rhodesian politics and in 1918 the long disputed legal position at last became clear. The Judicial Committee of the Privy Council now gave its decision on the case presented in 1914 and it went squarely against the Company. The

[1] See Long, B. K. *Drummond Chaplin: his life and times in Africa.* Oxford university press, 1941, p. 217–219

'Charter', in its commercial capacity, had no right to the unalienated land. The Lippert Concession was worthless as a title deed, and though the document might help to explain how and why the Company obtained governmental powers in Southern Rhodesia, it could not confer land ownership. The Company only conquered the country on the Crown's behalf. The Crown, through Orders in Council, put in the Company as its administrator. The Crown sanctioned the system of white settlement and native reserves and assumed the right to dispose of all land not in private ownership.

The Privy Council at the same time had to consider the African case, put forward by the Aborigines' Protection Society and backed by many missionaries and Matabele tribesmen. Earlier on, before the Great War, the Administration had made sure that Lobengula's legitimate heirs could exert no further political influence; in 1910 Njube, a royal prince, died, and Nguboyena, a highly educated man, withdrew into sullen melancholy. Nyamanda, another descendant of Lobengula, subsequently launched a land campaign, demanding a Matabele National Home where the people would be protected from the kind of eviction of which Nyamanda had himself had personal experience. Nyamanda met with support from the older men amongst the tribe, from educated Matabele clerks and teachers, from the leaders of Ethiopian Churches and from African solicitors in Pretoria and Johannesburg who tried to assist his case. In 1919 the Rev. H. R. Langalibalele Ngciyaya, a minister of an Ethiopian church in South Africa, met Nyamanda in Rhodesia and subsequently lobbied the Colonial Office in London.[1] Politically-minded Matabele favoured the new technique. Nothing comparable developed in Mashonaland; here links with South Africa remained weaker, Ethiopianism had as yet made no real impact, and African religious independency emerged, in the later 'twenties, in sharp opposition to the chiefs whose traditional rules of succession worked in favour of old and often incompetent men.

African agitation, however, failed to make any impact in Britain, and when the Aborigines' Protection Society pleaded the black man's cause before the Privy Council, their Lordships made short shrift of the argument that the natives should be regarded as owners of the unalienated land. The estimation of the rights of aboriginal tribes was always inherently difficult. Some tribes—argued the Council—were so low in the social organization that their usages could not be reconciled with the legal institutions of civilized society. There was no point in imputing to such

[1] Ranger, T. O. *Traditional authorities and the rise of modern politics in Southern Rhodesia: 1898–1930*, a paper read at the History of African Peoples' Conference, Rhodes-Livingstone Institute, Lusaka, 28 May–1 June 1963

people the shadow of rights familiar to British law and then transmitting these into the substance of transferable property rights as known today. Admittedly, there were some indigenous races whose legal concepts were hardly less precise than those of British lawyers. But between primitive and more evolved native peoples yawned a wide gulf, and the aborigines of Southern Rhodesia approximated to the lower rather than the higher type. Lobengula's duties, even if describable as those of a trustee, were duties of imperfect obligation. Except by fear or force, he could not be made amenable. If the natives before 1893 were owners of the whole of these vast regions in such a sense that without their permission neither travellers nor settlers could enter the country, these rights were fatally inconsistent with white settlement. Colonization however was the whole purpose of the forward movement pioneered by the Company and controlled by the Crown; this object was successfully accomplished, with the result that the aboriginal system gave way to another, prescribed by Order in Council. With conquest, sovereignty passed to the Crown, and the Crown thereby took over the land rights.

The settlers' own argument fared a little better, but not much. The Elected Members contended that the unalienated lands formed the property of the Crown, but that the Crown's power of dealing with this great asset was now limited. They considered that once the Company's administration ended, the land should pass to the Company's administrative successors and the new Government should treat the unalienated lands as an asset for the country's benefit. But the colonists' case involved the proposition that the Crown was already bound by some action or other. This contention was quite untenable. The Crown could do what it liked with its own, and when the Company's tenure of office came to an end, the Crown would remain free to dispose of the unalienated land by any lawful means.

The upshot was that the Company could only sell the unalienated land as long as it administered the country, and must apply the land revenue to administrative expenditure for current or past years. Once the Imperial authorities put an end to Chartered administration, the Board could look to the Crown for reimbursement of past advances made for the administration of Rhodesia.[1] This reimbursement could be made either from public funds or from the sale of the Crown's unalienated land in Southern Rhodesia. The new Southern Rhodesia Government, in other words, would not be able to use the unalienated land to its own profit until the Crown's debt had been cleared.

[1] Great Britain. Privy council. Judicial committee. *Special reference as to the ownership of the unalienated land in Southern Rhodesia: report . . . 1918*

A bitter dispute then broke out as to the size of the Company's prospective bill for administrative deficits. The Company's experts, not inhibited by excessive modesty, put the total at £7,666,000, a large sum for the time, and most financial experts saw the country's future in a very dim light. A self-governing Rhodesia would contain no more than about 33,000 whites and some 770,000 blacks, most of whom were still leading tribal lives in the reserves. The country would bear heavy financial commitments; the new government would own neither railways nor mineral rights and until the debt was paid even the Crown lands would be beyond its grasp. Chaplin thought that a Responsible Government administration would therefore have to resort to heavy taxation, and was accordingly struck by 'unmistakable signs of hesitation on the part of those who have anything to lose' in the country.[1] The Company itself thought that Southern Rhodesia was unlikely to make a go of autonomy. Phillip Lyttelton Gell, the Company's President since 1920, privately wrote to Chaplin that Rhodesians did not understand the world-wide scarcity of capital; he also feared that the Responsible Government party's lack of financial integrity in refusing to assume responsibility for the administrative deficits would get Rhodesia black-listed on the London market. The country was economically vulnerable, and the British—much poorer than the Rhodesians—could not be expected to give financial help.[2]

Since the Imperial Government had no taste for further commitments, a South African solution seemed the best possible alternative. Prospects south of the Limpopo were now looking much brighter from the 'Charter's' point of view. In 1919 Jan Christiaan Smuts succeeded Botha as Prime Minister at Pretoria, and South Africa was now run by a man thoroughly trusted by South African Unionists.[3]

Smuts co-operated with British mining interests, and was as sound as a bell on the social question! As Minister of Defence, he had previously quelled two serious European strikes on the Rand and deported their leaders. In 1922 he added further laurels to his reputation by smashing an armed miners' rising in Johannesburg. But Smuts stood for infinitely more than just gunpowder and grapeshot in defence of the established social order. A former Boer leader turned British General, a convert from Commando captain to Commonwealth War Cabinet Minister, a philosopher, and statesman of international stature, he represented perhaps the Empire's greatest living asset and therefore made a genuinely personal

---

[1] Sir F. P. D. Chaplin to Sir T. Smartt: 28 Feb 1921 (in CH 8/2/1, Nat Arch MS)

[2] P. L. Gell to Sir F. P. D. Chaplin: 8 Mar 1921 (in CH 8/2/2/6, Nat Arch MS)

[3] As early as 1915 Sir Percy Fitzpatrick had commented on Smuts's personal loyalty, preferring Smuts to Botha. Sir P. Fitzpatrick to Sir F. P. D. Chaplin: 10 Dec 1915 (in CH 8/2/1, Nat Arch MS)

appeal to Chartered policy-makers. In addition, the Board now had sound financial reasons for looking towards Smuts, for South Africa, with its comparative affluence, could buy out the Company on satisfactory terms, whilst the accession of a new bloc of British voters would strengthen the General's position in Pretoria.

Within Rhodesia two opposing political forces began to marshal their strength, and something like modern political parties began to emerge. The supporters of Smuts founded the Rhodesia Unionist Association in 1919 and received much help from the mining industry. The Association's headquarters lay in the Gold Fields Building in Bulawayo. Herbert T. Longden, a Bulawayo lawyer like Coghlan, served as Chairman; but James Gordon (later Sir James) McDonald and Sir Bourchier Wrey, both well-known mining men, stood out as the Association's most influential supporters. In an interview with Winston Churchill their delegation rightly pointed out to the British Colonial Secretary that they represented a good deal of Rhodesian capital; they feared national bankruptcy under Responsible Government, unless the Imperial Government would step in with financial help. South Africa on the other hand would probably levy lower taxes than an autonomous Rhodesian Government, and could give the country more favourable railway rates. Admittedly Union might lead to an influx of poor Dutchmen from the South, but people of that kind were good pioneers and would open up land that few British people would care to tackle.[1] People like Wrey and McDonald could also rely on support from most of the senior civil servants in the country, men such as Ernest William Sanders (later Sir Ernest) Montagu, the Secretary for Mines, and Percival Donald Leslie (later Sir Percy) Fynn, the Company's Treasurer, whose financial orthodoxy was unimpeachable, and who then had little faith in government by bush-lawyers and backveld farmers. The Union issue of course never became a real class struggle pure and simple. Some poor Europeans, including a number of Afrikaans-speaking immigrants, favoured the South African cause. Many families were divided, so that Dr Godfrey Martin Huggins, a prominent surgeon from England, favoured Union, whilst his wife remained a passionate advocate of Responsible Government, the two agreeing at the subsequent Referendum that neither should go to the polls. But by and large the people with bigger bank balances stuck to Smuts, and the less prosperous preferred Responsible Government.

In the meantime the advocates of Responsible Government managed to steal a slight march on their opponents. The scattered white population

[1] L. Ludlow [of Gold Fields Rhodesia Development Company] to Sir F. P. D. Chaplin: 17 Dec 1921 (in CH 8/2/1, Nat Arch MS)

was always hard to organize, and for long the Rhodesia Agricultural Union, first formed in 1904, had played a major part in local politics. The Union's annual congresses became important occasions which senior civil servants and prominent politicians would attend, in addition to delegates of Farmers' Associations from all over the country. The Union, which thus controlled a rudimentary political machine throughout the territory, became an important group which frequently voiced bitter criticism of the Administration, sometimes also clashing with the two Chambers of Mines in the country. Many farmers favoured Responsible Government, and in 1917 a Responsible Government Association came into being which determined to secure the country's internal autonomy. The Association's most prominent speakers included Robert Alexander Fletcher, one-time President of the Rhodesia Agricultural Union, a forceful but wayward man who later resigned from the Association. Another prominent farmer was William Muter Leggate, a tall, lanky Scotsman who once distinguished himself at Edinburgh University by coming out as a double medallist in economics, and subsequently farmed in the Hartley district, becoming President of the Rhodesia Agricultural Union in 1919. The Association's leading 'intellectual' was Mrs Ethel Tawse-Jollie, the widow of Colquhoun, the country's first Acting Resident Magistrate in 1890, a handsome and well-spoken Englishwoman, an ardent supporter of Empire and also an experienced organizer with various books and articles to her credit.[1] The Responsible Government Association also attracted many former supporters of the 'Gwelo Programme', but its influence at first remained rather limited. In 1919, however, the group received a major access of strength. Sir Charles Coghlan at last decided to support the movement and become its leading spokesman, much to the annoyance of old campaigners like Captain Harry Bertin who remarked in private that men like McChlery and himself led the way rather than jumped on the band wagon later.[2] Coghlan, a forceful speaker and, for all his abrupt and sometimes rude manner, a person of integrity, proved an important electoral asset and made an effective President. The most able man on the Responsible Government side, however, was Sir Francis James Newton, a sparse, quiet-spoken civil servant, a man who not only possessed brains but also gave the necessary 'tone' to the movement. Born in the West Indies, young Francis later went to Rugby and Oxford, subsequently making a name for himself in Southern Africa, where he became Resident

[1] Her work *The real Rhodesia*. Hutchinson and co., 1924, gives an outline of the Responsible Government campaign. She later became a member of the Southern Rhodesia Legislative Assembly, and at the same time the Empire's first woman parliamentarian.
[2] H. Bertin to J. McChlery: 16 June 1920 (in MA 15/1/1, Nat Arch MS)

Commissioner in the Bechuanaland Protectorate at a time when the territory was developing into a key position for further British penetration inland. During the Jameson Raid days Newton rather blotted his copybook and incurred bitter criticism for failing to report the Company's preparations. For a time he was rusticated to the West Indies, but the Company looked after its own and in 1903 appointed him the first Treasurer for Southern Rhodesia. Newton held office for sixteen years, turning the Treasury into the key position in the country's developing administrative structure. In 1919 he retired from the Company's service, but apparently he never quite forgave the 'Charter' for not making him Administrator when Milton left in 1914; on his retirement he felt aggrieved over his pension rights; besides he felt strongly about the Dutch question in South Africa, and he now threw his influence heart and soul behind the Responsible Government campaign.[1] Chaplin regarded him as the most dangerous man on 'the other side', for Newton had, what a South African like Coghlan lacked, an 'Imperial background', excellent connexions at the Colonial Office, and a thorough training in financial and administrative affairs, which the Responsible Government Party badly needed.

In campaigning for Responsible Government Coghlan and his associates enjoyed a number of considerable advantages. Rhodesia, despite its substantial foreign minorities, felt itself to be an intensely British country;[2] during the War something like a quarter of the white population served in khaki and these people loyally looked up to the Union Jack. Surely, argued Responsible Government men, Rhodesians would fare better as citizens of a purely British colony, based on British ideals, that in time would take the lead in Central Africa, than as offshoots of a powerful neighbour in the South, which sooner or later would go to the Afrikaner Nationalists. Rhodesia, moreover, remained a youthful community with a very high birth-rate, a land almost without grandmothers, displaying all the cheerful optimism and self-confidence which such a demographic condition usually engenders. At the same time the country was beginning to settle down; the excess of men over women, characteristic of any frontier community, was fast diminishing and the country was evolving a stable kind of family life.[3]

[1] Sir F. P. D. Chaplin to Sir D. O. Malcolm: 27 June 1921 (in CH 8/2/2/11, Nat Arch MS)
[2] The 1921 Census gave the proportion of British subjects as 94·26 per cent. 8,308 were born in Southern Rhodesia, 11,634 in the Union of South Africa, 10,544 in the United Kingdom, nearly two-thirds thus being of South African birth. The main ethnic-religious minorities were the Afrikaners, adherents to the Dutch Reformed Church numbering 6,537 out of 33,620 people, and the Jews, comprising 1,283 persons.
[3] The birth-rate in 1920 amounted to 29·77 on the basis of an 'adjusted population' (which reduces the excess of males to 4 per cent of the adjusted total, so as to make figures more easily comparable

At the same time white Rhodesians still felt themselves geographically isolated; the weary trip to the Union took several days by train, and Cape Town seemed very far away in those days when motor cars were few, and regular air passenger routes to the South did not yet exist. Besides, Coghlan was campaigning 'agin the Government' and big business, and thereby naturally had an easier task than Company men. Union, of course, might offer certain advantages. But all the same Rhodesians ought not to sell their birthright for a mess of pottage. A contemporary cartoon showed a tall, clean-cut, pipe-smoking Rhodesian wearing a broad hat and shorts, turning contemptuously away as Smuts, in the guise of an oily, disreputable peddler, tried to unload a whole consignment of promises, with Rhodes looking disapprovingly from his pedestal. Rhodesians felt a genuine patriotism for their country, and many believed that their kind of 'proto-nationalism', a composite of Imperial and territorial loyalties, was incompatible with joining their southern neighbours.

Responsible Government men moreover could draw on a number of hard economic arguments. Many of the younger civil servants, for instance, felt considerable distrust of centralized rule from Pretoria and the Union's policy of bilingualism which might interfere with the promotion of English-speaking officials. Farmers and smallworkers felt scared lest Union might be instrumental in depriving them of their native labour which was being attracted in increasing numbers to the Rand, with its higher rates of pay. Moreover South Africa was beginning to develop secondary industries of her own; influential South African groups spoke in favour of protecting their industries by high tariffs to cut out competition from Britain and other countries. South African protectionism would probably not have affected Rhodesian mining companies which bought much of their highly specialized machinery from South Africa. Union tariffs, however, were liable to interfere with Rhodesian raw material producers. For as long as the country only turned out a few primary materials for export, her interests would be best served by a policy of low duties which would cheapen consumer goods, and attract immigrants. Rhodesia should attract more people; but Rhodesians argued that the country needed, not poor *by-woners* from the south who might be allotted land for political reasons, but people with capital who would buy land in Rhodesia's empty acres and thereby help to improve the value of real estate, an important consideration in an under-developed country where land was a major form of investment. The Responsible Government men also argued that South African taxes and tariffs were higher than

between countries). In the meantime the 'masculinity' of Southern Rhodesia dropped from 245·76 in 1904 to 129·75 in 1921, the figures expressing the number of males to 100 females.

Southern Rhodesia's, that the Union Government would take the major share of public revenue, leaving the Provinces with only a relatively small proportion of the public income, and that Southern Rhodesians would be heavily outvoted in the Union Legislature.[1]

Responsible Government moreover made a strong appeal to the European working class who formed a substantial portion of the European population.[2] White working men found that the post-war boom had put them in a relatively favourable bargaining position, and again a number of strikes broke out, labour politics to some extent cutting across the Responsible Government issue. In defence of strike action the workers pointed to the steadily rising cost of living, which a subsequent commission of enquiry put down to a whole variety of factors. The price of imported goods was going up as the result of world-wide inflation, the prevailing shortage of commodities and the general economic disruption brought about by the war.[3] In addition traders had to meet high freight bills; at the same time company profits were going up, so that discontent grew apace, not only amongst miners and railwaymen, but also amongst civil servants, posts and telegraph employees and even policemen. Post-war immigrants from Britain and South Africa moreover brought in novel ideas about trade unionism and even syndicalism, whilst a large section of the poorer Europeans supported increased militancy.

In 1919 Herbert Walsh, a boiler maker and General Secretary of the Rhodesian Mine and General Workers' Association, helped to organize a fairly widespread miners' strike. At Wankie salaried officials carried on and raised some coal, but the railwaymen refused to take it away. At

[1] For the Responsible Government case, see for instance Tawse-Jollie, E. *Points for Unionists*, a pamphlet printed by the Argus press at Salisbury; W. M. Leggate's address at the Drill Hall, Salisbury, in *Rhodesia herald*, 19 Apr 1920; and Coghlan's address at Bulawayo in *Bulawayo chronicle*, 23 Apr 1920

[2] According to the 1921 census, the country's white occupational distribution was as follows:

Occupational group	Income earners	Proportion per cent of population dependent on each occupation
Public services	2,150	14·55
Professions	655	4·43
Mining	1,897	12·84
Agriculture	3,626	24·54
Industries	1,492	10·10
Commerce	2,481	16·79
Commercial services	740	5·01
Railways	1,637	11·08
Independent means	98	0·66
	14,776	

[3] See Southern Rhodesia. *Report of cost of living committee, 1921.* Salisbury, printed by the Government printer, 1921 (*A 2–1921*)

Rezende work continued with officials and native labourers, Chaplin hoping fervently that the public would now realize that a good many highly-paid white workers might be got rid of, if only Africans received more scope.[1] A year later the railwaymen came out, securing an eight-hour day, improved wages and other benefits for themselves.[2] Even more dangerous to the Chartered Government was the fact that white workers began to co-operate between themselves. In 1920, for instance, postal workers and railwaymen concluded a temporary alliance, the industrial situation becoming further complicated by the fact that the Executive Committee of the Civil Servants' Association at Bulawayo sympathized with the strikers. Trouble even broke out amongst police recruits, the Commandant-General feeling convinced that if the strikers were dismissed, the whole police force would stop work.[3] Coghlan's cause benefited from working-class discontent, even though he sympathized with the Government's difficulties and agreed with Chaplin on the dangers of collaboration between railway and postal workers. According to Coghlan, the country needed legislation on the Australian model to prevent the community from being paralysed. Trade unionism, Coghlan argued, was all right, but syndicalism was not, and this dangerous doctrine was now being taken up on the railways.[4]

The extent of Rhodesia's trouble should not, of course, be exaggerated. The country still remained an industrial backwater, and was never shaken by the violent labour disputes that were then rocking South Africa. Early in 1922 white miners on the Rand started a bloody rising, determined that the 'Rand Lords' should not undercut Europeans with cheaper-paid African labour. For a short time armed European workers controlled almost the whole Rand. The Union High Command found that many soldiers in the Citizen Force sympathized with the strikers and refused to fight; and towards the end of February practically the whole of the Union's Permanent Force had to be sent to the Rand. Pretoria remained unprotected, and had a similar outbreak occurred there the situation would have become exceptionally grave for the Government. As it happened the revolutionaries made a great many mistakes. They failed to destroy the telegraph lines or to put the railways out of action, their whole revolution suffering badly from lack of central control.[5] But for a moment the position looked desperate, and many Rhodesian middle-class people became

[1] Sir F. P. D. Chaplin to P. L. Gell: 24 Dec 1919 (in CH 8/2/2/6, Nat Arch MS)
[2] See *Rhodesian railway review*, no. 3, Nov 1921
[3] Sir F. P. D. Chaplin to P. L. Gell: 27 Feb 1920 (in CH 8/2/2/6, Nat Arch MS)
[4] Sir C. P. Coghlan to Sir F. P. D. Chaplin: 3 Mar 1920 (in CH 8/2/2/7, Nat Arch MS)
[5] General staff, Defence headquarters, Pretoria. Military report re industrial upheaval on the Witwatersrand . . . January to March 1922 (copy in B 2/2/10, Nat Arch SR)

convinced that their territory should not throw in its lot with such a turbulent country.

Rhodesian workers for their part were likewise determined to have nothing to do with South Africa. Smuts might be a hero to Imperialists, but many working-class people now regarded him as a kind of South African Cossack who would shy from nothing to beat the poor about the head. Rhodesia had a much more conciliatory Administration; the danger from native competition remained infinitely less, and white workers drew substantially bigger pay packets. 'Utter madness to join South Africa,' wrote Laurence John Walter Keller, a fearless and outspoken Bulawayo railwayman. The South African Railways paid much less money; strikers down south were subject to severe penalties, and the first thing South African capitalists would do after getting their claws on the country, would be to smash the Rhodesia Railway Workers' Union and increase working hours.[1] Responsible Government, therefore, acquired a wide social backing from both wage-workers and middle-class people, and became a powerful political force.

The groups 'marginal' to European politics likewise tended to favour Responsible Government. Indian and Coloured people preferred the milder Rhodesian regime and so, as far as one can tell, did Africans. Coghlan publicly spoke out in favour of Rhodes's dictum of equal rights for all civilized men south of the Zambezi. 'We have no right to keep back the natives from becoming civilized,' he told a meeting in Bulawayo, and 'if a man is a civilized citizen he should be admitted to the franchise irrespective of his colour. This is the right in the Cape, and I have never heard it has done any harm there'.[2] Admittedly, thought Coghlan, the existing clause in the Southern Rhodesia Order in Council of 1898, allowing Africans to hold land anywhere in the Colony, should be altered; but then it was precisely the liberal-minded Rhodesians who held that Africans would, in fact, do better if separate native purchase areas were marked out for them, since black men were unable to compete with whites in the real estate market. Rhodesians moreover believed their record in native matters to be better than that of either the Union or Nyasaland and, as far as one can judge, educated Africans agreed. Certainly no African body at the time raised its voice against Responsible Government. In 1921 a few black people, sufficiently well informed about politics to read the 'Legco' Debates, presented a statement to the Elected Members outlining

[1] Keller, J. W. 'Responsible government or union' (in *Rhodesian railway review*, no. 2, Oct 1921, p. 1–5
[2] Coghlan, Sir C. P. *Responsible government: the draft constitution: an explanatory address.* [Bulawayo, Responsible government association], 1922

various complaints; this petition, however, merely concerned itself with local issues, and Responsible Government never entered the debate.

The missionaries on the whole likewise backed the cause of Responsible Government. Rhodesia as yet completely lacked a native-born white intelligentsia of its own; the place of the 'Outsider' in politics was taken by white clergymen who generally lacked a direct stake in the settler community and propounded a faith which the majority of colonists— Deist more than Christian in their personal convictions—shared only in theory.[1] The 'Outsider' now also spoke up against Union, throwing his lot in with that of the majority of whites. White advocates of internal autonomy were perfectly willing to concede Imperial guarantees for Africans. Responsible Government men moreover comprised within their numbers an outspoken Negrophile like Francis Leslie Hadfield, a missionary and a Labourite in his sympathies.[2] The clergy, like the poorer white settlers, had long been criticizing Company rule; at the same time they objected to South African native policies and wanted to uphold the colour-blind franchise. This of course did not mean that they wished to see African participation in Government; even the clerical extreme left wing, composed of Arthur Shearly Cripps and John White, merely confined its political demands to a cautious request for native advisory councils, which ultimately would select white men to represent black in the Legislative Assembly. Africans, explained John White, still remained a 'politically dumb people', and advisory councils represented the best solution for the time being. Cripps agreed, adding that Union Government would be even worse than the Chartered regime, which, at any rate, represented 'dual control' and gave some say to the Imperial power.[3] But Company rule ought to go and local Europeans should take over.

The Company was under the necessity of waging a political battle on two fronts. On the one hand it was fighting Coghlan and his friends. But in addition it became subject to bitter criticism because of the recommendation of the Native Reserves Commission in 1917 that African tribal areas should be diminished by about a million acres. This caused Cripps,

[1] The census of 1921 stated that only 46·20 per cent of the white population was in touch with the clergy and recorded by them as Church members. Of the total population only 9·7 per cent attended public worship. On the other hand only 70 persons out of 33,620 described themselves as atheists, agnostics or free thinkers.

[2] The Responsible Government cause was backed by three Labour men, John Stewart, a railway clerk, Captain W. D. Douglas Jones and F. L. Hadfield. The first Rhodesian Labour Party was organized in 1920, led by Stewart and Hadfield, but showed itself so mild in its programme that the miners' and railwaymen's unions would not support it. Hadfield resigned in 1921, and the Party drew nearer to the unions, but the Party's new programme, issued in 1923, was much less forceful than even the rather nebulous socialism that most trade unionists thought desirable.

[3] Southern Rhodesia missionary conference. *Proceedings . . . July 1922*. Bulawayo, Argus printing and publishing company, limited, 1922, p. 24

a Christian Socialist of the 'Utopian' variety, to begin a bitter campaign against the Chartered Company, in which he received powerful support from the Aborigines' Protection Society, then the stronghold of middle-class reformism in colonial affairs. The campaigners successfully employed accepted methods of political agitation, pamphleteering and questions in Parliament, with the result that the Secretary of State weakened and in turn 'put the screw' on the Company. It accordingly had to give way on three of the major areas under dispute, the Sabi and Chiduku reserves and a new Inyanga reserve, and the Order in Council of 1920 included these modifications.[1]

The new settlement involved a serious political defeat for the Company, for missionary propaganda had now put it in bad odour all round. Cripps, an emotional man, a poetic dilettante of prolific output, who hated capitalism for spiritual reasons and dreamt of a golden age when accursed innovations like the Compulsory Dipping Ordinance were unknown to the primaeval African paradise, in fact went much further than his fellow clergymen. 'He is like a hysterical woman in his wriggling, inveracity and obsession,' furiously wrote Gell to Chaplin after an interview with 'that fanatical negrophile' at the Company's London offices. According to Gell, Cripps broke down when confronted with false statements concerning forced labour; he perforce agreed that every abuse forwarded to Chaplin had ceased, admitted that the Native Department officials were extremely fair, and promised both to co-operate with Native Commissioners in the future and to place the facts before Chaplin before making unwarranted charges.[2] But neither Cripps nor the Aborigines' Protection Society let up in their campaign, which was so effective that Gell shortly afterwards complained about the 'A.P.S.' having 'captured' the Labour Party.[3] John H. (later Sir John) Harris, the Society's Secretary, published a bitter book which mixed historical facts and fiction in about equal proportions, concluding that the Charter deserved no sympathy. White settlers, on the other hand, were in a very different category. They were to be pitied rather than envied, for the colonists were having a hard time in Rhodesia where the cost of living had soared and three gold sovereigns bought less than one in England. The colonists were facing tremendous difficulties, but nevertheless were fine people, possessed of a keen sense of justice and of sufficient ability to run the country.[4] Harris's view represented the

---

[1] For an account sympathetic to Cripps, see Ranger, T. O. *State and church in Southern Rhodesia, 1919 to 1939.* Salisbury, Historical association of Rhodesia and Nyasaland [1960 ?] (*Local series*, 4)

[2] P. L. Gell to Sir F. P. D. Chaplin: 6 May 1920 (in CH 8/2/2/6, Nat Arch MS)

[3] P. L. Gell to Sir F. P. D. Chaplin: 11 May 1920 (in CH 8/2/2/6, Nat Arch MS)

[4] Harris, J. H. *The Chartered millions: Rhodesia and the challenge to the British commonwealth.* The Swarthmore Press ltd, 1920, p. 236, 286-287

'progressive' orthodoxy of his day, though not Cripps's own views in the matter.

Chartered policy-makers for a time, however, had some grounds for political optimism. The Privy Council judgement was by no means unwelcome to 'London Wall', for the Crown now became responsible for the administrative deficits. Experts welcomed a political handover from the business point of view and were in fact anxious to get rid of the responsibility of government. 'My experiences as Commercial Representative in Rhodesia', wrote the Resident Director, 'always showed me that . . . the fact that the Company was responsible for the Administration undoubtedly hampered one in the prosecution of commercial enterprises.'[1] The Company possessed a powerful friend at court. In 1919 Milner took over from Long as Colonial Secretary and the new man, an Imperialist of the old school, felt no doubt that Southern and possibly even North-Western Rhodesia should become part of the Union, whilst North-Eastern Rhodesia should link up with Nyasaland, the former German East Africa, Uganda and Kenya, in a London-governed tropical dependency.[2] To him the issue seemed clear cut. Southern Rhodesia would strengthen the British cause in South Africa, a main hinge of Empire. Milner, a stern and realistic administrator, firmly wedded to prevailing doctrines of financial retrenchment, had no desire to set up yet another Crown Colony administration, and professed much anxiety to retrieve from the future owners of Rhodesia the sum payable by the Crown under the Privy Council judgement, feeling convinced that only South Africa would be in a position to afford such a heavy outlay.

In Southern Rhodesia, however, the Unionists could make no headway. In 1920 a Commission presided over by Lord Cave concluded its deliberations concerning the debt outstanding to the Company, reducing the Chartered claim to £4,435,225.[3] A few months later the Legislative Council by a great majority passed a resolution in favour of Responsible Government.[4] Milner, objecting to Cabinet policies in Egypt, retired from the Government, and Churchill, the new Secretary of State, proved an easier man for Coghlan to deal with. In 1906 Churchill had helped to steer self-government for the Transvaal through the House—fifteen years later he could hardly help feeling some sympathy when men of British stock put up similar demands. Churchill, an imaginative and warm-hearted man, was moreover deeply moved when he learned of the extent of Rhodesia's war sacrifices in the Imperial cause. Besides, a politician like Coghlan—

---

[1] P. O. Inskipp to Sir F. P. D. Chaplin: 23 Apr 1919 (in CH 8/2/1, Nat Arch MS)
[2] Sir D. O. Malcolm to Sir F. P. D. Chaplin: 16 Apr 1919 (in CH 8/2/2/11, Nat Arch MS)
[3] Cmd. 1129, A and B (1921)
[4] Southern Rhodesia. *Legislative assembly debates*, 12 May 1920, p. 47–92; 13 May 1920, p. 92–222

Catholic, Irishman and Imperialist all at the same time—seemed almost too good to be true at a time when Churchill was desperately trying to settle the bitter civil war in Ireland.

The Colonial Secretary then appointed a Commission, headed by Earl Buxton, a former High Commissioner for South Africa and sympathetic to the Rhodesians' cause. The Commission pointed out that as long as the Company believed itself to be the owners of the land it was willing to spend money liberally in administering the country. Now, however, the Company would no longer disburse the shareholders' funds without hope of reimbursement at a profit. Southern Rhodesia therefore had to decide on the question of Responsible Government, and should make up its mind by means of a Referendum. If Southern Rhodesia decided for autonomy the country should at last cease to be a Protectorate and be annexed to the Crown as a Colony. The Commissioners at the same time outlined a constitution, fashioned in the main on the instrument which had granted self-government to Natal. The country would be headed by a constitutional Governor, and effective power would lie in the hands of a Cabinet responsible to an elected Legislature. As far as the native question was concerned, the Commission noted a declaration made by Coghlan in the Legislative Assembly in 1920 that the Imperial Government was welcome to uphold all the conditions obtaining under the Chartered administration, and that the colonists would conform to any guarantees which the Imperial authorities would lay down.[1] The Commissioners thus recommended that all existing safeguards for Africans should continue, and that appointments in the Native Department should still be subject to the High Commissioner's consent, a recommendation which greatly impressed negrophile opinion.

'London Wall' bitterly resented the Buxton Report, and Smuts privately expressed his disappointment to Chaplin, arguing that the document had prejudiced the whole Union issue and given the electorate no real alternative.[2] Rhodesians ought to choose between a definite scheme for Responsible Government on the one hand and Union on the other, Smuts's supporters now being anxious to acquire Rhodesia for the sake of her votes.[3] Smuts became all the more hopeful when in 1921 his own South African Party fused with the Unionist Party and he won the election with a great majority. Shortly afterwards Sir Abe Bailey and S. B. Joel, two powerful South African mining magnates, confidentially interviewed Coghlan, indicating in rather circumspect fashion that he could have a

[1] Cmd. 1273 (1921)
[2] J. C. Smuts to Sir F. P. D. Chaplin: 21 May 1921 (in CH 8/2/1, Nat Arch MS)
[3] Sir J. G. McDonald to Sir F. P. D. Chaplin: 7 July 1921, reporting a conversation with W. J. Jagger, member for Cape Town in the House of Assembly (in CH 8/2/1, Nat Arch MS)

R

South African Cabinet post, if only he turn Unionist.[1] Coghlan however refused the proffered bribe. Few genuine Rhodesians, he thought, would be able to afford to sit in the Union Legislature. If the country decided to throw in her lot with South Africa she would be represented only by 'carpet baggers' in the Union Parliament. Rhodesian interests would be neglected there because Rhodesian parliamentarians would be bound to support Smuts against the Nationalists, whatever happened.

The focus of Rhodesian politics then shifted to London. Coghlan took a delegation there to interview the Colonial Secretary, presenting his case with vigour and trenchancy. He was glad to find that the British Cabinet greatly appreciated the Rhodesians' loyalty at a time when Egypt, Ireland and India were all giving trouble. He also made a good impression on British left-wingers; discussions took place with the International Advisory Committee of the Labour Party and Coghlan explained with much relish how John Harris, the Secretary of the Anti-Slavery Society, 'worked both meetings, not at our request, but on his own', and that Harris 'seems to be cordially in with us'. High finance—like Smuts himself—still opposed Responsible Government, however, and Coghlan found to his distress that loans would be impossible to obtain in the City where 'no one would give us a cent'.[2] Churchill himself, though friendly enough, insisted that the Rhodesians must first find out the Union's terms and in 1922 Smuts published a definite offer.

Smuts did not believe in spoiling his case by penny-pinching, and his terms turned out to be extremely generous. Rhodesia would become South Africa's fifth Province and be represented in the Union Parliament by ten and ultimately by seventeen members, with four seats in the Senate. A separate Provincial Council would control various important local services, as elsewhere in South Africa. The Union would take over the railways and give particular importance to expanding the small port of Beira, now a vital link in the Rhodesian communication system. South Africa moreover would guarantee to spend no less than £500,000 over the next ten years on development, and at the same time buy the Company's land and mineral rights. Land settlement would be encouraged through a Land Board consisting of Rhodesians, whilst public servants would continue to enjoy their rights and privileges, and the natives be left undisturbed in their reserves.[3]

---

[1] Sir C. P. Coghlan to Mrs B. Buller, his sister: 22 June 1921 (in CO 8/1/3, Nat Arch MS), printed in Wallis, J. P. R. One man's hand: the story of Sir Charles Coghlan and the liberation of Southern Rhodesia. Longmans, Green and co., 1950, p. 176–178

[2] Sir C. P. Coghlan to H. U. Moffat: 27 Oct 1921 (in CO 8/1/1, Nat Arch MS)

[3] Published in the British South Africa Company government gazette extraordinary, 31 July 1922, and the Gazette of 25 August 1922. The latter also contained the alternative Draft Letters Patent providing for the constitution of Responsible Government on which voters were to decide.

The South African Prime Minister personally visited Rhodesia, but Chaplin, cold and clearsighted as ever, had no illusions about the outcome. The Unionists' chances might have been better, he privately wrote to Smuts, had more time been allowed to elapse between the date of publication of the Union's terms and the Referendum. The short-lived post-war boom was at an end; if only the farmers were to suffer another six months of depression they might throw in their lot with Smuts. But as things stood the Unionists were not making sufficient headway. They had plenty of money, but lacked a strong party organization or effective speakers, and their whole approach was too rational and their tactics too defensive.[1] Coghlan, on the other hand, showed some imagination; for instance, the colours 'Red and Green', selected as a play on the initials of 'Responsible Government', made an effective appeal. The powerful Argus Press backed the Union cause, but the Rhodesian electorate refused to vote as their morning papers told them. The women especially, thought Chaplin, would vote for Coghlan because of the prevailing anti-Dutch feeling. Trade Unionists, many commercial clerks and also a proportion of the civil servants believed that they would hold a much stronger bargaining position under Responsible Government; and yet Coghlan was able to exploit the satisfactory state of the country's finance for which men like Chaplin were responsible. The Public Services and Posts and Telegraphs associations backed Coghlan; so did the teachers, whom Chaplin privately accused of apparently having carried out widespread 'R.G.' propaganda. The Indians and Coloureds supported Responsible Government, as did most of the clergy—except the Dutch Reformed Church—despite the fact that some Anglican Africans asked their Bishop to support Union.

Chaplin turned out to be right. On 6 November 1922, a great crowd collected outside the Court House at Bulawayo and at half-past five the Acting Civil Commissioner came to announce the results. Throughout the country 8,774 votes were cast for Coghlan, 5,989 for Union.[2] Coghlan stepped out to address the crowd and received a tremendous ovation. Rhodesia had made up its mind, and Rhodes's dream of a united Southern Africa was at an end.

A good deal of hard bargaining then took place in London, over-shadowed by the vastly greater problems of Anglo-French differences over Germany, the Irish 'troubles' and questions arising out of the post-war settlement in Europe. The Chartered Company put in a Petition of Right, claiming to be paid in cash for its administrative deficits before Southern

[1] Sir F. P. D. Chaplin to J. C. Smuts: 30 Oct 1922 (in CH 8/2/1, Nat Arch MS)

[2] Nearly 26 per cent of the registered electorate did not go to the polls, but registrations were not easy to check, so that the roll contained both 'dead' and 'dud' votes, whilst electors in the backveld found difficulty in getting to the polling booth.

Rhodesia could take over the unalienated lands. The Colonial Office for its part dreaded the idea of approaching the Commons for money to pay the Company, and time slipped by whilst Southern Rhodesia continued in a state of constitutional uncertainty. Newton hastened to London to look after the Elected Members' interests, the final settlement owing a good deal to his ability.

In the end Company and Colonial Office came to an agreement involving both Southern and Northern Rhodesia. The Crown abandoned its demands for advances made to the Company for special war-expenditure and agreed to pay to it £3,750,000 in settlement of the Board's own claims. The Crown at the same time took over all unalienated land, public works and buildings in the two Rhodesias, whilst the Company kept its mineral rights both north and south of the Zambezi, and received cast-iron protection against any tampering with its railway assets. The Company in turn withdrew its Petition of Right, whilst the new Southern Rhodesia Government had to pay £2,000,000 to the British Government, thereby reducing the total Imperial cost of acquiring the two Rhodesias to just £1,750,000.[1] Southern Rhodesia for her part obtained her public works and unalienated land, the Southern Rhodesian settlers becoming the only community in Imperial history which has ever had to pay for the privilege of self-government. In order to meet their bill, which amounted to more than the country's entire annual revenue, the Rhodesians were allowed to raise a loan.[2] Had their request for self-government been met in 1920 they would have had two bumper years to establish their position; but now they had to take over the Administration at a time when the economic position was getting worse. The Chartered Directors privately groused about the terms but they had gained a better deal than they imagined. Within less than a decade the Company's mineral rights shot up in value in a way which not even the most optimistic investor envisaged in 1923, and Rhodes's dream of a 'Second Rand' came true on the Copper Belt. In Southern Rhodesia the Company likewise retained a dominant economic position; it relinquished its administrative chores, whilst receiving a substantial amount of liquid capital which, together with the Company's intimate knowledge of local conditions, enabled it to continue playing a major part as a supplier of capital.

The country was formally annexed to the Crown as a Colony. The new Administration was headed by a Governor who represented the Sovereign and acted as the country's formal constitutional and ceremonial head. The Governor formed the recognized link between Salisbury and London; his

[1] See Cmd. 1914 (1923) and Cmd. 1984 (1923)
[2] The approximate receipts for 1923/24 were £1,510,103.

despatches and reports provided the Imperial Government with detailed and up-to-date information on the political and economic situation within the Colony, whilst Southern Rhodesia received a great deal of political, commercial and other kinds of intelligence from London which she could never have collected on her own. The Governor presided over the Executive Council, a formal ratifying body, composed of Ministers. A keen and energetic Governor could exert some influence in tendering advice, and in insisting on being heard and informed on all major issues. In the early days, when Ministers were not so familiar with the constitutional niceties, the Governor also played a valuable, though informal, part as constitutional adviser; no Rhodesian politician had as yet sat in a Cabinet; Sir John Chancellor, the first Governor, a man with extensive experience as Secretary to the Colonial Defence Committee and as Governor in Mauritius and the West Indies, could therefore always make his views felt. The Governor, who at the same time acted as the Colony's formal Commander-in-Chief, made certain that the country should not step out of line on major issues, such as in laws affecting the currency, in the imposition of differential duties, or measures inconsistent with British treaty obligations or affecting the property rights of British subjects not residing in the Colony. Imperial trusteeship, in other words, backed the interests of British investors, especially the Chartered railway and mineral rights.

At the same time, the new Constitution made provision for looking after native interests; the terms of the Letters Patent protected Africans against possible abuses rather than promoted development, native affairs being envisaged as a highly specialized function which could be neatly sliced off from the remainder of public affairs. The Constitution prevented discriminatory legislation against Africans, except with regard to the supply of arms, ammunition and liquor; the Reserves remained vested in the High Commissioner, and the Letters Patent guaranteed a free and colour-blind land market outside the tribal areas. The Native Department retained its special status; all appointments were made by the Governor-in-Council with the approval of the High Commissioner for South Africa, Imperial policy thus leaving the Native Department as almost a state within a state.[1]

The Colony thus remained closely tied to the Imperial connexion; it controlled its own local defence forces but could not carry out an

[1] For the full details, see *Southern Rhodesia constitution. Letters patent* . . . , 1 Sep 1923; Southern Rhodesia. *Letters patent . . . constituting the office of Governor*, 1 Sep 1923; *Instructions . . . to the Governor and Commander-in-chief of the Colony of Southern Rhodesia*, 1 Sep 1923 (in *Statute law of Southern Rhodesia from 1st January to 31st December, 1923*. Salisbury: Government printer, 1924)

independent foreign policy. The Imperial power retained a right of surveillance over all important legislation, London being consulted in detail before reserved bills went to the Legislature. Within these limits, however, the Colony now took full charge of its internal affairs. Government was exercized by a Cabinet, headed by a 'Premier' whose status was subsequently raised to that of 'Prime Minister'. Ministers formally owed their appointments to the Governor but remained responsible to a Legislative Assembly of thirty members elected by a limited electorate on the non-racial though property-weighed franchise inherited from the Cape; the number of voters remained sufficiently small to obviate the creation of great impersonal machines, whilst Ministers remained in close personal touch with their constituencies.

The road to political advancement did not lie in service to a party bureaucracy, but in getting to know people in law, business or farming. Attorneys like Coghlan—men trained to speak in public and familiar with the law—played a particularly important part. Other politicians made their names in a managerial capacity in trade, mining or banking, or in the Rhodesia Agricultural Union. A further group of public men consisted of people who had learnt the art of public administration in the Chartered Company's civil service. There were also other ways of getting to be known in politics, such as taking an active interest in municipal or trade union affairs, but these were less effective.

Substantive political power thus passed from London to Salisbury, into the hands of local notables, some of whom soon displayed considerable personal ability. The system as a whole rested on a complicated balance of power between local and Imperial interests, and much of the country's subsequent political history revolved on the problem of how the remaining shackles on local executive control should be removed. In this respect white Rhodesians at first remained much more concerned with the mineral rights and railway issues than with African affairs, which experts during the 'twenties and early 'thirties continued to regard as 'non-political' in nature. Within these limits Responsible Government men were satisfied with what they had got; no one in those days ever thought of claiming dominion status for the Colony, the existing partnership between the Imperial and the Southern Rhodesian authorities being regarded as part of the natural order of things, which would never break up. Coghlan himself rejoiced over what he regarded as a great victory, and when on 1 October 1923 the burly Irish lawyer—now a sexagenarian—solemnly took his oath of office, Southern Rhodesia at last entered upon an autonomous political career.

Chapter Seven

'White Rhodesia'

I

Coghlan in charge: 1923–1927

Constitutionally, Southern Rhodesia had made a big step forward; in day-to-day administration the change seemed less obvious. With the grant of Responsible Government the Governor called on Coghlan to form an initial Cabinet which would hold office until elections took place. The new Administration, despite a certain amount of agitation from job-hunters, made no attempt to 'Rhodesianize' its perfectly efficient and honest civil service; work in Government offices continued much as before, even though Heads of Departments were now responsible to Ministers, themselves answerable for their actions to an elected Legislative Assembly. Otherwise Coghlan made no startling innovations; in some cases he even preferred to work with former Unionists, secretly cursing irreconcilables and disappointed place hunters within his own party. Fynn, the Company's old Treasurer, continued in charge of the country's finance and stayed on, with his special knowledge, as a 'fixture' in successive Cabinets to come. Newton became Colonial Secretary for two years until 1925 when he left for London to take charge of Southern Rhodesia's vital Imperial relations as her High Commissioner in the United Kingdom. Robert James Hudson (later Sir Robert), a successful barrister, born at the Cape, trained at Cambridge, with a fine war record, was the first Attorney-General and Minister of Defence. Leggate was made Minister of Agriculture and Lands, a popular appointment with his fellow farmers. In 1925 Leggate was replaced by John Wallace Downie, a self-made Scottish immigrant who had worked his way up from a humble job on the Railways to a partnership in a Rhodesian shipping and forwarding house, and who later became Manager of the Salisbury Farmers' Co-operative. Howard Unwin Moffat, formerly General Manager of the Bechuanaland Exploration Company, one of Sir Edmund Davis's many financial interests, assumed a key position as Minister of Mines and Public Works.

Davis thought highly of Moffat's ability; he pressed him to take up politics and displayed much more confidence in the new government than did many other London financiers.[1] Old stalwarts like Mrs Tawse-Jollie got nothing, Coghlan insisting that he would not have the lady in the Cabinet, even though she might prove troublesome when left out.[2]

In the party political field Coghlan decided to bury the hatchet with the Unionists, the new course being symbolized by altering the party's name from Responsible Government Party to Rhodesian Party.[3] Die-hards in Coghlan's camp strongly resented the change, but Coghlan had no patience with them. McDonald, a staunch conservative, privately circulated a memorandum which explained to leading companies that the new Assembly would represent an electorate of some 18,000 people of whom three-fourths possessed but little property. The mining and land-owning concerns would therefore become the main source of revenue and should safeguard themselves against increased taxes on income and possible imposts on unoccupied land; Union with South Africa no longer formed a practical issue and Unionists would no longer put up candidates of their own. Instead former Unionists should support the 'best men' and, at the same time, contribute to a fund opposing Labour propaganda, lest their case should go by default and their financial interests suffer.[4] Richer people now put their trust in the Government Party, and even though a few old stalwarts like Sir Ernest William Sanders Montagu, the Company's former Secretary of Mines and Works, continued to sit in Parliament as a representative of extreme conservatism, Unionists as an organized group ceased to count, and the Party wound up.

Slightly more dangerous to Coghlan was the opposition from the left, consisting of white trade unionists and dissident farmers. Keller, now secretary of the Rhodesia Railway Workers' Union, tried to organize European workmen as a separate force, but did not get very far. The new Labour Party relied largely on the Railway Union for supporters and funds, and even though its programme was confined to reformism of the mildest kind, Labour could make little progress outside Bulawayo. W. Morsman, the Party's Secretary, frankly wrote in the Union's journal that Labour was not as yet 'sufficiently educated politically to govern',[5] and when a leading party functionary himself wrote in such a strain the

---

[1] In 1925 Davis became a Director of the British South Africa Company, his new position helping to correct the Company's bias against the new Southern Rhodesian administration.

[2] Sir C. P. Coghlan to Sir F. Newton: 5 Dec 1922 (in NE 1/1/1, Nat Arch MS)

[3] Sir C. P. Coghlan to Mrs Buller: 16 Dec 1923 (in CO 8/1/3, Nat Arch MS)

[4] McDonald, J. G. 'Memorandum re the new political situation in Rhodesia': 20 July 1923 (copy in FY 1/1/4, Nat Arch MS)

[5] Morsman, W. 'A Rhodesian labour party and its objects' (in *Rhodesian railway review*, no. 17, Jan 1923, p. 16)

public could hardly be expected to disagree. Labour never even considered strengthening its base by mobilizing native workmen in its support. Unskilled African workmen, politically quiescent and totally unorganized, played no part in politics, and Labour opinion simply looked upon them as potential blacklegs whom employers might use one day to undercut white wages. The Rhodesian Party, therefore, met with relatively little opposition when the first elections were held in 1924. Coghlan commanded a reasonably efficient party organization with real personal loyalty to himself, and his group accordingly swept the board.[1] Only four independents managed to get in; the remaining 26 members supported Coghlan in the Legislative Assembly which, for all practical purposes, became a select kind of Rhodesian Party club.

The politicians in the new Assembly now faced economic problems similar to those which had troubled Chaplin. The Colony worked on a small budget but in addition to ordinary expenditure now had to pay £2,000,000 to the Imperial Treasury, as well as another £300,000 previously advanced to the country in 1922. Newton skilfully managed negotiations at the London end and secured support from the Bank of England which agreed to give excellent terms, hoping thereby to secure future Rhodesian loan business.[2] Rhodesia at the same time settled its relations with South Africa, where a Nationalist Government, resting on a coalition between Afrikaans farmers and intellectuals on the one hand and white workers on the other, came into power in 1924. Coghlan himself much preferred General Hertzog's new South African Government to Smuts's administration, finding Hertzog's attitude friendlier than that of Smuts. A good deal of hard bargaining nevertheless remained to be done over the customs question. Commercial relations between the two countries had always been close, Southern Rhodesia having joined the South African Customs Union in 1903 with special arrangements enabling

[1] Party organization was based on local branches, any group of ten or more members being allowed to form a branch, and to elect their own officers and committee after obtaining the approval of the Central Executive. The branches therefore enjoyed considerable independence, a characteristic feature of Rhodesian politics, but the Central Executive nevertheless maintained general control through its hold on the party's finances and policy, and the right to select Parliamentary candidates. The Central Executive itself was divided into a Mashonaland and a Matabeleland section. Constitutionally the party was subordinated to the Party Congress. This consisted of one delegate from each branch with additional delegates from the stronger branches. In addition all members of the Central Executive and all Rhodesian Party members in the Legislative Council were automatically members of the Congress. Congress, in turn, elected the Central Executive, the President, Vice-Presidents for Mashonaland and Matabeleland and the Chairman. These, together with the other members of the Central Executive, held office until their successors were appointed at the succeeding annual Congress. They were, however, eligible for re-election and the Party, in fact, enjoyed considerable continuity in leadership. Its administrative work fell to a General Secretary, Coghlan's principal lieutenant in this capacity being Tom Brown Hepburn, a Bulawayo accountant.

[2] Sir F. Newton to Sir C. P. Coghlan: 20 Nov 1923 (in NE 1/1/1, Nat Arch MS)

the territory to grant greater preference to British goods under the so-called 'Rhodes Clause'. The Convention was modified in 1910 when the four southern colonies united, and after various revisions, Southern Rhodesia in 1924 concluded a new agreement on very acceptable terms. The Colony held good cards since Southern Rhodesians only sold between £300,000 and £400,000 of cattle and tobacco down south, accepting in exchange South African manufactured goods valued at about £1,000,000.[1] The South Africans, acting under pressure from their own backveld farmers, succeeded in keeping out Rhodesian tobacco of the poorer sort as well as scrub cattle of low weight. In exchange they granted a fairly substantial payment to Rhodesia; trade between the two countries otherwise suffered very few restrictions, whilst South African unwillingness to admit Rhodesian agricultural produce of inferior quality provided a stimulus for Rhodesian farmers to improve their methods.[2] Relations with the Portuguese remained equally friendly. Southern Rhodesia's Latin neighbours much preferred dealing with a small, self-governing British Colony than with an overweening South Africa stretching from the Cape to the Zambezi, and Rhodesian ministers always met with a good reception when they went to Mozambique. The Rhodesians for their part depended on Beira, which now was handling some 80 to 90 per cent of their country's imported and exported tonnage; their main complaint centred on the congestion of Beira's port facilities at a time when Rhodesian trade was increasing fast. But British investors stepped in, with the result that in 1929 an important new deep-sea wharf was opened by the side of the Indian Ocean.

The new Administration also took steps to encourage land settlement, and in 1924 established the Land and Agricultural Bank of Southern Rhodesia.[3] The Bank was controlled by the Treasury and made loans both to farmers and co-operative societies, following in general a soundly conservative policy in their affairs, much to the disgust of men like Downie who would have preferred a somewhat more venturesome approach. Easier rural credit facilities in turn stimulated tobacco farmers whose output shot up in a phenomenal fashion.[4] The Rhodesia Tobacco Warehouse and Export Company, a co-operative concern, put up a modern warehouse in Salisbury, with the latest equipment, and the Rhodesian capital now became an important marketing centre. Newton in

[1] Sir C. P. Coghlan to Mrs Buller: 27 July 1924 (in CO 8/1/3, Nat Arch MS)

[2] Customs agreement: Southern Rhodesia and Union of South Africa, 1924, in Southern Rhodesia. Controller of customs and excise. *Report . . . for the year 1926.* Salisbury, Government printer, 1927 (C.S.R. 21—1927), p. 1–4

[3] The Land bank act, 1924

[4] Production increased from 2,405,904 lb in 1924/5 to 24,889,244 lb in 1927/8.

London worked hard to get more customers for his country's leaf and British manufacturers gradually listened to him. Newton, of course, faced many obstacles. Much of the country's production remained poor in quality; Rhodesian tobacco exports met with a good deal of opposition from American competitors; British smokers turned out to be a conservative lot; advertising proved expensive. Nevertheless the country made good progress; a major step forward came with the Imperial Tobacco Company's decision in 1927 to establish themselves in Southern Rhodesia, the Company later agreeing to handle 'Rhodian' cigarettes, a cheap brand which helped to put Rhodesia on the map as a tobacco producer.

The Government likewise took steps to encourage meat exports, thereby benefiting both white and black breeders of cattle. The number of beasts in the country kept increasing, and it could no longer easily sell its surplus without breaking into overseas markets. The Government approached several firms, but only the Imperial Cold Storage Company was willing to deal in scrub cattle. The position was becoming all the more serious because of the Union's embargo on scrub animals, and the Government therefore gave special facilities to the Cold Storage Company which, in exchange, agreed to put up refrigerating works capable of dealing with no less than 20,000 head of cattle a year.[1] Coghlan met with a certain amount of opposition from the left of his own party, who complained about the Government's alleged hobnobbing with monopolists; but leftists like Frederick Philip Mennell, a well-known geologist who represented Bulawayo District in Parliament, and Francis Leslie Hadfield, did not carry much weight within their party which looked askance at the advocacy of large scale expenditure.

The Coghlan Government also faced the problem of high railway rates, both mining companies and farmers claiming that the cost of freight was interfering with their profits. The Constitution, on the other hand, gave special protection to Chartered railway interests, the Letters Patent providing that railway legislation must remain reserved for Imperial approval until the country adopted legislation on the lines of the British Railways Act, 1921. The Government then set about finding means to obtain the necessary control and, in 1924, General F. D. Hammond, a recognized expert on communications, was appointed to conduct an enquiry. Hammond produced a massive work which pointed out the high rate of profits earned by the companies and stressed the handicap suffered by Rhodesian farmers who had to compete against Union products and, at the same time, pay high railway rates. Hammond admitted that the

[1] Chilled and frozen meats export act, 1924

Company had provided railways at low cost, but came down in favour of control by agreement which he preferred to state-ownership.[1] Railway control in turn entailed inter-territorial co-operation between the two Rhodesias and Bechuanaland. Coghlan, together with Moffat and Downie, therefore went to London where they discussed the question with the Imperial Government and the Chartered Company. The negotiators agreed to set up a Railway Commission on which the two Rhodesias and Bechuanaland would all be represented, the new arrangement limiting shareholders' dividends by an agreed amount.[2]

The railway problem gave the first impetus towards pushing Southern Rhodesian politicians away from their accustomed isolationism. A decade earlier Responsible Government men fought the Company's amalgamation scheme for all they were worth. Now a number of Cabinet members began to have second thoughts. Their reasons of course were rather different from those of later years. Northern Rhodesian mineral wealth still seemed a very speculative asset. No white man as yet imagined that one day African nationalists would demand the creation of black states north of the Zambezi. Moffat did, however, realize that Southern Rhodesia on her own could not control a railway system half of which was situated outside his country's borders; in 1925 he made a speech pointing out that only a single government would be able to run rail communications throughout the two Rhodesias.[3] Had the Southern Rhodesians taken up the question with greater vigour, and had the Northerners co-operated, they might conceivably have succeeded. Colonial Office officials in Northern Rhodesia admittedly opposed a 'southern' solution; so did other experts in London who feared that a deal with Southern Rhodesia might encourage South Africa to raise the question of the three Protectorates under the High Commissioner's care. But many of the permanent officials in London were more amenable. Newton privately reported to his chief a conversation with Sir Charles Davis, the Permanent Under-Secretary of State for Dominion Affairs, who told him the Colonial Office would be quite willing 'to get rid of the whole thing', giving the eastern portion of Northern Rhodesia to Nyasaland, leaving Barotseland as a reserved enclave, and possibly handing the central portion to Southern Rhodesia. The Treasury especially, thought Newton, would be glad to let Southern Rhodesia have the territory, if Coghlan could 'harden his heart' to take it over.[4] Newton moreover got on extremely well with Imperial ministers;

---

[1] Hammond, F. D. *Report . . . on the railway system of Southern Rhodesia.* Salisbury, Government printer, 1926 (C.S.R. 2—1926), 3 v.

[2] Railways act, 1926

[3] *Bulawayo chronicle*, 2 Dec 1925

[4] Sir F. Newton to Sir C. P. Coghlan: 20 and 23 July 1925 (in NE 1/1/1, Nat Arch MS)

he thought well of James Henry Thomas, a right wing trade unionist who served as Secretary of State for the Colonies in the short-lived Labour Cabinet of 1924. The High Commissioner enjoyed even better relations with the Conservatives; he acted as a channel between the British Conservatives and the Rhodesian Party, a role which gave him some qualms as a conscientious civil servant, though it did not bother Coghlan, who cheerfully wrote back that he would not object to similar services from the High Commissioner for any other party![1] In 1925, moreover, the Dominions Office was set up as a separate organization, taking over from the Colonial Office Imperial relations with the Dominions, Southern Rhodesia and the Irish Free State; Southern Rhodesia accordingly came under the care of officials who dealt with countries like South Africa and New Zealand. Southern Rhodesia gained from the change, and in 1927 Moffat brought up the subject of closer union once more. He made a fine speech at Gwelo, in which he foresaw that one day a great British dominion would come into being comprising both the Rhodesias and Nyasaland;[2] *The Times* commented favourably,[3] but Moffat himself insisted that the first move should come from the north. White politicians beyond the Zambezi were, however, divided on the subject; influential colonists like Frank Leopold Moore, a Livingstone chemist and newspaper owner, considered that Northern Rhodesia could ultimately get Responsible Government on its own, and for the time being the question dropped.

Whilst Southern Rhodesian relations with the Imperial 'Establishment' remained excellent, the colonists' honeymoon with 'negrophilists' was drawing to a rapid end. Within the Colony African protests about the Government became a little more outspoken. Chiefs complained to visiting dignitaries that the reserves were becoming too small, that wages were too low and taxes too high or, alternatively that shopkeepers were charging too much. Chiefs, as a whole, became more worried as labour migration began to affect women and children; they claimed that women nowadays would no longer obey their husbands, that youths in urban compounds were growing up as loafers beyond control, and that some African women were going to town to become harlots. A number of educated Africans, mostly of South African origin, encouraged by the Rev. T. O. Beattie, banded themselves together into the Southern Rhodesia Native Welfare Association, headed by D. F. Gwebu, alias 'Fish', an intelligent young Matabele chief who spoke English well and

[1] Sir F. Newton to Sir C. P. Coghlan: 9 June 1927 (in NE 1/1/1, Nat Arch MS) and Sir C. P. Coghlan to Sir F. Newton: 7 July 1927 (in NE 1/1/1, Nat Arch MS)
[2] *Gwelo times*, 5 Aug 1927   [3] *The Times*, 13 Sep 1927

showed particular interest in the land question. Africans from the south at the same time were becoming more influenced by the growing race consciousness developing in the Union; they maintained contacts with the South African National Congress, criticized Southern Rhodesian land policies, and demanded to be represented in the Assembly by two Europeans, thereby echoing earlier missionary demands in this direction.[1] Small societies of this kind, 'quasi-Christian and constitutional in character' did not of course as yet represent a danger to existing rule. They did, however, express a certain amount of underlying discontent which found popular expression in the sermons of village prophets, many of them Nyasalanders, who used the Old Testament as a revolutionary's handbook. Itinerant preachers proved by quoting Isaiah and Amos that the existing order must one day crumble into dust, and that black men would inherit the white men's riches, life sometimes being made very unpleasant for villagers who would not conform to this teaching. In the Lomagundi District especially seers visited the villagers at night, urging them to be baptized. The Elect, once properly 'dipped', would see their ancestors in the water and would turn white; God would then come with a 'big wind' and blow out the Europeans. On the appointed day Africans would take over all farms and stores, and chiefs would once more rule their people. Admittedly there was no insurrectionary feeling in the country, and the Acting Chief Native Commissioner insisted that his officials must on no account employ illegal methods to suppress the prophets. But it was generally agreed that Africans were becoming less respectful to established authority, and were taking the view that everything not specifically forbidden by the Government was allowed. The Government tried to deal with this situation by restraining white backvelders, by strengthening the authority of Native Commissioners and by making some mild reforms. Coghlan, who all his life thought of himself as a 'Liberal and a Democrat', sharply resisted white farmers who tried to profit from the tobacco boom by some kind of forced labour. In a private interview with the Governor, he told Sir John Chancellor that he would not, for the time being, advise the Secretary of State to remove from the constitution the existing restrictions on the control of native affairs. At the same time the Premier maintained a tight hold over the missions which, in any case, depended on the Government for permission to enter the reserves and for financial grants for education. The Southern Rhodesian Missionary Conference nevertheless maintained its independence and successfully resisted a draft bill for the compulsory registration of native

[1] Superintendent of Natives, Bulawayo, reporting on a meeting at Gwelo market hall on 11 July 1927 (in S 138/18, Nat Arch SR)

preachers, Cripps arguing hotly that the measure would contravene British traditions of fair play and Christian freedom.[1]

Many missionaries as well as 'A.P.S.' enthusiasts also began to oppose other kinds of legislation, their interference sometimes based on the apparent assumption that the authorities in Salisbury must always be acting on the worst possible motives. In 1926 the Government brought in a new Act, designed to prevent the worst abuses of child labour. Juveniles under fourteen now required a certificate from the Native Commissioner before they could seek work, the parent or guardian having to give his consent. Youths outside parental control received special protection. Native Commissioners became entitled to terminate contracts on the grounds that the employer was an undesirable character, or that the job was dangerous or immoral. Native Commissioners could inspect employers' premises and were allowed to send youths in employment home at their guardian's request. Officials at the same time received added disciplinary powers, being able to sentence juvenile offenders to a maximum of ten light strokes of the cane.[2]

The Aborigines' Protection Society then let off a bitter and biased protest, arguing that the Act would enable, if not force, youngsters to seek employment without their parents' consent, that Native Commissioners stood in danger of becoming labour recruiters, being enabled to dispose of black youths as they thought fit, and the 'A.P.S.' theoreticians doubted whether in a country where tribalism continued, there could really be any number of friendless or destitute children. The 'progressive' gutter press took up the issue, and their readers overseas could read, with a humanitarian shudder, of little ones being flogged in Southern Rhodesia to make them work in the local plantations.[3]

The Coghlan Government further strengthened the existing Native Regulations by permitting Native Commissioners to try contempt of their own courts and by increasing the punishment for juvenile offenders to a maximum of fifteen strokes with the cane. A new Act consolidated previous legislation defining the powers of chiefs as constables, and regulated appeals, an offender having the right ultimately to take his case to the High Court of Southern Rhodesia.[4] To the Government's surprise both the Southern Rhodesia Missionary Conference and the Aborigines' Protection Society sharply attacked the measure, many critics assuming that this legislation constituted a new departure. In this belief they were in

---

[1] *Proceedings of the Southern Rhodesia missionary conference held at Salisbury . . . 1924.* Salisbury, Argus printing and publishing company limited, [1924], p. 9
[2] Native juvenile employment act, 1926
[3] Article by A. Holt in *No war*, April 1927   [4] Native affairs act, 1927

fact mistaken; it was not that white Rhodesians were becoming more reactionary; what was happening was that British progressives were becoming disillusioned with Rhodesian settler rule; the Fabians were forgetting their old belief in the virtues of Empire, and the post-war climate of opinion in England was undergoing a profound change with regard to colonial matters. The Southern Rhodesian Missionary Conference was influenced to some extent by the changing tide, and its Executive argued that the new Act allowed a Native Commissioner to be a judge in his own case, the whole idea being opposed to the basic concepts of British justice. John White and the 'A.P.S.' went considerably further; the experts at 'Denison House' criticized the whole idea of beating juveniles, and also objected to the allegedly novel principle that chiefs should act as constables or that their tenure should depend on good behaviour, a provision which would interfere with the hereditary principle and make them mere Government nominees. Salisbury was somewhat taken aback. The Rhodesian authorities pointed out that Magistrates already possessed the right to cane both white and black juveniles and that no one had ever objected before. They explained that chiefs and headmen did not, as alleged, receive 'new and far-reaching powers'; the Act merely reiterated previous legislation in this respect, and appointments of native dignitaries had always been dependent on good behaviour. Judicial officers always had the right to deal with contempt of their own courts, the only exception having been Native Commissioners. In the past contempt against a Native Commissioner used to be tried by another magistrate or Native Department official, but the procedure was cumbersome, injurious to the Native Commissioner's prestige, and not even appreciated by the accused. The Imperial authorities agreed with the white Rhodesians' reasoning, and the Act passed on to the Statute Book, but relations between Salisbury and the 'negrophilists' remained more strained than ever.

On the other hand the Coghlan Government gained a number of good marks by encouraging African education. In addition, the new administration introduced a major reform of the jury system. Until 1899 Rhodesian courts had held their trials under a judge sitting with three assessors, an excellent system in view of the high quality that always characterized the Rhodesian judiciary. Public opinion had, however, insisted on the introduction of juries, which British immigrants regarded as their birthright. In Africa, however, the system worked badly. Criminals, white or black, then had to plead their case before jurymen drawn from the voters' list, which, in practice, meant that black people depended on 'white' verdicts. European jurymen believed themselves to be surrounded by hordes of black savages, and often lived lonely lives on farms and trading stores fifty or a hundred miles from the nearest police station; under those conditions they felt convinced that only a harsh discipline would ensure the safety of their womenfolk, and of their persons and property. Trained lawyers like Coghlan, on the other hand, disapproved of a system which they thought incompatible with the basis of British justice. White Rhodesians admittedly did not practise lynch law, but several miscarriages of justice occurred through prejudiced juries. Before the First World War, for instance, Titus, an African newspaper vendor, for several months had attempted to make immoral suggestions to a fifteen-year-old white girl, offering her money and indecently exposing himself. When at last her father, a respected Bulawayan, heard about this, he got hold of the man by his collar, stood him up against a wall and shot him, subsequently taking a cab to the nearest police station to give himself up. The accused person acted under provocation, but the facts of the case were quite clear; the judge explained to the jurymen that the accused could not plead the right of self-defence, which only arose when there was an *immediate* need to protect life, liberty, person or honour. The white jurors could not agree amongst themselves, but during a second trial the accused was acquitted, though the *Rhodesia Herald* resolutely repudiated the idea that every white man should have the right to be judge, jury and executioner in his own case. Coghlan, a conscientious lawyer, raised the question in the old Legislative Council and moved a resolution that the existing jury system was unsuitable in cases involving crimes of violence between black men and Europeans;[1] as a result the Administration then introduced a new special jury.[2] But the Rhodesian judiciary still disliked the whole system. Hudson, Coghlan's Attorney-General, argued that juries had, since 1899, sometimes shown race prejudices and had in other cases passed inexplicable verdicts. The bulk of the people in the country were Africans—black men were not being tried by their peers. Coghlan's administration therefore put a new law on to the Statute Book which allowed accused persons charged upon indictment before the High Court to opt for trial by a Judge and Assessors. Africans from now on could stand their trial before at least one Judge and two Assessors, both of whom were required to be Native Commissioners of long standing,[3] and thus a 'settler-government' at last did away with a long-standing abuse.

Coghlan did not live much longer. His health had long been failing and

[1] Southern Rhodesia. *Legislative assembly debates,* 19 Dec 1911, p. 174–191

[2] For the jury legislation, see the Juries ordinance, 1899, and the Special juries ordinance, 1912. For a discussion see Mason, P. *The birth of a dilemma: the conquest and settlement of Rhodesia.* Oxford University Press, 1958, p. 295–311

[3] The Criminal trials (High Court) act, 1927

S

he knew that the end might come at any moment. The ailing Premier was getting weary of public life; work and worry were imposing a heavy strain, his personal problems not being made easier by the fact that he was short of capital and could not provide for his dependents. In a last letter, to be opened only at his death, he asked his country 'for some moderate provision or pension to enable my wife and daughter to live in moderate comfort and dignity when I am no longer there'.[1] Less than a year later, on the morning of 28 August 1927, he suddenly collapsed in his house. Moffat and Leggate rushed to his bedside, but before the day was out he died, fortified with the last rites of the Catholic Church; his body found a final resting place in the Matopos.

II

Politics and Land Apportionment: 1927–1930

Coghlan stood out head and shoulders above his colleagues in qualities of leadership and judgement. When his health began to fail the question of a successor gravely troubled the country. Southern Rhodesia's small white population did not provide a great reservoir of political ability, civil servants not being allowed to involve themselves in party affairs whilst many other prominent people were too busy with their private business, or too much taken up with their British or South African interests, to go into politics. The Cabinet of course did contain men of some stature. There was Downie, a successful and self-confident businessman, a bitter critic of the Railways, but inclined to be somewhat overbearing and to rub people up the wrong way. Leggate's record as Minister of Agriculture and also his sharp tongue made him many enemies, whilst Major Hudson, an able Attorney-General, lacked political ambitions and was more suited for a seat on the Bench. Fynn made an admirable Treasurer, but his many years as a civil servant had left a mark, robbing him of flair in dealing with the public and wearing away his initiative. Fynn moreover remained associated in the public mind with the Chartered Company, still a perennial bugbear, whilst his presence in the Cabinet acted as a constant check on expenditure. Newton, for all his knowledge of administrative affairs, was little known in the country, and many white Rhodesians still persisted in regarding him as an ex-Company man. There remained Moffat, who enjoyed universal respect for his transparent honesty. Moffat nevertheless suffered from serious personal disabilities as a leader; he worked hard but

---

[1] Printed in Wallis, J. P. R. *One man's hand: the story of Sir Charles Coghlan and the liberation of Southern Rhodesia.* Longmans, Green and co., 1950, p. 244

could not easily make a decision; gnawing self-doubt tortured his mind and despite his public career he remained so over-conscientious that criticism concerning the state of some country road in some remote back-veld area would make him search his soul whether he was really the right man to occupy the high office of Minister of Mines and Public Works!

Moffat thus seemed an unlikely man to assume the Premiership and guide the country through what turned out to be one of the most critical periods in its history. The Governor himself would have liked Murray Bisset, the Senior Judge, to form a Government, and Moffat himself might have been willing to serve in such a Cabinet. Hudson, however, strongly resisted the Governor's suggestion. Bisset was a relative newcomer, little known by the public; his appointment as Senior Judge had occasioned some criticism in the Press, and Hudson suggested Moffat. Hudson's colleagues concurred, and on 2 September 1927 Moffat stepped into Coghlan's shoes as Premier and Minister of Native Affairs.

In taking over office Moffat at first found himself in a relatively fortunate position. The country was still doing quite well; immigrants were still coming in; Downie as Minister of Agriculture, with a 'leftish' bent, gave preference to younger people from 'Home' with agricultural experience and rural background, and insisted that ex-Colonels and ex-Majors should receive no special preference, a decision criticized by more conservatively minded people who argued that ex-officers were in fact making fine settlers. Tobacco, between 1927 and 1928, reached a record production of some 25,000,000 lb as compared with 19,500,000 lb in the previous year, and gold was doing well, even though the industry had never managed to get back to its record output of 1916. Politically, moreover, Moffat did not face any very serious threat. The leading light in the opposition was Lieutenant-Colonel Frank William Johnson of Pioneer fame, who had since won a D.S.O. in North-West India and a reputation amongst right-wing Tories there as a tough-minded administrator who would stand no nonsense from *babus*. In 1927 Johnson stood for Salisbury South, a constituency containing many white working-class voters. Johnson, a forceful, courageous, bullet-headed kind of man, an excellent speaker who could bewitch his audience by vigorous argument and a flood of inaccurate statistics, stood out as one of the foremost representatives of right-wing radicalism. Johnson strongly opposed the Chartered Company and never tired of denouncing the Railways for sucking out the nation's life-blood. Johnson at the same time wished to develop the country in a more vigorous fashion, and never tired of thinking out new schemes, some sound, some unsound, for exploiting its potential. He believed for instance that Rhodesia needed a West Coast port, and argued that Walvis

Bay could become a new outlet. He clamoured for a 'Whiter Rhodesia', arguing that the country should intensify its agriculture and that this could best be done by getting smallholders to cultivate farms of a few hundred acres, helped only by a handful of native labourers. Johnson also opposed the Chartered Company's mineral rights, and held that the Colony should take the initiative in a 'Greater Rhodesia' programme. In Parliament Johnson could rely on a few left-wing malcontents from the Rhodesian Party, and in 1926 the opposition organized itself into the Progressive Party, where Johnson and the arch-conservative Montagu made strange bed-fellows.

The Opposition could not agree amongst themselves. Montagu and Fletcher remained convinced that in Rhodesia only larger farms could operate as economic units, whilst Montagu objected to Johnson's radical views on public finance. The white rural voters were also divided. The Rhodesian Agricultural Union would not consent to step into politics itself, but some discontented farmers banded themselves into the Country Party which stood as a separate group. The Labour Party remained a small sectional organization, appealing mainly to mine and railway workers, and holding out for a programme that would not have dismayed British right-wing Tories, asking for free education, an eight-hour day, unemployment insurance and old age benefits as well as a tax on unoccupied land. White Rhodesian workers, many of them owning a little bungalow, a life insurance policy, or a small bank account, had no reason to look upon themselves as exploited proletarians and some in fact supported Moffat. When the country went to the polls at the next General Election in 1928 the reluctant Premier thus won an overwhelming victory. Montagu lost his seat and retired from politics. Johnson likewise failed to get re-elected and Parliamentary opposition to the Rhodesian Party withered. In 1930 the Progressive and Country parties at last merged as the Reform Party, with Johnson as one of its Vice-Presidents and acting at first as the Party's real leader. Johnson, however, subsequently decided to go back to England, and the Reform Party remained a small opposition group which could only command four votes in the Assembly. Moffat then accepted a repentant Fletcher into the Cabinet as Minister for Agriculture and Lands, the Government once more settling down to a cautious policy of reform, secure in the possession of an unshakeable majority.

The Legislature imposed a small tax on unimproved land and revised the law concerning married women's property. It also passed a new Act for the protection of children and, more important still, in 1930 introduced compulsory education for European youngsters who had attained their seventh, and not yet their fifteenth, birthday. In addition the Government put a Workman's Compensation Act on the Statute Book as well as additional legislation to provide for increased compensation on the injury or death of African labourers. The Moffat Cabinet also made an important administrative innovation by setting up a Public Services Board in 1928, designed to make recommendations on the recruitment, promotion and discipline of civil servants. One of its three members was appointed by the Public Services Association, the measure as a whole being designed to allay the considerable discontent within the civil service which had never quite evaporated since Chartered Company days.[1]

Moffat, despite his cautious reformism, encountered a certain amount of opposition from the more radical element of the European working class. Early in 1929 a railway strike broke out which the Premier handled with an almost exaggerated deference to the white railwaymen. The Premier hurried off to Bulawayo, but failed to gain an undertaking from the strike leaders for reasonable time to examine the situation. When he arrived in Bulawayo, the country's 'other capital', he found to his humiliation that the strike had already begun. On a second trip Moffat—characteristically —went by railway trolley, whilst Keller made a spectacular air-flight to Salisbury and back at Government expense! Finally, however, a Court of Enquiry assembled to consider the workers' grievances, and decided that the workers had no real case; Southern Rhodesian railwaymen in fact enjoyed better conditions than their colleagues south of the Limpopo!

Moffat also had difficult problems in inter-territorial relations. The British Government despatched a Commission to Central Africa, headed by Sir Hilton Young, a noted lawyer and financial expert, to investigate the problem of associating the two Rhodesias more closely. The Commissioners took evidence all over the country, but amalgamationists met with heavy opposition. Chaplin, now a director of the British South Africa Company and of the Anglo-American Corporation, put up a strong case against Moffat's favourite project. He stressed the existing financial links between South Africa and Northern Rhodesia and predicted that sooner or later South Africans would come to realize the advantages of Empire, despite present controversies. A possible extension of South African rule to Northern Rhodesia would not necessarily injure African interests, and Northern Rhodesian mining and business interests were more likely to look towards South Africa than to Salisbury. The Southern Rhodesia Government was partly living on borrowed money,

[1] See respectively the Land tax act, 1928; the Married persons' property act, 1928; the Children's protection and adoption act, 1929; the Compulsory education act, 1930; the Workmen's compensation act, 1930; the Native labourers compensation amendment act, 1930 (supplementing existing legislation passed in 1922); and Government notice no. 161 of 2 Mar 1928

and even though it was not financially extravagant, Salisbury might well run into financial difficulties in times of economic crisis. Southern Rhodesia thus might be unable to take over another large territory, whilst Northern Rhodesia badly needed Imperial funds.[1] Immediate amalgamation was therefore inadvisable. The Commissioners themselves could not arrive at a solution. The Chairman suggested that Northern Rhodesia should be partitioned, the Railway Belt being linked to Southern Rhodesia. The majority advocated the status quo, evading the main issue on the somewhat unconvincing grounds that the future of the mining industry in Northern Rhodesia as yet remained too uncertain, and that Southern Rhodesia should first solve its own problems.[2]

The Imperial Government agreed with the majority, arguing that native areas like Barotseland and north-eastern Rhodesia should not be handed over to a white self-governing community. Northern Rhodesia's mineral wealth should remain under London control on account of its importance to Imperial trade and defence, Northern Rhodesia being likely to become the world's greatest copper producer. The agricultural areas north of the Kafue should also remain associated with the mines as food producers, and Southern Rhodesia might at best receive an area of some 30,000 square miles between the Kafue and the Zambezi, including the township of Livingstone. On 2 July 1931 the British Government therefore announced in Parliament that amalgamation could not be sanctioned for the moment, even though it need not be rejected in principle. In any future scheme, however, Barotseland must receive special treatment, whilst the boundaries of the area to be joined to Southern Rhodesia would not necessarily be co-terminous with Northern Rhodesia's existing borders.

The Imperial decision bitterly disappointed Moffat, who at the same time was facing Afrikaner Nationalists in the South. British-born Rhodesians resented the way things were going on the other side of the Limpopo, the South African flag question occasioning heated comments in Salisbury as well as in Cape Town and Johannesburg. The customs question formed an even more pressing issue. South Africa, seeking to widen her markets, entered a reciprocal tariffs agreement with Germany. In the normal course of events this would have to be extended to Southern Rhodesia, and Salisbury accordingly asked for a new customs conference. The Southern Rhodesians insisted that they should be able to fix their own customs duties; they also demanded free exchange of cattle and other

[1] Oral evidence given by Sir F. P. D. Chaplin to the Hilton-Young commission: 17 Apr 1928 (in CH 8/2/1, Nat Arch MS)
[2] Cmd. 3234 (1929)

agricultural produce, offering at the same time to admit a broad range of Union manufactures. Salisbury in fact held a strong hand, for the Colony imported much more from South Africa than it sold there. The Union Government however, acting under pressure from its own tobacco growers, inclined to favour the *platteland* rather than urban interests: the South Africans thus asked for further restrictions on Rhodesian tobacco imports as well as other concessions, and negotiations for a time broke down.

In 1930 the two countries tried again and negotiated a new agreement, the Southern Rhodesians to their fury discovering that Northern Rhodesia would not join them in a common stand. The Colonial Office argued that Northern Rhodesia would not benefit by placing high tariffs on South African imports just to please Southern Rhodesia: the northern protectorate was still importing a good many manufactured goods from the Union, including specialized mining equipment, and therefore preferred to nego-tiate on its own, Southern Rhodesians thereby learning another lesson in the value of amalgamation. The final agreement favoured Pretoria rather than Salisbury. The Union continued to ban Rhodesian scrub cattle, and at the same time limited the duty-free importation of Southern Rhodesian tobacco to 2,400,000 lb, thereby cutting a large slice out of Rhodesian export markets. Union manufacturers on the other hand continued to occupy a most favourable position. An ingenious arrangement allowed the duties payable on manufactured goods to be paid directly from the Union Government to the Rhodesian Treasury and not by the exporter or importer. The consumer and revenue collector north of the Limpopo benefited since the price of goods did not reflect the duty paid. Rhodesian manufacturers, on the other hand, had to compete with old-established Union industries without being sheltered by protective tariffs, so that South African industrialists had no incentive to set up factories north of the Limpopo.[1]

Moffat's most serious problem, however, remained the land issue. Earlier on, when Rhodesian delegates were negotiating for Responsible Government in London, the question of territorial segregation had already come up. Churchill in a published dispatch promised that His Majesty's Government would consider changing the existing law if a full and impartial enquiry should pronounce in favour of territorial segregation, after the achievement of Responsible Government.[2]

---

[1] See Customs and excise amendment act, 1930, and attached customs agreements between South Africa, Northern Rhodesia and Southern Rhodesia.
[2] W. S. Churchill to High Commissioner: 22 Dec 1921 (in *Southern Rhodesia government gazette extraordinary*, 19 Jan 1922)

The country's subsequent economic progress confirmed white farmers in their demand for the separation of white and black land. In 1925 a Commission finally assembled under an Imperial chairman, Sir Morris Carter, a distinguished legal man who previously had held high office in Uganda and in Tanganyika as Chief Justice. The Commission's final report is too long to be easily summarized, but the Commissioners approved of a form of territorial *apartheid*, having found that Europeans and Africans both preferred things that way. The investigators also stressed that separate areas should be set aside where Africans alone might buy holdings on individual tenure. Native purchasers would thereby be able to acquire land at lower prices than if they were competing with white farmers in the scramble for real estate. The African admittedly would thereby lose the right to buy land anywhere in the Colony, but would in fact benefit from the creation of a protected land market.[1]

In framing their proposals the Commissioners thought in terms of rural rather than urban African needs, an attitude understandable at the time when only about 3 per cent of the country's Africans were living in townships or mine compounds.[2] Like practically all their contemporaries, they looked upon the townships as European areas, though they did envisage the need for setting aside separate quarters where at some future time African shopkeepers and professional men might lease land for business purposes, and they also recommended that municipalities should set aside residential suburbs for better-off Africans. But the bulk of workers were regarded as migrant labourers—which in fact they mostly

---

[1] See Southern Rhodesia. *Report of the Land Commission, 1925*. Salisbury, Government printer, 1926 (C.S.R. 3—1926). The proposed division was as follows:

	Acres
Total area of Southern Rhodesia	96,226,560
Existing native reserves	21,594,957
Matopo National Park	224,000
Urban areas	149,033
Forest area	670,000
Native Purchase Areas	6,851,876
Land alienated to Europeans	31,033,050
Land still available to Europeans	17,423,815

The European areas would thus amount to 48,605,898 acres, including urban areas, land then classed as Crown land and 32,875 acres then alienated to Africans, a total of about 62 per cent of the whole land area.

The Native areas would total 28,933,362 acres, including the reserves, land then classified as Crown land, 473,915 then alienated to Europeans, etc., amounting to about 37 per cent of the total.

[2] The native population was given as follows:

	Total	Percent
In native reserves	516,335	63·44
On alienated land	150,650	18·50
On Crown land	122,088	15·00
Towns and mines	24,874	3·06

were—and the Commissioners professed themselves to be quite satisfied with the work already being done by municipalities to improve the locations. The main concession made to 'detribalized' Africans occurred in the proposal that special townships might be set aside in native areas where black craftsmen and professional people might serve their fellow-Africans, though the Commissioners had nothing to say as regards the economic purpose of such settlements.

Coghlan had threshed out the question at great length with the Imperial authorities, who approved of what he did. Coghlan, however, died before he could settle the matter and Moffat found himself faced with the task of putting through the required legislation. The new Premier privately criticized General Hertzog's land policy in South Africa, feeling convinced that Africans there were suffering great hardships, especially in the Eastern Cape, which he knew personally, and where the native communities no longer possessed enough land for cultivation and had become solely dependent on wages.[1] Southern Rhodesia's existing constitutional right allowing Africans to buy land anywhere they liked was all very well in theory, but in practice was proving no more than a 'paper right'. By 1930 white settlers had purchased something like 31,000,000 acres—Africans during the same period managed to acquire no more than 45,000 acres. Moffat imagined therefore that Land Apportionment legislation would lay the foundations for a new native policy, and received confirmation in this view from the foremost authorities south of the Limpopo, including liberal-minded men like J. W. Sauer, Sir James Rose-Innes, a famous Judge, and Dr C. T. Loran, a well-known educationist.[2]

Whilst deliberating on his policy the Rhodesian Premier for the first time found himself facing a small emergent 'Africanist' movement, which still drew its main inspiration from South Africa. In 1927 the native mine-workers at Shamva suddenly came out on strike, the secrecy of their organization and the efficiency with which the dispute was directed coming like a bombshell to the administration. Moffat, a diffident and conciliatory kind of man, at first wanted to concentrate the police at Mtoko, at a considerable distance away, so as not to appear to be panicking, but the Governor supported the Commandant of the Defence Force and strongly advised that police should be rushed to Shamva on motor lorries. The strike soon broke up, the labour force itself being divided. Practically all the labourers came from north of the Zambezi. About 2,000 of them drew their wages from the mine; the remaining 1,500 were employed by

---

[1] H. U. Moffat to Sir F. Newton: 6 May 1929 (in NE 1/1/7, Nat Arch MS)
[2] H. U. Moffat to Sir F. Newton: 15 June 1929 (in NE 1/1/7, Nat Arch MS)

private contractors, Europeans well-known amongst and popular with their gangs. The contractors' 'hands' went back to work first, with the result that the strike collapsed, 22 ringleaders, 'alien natives' all of them, being fined and deported.

The Government wrongly believed the strike to have been fomented by the Industrial and Commercial Workers' Union (I.C.U.), a South African organization which during the 'twenties began to open branches in Southern Rhodesia. The I.C.U. did not form a trade union in the modern sense of the word, but a compound between a workers' association, welfare society, political party and social protest movement, which aimed to unite within its ranks all black labourers, irrespective of their jobs, a policy inevitable at a time when few African workers acquired a permanent stake in any one industry. In Southern Rhodesia the movement was first organized by Thomas (or Robert) Sambo, a Nyasalander and a relative of Clement Kadalie, the Union's Nyasaland-born head in South Africa. The Government then deported Sambo and leadership fell to Masotsha (Masoja) Ndhlovu, and Thomas Sikaleni, the latter a clerk in the Native Department who was accordingly discharged. The I.C.U. began work in Bulawayo, subsequently building up small branches in other townships and spreading into the reserves, where speakers agitated against the compulsory destruction of diseased stock, the practice of enforcing unpaid labour on local roads and other grievances. The I.C.U. attracted to its ranks people like Charles Mzingeli, a Matabele mission scholar from Mariannhill, who at the age of fourteen ran away from home to seek work in Francistown. Mzingeli later worked in Bulawayo and in Northern Rhodesia; he then returned to Bulawayo where he served as a hotel waiter before taking a post as a cook with a railway official. In 1927 the young man, now 22 years old, resolved to join the I.C.U. Mzingeli's employer was furious when he heard that his servant was addressing public meetings, and Mzingeli decided that he could never take an active part in trade union work as long as he remained in European employment. He had no quarrel with the whites who had given him work but felt strongly about the black workers' low wages and poor conditions in general; in addition he bitterly resented personal discrimination against African people, a practice unknown on the mission, but one which occasioned harsh resentment in the sparsely-built, intelligent youngster when he first came to town.

The movement subsequently attempted to oppose the Land Apportionment Act, the Native Registration Act and the Industrial Conciliation Act, which politically conscious Africans began to describe as the 'three-legged stool' of white supremacy; the Union also demanded better pay

and more considerate treatment of Africans at the offices of Native Commissioners, and allied reforms. The I.C.U., however, did not attain much
success. Southern Rhodesia's migrant black labour force remained difficult
to organize; many members could not or would not pay their subscrip-
tions, and numbers fluctuated sharply; Mzingeli himself estimated the
number of supporters and well-wishers at about a maximum of 10,000
in the 'thirties, but the organization's income remained irregular and
Mzingeli helped to raise money by organizing social occasions and playing
the piano and violin. Under those conditions the I.C.U. could not afford
to pay regular salaries to its officials; there were bitter personal quarrels in
its ranks, and the organization suffered from all the weaknesses of remote
control. Headquarters remained at Port Elizabeth; it was supposed to
receive 25 per cent of the Rhodesian Union's revenue; it supplied the
Rhodesian branches with literature and also with directives which
generally bore little relevance to local conditions. The Rhodesian I.C.U.
officials moreover had no faith in the strike weapon. Feeling convinced
that labour stoppages would not succeed in raising wages, they confined
themselves to passing their views on to the Native Department, which took
little notice of their criticism.[1] In 1936 the I.C.U. finally collapsed in
Rhodesia and Mzingeli himself opened a shop in Salisbury, thereby
entering the ranks of Southern Rhodesia's embryonic African lower
middle class.

The I.C.U. and other comparable organizations all had this much in
common: they endeavoured to put pressure on the Southern Rhodesia
Government rather than Downing Street, fully grasping that the effective
seat of power had now shifted from London to Salisbury. But they remained small and suffered from bitter disputes between themselves. The
I.C.U. for instance seems to have distrusted both the Southern Rhodesia
Native Association and the Bantu Voters' Association, the latter supported
by some of the more prosperous Africans, Fingo immigrants and Matabele
aristocrats. The I.C.U. leaders argued that their opposite numbers were
no more than government 'stooges', out to gain pass-law exemption
certificates for their own members, but otherwise anxious to remain in the
Native Department's good books. In addition these indigenous organizations met competition from societies like the Mashonaland Native Welfare
Society, founded in 1930 with the blessing of the Bishop of Southern
Rhodesia and putting forward an ultra-'loyalist' programme. African
'modernists', anxious to organize their people on European lines, also had
to reckon with backward-looking movements like the Matabele Home
Society, a traditionally minded body, which began to displace the Bantu

[1] Information supplied by Mr C. Mzingeli of Harari, Salisbury.

Voters' Association in the affection of many Matabele. The Society aimed at rebuilding the 'fallen nation', and at the same time unsuccessfully tried to act as a channel of communication between the Matabele and the Rhodesian authorities. Rhodes Lobengula, a grandson of the last Matabele king, and the only descendant of Lobengula to wield any influence amongst his people, was elected secretary, despite the fact that the Government had previously forbidden Rhodes to accept the chairmanship of the Bantu Voters' Association. The Society took up a Matabele demand of long standing, one reiterated over and over again in the past, that a Paramount should once again rule over his people. The Society would have liked Rhodes Lobengula or some other important dignitary to be appointed 'Chief of Chiefs', but the Native Affairs Department wanted nothing to do with the scheme, and it petered out.

Moffat showed much greater personal sympathy to people like Mzingeli than did the rank and file of Native Affairs Department officials, though he explained to Mzingeli that the powers of even a Prime Minister remained strictly limited. Nevertheless, Moffat argued, Africans should have some outlet for their ambitions and he therefore favoured the creation of advisory Native Councils in the reserves. The Premier would also have liked to scrap the existing African suffrage, which in fact was benefiting only a few, and at one time thought of offering as a *quid pro quo* separate representation for natives in Parliament. Sir John Chancellor, the Governor, however, strongly opposed this suggestion. Striking native voters off the roll would only arouse unnecessary opposition overseas. Separate African representation in Parliament was in any case premature, for no such demand from Africans in fact existed. A system of such a kind, according to Chancellor, might lead to political rivalry between white and black, and the Governor strongly objected to any kind of arrangement which in the long run might effect a transfer of power from white to black people.

Far more important to the Premier was the economic question. Some African agriculturists were reaping a modest gain from the prosperity of the 'twenties; native peasants owned more cattle, ploughs and draught animals than ever before; the acreage under cultivation went up slightly even though the average yield of maize, already low, diminished further.[1] Agricultural standards remained low, and black cultivators got poor crops

[1]	*Estimated number of*	1920	1930
	Cattle	744,402	1,558,075
	Donkeys, mules and horses	8,360	40,946
	Ploughs in use	14,429	50,189
	Acres under cultivation	1,224,000	1,378,000
	Average yield per acre	2·7 bags	2·2 bags

even on fertile soils, because of their tendency to plant in mixtures or too thickly, and to let their gardens be crowded out by weeds. The misguided use of the plough often made matters worse by increasing the acreage of poorly tilled land which in fact might produce lower yields than women used to secure with the old hand hoe. The plough meant a social revolution, putting the men on the fields instead of the women, but unskilled tillers would often exhaust the soil, while untilled areas of worn-out land provided but poor grazing for cattle.

The Government made an important move to remedy the situation in 1924 when African students first began to enrol in the Government Industrial Schools at Domboshawa and Tjolotjo to train as farming demonstrators. The authorities fortunately secured a first-rate man to run their improvement programme. Emory Delmont Alvord, a Utah-born expert with plenty of experience in agriculture, soil conservation and teaching, first joined the American Board Mission in Southern Rhodesia in 1919. The American, a splendid farming man, an excellent athlete and a tough boxer to boot, stood out as a text-book representative of muscular Christianity, a person who would have delighted David Livingstone. In 1926 the Government called on Alvord to take charge of its agricultural demonstrators and, despite considerable resistance from the more conservative tribesmen, Alvord and his men began to make some headway. In 1929 Alvord came under the newly organized Department of Native Education, headed by Harold Jowitt, and village schools began to provide agricultural training. The Government strongly backed the scheme, and continued to increase the Development vote even in the crisis year of 1930/31 when allocations for other departments were sharply cut on account of the Slump. The authorities rightly argued that the old methods would no longer meet the needs of an expanding black population and their growing herds; they determined that Southern Rhodesia should not develop dust-bowls, and also argued that improved methods of food production would help to release peasants to sell their labour for a cash return. Alvord himself aimed first of all at producing more food from the same acreages, and decided to 'centralize' arable land in the reserves so as to protect the soil and get better crops, large areas being set aside at the same time for permanent grazing. A pilot scheme in the Selukwe Reserve yielded excellent results and after a good deal of hard, grim slogging the demonstrators' example slowly caught on.[1]

Moffat and his advisers, however, wished to go further. Economic improvement, the argument went, could only come about on the basis of

[1] See McHarg, J. *Influences contributing to the education and culture of the native people in Southern Rhodesia from 1900 to 1961.* Duke university, D.Ed. thesis, 1962

individual land tenure, leading to the creation of a stable and progressive class of native freeholders. Applications for land moreover were coming in from as far afield as Bulalima-Mangwe in the south, from the Gwaai District in the south-west and Melsetter in the east. Southern Rhodesia was witnessing the first beginnings of an African middle class which wished to invest its capital in the soil. There were a few relatively rich men like Mupe Sipopa from Bulalima-Mangwe, owning £250 in cash, 4 ploughs, 199 large and 50 small stock as well as a wagon and a donkey cart, who was asking to buy 1,000 acres of land. Sipopa was rather exceptional, but there were others, like Oliver Somkence from Bubi, who wished to acquire 100 acres, his worldly wealth amounting to £50, a plough, a bicycle, 46 large and 96 small stock, or Paul Mandiki, a Salisbury man, with £20, two ploughs, 33 large stock and a motor lorry.

The setting apart of land on individual tenure would of course help up-and-coming people like Sipopa or Mandiki. More important still, the end of the traditional system would end tribal conservatism. For under existing conditions, the experts explained, Africans would not take the trouble of constructing dips, dams and other permanent buildings, planting fruit trees or making other kinds of improvements. Moffat, following the advice of Sir Herbert Taylor, the Chief Native Commissioner, therefore wished to encourage the creation of native purchase areas, and looked forward to that more distant day when all reserves would be parcelled out to small peasant owners.

Southern Rhodesian thought thoroughly fitted in with the more 'progressive' kind of Imperial ideology, and in some ways indeed rather went beyond Colonial Office practice north of the Zambezi. The discrepancy between the extent of land-holdings in white and black possession respectively owed much to the operation of a free and unfettered land market. This had been postulated by 'Imperial' thinking as expressed in the provisions of the Southern Rhodesia Order in Council of 1898. Moffat, however, now saw that the 'free for all' principle required some modification. A 'new deal' would admittedly leave far more land in white than in African hands. But, argued the Premier, native peasants with little capital and only a few dozen head of cattle could work but a few hundred acres each. European farmers, operating with more capital and higher profit margins, required larger economic units. This contention was not disputed in London, where Colonial policy makers were encouraging white farmers to go to Northern Rhodesia so as to provide the expanding Copper Belt with a regular supply of food, as they thought that native subsistence cultivators would not be able to produce grain and cattle in sufficient or predictable quantities. Moffat held that Southern Rhodesia's vast empty acres could still give employment to growing numbers of white immigrants, a view acceptable even to a left-wing reformer like Lord Olivier who agreed that the Rhodesian Land Commissioners proposed to give as much land to the natives as they could then use or were likely to use for a reasonable period.[1]

Segregation still remained an accepted part of Imperial orthodoxy—the concept of territorial separation not yet having been relegated to Satan and the sinners of Stellenbosch! Imperial theoreticians thought in terms of strengthening native societies by enlarging their administrative powers; anthropologists discovered the real or supposed virtues of tribal communities in an assumed state of social equilibrium, to be guarded against the perils of 'culture contacts'. Clergymen hoped to protect their black flocks against the vices of the city and the moral contamination that befell black labour migrants when they worked under 'low whites', European workers who used bad language and preferred a 'sundowner' to a Sunday sermon. *Apartheid* was in the air, and in this respect there was little difference between conservatives and a Utopian Socialist like Arthur Shearly Cripps, who regarded the white Rhodesian as an unworthy Dives and the black man as an ill-used Lazarus. Cripps himself advocated territorial separation as the best solution for the country's multi-coloured society.[2] Very few theorists of those days thought in terms of cultural assimilation; even Marxists, though for very different reasons, believed in setting up a separate black republic in the American Deep South, and argued that cultural assimilation must remain 'absolutely excluded from the arsenal of Marxism-Leninism as being an anti-popular and counter-revolutionary policy'.[3]

The Premier accordingly met no serious opposition from local clergymen, and when he presented his case to the Southern Rhodesian Missionary Conference the reverend gentlemen congratulated the Government and the members of the Legislative Assembly on the fact that the principle of land segregation as enunciated in the report of the Morris-Carter Commission of 1925 was accepted with such practical unanimity.[4]

The Imperial Government vetted and revetted the land legislation to the last comma and colon. Moffat finally introduced the Bill in the Legis-

---

[1] Olivier, S. *The anatomy of African misery.* Hogarth press, 1927, p. 100–101

[2] For an expression of these views, see Cripps, A. S. *An Africa for Africans; a plea on behalf of territorial segregation areas and of their freedom in a South African colony.* Longmans, Green and co. ltd, 1927

[3] Stalin, J. V. 'The national question and Leninism' (in *Works,* v. 11, Mar 1928–Mar 1929. Moscow, Foreign languages publications house, 1954, p. 360)

[4] *Proceedings of the Southern Rhodesia missionary conference held at Salisbury, Southern Rhodesia, 26th to 29th March, 1928.* Salisbury, Rhodesian printing and publishing company limited, 1928, p. 5–6

lative Assembly, and was able to put forward what had in fact become an Imperial measure. In doing so he faced a legislature where the agricultural interest was strongly represented. Farming then employed more white people than any other industry,[1] and the Premier could therefore expect to meet some opposition. Fortunately for himself, the dispute did not, however, become a party issue. Native affairs were still regarded to some extent as sacrosanct, an issue to be left to experts who should stand above politics. The Constitution in practice entrenched the Native Affairs Department as a 'state within the state', and only a few politicians dared to criticize such a technical piece of legislation. The Bill accordingly had a fairly good passage. The new legislation—Moffat argued—would lay the cornerstone of a native policy built on Lord Lugard's principles. Segregation would meet the needs of the farmers and at the same time would avoid the predicament of South Africa, which only put segregation in force in 1913 when most of the available land had already been alienated to Europeans. Many missionaries, Moffat argued, were objecting that at least a portion of the 17,000,000 acres of the unassigned land should be specifically reserved for natives. But the legislation would include a special clause requiring the High Commissioner's approval for the setting aside of any land to Europeans or Africans in these unassigned areas. The native purchase areas would provide for about a quarter of the African population, who would be able to acquire land on lines following those of the Cape's Glen Grey Act for the Transkei; this would do away with 'kaffir farming', whereby white landowners allowed their farms to be run by African tenants who ruined the soil and provided some farmers with an ill-merited income. This problem was particularly difficult in central Matabeleland where Europeans were granted large areas after its conquest, and the original occupiers were allowed to stay on in return for rent or services.

In putting forward these views Moffat met with a certain amount of opposition. Huggins, though supporting the Government, argued that, by relinquishing a free land market, white men were making a bigger sacrifice than the Africans. Many farmers were objecting that they had to compete with African growers, and therefore felt that natives should not

---

[1] The occupational classification of Europeans in the main industries stood as follows in 1931:

Agriculture	4,325
Commerce and finance	3,886
Public administration and defence	3,080
Transport and communications	2,850
Mining and quarrying	1,880
Building and contracting	1,529
Professions	1,359
Personal services	1,162

be allowed to purchase land more cheaply than could Europeans. A more devastating attack came from Harry Herbert Davies, a white Labour leader who believed that the bill really pointed the way to ultimate integration, and would thereby endanger the future of white artisans. Max Danziger, an able Jewish attorney, took a similar line, and put forward the case for complete segregation. The country had to protect its white workmen from being undercut by blacks. Africans on the other hand could not be kept down, for the country was bound to develop a black intelligentsia which in time would take the lead in stirring up the masses. There was only one solution, and that was to give to the Africans a large area near Bechuanaland which would ultimately absorb the whole of the Colony's black population, Danziger envisaging a population transfer comparable to the kind which a few years earlier had shifted all Greeks from Asia Minor.[1]

Outside the House the Land Apportionment Bill met with a certain amount of hostility from white farmers who considered the Premier to be 'negrophile' in his approach. Educated Africans for their part held that the natives should have gained more land, though they did not object to *apartheid* as such. Earlier on, in 1926, the Southern Rhodesia Native Welfare Association held a meeting at Gwelo where educated Africans were present as well as a few chiefs. The Association considered that the Land Commission's report was unsatisfactory, and that the chiefs who gave evidence really wanted the 'loaf to be halved', so that Southern Rhodesia would be equally split between white and black men. No one, however, doubted the merits of segregation, and a year later the Native Welfare Association agreed that, though the extent of the African purchase areas should be increased, the principles of separate purchase areas for white and black men must be approved.[2] In all these discussions the question of African urbanization received very little attention. Moffat explained to the House that segregation must also be enforced in the townships, but that Government would have to leave this question to the Municipalities concerned. So long as the towns took no action the existing situation would continue, and natives might go on buying land in towns. The Municipalities would now be enabled to set aside areas for occupation by Africans alone, and once they decided on such a step, Africans would no longer be able to own stands in any other portion of the city.

Moffat, in other words, never even considered the possibility of a

[1] See Southern Rhodesia. *Legislative assembly debates*, 1930, p. 12, 1379, 1613–1628, 1866–1874, 1915–1916, 1939

[2] Native Commissioner, Gwelo, to Superintendent of Natives, Bulawayo: 30 July 1927 (in S 138/18, Nat Arch SR)

T

large-scale permanent African influx into the towns or the emergence there of a substantial African middle class. But neither, it should be added, did educated Africans at the time make an issue of the matter. At this time the African intelligentsia was still maintaining close personal links with the villages, and as far as general attitudes towards urbanization were concerned, there was not all that much difference between white Rhodesian landowners, African schoolmasters and Imperial experts overseas. The intellectual climate of opinion differed from the accepted thought of the following generation; this after all was the period when a famous anthropological pioneer like Bronislaw Malinowski could describe indigenous society in a South Sea island without even mentioning such regrettable intrusions as white stores, mission stations and administrative posts, not to speak of cruisers or gunboats! Many Colonial theorists still regarded 'detribalization' almost as a dirty word, and extolled the merits of tribal peasantries which were supposedly more 'crisis-resistant' and also less troublesome than urban proletariats, black or white. North of the Zambezi Imperial administrators thus for many years continued to resist the 'stabilization of labour' on the Copper Belt on the grounds that metal prices tended to fluctuate sharply, with the result that a permanent labour force would be exposed to constant threats of unemployment and distress, and that black workers accordingly should maintain their links with their tribal lands.[1]

In Britain the Conservatives proved reasonably co-operative and Labour was by no means hostile. In July 1929 Ramsay MacDonald's second Labour ministry assumed office in place of Baldwin's Conservative administration; Sir Francis Newton, the Southern Rhodesia High Commissioner, joyfully wrote back to Salisbury that Sidney James Webb (Lord Passfield of Passfield Corner), the well-known Fabian theorist, had taken over the Dominions and Colonies, rather than Sydney Olivier (Lord Olivier of Ramsden) whom Newton regarded as an 'extremist' and as very unpopular in the House of Lords.[2] Olivier objected that the Europeans were getting too much land, and that the measure was premature. But the 'pro-Rhodesians' justly pointed out the danger of waiting too long, as in South Africa. Lord Buxton, always a strong advocate of Responsible Government for Southern Rhodesia, argued that, as the result of future immigration, the white population in the Colony was bound to grow much more quickly than the number of Africans. Europeans, with their more highly developed farms, required more land than African peasants. He added that Southern Rhodesians might be over-

[1] See Gann, L. H. *A history of Northern Rhodesia*. ... Chatto and Windus, 1964, p. 298–299, 361–363
[2] Sir F. Newton to H. U. Moffat: 12 June 1929 (in NE 1/1/7, Nat Arch MS)

estimating the existing African demand for private property in land, and thought that the authorities in Salisbury would be well advised to make provision for the purchase areas to revert to the reserves, if necessary.

The main opposition came from the Labour Party's left wing, from the Aborigines' Protection Society and from the *Manchester Guardian*, with the effect that Passfield began to waver. He was particularly influenced by the *Manchester Guardian*, and was always inclined to bow to whichever pressure happened to be stronger. At one time Moffat even cabled to London that if the Bill was not assented to he would have to resign.[1] But Newton wrote back soothingly that Passfield recognized the sincerity of the Premier's aim, 'namely to improve the condition of the native under this Bill',[2] and things never got to a breaking point. Moffat for one thing had not the slightest intention of unnecessarily alienating the Imperial Government, whose support he wanted on the question of amalgamating the two Rhodesias. He also needed British support for Imperial preference to Empire-grown tobacco, which many Labour free-traders opposed. But the Southern Rhodesia Government had the best case and in time managed to convince all its opponents. Sir Charles Davis, the Permanent Under-Secretary for Dominion Affairs, took Moffat's part, and towards the end of 1929 William Muter Leggate, the Southern Rhodesian 'Colonial Secretary' (that is the Minister concerned with Internal Affairs), travelled to London. Leggate interviewed Harris and T. Buxton, two leading lights in the Aborigines' Protection Society, and soon got the better of the argument. Leggate stressed the difference between South African and Southern Rhodesian policies. He pointedly asked Harris what his society would have said if General Hertzog had set aside 7,500,000 acres for native purchases, and Harris 'rather winced' at this point. The Africans' right to buy land anywhere in the Colony was no more than 'a paper right, a barren right', and Harris was won over. Harris no longer took any exception to the Bill itself, and only hoped that a better arrangement might be found with regard to the undetermined area.[3] Leggate also wrote a forceful letter to Charles Prestwich Scott, the Governing Director of the *Manchester Guardian*. He strongly criticized the paper for articles which described the Rhodesian policy as aiming at 'exclusive white land owner-ship controlling a landless, homeless and legally controlled proletariat worker'; he pointed out that his Government was aiming at precisely the opposite, and that, if nothing was done now, the opportunity of creating

---

[1] H. U. Moffat to Sir F. Newton: 15 Jul 1929 (NE 1/1/7, Nat Arch MS)
[2] Sir F. Newton to H. U. Moffat: 24 Jul 1929 (in NE 1/1/7, Nat Arch MS)
[3] Interview between W. M. Leggate, J. J. Harris and T. Buxton: 19 Nov 1929 (in MO 13/1/1, Nat Arch MS)

an independent African peasantry would disappear.[1] Again the Rhodesian's argument carried the day, and a few days later Newton was able to report back that nothing more need be feared from the formidable *Guardian*.[2]

The main British pressure groups having been disposed of, the battle was practically won. The Labour majority in the House of Commons paid little attention for colonial debates emptied the House. Only Colonel Josiah Clement Wedgwood, a Labour stalwart, objected to the law which, according to him, deprived the natives of an opportunity of living in their own country.[3] In addition Charles Roden Buxton, the Labour M.P. for the Elland Division of the West Riding, made a few mild criticisms. Buxton cautiously argued that the Southern Rhodesia Government might in fact make out 'quite a reasonable argument' to the effect that the natives would be better off under the new dispensation, though the Secretary of State might have obtained improved terms for them. But even though the terms might not be fair the principle was just, and no Labour speaker really had an argument to oppose William Lunn, the Parliamentary Under-Secretary, who pointed out that, if nothing was done now, the Europeans would 'collar' all the land.[4]

The only remaining difficulty was a purely legal one. The Land Apportionment Act ran counter to the Southern Rhodesia Constitution Letters Patent which required amendment before the Act could go on to the Statute Book. This done, the bill was introduced once more into the Assembly and only four members, including all three Labour representatives, voted against it. The law finally received the royal assent and was promulgated on 10 October 1930.[5] The makers of the Act regarded their handiwork as an essay in trusteeship. The Act provided Africans with an area only slightly smaller than that of the whole of England. The indigenous folk, in terms of land, thus fared a great deal better than the Red Indians of North America, the Maori of New Zealand or the Araucanians of Chile. The land available to black people subsequently expanded; so did the cultivated acreage in African occupation.[6] Africans moreover secured some good land though the white men had the best of the deal.[7]

---

[1] W. M. Leggate to C. P. Scott: 19 Nov 1929 (in MO 13/1/1, Nat Arch MS)

[2] Sir F. Newton to H. U. Moffat: 21 Nov 1929 (in NE 1/1/7, Nat Arch MS)

[3] House of commons. *Debates*, v. 237, 26 Mar 1930

[4] House of commons. *Debates*, v. 240, 26 June 1930

[5] The Land apportionment act, 1930. The opposing members were M. Danziger and the Labour members—H. H. Davies, L. J. W. Keller and H. Malcolm.

[6] In 1946 designated African agricultural areas in Southern Rhodesia amounted to 20,322,700 acres. Of these 17,954,400 were described as usable for cultivation or grazing. In 1961 the total acreage of designated African land amounted to 40,362,700 and the usable acreage amounted to 30,624,100. By then the usable acreage available to Africans was about equal to the total acreage devoted to cultivation and grazing in Great Britain in 1926.

[7] For a detailed comparison of the amount and quality of land available to whites and blacks

Black cultivators thus sustained both losses and gains from the European impact. On the credit side, they acquired new implements such as ploughs and carts, improved breeds of live stock, new methods, as well as public works such as roads, dips and dams. African farmers could earn cash for their produce. European farming itself sometimes gave a stimulus to African cultivation, as the more specialized newcomers, tobacco growers and dairy men, themselves often bought African maize or meat. Generally speaking, the pacification of the country allowed the weaker African communities to utilize their land resources more effectively, since villages no longer had to be built with an eye to defence, and peasants could move further afield in search of new land. On the debit side Africans lost the use of the greater part of the country, over an area which appreciated in value as Europeans brought capital, 'know-how' and new technical methods to develop their farms.[1]

The settlement also led to hardships. The Rhodesian legislators believed that the existing reserves could carry a much larger native population—including most of the Africans then living on Crown and private land—an assumption proved wrong in practice. Besides, they looked upon the whole land problem in purely rural terms, and like their colleagues north of the Zambezi, saw labour migrancy as part of the natural order of things. The whole question of African urbanization was therefore not squarely tackled at a time when the territory still had the opportunity—even in terms of a purely segregationist philosophy—to formulate a national policy for planning native townships which might be sufficiently accessible to white quarters to obviate transport problems, and sufficiently attractive to promote the creation of a stable class of African urban house-owners. Instead the problem was mainly left to the municipalities. They did their best, but possessed neither the financial means nor the administrative resources to shoulder the task. But facts were already beginning to outrun theory. Bulawayo, the main commercial centre, presented the worst problem, and a locally appointed commission issued a forceful report

respectively, see the table in Appendix 1 of: Federation of Rhodesia and Nyasaland. *An agricultural survey of Southern Rhodesia. Part I: Agro-ecological survey.* Salisbury, Government printer, 1961.

[1] The figures for land occupation stood as follows for 1931 and 1962 respectively:

	1931	1962
European areas	49,149,000 acres	36,834,000 acres
Native reserves	21,600,000	21,020,000
Native purchase areas	7,465,000	4,216,000
Special native areas	—	19,150,000
Unassigned or unreserved	17,793,000	5,416,000
Wankie Game reserve	—	3,324,000
Forest area	591,000	6,650,000
Undetermined areas	88,000	—
Total	99,686,000	96,610,000

which in turn evoked a strong protest from the municipality. Sir Cecil Rodwell, the new Governor, himself thought that the City Fathers had a case, that the Commissioners had not given enough credit where praise was due, that there was no fault with the general lay-out of the location or the type of building erected, that the sanitary system was satisfactory and the water supply excellent. The living conditions in the locations appeared to him to compare very favourably with those of the coloured population in urban areas in other tropical countries of which he had knowledge. But nevertheless the location in no wise met the needs of an emergent urban working-class population. Guka Kumalo, the treasurer of the otherwise arch-conservative Matabele Home Society, saw the problem much more clearly. In 1930 he pointed out to the Superintendent of Natives in Bulawayo that many black people in town had been working there for years, that they knew nothing any more of farming, and that they no longer wanted to live in the reserves. What they wished was a better town. Existing facilities in Bulawayo, however, were quite inadequate. The houses were small and dirty; for the first time the streets were being made unsafe by thugs and spivs who had learned their trade in Johannesburg and returned to Bulawayo; here they formed gangs, from members of the same tribe, who roamed the roads with bicycle chains and knuckle dusters, ready to beat up members of opposing street corner mobs when they chanced to meet.[1] In a very small way Bulawayo was beginning to develop the problems that assail all industrial communities—and these were largely put aside, to be solved perhaps in the more distant future.

III

Slump and Reform Party

When Moffat took over the reins of Government, the country was still doing relatively well; immigrants, many of them farmers with some capital, were making new homes for themselves and the country's white population increased so swiftly that its rate of expansion stood out as one of the highest in the world.[2] The country's prosperity nevertheless rested on somewhat slender foundations. Administration remained an expensive

[1] Memorandum by the Superintendent of Natives, Bulawayo: 24 Sep 1930 (in S 138/2, Nat Arch SR)

[2] See Clay, H. *Report on industrial relations in Southern Rhodesia.* Salisbury, Government printer, 1930 (C.S.R. 3–1930). Clay calculated the growth of European population between 1921 and 1926 at 33 per 1,000 per annum. During the period 1881 to 1921 the comparative rates for other immigrant countries were: New Zealand 23, Australia 22, U.S.A. 19, Canada 18. England and Wales increased at only 8 per 1,000 per annum.

affair, for the Government had to provide all the services required by a civilized community, without being able to use them to their full capacity. The railways, the merchant firms and banks could all have handled a much greater volume of business; transport remained expensive, and in addition to high railway rates Rhodesians had to face considerable shipping charges. Rhodesia, wrote Professor Henry Clay, a well-known Manchester economist, resembled a firm with heavy overheads and an inadequate turnover. Matters could only improve by attracting more immigrants and more capital, and by increasing African purchasing power, which in turn depended on the state of the world market, which Rhodesians could not influence.

The Rhodesian 'firm' moreover depended on a few selected 'lines', such as maize, tobacco and gold. Many immigrant farmers ran into difficulties; they endeavoured to develop their holdings too quickly and tried to do in a few years what had taken other countries several generations. Large sums went into buildings, stumping, fencing and other permanent improvements; this outlay might have been spread over a longer period of years thereby avoiding financial embarrassment to the settlers when the lean years came.

Mining remained limited in extent, whilst secondary industries were in the main confined to the processing of agricultural products like cheese, bacon and tobacco. The country also boasted of a few additional works— flour mills, breweries, cement and fertilizer plants as well as some consumption industries preparing goods like soap, biscuits, and furniture, and clothing for the native trade. These industries, however, as yet had little importance, the railway system, with its important transit route to the Northern Rhodesian Copper Belt and Katanga, standing out as the only other major economic asset.

Southern Rhodesia's economy admittedly remained more diversified, and thus more 'crisis-resistant', than, say, that of its sister-colony beyond the Zambezi, but the country nevertheless remained underdeveloped and badly exposed to fluctuations in world trade. The first danger signal appeared in 1928. Following an increase in Imperial Preference, the production of leaf—much of it inferior in quality—shot up from 2,400,000 lb in 1925 to 24,900,000 lb in 1928. But then growers found their markets saturated; unsaleable stocks accumulated in warehouses overseas; London merchants began to complain of a glut in Empire tobacco and refused to place further orders. Rhodesian tobacco farmers suffered another blow when in 1930 South Africa imposed a quota on duty-free tobacco from Southern Rhodesia, and by 1931 about half the flue-curing barns in the Colony were standing unused.

In the meantime the country was caught by the great economic blizzard that was sweeping across the world, and all raw material producers were finding themselves in similar straits. Maize remained the country's main agricultural standby, and some mealie growers had considerably improved their methods. Earlier on in the century farmers used to grow various kinds of white and yellow maize, but found that white varieties yielded better crops and commanded a ready market overseas, with the result that certain areas were declared 'white maize areas', the 'White Flat' produced in Rhodesia acquiring an excellent reputation. Maize-growers nevertheless made mistakes. A few experienced men managed to produce yields of about nine bags an acre, but the ordinary farmer turned out no more than five, better than the general South African average, but not very good when compared with the best results achieved elsewhere. Worse still many farmers neglected to adopt green manuring and other improvements; when they did so, at long last, the awakening came too late, and land-owners found that, at a time when prices were dropping, they lacked the means to restore their ruined fields to productivity. The world slump wiped out most available markets and by the end of 1930 most maize farmers were facing bankruptcy.

Pastoralists meanwhile were facing similar difficulties. In 1924 European stock-owners owned more cattle than all the Africans between them; five years later the proportion of white-owned beasts had considerably decreased, many Europeans having changed over to dairying or dairy ranching, whilst others had sold their animals altogether and put their money into tobacco or cotton. Some breeders tried to improve their stock but faced many technical difficulties, with the result that 75 per cent of the cattle exported remained of the native type, most of the better grades going to Johannesburg, and only a small proportion being sent to the United Kingdom.

Farmers had other and more general headaches. A subsequent Committee of Enquiry headed by Danziger, a sharp and clear-headed man, pointed out that whilst agriculturists were getting much less money for their own products, they still had to pay relatively high prices for imported implements or other manufactured goods. Many co-operatives suffered from bad management, from high overheads, from the disloyalty of members or competition from outsiders. South African competition continued, the Rhodesian producers' position being made worse by high rail freights. Professional agriculturists were also running up against 'part-time' farmers who often managed to undersell regular producers. The burden of debt remained heavy and so did the farmer's outlay for 'domestic' services such as education, transport and medical treatment.

Besides, numerous farmers initially bought their land at too high a price—to find themselves faced later on with heavy expenditure for development. Many settlers were used to a relatively high standard of life which put them at a disadvantage in competing with backveld farmers, a serious problem made worse for immigrants who acquired their land in unsuitable areas or allowed their farms to deteriorate, or failed to keep proper records to show them where they made their losses. In addition the less efficient European farmers now had to face competition from native producers. Africans of course could not compete in more highly specialized lines like tobacco farming or dairying, requiring skill and capital beyond their resources, but many black growers did manage to supply local markets with low-grade meat and mealies at a cost below the white man's.

The farmers as a whole formed a well-organized pressure group and the Moffat Government generally complied with their wishes. Financial experts argued that between 1928 and 1933 about £1,000,000 was spent in the way of debt liquidation or reduction, publicity, export bounties, rebates and research. The Government set up a tight machinery of control to keep up domestic prices and protect producers, Southern Rhodesia in some ways working out a 'New Deal' of her own, an extensive assistance programme that owed nothing to theory but developed as a series of *ad hoc* measures.

Tobacco growers probably managed to weather the storm with more success than other farmers. When returns from their leaf began to fall, the smaller men urged the formation of a Tobacco Control Board whereby farmers would be able to keep up prices and improve the conditioning of their crops for export—a highly technical process which backveld growers could not tackle with 'rule of thumb' methods. The larger producers and important buyers like the Imperial Tobacco Company and the United Tobacco Company preferred a free market, but Government sided with the lesser men. The Legislature set up the Tobacco Control Board with extensive powers; a tobacco levy forced growers to finance various measures of general benefit to the industry, whilst a sharply worded Tobacco Pest Suppression Act protected the precious crop against disease.[1]

Growers gradually improved the quality of their merchandise and found to their joy that British sales went up. In the United Kingdom the Empire Marketing Board conducted an extensive 'Buy British' campaign. In addition Rhodesians benefited from the United Kingdom's Imperial Preference policy. They also gained an unexpected boon from the very

[1] See the Tobacco sale and export control act, 1930; the Tobacco levy act, 1933; and the Tobacco pest suppression act, 1933

fact that Rhodesian leaf fetched so little, since the Slump forced ordinary people in Britain to look for cheaper brands. After a disastrous year in 1931, when output barely exceeded one-eighth of the record figure attained in 1928, the industry picked up and by 1934 the Colony was turning out more leaf than ever before, even though prices still remained low.[1]

Pastoral farming likewise received some assistance. The Government imposed a levy on cattlemen, the money to be used for promoting the export of meat and live beasts.[2] In 1933 the Colony sent its first regular shipment of chilled beef to the United Kingdom and the pastoral industry gained some additional benefit when in the same year Liebig's (Rhodesia) Ltd opened a factory at West Nicholson for making extract of meat. The dairy industry had now increased to a point where the Government was able to set up a Dairy Control Board, which enforced a small levy from butter and cheese manufacturers. The Governor was empowered to issue stringent regulations designed to make Rhodesian dairy exports more acceptable overseas.[3] As a result dairymen got more stable prices; farmers improved the feeding and management of their herds, and dairying became the pastoral industry's most encouraging branch.

The maize growers' plight presented the Government with a more difficult problem. During the year 1929/30 Rhodesian farmers planted some 340,000 acres of 'mealies'—nearly double the acreage worked at the beginning of the decade. When prices began to drop, Moffat in 1930 announced that the Government under certain circumstances would pay an export bounty on every bag of maize sent abroad. Prices, however, did not recover and farmers often received no more than 5/– a bag which did not even cover their production costs. European maize growers at the same time began to meet with competition from Africans who were gaining a knowledge of European farming methods, not only from agricultural instructors but also from white employers themselves. A Committee of Investigation found that Africans were turning more and

---

[1] More detailed figures are:

Year	Total yield Virginia type in lbs	Total yield Turkish type in lbs
1928	24,491,464	451,580
1929	6,704,936	337,478
1930	5,494,063	350,140
1931	3,268,926	375,464
1932	14,448,440	577,726
1933	13,777,286	393,356
1934	26,097,888	694,204

[2] Cattle levy act, 1931
[3] Dairy control act, 1931

more from other indigenous foods to maize; this yielded better food value and could also be milled in European establishments, the grain mills doing away with the women's age-old drudgery of grinding corn in the kraal. African growers in the reserves, unlike European farmers, enjoyed the additional advantage of not having to pay rent or mortgage charges for their land; their standard of living remained lower, and even though the quality of their product was generally inferior, African farmers began to play a serious part in the market economy.[1] The Committee stated that during 1928/29 the total European-grown crop amounted to 1,826,000 bags. The estimated native-grown maize on the market amounted to 140,000 bags; 748,000 bags of European-grown maize were exported and 372,000 retained for farm use. No native-grown maize was exported, the whole lot being retained for local consumption. Rhodesians could not eat all their own maize. The surplus had to be exported but overseas buyers, faced with a world-wide glut, could pay very little. To help mealie farmers, Government continued to protect internal prices, and in 1931 the Assembly passed an Act for the compulsory control of maize and maize meal sales.[2] The new law provided for a Maize Control Board with extensive powers, and aimed at giving all producers a share in the relatively more profitable home market whilst bearing a proportion of the un-remunerative exports. For political reasons, however, some regions at first remained exempt from the provisions of the Act, with the result that producers and traders sent their maize to 'controlled' areas, thereby obtaining the benefit of the controlled price, whilst contributing nothing to the cost of financing exports.

The legislation also raised questions of more general policy on which opinion differed sharply. The missionaries opposed the law, the Rev. G. S. Murray explaining to the Southern Rhodesia Missionary Conference that the measure benefited larger European producers rather than African growers; black farmers lived further from the railway line, lacked transport and could not afford to wait for their returns, with the result that traders could pick up native grain for as little as 2/6d a bag.[3] The Chief Native Commissioner for his part considered that the existing marketing organization was inadequate, arguing that Africans could in fact expand their production if only improved sales facilities became available. The Maize Control Board, on the other hand, defended the law as it stood, and

---

[1] See *Southern Rhodesia: report of the maize enquiry committee*. Salisbury, Government printer, 1930 (C.S.R. 2–1931)

[2] Maize control act, 1931

[3] *Proceedings of the Southern Rhodesia missionary conference, Victoria Falls, 23rd to 28th June, 1932.* Morgenster, mission press, 1932, p. 17–18. The mission conference passed a resolution against the Act.

so did the Rhodesia Bantu Voters' Association.[1] In the end Native Commissioners themselves took a hand in marketing African grain, with the result that traders had to pay better prices, and the Chief Native Commissioner finally declared himself satisfied.

The mining industry in the meantime also suffered severely, largely because of rising costs. After 1916 gold output in Southern Rhodesia went down, and even though the early 'twenties saw a temporary recovery, the industry declined once more towards the end of the decade. Prospectors lost interest; many small workers went out of business; Shamva mine, an important producer, closed down in 1930; most remaining companies preferred to play for 'safety first', so that by 1931 the Colony was turning out less of the yellow metal than at any time since 1907. Opinion in the country sharply differed on how the situation might best be remedied. Smallworkers argued that the Government should have subsidized the industry by bounties on gold when times were good, but Leggate, a farmer, would not hear of it. The Government believed that such a step would only cause a boom resulting in the selling of worthless claims at high prices, and instead made the mistake of levying an extra tax on the industry to help balance the budget.[2] The Chartered Company for its part held that the Government ought to have given special grants to large concerns on the lines employed in Northern Rhodesia, claiming that only large-scale, scientific, methods would produce results, a contention bitterly denied by lesser entrepreneurs.[3]

The country's base mineral industry also suffered severely. Rhodesia possessed huge deposits of high-grade chrome, but in 1931 output fell disastrously for the overseas buyers—most of them Americans—found that the depressed state of world industries no longer warranted many purchases. Rhodesians moreover faced special problems as chrome producers. The mining cost of this metal always remained relatively low in comparison with railage charges and ocean freights, so that the country's geographical position put its producers at a particular disadvantage. The asbestos industry declined in similar fashion, Rhodesians having to face sharp competition from Russia. Coal fared no better, for even though the country could boast of almost astronomical carbon reserves, Rhodesians found that prices at the pithead remained higher than in the Union, whilst rail charges further limited the expansion of the coal industry.

Grim as the economic outlook appeared, Southern Rhodesia in some

[1] Chief Native Commissioner to Superintendent of Natives, Bulawayo: 8 Mar 1931 (in S 138/18, Nat Arch SR)

[2] See *New Rhodesia*, 31 Dec 1932, 11 Feb 1933 and 8 Sep 1933. The tax was raised through the Gold premium tax act, 1932.

[3] Sir H. Birchenough to H. U. Moffat: 19 Nov 1931 (in MO 13/1/1, Nat Arch MS)

ways escaped the effects of the Slump more lightly than many other African countries. The Northern Rhodesian copper mines continued development for a time, and Southern Rhodesia garnered some benefit from its extensive transit trade to the north, giving employment to the railways. Southern Rhodesia, Birchenough wrote bitterly, was from the railways' point of view in fact profiting from the fortunate accident of lying on a successful route to which it was not contributing enough traffic,[1] and this advantage lasted till 1931. The first rumblings of danger from the north came in February of that year when Bwana Mkubwa, a high cost producer, closed its gates. Later the copper companies suspended development work at Nchanga, Chambishi and Kansanshi, and by the end of the year only Roan and Nkana continued at work in Northern Rhodesia.

The blow to Southern Rhodesia's economy struck hard, but again the country experienced a stroke of luck. Britain decided to depreciate her currency so as to boost her export trade, and abandoned the Gold Standard. On 12 October 1931 Southern Rhodesia followed suit. She now found herself in a relatively favourable position. South Africa, her chief competitor, continued to adhere to gold for more than a year after, and purchasers of raw materials preferred to buy Southern Rhodesian goods with depreciated sterling currency rather than spend their money on merchandise from south of the Limpopo. The price of the yellow metal rose sharply; the Southern Rhodesian gold mining industry suddenly made money, and gold prices continued to move up until their stabilization during the Second World War. Ageing prospectors once again took out licences to search the veld; smallworkers went back into business; the minor entrepreneurs' share in the industry went up after many years in the doldrums.[2] The Southern Rhodesian mining industry also gained a few minor successes. The Rhodesian and General Asbestos Corporation Ltd, which controlled practically the whole of the country's output, managed to come to an agreement with the state-owned asbestos industry in the Soviet Union. This ensured that supplies from both countries would be

[1] Sir H. Birchenough to H. U. Moffat: 19 Nov 1931 (in MO 13/1/1, Nat Arch MS)

[2] *Chambers's Encyclopaedia*. London, G. Newnes ltd, 1950, v. 6, p. 417, gives the following figures for the average price of gold in London: 1930: 100; 1931: 109; 1932: 139; 1933: 147; 1934: 162; 1935: 168; 1936: 165; 1937: 166; 1938: 168; 1939: 183; 1940: 198. Between 1931 and 1932 the value of the country's gold output went up from £1,054,443 to £2,751,713. Details of the output are:

Year	Ounces of gold produced	% share of major producers in total production	No of producers
1928	576,112	77·31	300
1929	560,813	73·59	290
1930	547,630	74·65	331
1931	532,111	68·93	449
1932	574,135	61·41	782

sold on an economic basis, Rhodesian experts gratefully concluding that had competition continued unchecked, their own asbestos industry would have gone out of business.[1]

The Slump also put a new emphasis on Imperial co-operation and in a somewhat roundabout fashion enhanced the Colony's international status. In 1932 delegations from the various Commonwealth countries assembled at an Economic Conference at Ottawa. Moffat led the Southern Rhodesian delegation and from the first asserted his right to be heard as well as seen. The Rhodesian delegates took part in committees and received all the consideration they could possibly ask for, the Ottawa Conference marking a considerable advance in the status of Southern Rhodesia since an earlier Imperial Conference held in 1930. The country nevertheless counted as small fry. Downie, one of the Southern Rhodesian representatives, found his stay somewhat disillusioning. The Conference produced no real leaders, just ordinary people like themselves. R. B. Bennett, the Canadian Prime Minister, stood out as the most important figure, while the United Kingdom delegation formed no more than a 'one man conference', the one man being Sir Horace Wilson, their Chief Industrial Adviser.[2]

The Conference aimed at tightening the bonds of Empire trade; Britain, having already committed herself to a policy of protection, conceded various new or increased preferences to Empire raw materials. The Dominions in their turn aimed at expanding the British market for their primary products. In addition they required British capital to build up manufacturing industries of their own, which in turn required protection from old-established competitors overseas. The Dominions accordingly made a number of small tariff reductions benefiting British industries, but raised duties against other countries, though at the same time coming to some reciprocal arrangements between themselves. Southern Rhodesia did not fare too badly, and in August 1932 the Colony concluded an agreement with Great Britain which secured for a period of ten years to Rhodesian tobacco the existing margin of preference over foreign tobacco. The Colony also concluded an independent agreement with Canada whereby Southern Rhodesian maize and citrus received certain advantages in return for specified privileges for Canadian wood, paper and certain classes of manufactured goods.[3]

The British South Africa Company in the meantime continued in possession of the country's mineral rights which the constitutional settle-

---

[1] Southern Rhodesia. *Ottawa conference: report of the committee appointed to investigate and report to the Government.* . . . Salisbury, Government printer, 1932 (C.S.R. 1–1933)

[2] J. W. Downie to W. M. Leggate: 7 Sep 1932 (in LE 3/1/1, Nat Arch MS)

[3] For the proceedings of the Conference, see Cmd. 4174 (1932) and Cmd. 4175 (1932). For the agreements with Britain and Canada, see *Southern Rhodesia government gazette,* 14 Oct 1932

ment of 1923 had secured to the Board. The Company, however, incurred strong criticism, the slump in minerals giving an extra edge to discontent. Some argued that Lobengula had no right in the first place to grant the Rudd Concession; others felt that the Company should only have been able to exercise its title in minerals as long as it administered the country. The whole issue aroused bitter controversy, not merely between the 'people' and Company, but also between conflicting groups of capitalists. Bodies as conservative as the two Chambers of Mines and the Rhodesian Mining Federation joined with the Rhodesia Agricultural Union, the smallworkers and the Reform Party in demanding a final settlement. The Moffat Government accordingly enquired of the Company whether it would be willing to submit the matter to a competent tribunal or—if necessary—to the Privy Council. The 'Charter' on the other hand considered that its shareholders undoubtedly owned the mineral rights, the continued security of the Company's title forming one of the conditions of Responsible Government, so that any interference with established rights would be a breach of faith.

The question became a major issue in which the interests of British investors overseas strongly conflicted with the claim of the local mining industry. The Moffat Government at first hoped that the 'Charter' might be edged out, but for all their theorizing about Trusteeship, the Imperial authorities strongly sided with the British South Africa Company, the short-lived Labour Government proving no more sympathetic than the National Government which took its place in 1931. The Southern Rhodesians found themselves in a difficult position. The Letters Patent providing for the constitution of Responsible Government specifically stated that any local law concerning the collection of mining revenue or the imposition of taxes on minerals must be subject to Imperial consent, so that Southern Rhodesia could not deal with the mineral problem through legislation, and only the way to the Privy Council remained open.

Moffat tried to bring up the subject at Ottawa in conversation with James Henry Thomas, the Dominions Secretary, but found Thomas ignorant of the matter, hopeless to talk to, and not particularly interested.[1] Moffat thought that Sir Edward Harding, the Permanent Under-Secretary, was the man who really counted, but though Harding proved friendly enough, the Rhodesian authorities failed to get much satisfaction. At the end of 1932 Harding in a published despatch informed the Rhodesians that the 1923 Agreement between the Secretary of State and the Chartered Company recognized the Company as owner of the mineral rights; this clause formed part of the final settlement giving self-government to

[1] H. U. Moffat to W. M. Leggate: 16 Aug 1932 (in LE 3/1/1, Nat Arch MS)

Southern Rhodesia. Even apart from the Devonshire Agreement and the Constitution Letters Patent, the Imperial authorities could see no reason for questioning the Company's position under the Rudd Concession, the Rhodesians thereby receiving a strong hint not to go on with the case.[1]

The Imperial Government's position was of course difficult; the 'Charter' obviously held good cards at law, and even had the courts pronounced against the Company, the Board would have had strong grounds for proceeding against the Crown by means of a Petition of Right. The Salisbury authorities for their part consulted various legal luminaries, getting differing advice, but Denis Nowell Pritt, a prominent Socialist and an outstanding lawyer, advised that the Rhodesians would be unlikely to succeed if they challenged the Company in court. Apart from the legal, there remained the political and moral aspects. The Company's opponents argued that the Rhodesian electorate did not know about the mineral reservation at the time of the Referendum, and that the special conditions were only later 'slipped in' to the Constitution. Sir Hugh Williams, a leading smallworker, went as far as to refuse paying royalties on the output of his mine so that his case went to court, but Moffat took a more conciliatory line. The Premier argued that the country was well aware of the mineral reservation during the Referendum period,[2] and after much discussion and correspondence his Government decided to settle with the 'Charter', thereby avoiding a lengthy, expensive and probably unsuccessful action before the Privy Council. Sir Edmund Davis declared himself, in a private interview, willing to approach the Company, if Southern Rhodesia would make an offer of £2,000,000.[3] In 1933 the purchase went through, and from the purely business point of view the Moffat administration made a good bargain. For £2,000,000 they acquired extensive rights which rising sterling prices of gold steadily put up in value. The 'Charter' for its part exchanged a speculative asset into first-class securities and greatly increased the liquid resources at its command.[4]

Politically the mineral rights purchase, however, did serious harm to the Moffat Government. Many Rhodesians thought that they were paying good money for something which should never have been recognized as

---

[1] See Sir E. J. Harding to J. W. Downie: 2 Nov 1932 and 10 Jan 1933, printed in Southern Rhodesia. *Copy of correspondence, opinions by counsel, documents and returns relating to the question of the ownership of the mineral rights in Southern Rhodesia.* Salisbury, Government printer, 1933, p. 1–3 (C.S.R. 18–1933)

[2] H. U. Moffat to R. J. Hudson: 16 Mar 1933 (in LE 3/1/1, Nat Arch MS)

[3] Interview between the Premier, the High Commissioner and Sir Edmund Davis: 5 July 1932 (in LE 3/1/1, Nat Arch MS)

[4] B.S.A. Company. *Report of the thirty-sixth ordinary general meeting held . . . on 28th February, 1934,* p. 8

the Company's property in the first place, and blamed the Government for not extricating them from the 'Charter's' clutches. The Moffat Government similarly sustained heavy attacks in connexion with allegedly high railway rates, the Reform Party and Labour men all feeling convinced that the Premier was knuckling down to London capitalists, and that the public was paying too much into company coffers. The Railway Commission set up in 1926 was not an impressive body, and critics of Government were not slow in pointing out its deficiencies. The Railway administration on the other hand had to invest a good deal of capital in its installations, especially in Portuguese East Africa, and when the Slump came the lines began to run into financial difficulties. Expenditure was cut, staff was retrenched, wages went down and goods and passenger services suffered curtailment. The Chartered Company provided some financial assistance, but in 1932 the Railway Companies had to apply for a moratorium.

The Government itself carried out a similar policy of retrenchment; expenditure was heavily reduced, especially in the vital Department of Agriculture, and civil servants had to accept salary cuts under a special law which involved a change in the Constitution.[1] Opposition against the ruling party accordingly grew more and more widespread. Discontented railway men and civil servants, artisans without a job and farmers in economic distress—most of whom had voted for Responsible Government—now began to turn against the Rhodesian Party, and Moffat experienced increasing difficulties in coping with the situation. The Premier —always shy and inclined to secrecy—lacked the ability to put over his case, whilst his Cabinet appeared 'a dull lot'. Downie, the most vigorous personality amongst his supporters, was away in London as High Commissioner, in succession to Newton. The unpredictable Fletcher, whom the good-natured Premier accepted into the Ministry to look after Agriculture, turned out to be a political embarrassment and was dropped. The Rhodesian Party sustained some defections in the House, where its majority became reduced and its internal cohesion began to weaken. A stronger man of course might still have managed to keep control. The critics of Government remained divided, Davies, Keller and Malcolm continuing to uphold Labour principles, whilst the main opposition derived from the Reform Party, now led by Robert Dunipace Gilchrist, a farmer of Scottish descent. Gilchrist could rely on support from Bertin, from Jacob Hendrik Smit, a respected merchant of Hollands origins who had worked his way up from a greengrocer's barrow to comparative affluence, and from Stephen Martin Lanigan O'Keefe, a former civil servant. Gilchrist, however, lacked all powers of leadership and possessed so little

[1] See Public services economy act, 1931

u

confidence in his party's chances that in 1931 he suggested to Moffat that the Slump made a general election undesirable.[1]

The Opposition however obtained a major new access of strength in 1931. Dr Godfrey Martin Huggins, who represented Salisbury North, a prosperous suburb of the capital containing many civil servants, resigned from the Rhodesian Party over the Public Services Economy Act and other issues, and crossed the floor. Huggins, an English stockbroker's son, Conservative in his leanings and staunch in his Imperial beliefs, first came to Rhodesia in 1911 on a short-term engagement as a *locum tenens*, but then decided to stay on, giving up his hopes for academic preferment in a London teaching hospital for the more solid financial rewards of a colonial practice. Huggins, an able and highly qualified surgeon, soon became a popular personality in a small country where 'Mr Huggins's' word carried a good deal of authority with his numerous patients in all circles of society. In a public meeting to explain his resignation, Huggins told his constituents that the Railway Act did not work, that the Government had failed the country in the matter of the mineral rights, and that not enough was being done for secondary industries, the damnable Public Services Economy Act only forming the last straw. Huggins also objected to the idea of Africans enjoying the same political rights as white men, and lastly he called for amalgamation with the north. At the end of his speech he received an ovation from his constituents, and a warrant to stay in Parliament as their representative.[2] Huggins had at first no serious alternative to put forward, but nevertheless made his mark as a witty and incisive speaker, forceful to the point of indiscretion, and much more likely to lead the Reform Party to victory than the somewhat ineffectual Gilchrist. Huggins himself never attended a decisive Reform Party Congress called to determine the leadership, but received strong backing from Smit and Patrick Basil Fletcher, an influential businessman and the son of R. A. Fletcher,[3] and when the discussions were over Huggins got a cable informing him that he had been elected to head the Party.

Many Government supporters now began to worry. Moffat became his party's scapegoat and the malcontents looked for a successor. The Bulawayo section would have liked Downie, but Downie preferred to continue in London as High Commissioner.[4] The Rhodesian Party's Salisbury wing supported George Mitchell, Moffat's Minister of Mines and Works since 1930, and a Party Congress elected Mitchell to be Vice-

[1] R. D. Gilchrist to H. U. Moffat: 12 Nov 1931 (in MO 13/1/1, Nat Arch MS)
[2] See *Rhodesia herald*, 4 Mar 1932
[3] P. B. Fletcher to J. H. Smit: 18 Nov 1934 (in SM 4/1/1, Nat Arch MS)
[4] W. M. Leggate to J. W. Downie: 25 June 1932 and Downie to Leggate: 10 July 1932 (both in LE 3/1/1, Nat Arch MS)

President for Matabeleland in place of Hudson who a year later accepted a well merited appointment to the Bench. Moffat had previously intimated his willingness to retire, and now found himself under heavy pressure from Allan Ross Welsh, a prominent lawyer and the Party's Chairman, as well as from Ernest Lucas Guest, Welsh's partner, who both felt the country needed a change. In the end the Congress compromised by re-electing Moffat as President for the time being, on the understanding that he would retire from the Premiership after the following Parliamentary session when Mitchell would succeed.[1]

Moffat, never an ambitious kind of person, loyally accepted this decision, and in July 1933 Mitchell formed the most short-lived administration in Rhodesian history. The new Prime Minister,[2] a tired, elderly businessman with greying hair and a neat moustache, an ex-bank manager and former President of the Chamber of Mines, was hardly the man to set the country on fire. Admittedly, the economic situation was beginning to ameliorate and Downie wrote optimistic reports about the improving export position. But discontent remained rife, at a time when white unemployeds were doing unskilled work at 5/– a day. Huggins made many converts and his task was made easier by the fact that organizing a party in those days did not require large funds.

The Reform Party then issued a new programme which was well designed to appeal to all European malcontents. The Party proposed to set up a State Reserve Bank, with enough loan capital to purchase all the gold produced in the country, for the purpose of controlling internal currency and bank credit, and it advocated a quasi-Keynesian policy of credit expansion. Huggins also stressed the need for developing secondary industries; he opposed monopolies and concessions harmful to the public interest, and at the same time promised to treat unemployment relief as a national responsibility. The Party also gave a pledge to improve educational and welfare services, and also to make the railways more amenable to public control. More important still, artisans angered by African competition received an undertaking that the Government would put new industrial legislation on the Statute Book to look after the white workers' interests. Huggins likewise promised 'gradual differential development of the European and native races upon a territorial basis', the removal of African voters from the common voters' roll, and the development of a Native Council system, proposals which did not seem very revolutionary

---

[1] See *Bulawayo chronicle*, 12 Nov 1932

[2] The Ministerial titles act, 1933, altered the title of Premier to that of Prime Minister; the Treasurer became Minister of Finance, the Colonial Secretary became Minister of Internal Affairs and the Attorney-General became Minister of Justice.

at the time, but subsequently caused Huggins considerable embarrassment. The programme was gilded with a Sweepstake Clause which provided for a referendum to decide whether the public wanted to indulge its gambling instincts through a public lottery.[1] In the General Election of 1933 the Rhodesian Party—with its constant harping on past achievements, its lack of vigour and its spineless speeches—failed to win. Moffat, Leggate and Mitchell all lost their seats, whilst the Reform Party gained a total of 16 constituencies, a victory which just allowed it to outvote the combined Opposition in Parliament. But its opponents were still numerically superior in votes; according to published press reports the Rhodesian Party scored 10,512 as against the Reform Party's 11,539 votes, the Opposition as a whole obtaining a total of 16,241 votes so that the Reform Party could not claim to have the majority of the electorate behind them.[2] The existing system of Parliamentary constituencies now, however, worked against the Rhodesian Party, which in the new Assembly had only nine seats against Labour's five. Fynn took over the leadership of the Opposition. The old ruling party was safely out, and 'the underdogs, the down and outs and all those with little stake in the country'—as Leggate now termed them with disgust—had made the running.[3] Huggins had got his doctor's mandate, and when on 6 September 1933 he assumed office as Prime Minister, the country seemed set for a more leftward course.

IV

Doctor's Mandate: 1934

When Huggins took office, he found himself in a difficult position. His Parliamentary majority was small and many forecasters feared a deadlock. The Opposition, however, came to the Prime Minister's rescue. Fynn decided to assist the Government, all the more so since the new Administration stuck to financial orthodoxy. Smit took over the Ministry of Finance, and promptly forgot all about his violent election speeches; he ran the national exchequer with the same caution as his own business, a conservative budget with a solid surplus disappointing the left wingers' hope of lavish public expenditure.[4] Huggins's native policy showed little difference from that of his predecessor. The Prime Minister abandoned the idea of setting up a special Commission to make policy recommendations,

[1] For the Party's full programme, see *New Rhodesia*, 14 July 1933
[2] *New Rhodesia*, 8 Sep 1933
[3] W. M. Leggate to J. W. Downie: 13 Sep 1933 (in DO 1/1/4, Nat Arch MS)
[4] Notes by P. D. L. Fynn for April to May 1934 (in FY 1/2/1, Nat Arch MS)

and instead continued to rely for advice on the Native Department which stuck to paternalism and cautious differentiation. Huggins himself explained in public that assimilation never worked even with American negroes, and that the country should aim at a policy of adaptation whereby Africans would develop on their own lines. He painted a somewhat optimistic picture whereby white and black civilizations would advance side by side, helping each other all the way. Nevertheless he insisted that African marketing facilities must be developed and that black people must be paid in cash for their produce, for he soon became convinced that, for administrative and economic reasons alone, a policy of rigid segregation would not work.

The Reform Party left wingers bitterly resented what they regarded as Huggins's policy of compromise with the 'Old Gang'. This resentment was typified in articles by Neil Housman Wilson, the Reform Party's most prominent writer, who bitterly attacked the control of Rhodesian banks and railways by outside influence. The country needed a national currency, a reserve bank of issue and an independent credit structure based on Rhodesia's local gold production. But outside investors continued to draw their income from loans made in London, and the Government refused to fight for financial independence. The country's native policy likewise stood in need of root-and-branch alteration. If things went on as they did, Wilson argued, the whites would gradually be driven out; the only salvation lay in a well-planned 'two pyramid' policy. The blacks in time would become their own bricklayers, merchants and solicitors and advance to the top of their own pyramid. The Europeans for their part should also have a pyramid of their own, where in time even the lowest steps would be occupied by men of their own race. Only in this way could the country hope to get rid of racial hostility, attract white immigrants in large numbers, give jobs to Rhodesian-born youngsters without special qualification, do away with its emergent 'poor white' problem, and prevent the African areas from being drained of their best men. The whites no longer had a hinterland where they might trek, as in South Africa's olden days, to escape from their problems, and the Government must act now. Fortunately the Colony still had a chance, for sufficient land remained available, and the Native Affairs Department had already made a start by preventing whites from moving into the reserves, and thereby had set up the country's only legalized colour bar.[1]

Huggins, a conservative upper middle class Englishman at heart, had, however, little patience with what he regarded as theorizing and, instead, devoted himself to the task of reducing more immediate pressures. Some

[1] See articles in *New Rhodesia*, 17 Nov and 8 Dec 1933

of the harshest clamour came from the smaller European maize growers who found that, despite existing legislation, they still could not keep their heads above water. Previous legislation had instituted a system of compulsory control, but this did not apply to all areas. The legislators moreover had at first intended that African-grown maize should share the burden of subsidizing unremunerative exports. But when the Maize Control Board came into being in 1931, the authorities decided that African maize, purchased by 'farmer consumers' for their own use, should be exempted from the contribution. European farmers, in other words, themselves bought a good deal of grain from their African neighbours, the 'white' and 'black' economies having already become far more dependent on one another than the planners assumed. This demand for cheap maize forced up prices paid to native growers, as European purchasers preferred to buy 'mealies' at up to 9/6 from black men instead of about 11/– from the Board. Disgruntled farmers complained that the benefit of being exempt from the contribution to the export burden went to Africans whose production costs remained lower, and who did not have to bear the added burden of rents and mortgages.

The Government therefore drafted a new Act which provided two separate pools and discriminated in favour of the small white as against both the larger white and the African grower. European crops surrendered to the Maize Control Board were divided according to a sliding scale. Smaller farmers were allowed to put a much larger percentage of their crop into the local pool which commanded a higher price, whilst big producers were only allowed a smaller share of the profitable home market. The scheme first of all intended that African producers should only receive a quota of about 12 per cent in the local pool, but neither the Governor nor the Chief Native Commissioner were satisfied with this arrangement, and the authorities then changed the legislation in such a way as to assure Africans of a quota of about 20 per cent for the first year. The Imperial Government consented to the scheme, and in 1934 the amended law passed on to the Statute Book.[1]

The new Act extended control over the whole country. Prices obtained by European maize producers varied in inverse ratio to their total production, so that smaller growers got more than bigger farmers. Africans surrendering maize to the Board received a price averaging that paid to *all* white growers, the authorities arguing that control would become unworkable if the great army of very small African producers all had to be registered. Ordinary traders could still buy African-grown maize for resale, but could not participate in the most favoured pool, so that their

[1] Maize control amendment act, 1934

African suppliers received no more than the prevailing export price. Black people on the other hand obtained some distinct advantages from the control machinery. They could sell their grain directly to the Board which thus competed with European and Indian traders, and this often gave Africans at a distance from the line of rail a better means of getting rid of their surplus. Africans also enjoyed certain privileges not available to European producers; they could still dispose of their mealies to registered traders, or to other Africans or to white prospectors for local consumption, so that the white farmers, who could do none of these things, benefited perhaps less from the Act than they imagined. The law as a whole was also unpopular with white merchants and miners who would have preferred a freer market economy; the larger farmers remained resentful, and even many small growers criticized the control system, which involved delayed payments as well as periodic inspections by Government graders.[1]

In addition the Huggins Government passed a Tobacco Reserve Pool Act,[2] which aimed at giving tobacco growers a better return for their outlay. The Act set up a pool designed to hold surplus stocks off the market until buyers had secured their normal needs. It compelled growers to contribute to the pool on a sliding scale that varied according to the size of the tobacco crop. Another law provided for a compulsory levy on all cattle, the money collected being used for a subsidy on cattle exported abroad.[3] Rhodesians in fact, though no one said so, were subsidizing consumers in richer and more industrialized countries overseas—especially Britain, which benefited from low-cost agricultural imports.

Huggins at the same time found himself under considerable pressure from European artisans who were suffering from the Slump, and dreaded being under-cut or unemployed. The white workers, dispersed in 'penny packets' in scattered townships, remained relatively weak; trade unionism did not achieve much success outside the Rhodesia Railway Workers' Union which Keller, a veteran from the Western Front, ran with considerable efficiency as General Secretary. The remaining workers' associations suffered from internal dissensions, from boundary disputes between small unions, and also from the general lack of stability which characterized the European labour force, many of whose members looked to Britain or South Africa as 'Home'. The immediate post-war years had witnessed a temporary rise of working class militancy, but this had proved but a flash in the pan. In 1919 for instance Herbert Walsh had formed the Rhodesian Mine and General Workers' Association, and for a

---

[1] See 'Open letter to Miner Frank from Farmer John' (in *New Rhodesia*, 5 Oct 1934, p. 5–7) for the point of view of the smaller white farmer *vis à vis* the mining interest.

[2] Tobacco reserve pool act, 1934   [3] Cattle levy and beef export bounty act, 1934

time succeeded in getting the scattered white mine workers to act in unison in a country which professional Union secretaries regarded as 'unorganizable'. Walsh, a Yorkshire boiler maker, who had learned his political creed from William Morris's Socialist Society and the pioneers of the Independent Labour Party in Bradford, possessed unusual ability. Having worked in the North of England, he went to South Africa before the Boer War for a job in Simonstown Dockyard, and later to Kimberley, where he opened a branch of the Boiler Makers' Union. Walsh soon got into trouble with his autocratic company over trade union matters and then emigrated to Rhodesia where he became a well-paid technician at the Globe and Phoenix Mine, and continued his Union work. But even Walsh could not solve the problem of keeping his union afloat in the face of fluctuating and uncertain membership and of sectional disputes with the mechanics, with the result that it disintegrated a few years later.[1]

Politically the white workers' position was little stronger. The Rhodesia Labour Party never attained much influence outside Bulawayo; during the Slump it demonstrated its general weakness by refraining from pressure for any social or industrial reforms till the country should get back to a sound footing.[2] Huggins himself firmly believed that Labour would never form a Government in the country; many Labour supporters secretly shared this view, so that the white artisans became no more than yet another pressure group which looked for favours from the ruling party, instead of aiming at supreme power for itself. The depression with its attendant unemployment greatly diminished the white workers' bargaining power; jobs were hard to get in a country possessing so few industries, and the artisans, therefore, put their trust in legislation more than strike action. Harry Herbert Davies, a Bulawayo estate agent and a prominent Labour supporter in Parliament, explained to the Assembly that Southern Rhodesia must aim at marching in step with other civilized countries by eliminating the antagonism between workmen and employers, and look to Roosevelt's New Deal as a pattern for social action.[3]

The artisans as a whole demanded that the community should secure them a living wage and what they called 'fair competition'. James Cowden, a building contractor, thus bitterly pointed to an instance where a white mechanic in a Salisbury garage was working for a miserable pittance of £5 a month, whereas he should be getting something like £30 or £40 for the same amount of work.[4] The European workers at the same time felt themselves threatened by poorly paid African artisans, and

[1] See *Rhodesian railway review*, Dec 1934
[2] See statement by H. H. Davies (in *Rhodesia herald*, 21 Sep 1934)
[3] Southern Rhodesia. *Legislative assembly debates*, 11 Apr 1934, p. 98
[4] *Ibid.* 10 Apr 1934, p. 26

applied the same yardstick to their black competitors as they did to white
ones. Black youngsters were receiving industrial training in the Government schools at Domboshawa (set up in 1920) and at Tjolotjo (established
a year later and transferred to Mzingwane in 1943). Mission instructors also
gave a certain amount of technical training; white artisans themselves
passed on some of their skills to black helpmates on the job, a practice
bitterly deplored by many trade unionists, but one which could not be
stopped as long as, for example, white building workers brought their
own 'boys' to the site. White artisans of course probably exaggerated the
position. Outside a few trades like brick-laying, carpentry and house-
painting, European workmen faced little competition, whilst the black
artisans' village background for long militated against habits like punctuality, consistency and reliability—qualities bred more easily in a
Western money economy where every man owned a timepiece as a matter
of course, and was brought up to be conscious of time from early child-
hood. Most African workmen as yet required a good deal of supervision;
highly skilled people remained scarce, the country's real problem lying
not in an excess of qualified men, but in a lamentable lack of trained labour
all round. An outstanding economist like Professor Henry Clay thus
felt not the slightest doubt that European labour could well hold its own
through its skill and adaptability. But the ordinary European did not see
matters in this way.[1] The number of African independent artisans was
rising,[2] and white workmen insisted that the Legislature should step in.

The Government for its part wished to conciliate white workers, but
also had other reasons for regulating industry. The country lacked any
statutory machinery for dealing with labour troubles, except for the Industrial Disputes Ordinance, 1920, which could only be invoked after a
dispute had started and which the authorities had in fact never used. The
authorities wanted legislation which would prevent strikes and lock-outs
that might dislocate the country's infant industries. They also had other
less apparent objects. Southern Rhodesia as yet lacked factory legislation,
and the Acting Solicitor-General argued that elaborate laws on overseas
lines would turn out to be more of a hindrance than a help, and could not
be enforced in such a sparsely-populated country. In addition the rising
generation of white youngsters should be given the chance of learning a

---

[1] See Clay, H. *Report on industrial relations in Southern Rhodesia*. Salisbury, Government printer,
1930 (*C.S.R. 3–1930*)

[2] *The report of the Chief Native Commissioner for the year 1930*. Salisbury, Government printer,
1931 (*C.S.R. 11–1931*), p. 7, stated that the number of Africans in business on their own increased
from 864 in 1929 to 1,586 in 1930, when there were 423 builders, 283 shoemakers, 179 carpenters,
93 hawkers, 74 painters, 54 brickmakers, 42 well sinkers, 40 transport riders, 27 cycle repairers.
Others included 2 mechanics and 2 photographers.

trade under suitable controls. Rigid apprenticeship legislation would not yet meet the case; each industry and trade should instead formulate its own conditions in accordance with varying circumstances in different areas.

The authorities, therefore, to cover these matters drafted a bill on the model of existing South African statutes and applicable to industry, though not to farming or the civil service, which possessed its own conciliation machinery. The law made provision alike for whites, Coloureds and Asians, but excluded Africans from its definition of 'employees', on the grounds that they were not yet ready to join trade unions. The Industrial Conciliation Bill met with opposition overseas on the grounds that it sharply discriminated between white and brown people on the one hand, and black folk on the other. The Governor replied that the Africans' interests were being protected through the Native Department and by existing legislation like the Native Labour Regulations Ordinance, 1911, and the Masters and Servants Ordinance, 1901. The Bill moreover did not set up an industrial colour bar in so many words. Conciliation Boards, composed of white employers and trade unionists, forwarded agreements to the Minister who could then make a formal declaration that these should be binding on both parties. If an Industrial Council or Conciliation Board reported to the Minister that the objects of an agreement were being defeated by the employment of lower-paid Africans, the Minister could prescribe wage rates for certain industries. These rates would be applicable to both white and black workers in specified areas. The law, in other words, turned the townships into protected fiefs for white workers. It compelled employers in these areas to pay identical wages to skilled Europeans and Africans; thereby in practice it gave European artisans, and to a lesser extent Coloureds and Indians, an overwhelming advantage, for employers had no reason to engage Africans unless they could thereby save money. Unskilled black men, who probably comprised more than 99 per cent of the African labour force, remained outside the provisions of the Bill; the white trade unions in the towns continued to exclude all but a few native artisans, the Bill giving the sanction of law to the white workers' policy of keeping up the wage rates in urban areas. European farmers, on the other hand, outside these urban areas, could continue to employ trained or semi-trained Africans on jobs like the building of homesteads and tobacco barns, whilst the native purchase areas and reserves remained outside the scope of the legislation.

The Industrial Conciliation Bill met with a good reception in the Legislative Assembly, Labour's only complaint being that the law did not go far enough. The Imperial Government, which then did not intend to encourage trade unionism amongst Africans, gave its assent, and in 1934 the Bill became law.[1] The new Act provided for the proper registration of both trade unions and employers' organizations and set up machinery for the prevention of industrial disputes through mixed industrial councils. It laid down special conditions for disputes affecting essential services, and provided for the way in which agreed terms should be applied to Africans; there was also provision for apprenticeship rules. Administration of the measure as a whole was assigned to the Minister for Internal Affairs who thereby gained a key position in industrial matters.

The Reform Party had not met with serious trouble from the Imperial power, but Huggins nevertheless felt convinced that he must provide against possible future eventualities. At this point the Prime Minister still believed in segregation and considered that this policy of separate development should be extended to the remainder of British Central and East Africa; he hoped thereby to solve the contradictions of his own native policy by providing opportunities for educated Southern Rhodesian Africans beyond the Zambezi. Huggins also dreaded the thought that African voters might one day dominate the voters' roll, a contingency all the more likely since the Land Apportionment Act aimed at an expanding class of African property owners. Huggins, like Moffat before him, nevertheless thought that Africans should be entitled to some kind of representation in the Assembly, and that the electoral law should accordingly be reformed. Huggins and his fellow Parliamentarians moreover felt resentful at Southern Rhodesia's remaining constitutional shackles, with their many attendant anomalies. He had little interest in Dominion status as such, dreading the trouble and expense which a change would involve and preferring the existing partnership between the local and the Imperial power. Nevertheless the terms of this partnership should be improved and the remaining powers in Southern Rhodesia of the High Commissioner for South Africa ought to be scrapped.

In the middle of 1934 Huggins and Colonel Clive Lancaster Carbutt, the Chief Native Commissioner and a firm segregationist, went to London to discuss with the Dominions Office the points at issue. The Southern Rhodesians put up a scheme whereby Central Africa would divide into separate white and black areas; Nyasaland would ultimately become a black country pure and simple; Northern Rhodesia would be split, and advanced Southern Rhodesian Africans find an outlet beyond the Zambezi for their energies.[2] The Prime Minister stressed his own incipient poor white problem; at the moment Southern Rhodesia counted no more

[1] Industrial conciliation act, 1934
[2] For Carbutt's views see Carbutt, C. L. 'The racial problem in Southern Rhodesia' (in *NADA*, no. 12, 1934, p. 6–11)

than 100 or 150 poor whites, but if things took their course, the country might face a position like that of South Africa which found itself with 300,000 of these unfortunates on its hands. He did not oppose African advancement; in fact a lot was being done in this direction: but it must not come about at the expense of the white taxpayer on whose goodwill the country depended for its African improvement programme. Carbutt, an able man of the old school, strongly backed his chief, but the Imperial officials remained sceptical. They felt convinced that the British Government would never sanction a project that denied black advancement over large areas in Northern Rhodesia, and that would encounter strong resistance from Parliament and mining companies. Carbutt's scheme would not of course embarrass the Colonial Office if confined to Southern Rhodesia, but the Colony must not be encouraged in a policy which might get the Imperial Government into trouble elsewhere. London could not initiate a policy less liberal than that of Pretoria, and Southern Rhodesian objections were urbanely swept aside.

A policy for breaking up Southern Rhodesia into 'colour-cantons' would have been expensive, but not perhaps impossible as a long-term venture. But educated Africans now shared the Imperial power's distrust of Carbutt's approach. They accepted the idea of segregation within Southern Rhodesia, but had no desire to go beyond its borders. Northern Rhodesia, they argued, had no attractions; many parts remained backward and disease-ridden; educated black folk from the south would never live under strange chiefs and stranger tribal customs. A northern native state might become no more than a reservoir of cheap manpower and, in any case, the time was now too far gone for a solution on Carbutt's lines. Labour migrants were absorbing new ideas; the African people were giving up their nomadic habits, and Southern Rhodesia must be regarded as a common home for black and white alike, where Africans should acquire a share in the making of laws.[1]

Huggins had no greater success in London with his franchise suggestions. He argued that existing African voters on the common roll might stay there but he was worried about the future. The number of Africans entitled to go to the polling booths was bound to grow; property qualifications for the vote remained low; the Land Apportionment Act in fact encouraged black people to acquire land on freehold tenure and thereby make enough money to qualify. Assimilation would not work; even in America Negro voters were being bought, bullied or beaten up, and

---

[1] Archdeacon S. J. Christelow, Hon. Secretary of the joint executive of the Southern Rhodesia Missionary Conference, in a covering letter to an article by African members of the Conference: 25 Jan 1935 (in *Rhodesia herald*, 1 Feb 1935)

Southern Rhodesian whites would never stand for a political hand-over. Representatives of the black people might ultimately sit in a Second Chamber, but there were too few able people of any race on whom to draw and it would involve a great deal of expense. Africans, however, did need some kind of representation, and Huggins suggested therefore that two members should sit in the Assembly to speak on their behalf whilst keeping aloof from any political party affiliation. The Imperial authorities, however, began to hedge. Africans would sooner or later insist on being represented by men of their own blood. In any case the British Government would have to consider the Colony's problems in the light of current practice in South Africa, where Africans at the Cape still enjoyed the franchise and racial policy was in the melting-pot. British public opinion would object if Southern Rhodesian Africans secured a lesser measure of representation than their brothers south of the Limpopo, and the existing franchise should remain for the time being.

Huggins also asked for modification of Clause 28 in the Constitution, which compelled the Governor to reserve legislation on certain matters, but he admitted that the reserve powers could not be completely removed until Southern Rhodesia acquired a Second Chamber. The Dominions Office, on the other hand, insisted that the reservation of differential native legislation must remain; the Office was always willing to consider Southern Rhodesian legislation sympathetically as in the case of the Industrial Conciliation Bill, but the Prime Minister must realize that a complete excision of the reserve clause would lead to political opposition in the United Kingdom. The reservation moreover gave a useful opportunity for discussing in advance legislation with which the Home Authorities disagreed, and no change could be entertained for the time being.

Huggins acquiesced, but found himself on stronger ground in dealing with the remaining powers in the Colony's affairs held by the High Commissioner for South Africa. The High Commissioner, for instance, still wielded extensive rights in connexion with Native Department appointments. The creation of a Public Services Board in Southern Rhodesia and the development of regular airmail services were, however, making these functions obsolete. The former now provided a strong and politically independent organ of control over the civil service, whilst letters from Salisbury now took little longer to arrive in London than in Cape Town. After further negotiations the Southern Rhodesians secured additional powers for their own Governor-in-Council, and in 1937 the majority of the High Commissioner's functions disappeared from the Constitution.[1]

---

[1] See Constitution amendment act, 1937, and Southern Rhodesia. Additional instructions to the Governor: 25 Mar 1937 (in *Southern Rhodesia government gazette*, 22 Oct 1937)

When the Prime Minister came back from London, he found to his sorrow that Charles Spearman Jobling, his Minister of Agriculture, had suddenly died from worry and overwork, and Huggins faced the vexed task of making a new appointment. Instead of choosing a member of his own Reform Party he selected an outsider, Captain Frank Ernest Harris, who did not even sit in the Assembly. Harris had to fight a bye-election to get into Parliament, but the Rhodesian Party decided not to oppose him, so as not to precipitate a General Election which—in their view—might gain them a few seats but would not enable them to form a stable Government.[1] The Reform Party's left wing was furious at the appointment, and sarcastically suggested that the new Minister's main qualification for office seemed to be his past service as Chairman of Stewards on the Bulawayo Turf Club! Huggins, however, thought highly of Harris, a successful businessman who had previously served on the Maize Control Board and as member of a commission headed by Danziger to enquire into the Colony's agricultural position. Huggins had all the traditional upper middle class Englishman's preference for the intelligent amateur over the specialist; as a doctor he himself would not interfere in public health matters, and felt convinced that Harris would do better than a technical expert. There could be no question of 'jobs for pals', for he did not know Harris well, and owed him no special debt of gratitude.

There was a new feeling abroad. Party politics as a whole were falling into disrepute and the Rhodesians' mood mirrored the widespread disillusionment with politicians that characterized much of the western world. The electors wished for a strong government and preferred Huggins the man to his party. They had before them the example of a National Government in Britain where Conservatives and right-wing Labourites had joined under James Ramsay MacDonald to cope with the Slump. Allan Ross Welsh, an influential Bulawayo lawyer and a prominent Rhodesian Party Parliamentarian, suggested to Fynn that the time might be ripe for a coalition.[2] Fynn then saw the Prime Minister and assured him that, if Huggins wanted to form a National Government, he would meet with a sympathetic response from the Rhodesian Party which would not make any conditions in the allocation of Cabinet seats. Fynn knew his man, for Huggins—forceful and determined—meant to get his way. Huggins asked for time to consider the matter, and early in September 1934 met his Party Congress at Gwelo where opposition was brewing up from his left wing.

The Reform Party dissidents argued that the Government was putting

[1] Note by P. D. L. Fynn: 14 Aug 1934 (in FY 1/2/1, Nat Arch MS)
[2] A. R. Welsh to P. D. L. Fynn: 15 Aug 1934 (in FY 1/1/4, Nat Arch MS)

too much stress on balancing budgets and condemned Huggins for not implementing former election promises concerning a national banking system. They also deplored continuing unemployment and emphasized the need for secondary industries. The malcontents had some personal ability, but no political sense, and chose their ground badly. Earlier in the year, for instance, Huggins had gone to Cape Town to negotiate a new Railway Agreement. N. H. Wilson went along as adviser to the Southern Rhodesian Delegation, and on his return published a detailed statement defending the arrangement. He showed that under the new dispensation Company dividends and overheads would contract, that the Railways would build up a reserve from savings, and the country would gain.[1] Later on, however, Wilson shifted his ground. He informed the public that his own acceptance of the Railway Agreement always depended on the inclusion of an option for Southern Rhodesia to purchase the system.[2] The left wingers in Parliament had refused to guarantee support to Huggins for the impending Railway Bill which, they felt, left 'Chartered' interests in a commanding position.

The left wingers at the Party Congress also claimed that more people were looking for jobs than ever before, but again could not put up a very satisfactory argument. Whether as a result of, or in spite of, local legislation, the country's economic situation was beginning to improve as the world slowly emerged from the Depression. Earlier on the authorities had hastily drafted a Work Colonies Bill to discipline white unemployables, but the measure turned out to be so Draconian that they did not dare bring it before the House. The Government, however, had not remained idle. It appointed a Commissioner of Labour who investigated the situation and found that by the end of 1933 there were 826 registered white unemployeds out of a population of some 50,000 Europeans, a proportion that compared favourably with conditions in Britain and Germany. The Government had set up relief camps and put white men on unskilled jobs like afforestation and road making,[3] and by the end of 1934 the crisis had at last begun to recede.

The left wingers within the Reform Party nevertheless resented the Prime Minister's personal rule as much as his deviation from the original Party line; and opposition came to a head at the Congress. Huggins

[1] Wilson, N. H. 'The 1934 railway agreement: a study of its probable effects' (in *New Rhodesia*, 1 June 1934, p. 1267–1273)

[2] *New Rhodesia*, 5 Oct 1934, p. 11. Wilson, in fact, had stated earlier that whilst he would have liked to see an option for purchase included in the Agreement, he realized that neither Southern nor Northern Rhodesia wanted such a solution at the time.

[3] See Wells, G. E. *Report on unemployment and the relief of destitution in Southern Rhodesia.* Salisbury [Ministry of internal affairs], 1934. A further report was issued by Wells as Commissioner of Labour in the following year.

insisted that his Members of Parliament must support him on every issue which he considered to be of national importance; they might have their say in caucus but must back him in the Assembly, especially in view of his Party's slender majority. Huggins managed the Congress extremely well, and when Reginald Herbert Bruce Dickson, a highly trained farmer and a member of the Opposition group, moved that no party member should negotiate with a view to forming a National Government, the majority stood by Huggins. The Prime Minister frankly told delegates that he would do what he thought best for the country and, if need be, he would ignore any such resolution.[1] Huggins then parleyed with Welsh and received a promise of support from the Rhodesian Party. During a dinner together Huggins mentioned that he would probably ask Sir Alexander Fraser Russell, the Chief Justice and Acting Governor, to dissolve Parliament. He explained that he was about to face a meeting of his Party's Executive at Gwelo; his Party's left wing would probably break away so that he would have no alternative but to fight a general election. Welsh then suggested that Huggins should avoid an election and rely on support from the Rhodesian Party, but Huggins would not commit himself. The Prime Minister was feeling unhappy about his own personal position; he was by this time virtually living as a pensioner on his medical partners, and was considering resigning in the following year to settle family affairs in England. Welsh asked Fynn to approach the Acting Governor and persuade him that the country needed stability. If Huggins had to fight the Rhodesian Party, Labour and his own malcontents together, he could not hope to get back with a working majority; an election campaign moreover would fray tempers to such an extent that a coalition would become even more difficult to achieve. The Governor therefore should use his good offices, in the same way as the King did in Britain before the formation of the National Government, to bring about a coalition.[2]

Huggins asked for a dissolution, but Russell would not give it to him, on the grounds that he still wielded a majority in the Assembly; the Prime Minister then braced himself for a final 'show down'[3] with the dissident minority within his Executive. Only an unconfirmed set of minutes, issued by Huggins, now survives from this vital Executive meeting, and they do not quite agree with the account given by Sir Hugh Williams on behalf of the Opposition members. At the meeting, Huggins complained that some Members of Parliament sitting for the Reform Party had refused to give him an assurance that they would support him on matters which he con-

---

[1] *Rhodesia herald*, 7 Sep 1934
[2] A. R. Welsh to P. D. L. Fynn: 14 Sep 1934 (in FY 1/1/4, Nat Arch MS)
[3] Information supplied by Lord Malvern.

sidered of major national importance. Some Reform Party members suggested that if they should vote against the Government on controversial matters, the Rhodesian Party could still see the Government through its troubles. But Huggins would not accept such terms, and advised the Executive to vote in favour of approaching other parties for the formation of a stable Government. The rebels pointed out that the Executive had no powers to take such a step as it would override the Party's constitution. But according to Sir Hugh Williams, the Party's Vice-President, Huggins cheerfully admitted that he had never read this troublesome document! The Chairman, Captain Frank Smith, ruled that the Executive had no powers to suspend the constitution, but in the end the meeting nevertheless voted by a majority of 27 to 11 that proposals by Huggins for the formation of a United Party should be supported. Huggins should carry out the negotiations and would receive loyal support as Leader of a United Party, so that the country might secure stable government over the next five years.[1]

The opposing factions then closed their ranks. The majority of the Reform Party and of the Rhodesian Party joined to form the United Party which tightened up discipline and gave Huggins a predominant say in the selection of Parliamentary candidates. Local branches of the United Party put their nominees forward. These were scrutinized by a Central Selection Committee, consisting of two Reform Party and two Rhodesian Party members, the Prime Minister wielding both an original and a casting vote, which gave him a firm grip on the Party's Parliamentary composition. Candidates had to sign a statement in which they promised to submit to Party discipline. Local branches of course still retained considerable power since local electors would often decry outside candidates as 'carpet baggers'. Nevertheless the United Party emerged as a fairly cohesive force, with extensive public support, whilst opposition to Huggins from within withered away. Huggins also approached Davies, the Labour Party's leader, to join him in a National Government; but Davies refused to become the prisoner of a conservatively minded majority, and when Huggins got his dissolution, Labour fought as an independent force in the ensuing general election.[2] The old Reform Party also went into battle on their own with the result that the opposition against Huggins remained divided. White artisans and railway men on the one hand, and the poorer farmers and smallworkers on the other, never managed to establish a common front, and this pattern continued as long

[1] Minutes of an Executive meeting, held at the Midlands Hotel, Gwelo, on Monday 17 Sep 1934, at 10 a.m. (cyclostyled copy in the possession of Colonel T. Nangle). Sir H. Williams's own account was published in *New Rhodesia*, 21 Sep 1934, p. 11–12.

[2] *Rhodesia herald*, 21 Sep 1934 and 8 Oct 1934

as Huggins remained in office. The 'P.M.' for his part, a debonair racing man with a gift for making the right joke at the right time, forceful and urbane, with the experienced doctor's gift for summing up people, now wielded a tremendous personal ascendancy. He moreover could point to some solid achievement. Agricultural controls were working well; the Industrial Conciliation Act reconciled many white workmen to the Government; the Railway Agreement stood out as an improvement on the old, and the country's economic future looked brighter. The United Party promised an extensive road building programme and improved education; it was now ready, if necessary, to override the finance and mining companies as well as the Protestant Churches in their dislike of lotteries, and to introduce a Sweepstake Bill; this measure was strongly supported by the electorate which subsequently approved of the scheme through a referendum.[1] In native affairs Huggins now hedged over segregationism. Old style Reform Party men angrily remarked that his new call for 'a just and logical native policy' leading to improved economic and social conditions for both races, sharply diverged from the Whiter Rhodesia ideal.[2]

Most important of all Huggins appealed to the country's desire for a 'strong' administration. The issue was quite clear, the Prime Minister argued in an 'Eve of Poll' message. If the people wanted stable government they should side with him. If, on the other hand, they desired a forceful Opposition, with plenty of elections on petty side issues, they should cast their votes for his opponents whose job-seeking, parish pump politics and class legislation might ultimately end in Union or Crown Colony Government. Huggins was by this time rather disillusioned with party rivalries and bitterly wrote to a prospective candidate in a private letter that the more a man got into politics, the more he would find how little the country, and how much intrigue, counted in public affairs. Huggins's mood, common amongst many people in the early 'thirties, found an echo in the country, and the Opposition's warning against personal dictatorship made but little appeal. The Rev. Arthur Shearly Cripps took up his evangelical lyre and, incongruously siding with the advocates of White Rhodesia, delivered himself of a somewhat creaking political philippic:

> 'Pause: Why omnipotence confer
> On your own pet practitioner?
> Will he, like Mussolini, foil
> His foes with flood of castor oil?

---

[1] The scheme was put into operation by the State lotteries act, 1935.
[2] Wilson, N. H. 'Native policy' (in *New Rhodesia*, 12 Oct 1934, p. 8–9)

"Doctors" mused Rhodes, that man astute
"Are bloody, bold and resolute".
Why foist a surgeon fond of steel
A Führer on our Commonweal?"[1]

The dictatorship argument, however, did not 'sell', and in the elections of November 1934 Huggins emerged with a crushing majority that stunned even the United Party's most convinced supporters. The United Party won 14,813 votes and 24 seats in the House. The five Labour members in the House secured re-election with reduced majorities, receiving 6,092 votes. The Reform Party rebels, on the other hand, suffered almost complete political extinction, obtaining only 2,237 votes and a single seat in Parliament.

Huggins thus emerged as what an opposition journal called a 'constitutional dictator on thoroughly democratic lines'.[2] A few days earlier Welsh could gravely ask Fynn to impress upon the Prime Minister the need for greater discretion in his statements, if he expected to remain leader of the United Party.[3] But now the mandarins from the old Rhodesian Party themselves counted for little. Huggins's new Cabinet consisted almost entirely of 'loyalists' from the old Reform Party: only Fynn came in from the Rhodesian Party as Minister without Portfolio, greatly chagrined at the poor recognition afforded to his faction, but feeling bound by the promise that there should be no haggling over Cabinet seats.[4] From then on Huggins governed at Salisbury with a doctor's mandate. As his opponents saw it, the Rhodesian 'Establishment', consisting of the senior ranks of the civil service, the chambers of commerce and of mines, the agricultural and show societies, the Salisbury Club, backed by the Argus Press and the Anglican hierarchy, was back in power. Effective opposition was at an end. Huggins ran the country, and his personality was to dominate the next two decades of its history.

[1] *Rhodesian railway review*, Nov 1934
[2] *New Rhodesia*, 9 Nov 1934, p. 3
[3] A. R. Welsh to P. D. L. Fynn: 1 Nov 1934 (in FY 1/1/4, Nat Arch MS)
[4] Notes by P. D. L. Fynn for Nov 1934 (in FY 1/2/1, Nat Arch MS)

Chapter Eight

Southern Rhodesian society in the early 'thirties

I

White men and brown

Statistics form the life blood of modern social studies. But Africa lacks adequate figures concerning its earlier development, and in this respect Rhodesia—though better provided than many other territories—forms no exception. Historians must therefore treat statements concerning past population movements with some reserve, for information, especially about the African peoples, remains largely based on intelligent conjecture. The white population fluctuated, and documentation remained deficient even for Europeans. The first real census was taken in 1904 when the country was divided into census districts; in the absence of an expert the work was organized by the Director of Education who—as an intellectual —was expected to be capable of doing his sums correctly! The authorities ran a second census in 1911, and from them onwards there was one about every ten years. But the Administration still lacked professional statisticians; the machinery for collecting information often creaked, and even though statistics concerning white, Coloured and Asian people can be accepted with some confidence, much of the information given about Africans rests on no more than approximate knowledge. As late as 1926 the Director of Census, a senior civil servant of proven merit, frankly concluded his report by pointing out that his 'national stocktaking' rested on amateur productions assembled by a 'scratch team' which lacked previous experience in the field of census work.[1] Later on matters improved; in 1934 the authorities appointed a highly trained Government Statistician, and Southern Rhodesian statistical services began to acquire a high reputation amongst professionals. But earlier work was sketchy, and people who delve into the country's past must approach their material with caution. Various Government departments and commissions nevertheless accumulated a good deal of valuable information, and writers may

[1] Southern Rhodesia. *Report of the Director of census regarding the census taken on 4th May 1926; part III.* Salisbury, Government printer, 1927, p. 28 (*C.S.R. 6–1928*)

therefore venture upon some cautious generalizations, especially with regard to the white people in the country.

The European population grew rapidly during the post-war period, and Europeans could boast of a faster rate of increase than almost any other community in the world.[1] The proportions of men and women began to even out, and the country was losing its old-time army-camp atmosphere. In the larger centres people could lead normal family lives, even though many smaller townships and isolated mining camps still retained the masculine atmosphere of the pioneering period, with drink aplenty and women in short supply.[2] Rhodesia at the same time remained a youthful country, a land lacking grandparents; the number of marriages went up, the birth rate was high and Southern Rhodesia continued to enjoy a 'baby boom' at a time when Northern Europe began to worry about its low birth rate.[3]

From the national point of view white Rhodesia remained strongly British in composition. In 1936 only 5·3 per cent of the European population had come from foreign countries. The Empire-born population on the other hand contained a substantial Afrikaans-speaking minority; nearly 18 per cent of the country's white population professed membership of the Dutch Reformed Church, a religious group nearly all of whose adherents spoke Afrikaans, and who formed a majority of the white population in some of the rural areas of Mashonaland including Charter, Chilimanzi, Gutu, Makoni, Melsetter, Mrewa and Ndanga. About one-fifth of the Europeans spoke a language other than English in their homes. Just under a quarter had come to Rhodesia from the British Isles, the immigrants from the United Kingdom containing a small but influential Scots component. About a third being Union-born, the Colony retained a strong South African flavour and a substantial body of people looked to Cape Town and Durban rather than London or Edinburgh for their political inspiration. The country at the same time contained many second-generation Rhodesians. By 1936 about 35 per cent of the white people had been born in Southern or Northern Rhodesia; this element gained preponderance as the largest component between the years 1931 and 1936.[4]

[1] In 1921 the European population amounted to 33,780; in 1931 there were 50,070 whites and in 1936, 55,408. The percentage increase between 1921 and 1926 amounted to 16·52; between 1926 and 1931 it was 27·41; and between 1931 and 1936 it was 11·02.

[2] The proportion of females per 1,000 males grew from 407 in 1904 to 515 in 1911; 771 in 1921; 796 in 1926; 830 in 1931; and 864 in 1936.

[3] In 1911, 373 per mille of the male and 666 of the female population above 15 years of age was married. The figures for 1921 were 503 and 650; for 1926, 522 and 629; for 1931, 551 and 629; for 1936, 408 and 448. The births stood at 27 per mille in 1911; 27 in 1921; 23·8 in 1926; 23·6 in 1931; and 23·4 in 1936.

[4] In 1936, 18,904 people or 34·1 per cent had been born in Southern Rhodesia. The corresponding figures for those born in Northern Rhodesia were 551 and 1 per cent, in South Africa 18,151 and 32·8

Economically, farming remained the country's largest industry, followed by mining, with railway communications not far behind. Rhodesia continued to rely on a few primary commodities for export, whilst secondary industries remained unimportant. The territory already possessed, however, a relatively large administrative and commercial superstructure, government forming one of its biggest industries. The white population also contained a professional element of doctors, attorneys and architects, as well as a fairly large number of clergymen, many of whom served Africans as teachers and missionaries.[1] Rhodesia's small backveld community on the other hand could not sustain a literary intelligentsia, and the country thus totally lacked that cultured, self-questioning and hypersensitive group of literary men and artists whom war and its aftermath fired into bitter criticism of the established order in wealthier countries overseas.

White Rhodesian society did not allow of great social distinctions and the average Rhodesian could rightly say that if he wanted to make any man's acquaintance, none would say 'no'. Snobbery of course never quite disappeared. Salisbury in particular retained a reputation for stuffiness which Rhodesians blamed on the civil servants. But Salisbury in terms of population still yielded second place to Bulawayo, the country's most populous and go-ahead township, the centre of the railway administration and in many ways the country's economic capital, which displayed a colonial egalitarianism that reminded newcomers more of a South African community than of a British colonial settlement. Salisbury and Bulawayo —opposing but complementary poles—dominated the country's life to such an extent that wits used to speak of its history as 'a tale of two cities', a high percentage of white Rhodesians leading the life of provincial townsmen rather than of colonial farmers.[2]

Rhodesia's small-town and farm society for the most part maintained an intensely British-South African outlook, a pride in the Union Jack, in

per cent, in England 9,249 and 16·7 per cent, in Scotland 2,739 and 4·9 per cent, and in Ireland 836 and 1·5 per cent. Foreign born persons amounted to 2,962 or 5·3 per cent. 9,859 or 17·8 per cent were members of the Dutch Reformed Church. Jews amounted to 2,220 or 4 per cent. The Greek community numbered 543 persons, or 1 per cent.

[1] In 1936, 4,093 white people were occupied in agriculture and forestry; 3,718 in mining and quarrying; 3,545 in government and administration, including 350 teachers and 214 nurses. 4,493 were engaged in commerce and finance; 2,503 in transport and communications. Metal industries occupied 968 persons; wood-working and furniture 105; private building and construction 1,002; clothing and leather 196; food, drink, and tobacco 553; other manufactures 602. 405 persons were employed by local government agencies. The census of 1936 lists 1,557 professional people, including 262 architects, 188 clergymen and 106 medical practitioners. 1,090 people rendered personal services as shop assistants, domestic servants, barmen, waiters, public house keepers and so forth.

[2] In 1936 Bulawayo had a population of 10,896 white persons, Salisbury 9,442, Umtali 2,134, Gwelo 1,295, Gatooma 742, and Que Que 553. The country as a whole had 55,408 white inhabitants in 1936.

King and Empire, a kind of patriotism already beginning to wane in the Mother Country. In the backveld British middle class and Imperial traditions retained greater vitality, even though they became curiously modified in an African environment where the Salisbury Hunt Club, instead of chasing foxes, magnificently rode to hounds after jackals! White Rhodesia began to emerge as a separate community with its own culture heroes, men like Allan Wilson, whose deeds had secured Rhodesia to the Empire and made white colonization safe in the interior. Rhodes's grave in the Matopos remained a national sanctuary and Pioneers, little honoured in the early days, acquired a national prestige inherited by their descendants and preserved in various societies. In 1935 the Government Archives of Southern Rhodesia came into being, its creation owing much to the historical interest and national pride that arose from celebrations commemorating the conquest of Matabeleland four decades before.

Rhodesian children were acquiring an accent of their own, a variant of South African speech, which gave them something in common, no matter whether they came from Lancashire or Lithuania. As early as 1912 the Director of Education addressed a warning circular to parents of Salisbury high school scholars on the subject. 'You have undoubtedly realized that the youth in this country are at a disadvantage in the manner of learning the correct pronunciation of the English language. More often than not their ears are accustomed to variants of the English language far from pleasant to hear and which, if acquired, would in later years betray a lack of cultured training.'[1] But official circulars did not stop the creation of a new speech, which itself formed one of the elements that went into an emergent 'proto-nationalism', linked to British patriotism, but based on an open-air ethos and an enduring faith in the white man's mission in Africa. The sense of forming a cultural vanguard remained strong in the Colony, physically isolated from 'Home', and mentally shielded from the disillusionment that hit so many British intellectuals in the aftermath of war. The post-war years did see the emergence of a social conscience, a greater sensitivity amongst Europeans towards the needs of Africans. Church synods and undenominational 'welfare societies' pressed for various betterment schemes, and a few white people like Hadfield, or Alderman Leslie B. Fereday, later a Mayor of Salisbury, worked hard to promote improvements. But Rhodesians on the whole as yet took little interest in the 'native problem'; they remained Victorians at heart. They lived in a country where unemployment pay and many other kinds of social welfare measures were unknown; they generally held that people

[1] Director of Education to Parents and Guardians: 10 May 1912 (circular no. 11a of 1912 in E 2/5/3, Nat Arch SR)

should look after themselves and that a man should be allowed to do what he liked with his own. The country continued to be governed by a small and cohesive electorate; there were no mass parties, no mass organizations, no mass press. The *Rhodesia Herald* and *Bulawayo Chronicle* gravely recorded long speeches made in the Legislative Assembly; white Rhodesians remained content to read solid extracts from official reports over their breakfast tables, and bathing belles and beauty queens did not make headlines.

White Rhodesians at the same time maintained a firm faith in their country's future. The history of Southern Rhodesia was in many ways a success story; within a space of just over forty years European settlers had created a modern economy and a complex machinery of government. Rhodes's dream of 'more homes' had become a living reality. Since the institution of Responsible Government the country had managed to make greater advances and to create better social services for its white and black people than Northern Rhodesia under Colonial Office rule, despite the fact that nature had bestowed far greater natural riches on the northern sister state, with its vast and as yet only sparsely exploited riches in copper, iron, coal and other minerals. Southern Rhodesia, far from receiving international help, had had to pay heavily for self-government; Southern Rhodesian tax-payers had provided £2,000,000 for the country's mineral rights and £2,000,000 for the land rights, carrying a burden never as yet laid upon any British community endowed with the privilege of Responsible Government. The country largely depended on British and South African capital, though after the Great War local re-investment from gold mining and investment by smallworkers assumed increasing importance.[1] Southern Rhodesia thus laboured under a considerable load of debt—yet the territory managed to bear the strain and confound the pessimists. White Rhodesians on the whole stuck to their traditional belief that, however many setbacks their country might suffer, prosperity was nevertheless waiting round the corner. Sooner or later more immigrants would come and exploit the country's enormous resources; land values would appreciate and more homes would spring up on the veld, each one destined to become yet another little cell of civilization. Disgruntled Rhodesians might rail at their 'Old Gang', but of genuine revolutionary feeling there was none, for few doubted that things were bound to get better in the end. The fear of tribal risings was gone, the fear of African

[1] See Frankel, S. H. *Capital investment in Africa.* Oxford University Press, 1938, especially p. 57 and tables facing p. 175 and p. 158. The total funded debt in 1935 amounted to £7,955,000 at an average rate of interest of 3·85 per cent. The total amount of invested capital in 1936 was calculated at £102,403,000.

nationalism not yet born; the country remained physically secure, and required but a modest military establishment to preserve the social order. White Rhodesians thus remained a warlike but not a militaristic people; the country contained a large proportion of civilians with military experience and aptitudes but the armed forces remained small. In 1926 a new Defence Act did away with the old Volunteer system and brought into being a European short-service militia with compulsory training, held together by a tiny professional cadre. The police, an élite force, continued to serve as the country's first line of defence, but white policemen formed less than one-half per mille of the country's total population.[1]

White Rhodesian society felt thoroughly secure. Now and then a missionary might step in to criticize some aspects of life, but most clergymen remained too much occupied with practical issues to interfere in politics. Missionaries in the backveld retained more of the old Victorian attitudes than their colleagues in England, who were exposed to a greater extent to modernist trends in theology and were often less aware of the black converts' manifold 'backsliding' than were the white parsons on the spot. Rhodesia admittedly produced a few exceptional clerics, the nearest thing to 'left-wing intellectuals' the country contained. The most outstanding of these was the Rev. Arthur Shearly Cripps, an Anglican of Oxford and Cuddesdon College, a high-minded Christian Socialist, who harshly criticized the settlers, and dreamt of a golden future where the hardy, country-bred virtues of Africans would one day redeem the land. But people like Cripps exerted not the slightest influence on their white fellow citizens. Cripps was laughed at for his inferior farming practices and resented for the vitriolic tone and negrophile content of his polemics. He thought in terms of 'an Africa for Africans', Christian but black, whereas the ordinary settler never doubted that Rhodesia would remain a 'white man's country', where natives remained at best a 'problem' and at worst an off-stage noise. The country's government revolved round European questions; native affairs remained the specialist's concern, and even the white politician's private correspondence hardly ever mentioned Africans at all.

Rhodesia's white top-stratum, ranging from senior administrators and wealthy businessmen to skilled artisans and backveld farmers, of course never formed a homogeneous whole; considerable differences of wealth

---

[1] Up to 1926 Southern Rhodesia in peace-time relied on the police and on volunteer soldiers. The Defence Act, 1926, provided for compulsory peace-time training for European citizens between the ages of 19 and 22. Training was limited to a continuous period of 14 days with 60 extra hours spread over the first year. During the following years the training period amounted to 14 days and 40 hours of extra time. In 1934 the permanent military nucleus amounted to no more than 55 men. The European police mustered 539.

remained. There was a good deal of poverty, and as late as 1942 a survey revealed that as much as 8½ per cent of white school children examined suffered from malnutrition. In some ways the 55,000 Europeans, on whose skill the whole economy hinged, stood out as a much more varied lot than the inhabitants of a British town with a population of similar size.

Their society at the same time remained exposed to considerable changes from within. Communications had vastly improved since the early days. In 1905 a Salisbury firm had imported the first Ford; later the 'Model T' became a familiar sight at many homesteads, and the internal combustion engine brought a social revolution to the backveld, allowing goods, ideas and people to circulate at greater ease than in the olden days of creaking ox-wagons. The white man became the man with a motor vehicle, the change affecting missionaries in just the same way as settlers and civil servants, so that Cripps called curses down on 'car-borne clerical vampires', who supposedly rushed round the veld without getting to know their black charges as of old. At the same time aircraft made world-wide communications easier; Imperial Airways set up a trunk route from London to Cape Town in 1932, and a local service, Rhodesia and Nyasaland Airways, began operations a year later.

The country moreover vastly extended its education services. Rhodesia in its pioneering stage, like Europe in the Middle Ages, at first relied on the devoted work of clergymen and nuns, the Dominican Convent at Salisbury and St George's College, a Jesuit school, providing the best teaching in the land. The passing of the first Education Ordinance in 1899 had marked the beginnings of an organized system of education, and by the time the Chartered Company relinquished its rule, solid foundations had been laid. In 1911 34·7 per cent of the white children between the ages of 7 and 14 had received no education whatever; ten years later the figure had dropped to 20·2 per cent and from then onwards illiteracy was largely eliminated. The Coghlan Government made further improvements and in 1930 Moffat introduced a measure for compulsory education which came into force in the following year. The Education Department also commenced correspondence courses for children on lonely farms in the bush, and boarding schools, formerly concentrated in the towns, were extended to the countryside through centralized boarding hostels run by local committees.[1] More youngsters accordingly managed to complete secondary school courses and go on to a university, either in South Africa or in England.

Rhodesians at the same time displayed a certain amount of scientific

---

[1] For an excellent statement regarding the ideals of white Rhodesian education, see Southern Rhodesia. *Report of the education commission.* Cape Town, Cape Times ltd, 1929 (*C.S.R. 27–1929*)

interest; in 1899 the Rhodesia Scientific Association held its first meeting, and in the decade preceding the Great War the Administration set up a number of scientific departments, including public health, veterinary and agricultural research stations which quickened thought in their special disciplines. In 1912 a Rhodesian Branch of the British Medical Association came into being, followed later by a mining association and similar bodies. White Rhodesians, however isolated physically, thus battled to reproduce the cultural institutions which they knew at 'Home' and retained their links with the scientific culture of the West. Deistic rather than atheist, secular-minded more than Christian, admiring Martha more than Mary, the European colonist stuck to the past century's inherited optimism, and sought to make the best of this world rather than search for salvation in the next.[1]

The Rhodesian immigrant population also included settlers from east of Suez; the term 'Asiatic' was used in a sociological rather than a geographical fashion and related to citizens from India, the handful of Turks, Palestinians and Chinese in the country being classed as 'Europeans'. White businessmen generally resented competition from brown-skinned traders, willing to work with low profits and small overhead expenses, organized in extended families, and always prepared to support necessitous kinsmen. From 1924 onwards Southern Rhodesia largely put a stop to further Asian immigration, though Rhodesians managed the matter more tactfully than their South African neighbours, excluding Indians on economic grounds rather than race, and showing a greater degree of liberality in cases of personal hardships.[2]

At a time when business remained difficult and Rhodesian markets limited, many Indian merchants in fact do not appear to have regarded these restrictions as an unmixed curse; the Immigration authorities after all often kept out potential competitors, and Indians in general preferred Southern Rhodesia's more politic approach to that of South Africa. Socially and politically Indian people in Southern Rhodesia occupied a position analogous in many ways to that of the Jews in nineteenth-century Russia: a large proportion made their living from commerce; but Indians also worked in the food, drink and tobacco industries, and some laboured as farmers and market gardeners. Predominantly Hindu in religion, but

[1] In the 1936 census barely 1 per cent described themselves as atheists, agnostics, free thinkers or of no religion. 42·94 per cent were Anglicans, 17·79 were Dutch Reformed, 11·41 Presbyterian, 8·88 Methodists and 8·44 Roman Catholics. 4·01 were Hebrew. Figures for active Church membership are difficult to obtain, but the number of Church attendances is unlikely to have risen since 1921 when the Census stated that 46·2 per cent described themselves as Church members, but no more than 9·7 per cent of the total population attended public worship regularly.

[2] In 1936 the Indian population amounted to 2,180. Out of 1,278 economically active persons 428 were employed in financial and commercial occupations, 153 in various industries and trades, and 134 in agriculture, including 14 farmers and 16 market gardeners and vegetable growers.

with Muslim and Catholic minorities, the Indians lived in small, self-contained communities. In some ways, however, Indians were becoming more Rhodesian than their white compatriots, for official restrictions pushed down the number of newcomers, leaving Asians with a larger proportion of Rhodesian-born persons than the whites.[1]

Indians, like Coloured people, enjoyed a kind of intermediate status between white men and black. They mostly possessed the property qualifications for the vote; they could take out General Dealer's Licences and did not fall under the Land Apportionment Act. They could not, however, attend white schools; they remained excluded from the civil service and did not receive peace-time military training; urban title deeds and leases often excluded them, whilst some complained that municipal authorities discriminated against them with regard to trading facilities.[2] Indians, unlike Russian Jews in the late nineteenth century, remained, however, physically secure from attack; some built up a modest prosperity, and they remained as averse from root-and-branch changes as their white fellow-countrymen. Politically Indians first supported Responsible Government; subsequently they backed Huggins's Reform Party in the 1933 elections; at a later date a visiting intellectual like Professor Ardaser Sorabjee N. Wadia from Bombay could completely identify himself with prevalent white race attitudes, contending that the idle and inefficient Negro needed the white man's strong guiding hand, though stressing that Indians too should enjoy equal rights for civilized men.[3]

Coloured people of mixed European-African or Asian-African ancestry occupied the lowest rung on the non-African colour ladder. Earlier on in Central African history Portuguese frontiersmen, many of them illiterate and always separated from home by the vast time-scale of slow-moving sailing-ships, made their way inland without womenfolk of their own; they consequently had children with African girls who either found acceptance as Portuguese or else went back to their mothers' communities. The Portuguese, however, made no permanent impact on the interior, and later immigrants, coming at a time when improved communications did away with the old-time isolation, soon managed to bring in women of their own colour. The cheap steamship ticket, a historian might argue, killed biological assimilation, and even though white housewives never quite managed to put an end to inter-racial affairs in the bush, they did succeed in imposing their own standards on the white community.

[1] The 2,180 Indians in the country comprised 949 persons born in Northern or Southern Rhodesia, 703 born in the Bombay area of India and 118 from Goa, the remainder coming from other parts of India or other countries.

[2] See Desai, D. M. *The Indian community in Southern Rhodesia*. Salisbury, The author, 1948

[3] Wadia, A. S. *The romance of Rhodesia*. J. M. Dent and sons, ltd, 1947, p. 128–134

Miscegenation soon became a term of reproach, and a dark cloud of illegitimacy fell heavily over the Coloured community. Europeans at the same time enjoyed tremendous prestige; educated Coloured people themselves looked with distress at Eurafrican children playing in African villages as 'natives', and therefore demanded for their community a recognized place of its own, as a poor second to complete acceptance into the European group. Most Rhodesian Coloureds knew no other home but Rhodesia. Their economic status for the most part remained low; the majority served as semi-skilled workers or foremen in agriculture and industry, or entered domestic service.[1] A few Coloured folk managed to make good as teachers or businessmen, the Coloured upper stratum including some people like Gaston Thomas Thornicroft, the son of a British J.P. from Fort Jameson. He came to Southern Rhodesia at the age of twenty, made his way as a farmer and storekeeper, and became in 1932 the first President of the Coloured Community Service League.

But Coloured folk found themselves socially isolated and politically powerless. They lacked the bond of a common creed, the national pride born of a distinctive religious or cultural heritage, and the conviction that they formed a people chosen rather than handicapped by history. Coloured people in Southern Africa made few attempts to better their lot by overseas emigration, by going, say, to countries like Brazil where their colour would have been no disadvantage to them. The Coloured community moreover suffered from tremendous internal cleavages; some Eurafrican children led the lives of black people in the reserves; others lived like Europeans. Many professed Christian creeds; a minority followed the faith of their Indian fathers.[2]

II

The Africans

When the Pioneers came to Mashonaland, they felt themselves to be harbingers of a new future. Their descendants regarded the Colony as a 'white man's country' and instinctively likened the territory to countries such as Australia, where immigrants formed the overwhelming majority

---

[1] In 1936 the Colony contained 3,187 Coloureds. Of these 2,287 were born in Southern Rhodesia, 737 in South Africa, 38 in Bechuanaland and 28 in Northern Rhodesia. 1,467 were children under 15. Of those in gainful employment, domestic service accounted for 201 (including 173 women); next on the list came agriculture with 156, followed by 112 in trade, 93 in mining and 69 in road transport, with a considerable spread over other industries.

[2] In 1936, 2,744 Coloureds professed Christianity, including 1,266 Anglicans, 741 Catholics, 355 Methodists and 229 Dutch Reformed adherents. Asian religions had 233 votaries, including 193 Muslims, 37 Hindus and 3 Confucians. There were 178 Coloureds who professed no religion.

and the 'natives' did not count. Rhodesian realities, however, never conformed to the immigrants' image. The small bands of nomadic hunting folk of Australia could not easily be absorbed into the white man's economy except in marginal occupations—as stockmen or trackers; if they failed to conform, they were driven out or crushed. But the vastly more numerous Bantu, farmers and pastoralists with a knowledge of metal working, possessed a much higher degree of material culture; they could therefore get employment in all kinds of subordinate jobs, as farm-hands and mine labourers, and later even as artisans and white collar workers, the Europeans finding a great reservoir of cheap though inefficient labour right on their door steps. The Rhodesian Bantu lost much of the land over which they had once roamed in the past. But they continued to live in tribal communities with sufficient land to prevent, for the time being, the emergence of a propertyless proletariat without a stake in the country, the labourers in township and mine compound retaining their link with the village. The Europeans, neither numerous nor ruthless enough to crush or anglicize the Africans, remained a hereditary caste, egalitarian within, closed against non-Europeans; their concepts of the social order followed that of India more than that of Australia, even though white Rhodesians would have been loth to admit the Asian parallel. Colonial society remained divided into sharply distinct communities, the Europeans generally regarding integration as contrary to nature, dreading nothing more than the idea that their descendants should intermarry with the indigenous people, and sink to the level of a backveld Coloured community.

The whites introduced new ways of mining and farming; they built up a network of communications; they brought Western medical and veterinary techniques to the country; tribal migrations and warfare came to an end, so that the indigenous people and their cattle rapidly multiplied. Exact statistics of course remain impossible to get; the official figures, based on incomplete information, have almost certainly always underestimated the number of black people in the country. Statisticians are probably right, however, in assuming that from the turn of the century onwards Africans doubled their numbers within a generation, whilst their herds increased thirtyfold.[1] The overwhelming majority of natives lived on the land; black town-dwellers made up but a tiny fraction of the whole. Most country-folk had their homes in the reserves, but there were substantial minorities on farms and Crown land in European areas.[2] The

[1] The estimated African population was 514,813 in 1902 and 966,015 in 1930. The corresponding figures for their cattle were 55,155 and 1,558,075 head.

[2] According to the Chief Native Commissioner the distribution in 1934 was as follows: 688,573 in native reserves; 163,284 on Crown land in European areas; 30,475 on Crown land in native areas; 192,182 on privately owned land; 1,710 on the Fingo location; 6,906 in mines and locations.

Land Apportionment legislation assumed that in time Africans would all live in their own areas, an almost impossible aim to achieve. Population transfers—though never pursued with the brutality that once marked many of the Highland 'clearances' in Scotland—continued to create great bitterness. Africans, whilst recognizing that Europeans brought all kinds of useful things, 'clothes, peace, ploughs, plants' as well as schools, churches and better communications, believed strongly that there was 'one bad action which they did to us, that is selling all the best land to farmers', whilst Africans settled on European property were made to 'pay two kinds of taxes, that is one to the government and the other to the owners of the farms where they happen to live'.[1]

But Africans at the same time vastly increased their output under the new dispensation. Black peasants managed to make some use of new economic opportunities, though the rate of change remained very uneven, depending on many different factors—the internal constitution of the various tribal communities, geographical conditions such as the fertility of the soil, the amount of rainfall in each area, distance from market, the degree of European penetration in the shape of stores, farms, mission stations and mines—so that generalizations for the country as a whole are impossible. In the more accessible parts of the country Africans began to improve their crops. Black farmers traditionally cultivated millet, beans, groundnuts, melons, vegetable marrows and some maize, but from the beginning of the century the Chief Native Commissioner began to remark on the increased acreage devoted to maize. For instance, by 1909 Africans in the Marandellas region, a European settlement area, were using the white man's varieties of 'mealie' to such an extent that the small native types were rarely seen. European traders introduced ploughs and wagons; the Government promoted the sinking of boreholes, whilst trained demonstrators showed how new methods vastly increased traditional yields.[2] In 1927 the Government agricultural service began a pilot scheme in the Selukwe reserve, where demonstrators taught the value of using kraal manure and winter ploughing, whilst the Native Commissioner urged the people to centralize arable land and allocate permanent grazing. The authorities managed to gain the people's confidence, so that the villagers came to look upon the project as their own, and a deforested, worn-out and over-stocked part of Rhodesia completely changed in

---

[1] Machiwanyika, J. *History and customs of the Manyika people*, translated by W. S. Musewe in 1943 (an unpublished manuscript in MA 14/1/2, Nat Arch MS)

[2] The most phenomenal increase in the cultivated area in the reserves occurred before the First World War when the acreage went up from 159,000 in 1904 to 936,173 ten years later. In 1924 the acreage stood at 1,186,761; three years later at 1,616,488.

appearance. The new ways slowly spread to other parts of the Colony, and traditional subsistence incomes came to be supplemented to a varying extent by money earned from selling grain to white men.

Large areas of Southern Rhodesia naturally form a stockman's country. Matabele and Mashona people alike traditionally placed a high value on cattle, the animals being regarded in some ways as members of the family, each with their own recognized individuality. Cows of course bear young, just like women; cattle thus served as a means whereby one exogamous patrilineage might obtain wives from another. Marriage formed a compact between two kinship groups rather than an arrangement between two private individuals, the exchange of women for cattle being regarded as a transfer of equivalent reproductive capacities.[1]

Cattle therefore had more than a purely economic value, and many tribesmen at first resisted the idea of selling their surplus beasts for cash, the Matabele being more resistant to change than the Mashona. The losses incurred during the Matabele War and the Rebellion gravely interfered with the institution of 'bride-wealth', and by the turn of the century the Chief Native Commissioner for Matabeleland imagined that the *lobola* custom was dying out for lack of animals. But from then onwards the number of beasts rapidly increased. Europeans brought in new varieties, the African tribesmen finding the hardy Afrikander cattle more to their taste than the highly bred varieties from overseas which needed much more care and could not so easily find their own living on the veld. The Government moreover encouraged native pastoral industry through the construction of boreholes and dips; more Africans got accustomed to the idea of disposing of beasts for cash, so that the number of native stock sold to white men between 1920 and 1930 probably quadrupled.[2]

At the same time communications expanded, and Africans from the backveld were getting more accustomed to modern means of travel. The railways carried a steadily increasing number of black passengers and made journeys easier for those Africans who shared in urban life. By the early 'thirties motor cars could make their way to most parts of the Colony, drivers benefiting greatly from a major road-bridge construction programme begun in 1925. In 1927 the authorities experimented with motor road services to supplement the railways. Private bus companies began to appear, and the internal combustion engine contributed perhaps more than any other agency to putting out-of-the-way villages in touch with the

[1] See Holleman, J. F. *Shona customary law.* Cape Town, Oxford University Press, 1952

[2] See Margolis, W. *The position of the native population in the economic life of Southern Rhodesia.* University of South Africa, M.A. thesis, 1938. The author gives the following estimates for the number of native-owned head of cattle sold to Europeans—1920: 21,460; 1926: 27,144; 1930: 79,248. With the Slump the number dropped to 41,156 in 1931.

remainder of the country. Bicycles were particularly useful on bush tracks. As early as 1894 Charles Duly, a Rhodesian business pioneer, cycled all the way from Johannesburg to Bulawayo. Later on he opened a cycle shop (which subsequently turned to selling cars) for the bicycle was a popular means of transport amongst Europeans before the first car appeared. Africans in the early days could not afford to buy two-wheelers for themselves alone, and bicycles became treasured family possessions, capable of carrying either a pillion passenger or a 200 lb bag of grain, so that people could get about more easily. Pupils who previously lived too far from school could now attend classes; teachers became more ready to accept appointments away from home; peasants could visit their friends in neighbouring villages, and news from the townships quickly became known in the surrounding country areas.[1]

Improved communications in turn quickened trade, and even in the more distant parts of the country Africans slowly got used to buying 'white' commodities like enamelware, cotton cloths, blankets, knives and axes, tea and soap and so on. Indigenous smiths, carvers and potters could not compete with overseas factories, as African tribesmen came to prefer the cheaper and more durable goods turned out by the machine, and much of the old domestic industry withered away. African villagers urgently wanted cash to pay for these goods, the need for money to purchase commodities by now forming a much more important incentive to accept paid employment than the pressure from taxation. By 1934 the country possessed a relatively large labour force; Southern Rhodesia knew neither debt bondage, peonage or slavery, and the white man's law was doing away with the traditional restraints on individual liberty such as hereditary servitude, the inheritance of widows and the pledging of children in marriage. The territory in fact formed a powerful magnet attracting migrants from neighbouring countries, the majority of black workmen employed within the country coming from beyond its borders; nearly a third of the total labour force was from Nyasaland.[2] A minority of Africans found jobs in the towns, but mining and agriculture between them

---

[1] See McHarg, J. *Influences contributing to the education and culture of the native people in Southern Rhodesia.* Duke University, D.Ed. thesis, 1962. McHarg found that the number of railway passengers carried in 1913 was 200,000. By 1926 this figure had risen to 300,000 a year. When fares were reduced in 1927 passengers increased to over 400,000 and the figure was about the same in 1935. In 1934 road services carried 16,745 passengers, accounting for a running mileage of 379,511, and thereafter the services increased rapidly. Southern Rhodesia did not register its bicycles; records of bicycle imports only began in 1930 when at least 16,000 bicycles were introduced into the country, whilst sixteen years later at least a quarter of a million bicycles were in use.

[2] 252,482 male natives were in employment in 1936. Of these 107,581 came from within the country; 25,215 from Portuguese territory; 46,884 from Northern Rhodesia; 70,362 from Nyasaland; and 2,440 from other countries.

Y

accounted for the majority of employees.[1] African wages in the early
'thirties, though higher than those in Nyasaland or Mozambique, remained
low and static, and black workmen at first benefited but little when
Southern Rhodesia emerged from the Slump. White rate-payers in fact paid
an indirect and largely unrecognized subsidy to employers by contributing
to the cost of African urban housing for which black workmen could not
afford to pay out of their own pockets. The vast majority of hired hands
possessed no qualifications, and looked forward to going home to the
village at the expiry of their contracts rather than to improving their skills.

Many factors contributed towards this state of affairs. The tribal lands
and ways of life continued to exert a strong pull, at a time when most
native areas had not yet reached saturation point. White artisans dreaded
competition from native workers, and training facilities for black men
remained limited. European farmers and smallworkers required but few
educated Africans, while few mines expected a sufficiently long life ahead
to warrant the setting up of permanent married quarters. The country's
outlets for a more diversified system of native agriculture remained
limited; and there were lacking industrialists anxious to build up a highly
trained African labour force or to expand the number of African customers.
The country in fact had remained South Africa's economic hinterland,
purchasing most of its manufactured goods from the United Kingdom or
the Union. A major departure in economic policy only came in 1935 when
pressure from South African backveld farmers, jealous of competition
from Southern Rhodesian tobacco and cattle men, did away with the
existing system of free trade between the two countries. South African
manufacturers complained bitterly, but Southern Rhodesia at last set up
its own customs houses, and began to look to its markets at home and to
the territories beyond the Zambezi as an outlet for infant industries.

By the early 'thirties the effects of incipient economic diversification and
of improved training facilities for Africans were beginning to make
themselves felt. The territory was giving employment to a small body of
African professional men such as pastors and schoolmasters, to a 'white
collar proletariat' of clerks, court interpreters, and to a few independent
tradesmen. Economic development was gradually breaking down the old
ways, but was bringing a whole range of new skills, the tailor's art, the

[1] In 1936, 20,177 Africans, male and female, were employed in Salisbury; 15,322 in Bulawayo;
3,566 in Umtali; 2,165 in Gwelo; and 1,718 in Gatooma. In 1936 domestic service employed 32,200
Africans; agriculture 83,270; mining and quarrying 84,337; food, drink and tobacco manufacturers
2,601; paint, candle manufacturers, etc., 289; metal manufacturers and repairs 734; leather goods 214;
clothing trades 1,484; wood and furniture 1,511; brick, tiles and lime 2,225; paper and printing 148;
water and electricity 836; building 2,688; roadworks 11,820; rail transport 5,781; road transport
2,927; other transport 700; persons in shops and offices 6,717; professionals 1,503; police and defence
1,715; warehousemen and storekeepers 3,408.

carpenter's and the bricklayer's, which were replacing the more traditional crafts; a tiny group, the original nucleus of an indigenous black bourgeoisie, was beginning to enter trade.[1]

The drift into paid jobs as yet hardly affected African women who remained in the villages and for the most part carried on their accustomed lives. Mission stations educated a small number of girls, but the great majority of African men did not like the idea of their daughters taking up paid positions, so that the number of African girls in employment remained negligible.[2] A number of African women did of course manage to make their way to the locations. Some followed their husbands; others —many of them apparently widows, unhappy wives or girls pledged in infancy to unsuitable husbands by their kinfolk—ran away to the towns, which thereby provided a personal escape-hatch and weakened the traditional controls over women. African elders complained bitterly at this influx, arguing that single girls became prostitutes and infected their men with venereal disease which seeped back into the villages with disastrous consequences. The missionaries agreed, feeling convinced that promiscuity had increased since Europeans stopped the ancient punitive customs whereby kraals harbouring fugitive women were burnt down, their cattle confiscated, and their owners mutilated.[3]

Traditional marriage customs, based on compacts between kin groups and the giving of bride-wealth (*lobola*), appear to have changed but little. Missionaries complained that in many places half the girls given in marriage were still pledged in infancy, as in the olden days, whilst the value of *lobola* steadily went up.[4] Most clergy believed that the rise in the cost of marriage should be stopped by law, but Africans generally disagreed. The question formed a hardy annual at Native Board meetings in the reserves, the younger men present often favouring a compulsory 'ceiling' on *lobola*. The majority of councillors, however, insisted on a policy of laissez faire, or suggested that any top limit should be a very high one. In defending the custom, conservatives argued that excessive

[1] In 1936 the Chief Native Commissioner stated that 3,043 natives were working in independent occupations. These included 612 builders; 344 cobblers; 283 carpenters; 182 transport riders; 170 tailors; 135 painters; 134 well sinkers; and 110 cycle repairers. The trading element comprised 135 hawkers and 25 general dealers.

[2] The number of African females in employment amounted to 1,628 in 1926; 1,066 in 1931; and 1,815 in 1936. The corresponding figures for African males were 171,970; 179,092 and 252,482 respectively.

[3] Hugo, H. C. 'A brief review of the Mashona marriage problem' (in *Proceedings of the Southern Rhodesia missionary conference held at Salisbury, Southern Rhodesia, 2nd to 5th August, 1926.* Salisbury, the Conference, 1926, p. 26–33)

[4] The Rev. H. C. Hugo considered that in Mashonaland the *lobola* traditionally amounted to 10 sheep and 10 goats or 50 native hoes and 12 yards of strings of beads. Later it went up; in 1926 it amounted to between 7 and 10 head of cattle and £2 to £5 in cash, additional gifts being given to the bride herself, her mother and the intermediary agent.

demands for *lobola* allowed a father to turn away undesirable suitors without giving offence, that *lobola* formed a check on youngsters disregarding the rules of courtship and marriage, that large reductions in the amount of *lobola* would result in more marriages between local women and black migrants from outside the country with consequent social complications, and that—in any case—the practice rarely resulted in litigation. The Government refused to intervene—wisely so, since the rise in bridewealth resulted from increased African prosperity rather than from the introduction of a purely mercenary element.[1]

Traditional marriage customs, based on an intricate network of kinship obligations, strongly clashed with missionary moral concepts. Christian clergymen put forward a very different ideal of society; they demanded that their converts should only have one wife; they asserted the primacy of the individual with his immortal soul over the tribal group and insisted that traditional arrangements must give way to a higher morality, though they often compromised with indigenous ideas in actual practice. By and large, however, the preachers' cultural self-confidence remained as unshaken as that of the colonists, and cultural relativism as yet had made but small impression on white clergymen. A small group, strong apparently within the Anglican Community of the Resurrection, was beginning to waver, holding that missionaries should be careful lest they destroy native cultures. The majority, however, stuck to the accustomed point of view. Father A. Burbridge, a learned Jesuit, made a vigorous stand for moral absolutism as against the contemporary social anthropologists' more permissive approach. Christians, he argued, must continue to make value judgements, and must sharply differentiate between harmless and wicked customs. Scholars could give but limited guidance in this respect, for many features which they described were in fact not essential to the functioning of society; anthropologists in any case could not agree amongst themselves; they were divided into sharply differing schools, whilst many research workers simply projected their professors' teachings on African realities. Outside forces beyond clerical control were, he felt, changing indigenous society in any case, and under these conditions believers must carry on the fight for Christian liberty.[2]

The missionaries thus tried to promote monogamy, and the law

---

[1] For an important discussion by an anthropologist, see Holleman, J. F. *Shona customary law.* Cape Town, Oxford University Press, 1952, p. 371–373

[2] For the two conflicting points of view in the Rhodesian missionary field, see Shropshire, D. W. J. *The church and primitive peoples.* Society for the promotion of Christian knowledge, 1938, and Burbridge, A. 'Missionary attitude towards heathen customs' (in *Proceedings of the Southern Rhodesia missionary conference held at Salisbury, Southern Rhodesia, 2nd to 5th August, 1926.* Salisbury, the Conference, 1926, p. 40–44)

permitted African converts to marry in church, like white men. This of course meant that an African husband, married as a Christian, became guilty of bigamy if he took a second spouse according to native custom. However, many African converts did so, wedding a first wife in church and afterwards a second wife in the traditional manner. The Chief Native Commissioner thus reported the characteristic case of an African who contracted a Christian union. The unfortunate man in due course succeeded to a chieftainship, but found that his wife—by now an invalid—could no longer carry on the duties of a chief's consort—particularly that of providing food for visitors. The chief then told his Native Commissioner that he would have to take a second wife, only to be told to his horror that he would thereby make himself criminally liable. Such cases were common and the courts in fact took a very lenient view of them. The Moffat Government, despite strong opposition from the Anglican bishop, introduced a new Act which tightened up existing legislation and required a special certificate from a Registering Officer before a clergyman might solemnize a native marriage, so as to prevent further scandal in future.[1]

The clash between tribal and individualistic values likewise affected property and inheritance. The Mashona, like their European neighbours, of course strove to acquire riches, but the African pastoralists' traditional concept of wealth sharply differed from that of their white countrymen. In the old Mashona society land could not be held in fee simple; livestock only had a limited economic value, for the tribesmen did not use manure as fertilizers, and only began to use oxen as draught animals when the Europeans introduced ploughs and carts. Beasts might be slaughtered for special occasions, but beef and milk did not form part of the villagers' regular diet, cattle being kept primarily for the purpose of making marriage payments or propitiating the spirits. The Mashona term for wealth, like the Latin word *pecunia* (from *pecus*) had the same root as the word for 'cattle', and when Mashona elders adjudicated on a question of inheritance, they primarily thought in terms of a kinship group's capacity to reproduce itself. Individual property rights largely remained limited to goods of a purely personal value, such as clothing, weapons, tools and ornaments, so that the indigenous system of inheritance was bound to come into conflict with that of the white man.[2]

But the Europeans brought in new kinds of property; their Land Apportionment Act allowed Africans for the first time to hold land on individual tenure and the law-makers considered themselves as liberators.

[1] For the relevant legislation, see the Native marriages ordinance, 1917, and the Native marriages amendment act, 1929.

[2] See Holleman, J. F. *Shona customary law*. Cape Town, Oxford University Press, 1952 ch. 8

Many Africans, Coghlan argued as early as 1925, were already carrying on civilized pursuits, and native law should not apply to such people, whatever Imperial legislation with its backward-looking cast of mind might say. The Southern Rhodesia Order in Council, 1898, specified that in African civil cases the High Court should apply native law, as long as this did not clash with natural justice or existing statute law. Emancipatory legislation, however, must become the rule, and civilized Africans should be allowed to free themselves from traditional custom by their own personal decision. The effect of excluding natives from the operation of the general European law had proved anything but beneficial to the progress of natives in the Union of South Africa, especially in Natal, and —Coghlan went on—he did not desire that a similar state of affairs should obtain in Southern Rhodesia. The Chief Native Commissioner on the other hand identified himself more with the old order of things. In the African view, Sir Herbert Taylor argued, a man's inheritance—that is to say mainly cattle—should pass to the nearest male relative on the agnatic side, its main purpose being to support a dead man's children. Property was administered by the family head, but belonged to the family, and Africans regarded with abhorrence the idea that a man should have power to dispossess his offspring. The customary tutelage of women should not be eliminated right away. To do so would only bring licence, disruption of family life and unhappiness to the many, quite out of proportion to the benefits bestowed upon the few. Native women had, over the last 30 years, in fact acquired increasing freedom from parental oppression through asylum at mission stations, through education and—unhappily also— through prostitution in industrial areas. Legislators, Taylor thought, should walk warily and abstain from suddenly breaking down existing usages whereby they would only deliver the indigenous people into the bondage of an alien law inapplicable to their needs.

The Native Affairs Department successfully clamped down on some of Coghlan's more far-reaching ideas, but gradually Africans too accepted the view that African Christians should be allowed to make wills in the European fashion. In 1933 a new Act laid down that Africans who married by Christian rites or civil contract might provide by will for the guardianship of their children, and that they might make testamentary disposal of immovable property, though a man's inheritance would still go to his heirs at native law in the case of an intestate succession.[1]

The whole issue as yet only affected a minority of Africans, many of

[1] Native wills act, 1933. See also the Administration of estates ordinance, 1907, already then on the statute book, which did not specifically apply to any one race and which lawyers later applied to Africans as well as Europeans.

them immigrants from beyond the Limpopo, and the Coloureds. A typical case was that of the heirs of Kosepg Komo, a Basuto who acquired a quarter share of 'Erichsthal' farm in the Victoria District. Komo left a widow, a Christian Basuto married to him in church; their daughter then wedded a Coloured person of partly African ancestry who lived with the Komo family under conditions resembling that of poorer Europeans. The Eurafrican husband died in his turn, his decease leading to a complicated legal tangle. The fundamental issue hinged on the question of whether an African might legally make a will, and the learned Judge decided that indeed he could.[1] Africans, in other words, could accumulate and bequeath property in the European fashion, and no legal barriers now prevented the hereditary descent and subsequent accumulation of personal capital.

Southern Rhodesia, under Responsible Government, also expanded the system of African education. The authorities approached their task with a number of preconceptions. White men had a moral obligation to lead their black countrymen forward, the burden of improving African social conditions forming part of their guardianship. The country at the same time needed a more efficient labour force, imbued with 'discipline, habits of work and punctuality, cleanliness and respect for authority' which education alone could provide. The country at the same time should grow more food in the reserves, thereby freeing more villagers for work in the towns, whilst safeguarding the natural resources through better soil management. To achieve this, educational advance must take place on a broad rather than a narrow front; educators should aim at mass literacy rather than the creation of a small, anglicized élite, out of touch with the villagers, inclined to question the existing social order and to demand jobs which a backward economy could not as yet provide. Missions should bear the main weight of education, for mission teachers would work for less money, and also inculcate new moral standards to take the place of dying tribal sanctions. Pedagogues ought to employ the vernacular in the lower forms and only switch to English in more advanced classes; missions should concentrate on practical matters and develop a syllabus suited to the children's home background. Government, however, would step in to provide more advanced technical education at schools like Tjolotjo and Domboshawa, whilst assuring adequate standards elsewhere through inspection and the judicious use of financial grants.

The missionaries themselves by and large agreed with this assessment of the country's needs. The various societies always found themselves short of funds, and could not have set up a more advanced system of education, even had they wished to do so. Missionary incomes to a large

---

[1] *Rhodesia herald*, 3 Aug 1935

extent derived from outside supporters and varied sharply with fluctuations in the world economy. Each mission moreover felt itself obliged to safeguard the interests of its own denomination and to provide the kind of statistics that would secure donations for its appeals, supporters at home preferring to dip into their purses to evangelize pagan primitives rather than to turn out black graduates. Free evangelical competition between the societies led to a certain amount of rivalry, duplication of effort and dispersal of resources. The missionaries moreover faced an exceedingly difficult staff problem, for teachers remained in short supply, and many Africans with scholastic training preferred to take better-paid jobs in industry and commerce. The missionaries tried to get over the difficulty by delegating work to poorly qualified black assistants, white schoolmasters concentrating on taking the more advanced classes and supervising the bush schools.

A mass literacy campaign made a greater appeal to Africans themselves. Villagers would rather see new schools than support the extension of existing ones; a village acquired enhanced status by having a school and a church of its own, so that headmen began to approach Native Commissioners with requests for school houses. African pupils at first found considerable difficulty in relating their teaching to the life they led in backward villages, and would not have benefited from more advanced training institutions. In native settlements where huts lacked artificial illumination enabling a man to read in bed, schooling could not easily be carried beyond the point of satisfying the people's demand for novelty. Most Africans remained content painfully to spell their way through a vernacular primer, or to just learn enough to write a letter from Harari to their folks at home. Parents showed impatience with prolonged schooling, young boys being needed at home to herd the cattle, whilst the prejudice against educating girls died especially hard.[1] African society, with its traditional values, sharply discouraged social climbing; black children for long lacked educational incentives; much time elapsed until African teachers and demonstrators acquired a new prestige, and even more until educated Africans themselves became numerous enough to shape public opinion on their own.

Village education nevertheless made progress, and standards slowly rose, though continuing to vary widely from one mission society to another.[2] In 1927 the Government created a Department of Native

[1] See McHarg, J. *Influences contributing to the education and culture of the native people of Southern Rhodesia.* Duke University, D.Ed. thesis, 1962, p. 35–47

[2] By 1934 there were 1,325 grant-earning native schools in the country with a total enrolment of 101,492 pupils and an average total attendance at any one time of 54,328. These schools employed 264 white and 1,659 black teachers. The two Government training institutions had a gross enrolment of

Education separate from the European department, and Harold Jowitt, the new Director, greatly improved the system. Jowitt considered that agriculture should form the basis of school work in the villages, the Government's agricultural improvement programme itself depending on strengthened educational foundations. The new Director strongly supported the Southern Rhodesia Missionary Conference in a successful move to engage Professor Clement Martyn Doke from Witwatersrand to report on the unification of the various Shona dialects; even though the Professor's suggested orthography did not find general acceptance, his linguistic work greatly eased the schooling problem.[1] Jowitt also got the Government to start the territory's first African newspaper which he used as a vehicle for his development programme, and began a vigorous drive to promote higher standards in the African teaching profession. He started a 'subsidiary' training programme for African schoolmasters without proper qualifications, and closed kraal schools that failed to come up to scratch. He likewise developed the training of 'Jeanes' teachers, itinerant pedagogues who went from village to village to promote development. Jowitt unfortunately clashed with Carbutt, and in 1934 resigned from the Southern Rhodesian service, but the country's educational system continued to advance and far out-distanced comparable work done under the Colonial Office north of the Zambezi.

The country was at the same time making a more determined effort to meet its health problems. Administrative medical services expanded; more hospitals opened their doors and preventive medicine improved in town and country alike. Southern Rhodesia used its Government District Surgeons, Native Commissioners and policemen to vaccinate Africans against smallpox, thereby bringing a dreaded killer disease under control. Doctors also made some progress in fighting diseases like yaws, an endemic form of syphilis, which in time became largely extinct. From its early beginnings the territory could also boast of two excellent native leprosy stations. Llewellyn Edgar Williams Bevan, a Government Veterinary Surgeon, first suggested that *Br. abortus* caused the so-called

---

382, with 10 European and 17 African teachers. In aided kraal schools the African teachers with the best qualifications were found to come, in descending order of standard (not of numbers), from the following nonconformist groups: African Methodist Episcopal Church, Presbyterians and the American Board Mission, Methodists, London Missionary Society, Church of Christ, Salvation Army, South African General Mission, Methodist Episcopal and Seventh Day Adventists. The Roman Catholics had the least number of teachers with Std IV, or higher, qualifications, followed successively by the Church of Sweden, Dutch Reformed, Brethren in Christ and Anglicans. Of these the Methodists, Salvation Army, Methodist Episcopal, Catholics, Dutch Reformed and Anglicans employed the highest number of teachers.

[1] Doke, C. M. *Report on the unification of the Shona dialects.* Printed for the Government of Southern Rhodesia by Stephen Austin and sons, ltd, Hertford, 1930 (*C.S.R. 25-1930*)

Malta fever, his observations being brilliantly confirmed when in 1924 Dr Leander Joseph Orpen managed to isolate the organism at the Salisbury Public Health Laboratory. Other qualified men carried out work on parasitic diseases, Dr William Alves subsequently making an important contribution by introducing the first rapid treatment for bilharzia through antimony injections. In addition the Government extended free rural dispensaries in the reserves so that European medicine slowly percolated into the remoter villages.[1]

The white doctor, like his missionary compatriot, thus clashed with native medicine men, the traditional healers, who continued to enjoy a high reputation amongst their own people and went on practising their craft. The Mashona held that medicine-men, like many gifted people in other walks of life, owed their special ability to a guiding spirit; the *nganga* was an 'inspired' person and supposedly could manipulate the forces of nature. He tried to protect the community against the supposed ravages of wizards and witches, depraved persons who inherited a spirit of evil and used occult powers to injure their neighbours. The witch-doctor largely relied on his knowledge of the mind and stood out as an artist *par excellence*. He used his dress and horns, his amulets and decorative beads to win his patients' confidence, and thereby managed to play a useful part in the treatment of simple psychological disturbances. But he also tracked down witches; European officials largely managed to suppress witchcraft executions and, since the turn of the century, witchcraft accusations had rarely lead to bloodshed. Professor Michael Gelfand, who has laboriously analysed great piles of old court records, has found that witchcraft quarrels seemed to play but a minor part in culpable homicide, murder and arson cases, and has concluded that the fear of witchcraft to some extent even helped to tighten up rules of good conduct, since any display of meanness, envy or other evil traits might lay a man open to the charge of being a wizard. The dread of witchcraft at the same time acted as a social equalizer, a defence against 'climbers' who boasted of their possessions, the villagers imagining that wealth would provoke a witch's jealousy. The philosophy of witchcraft, in other words, helped to make tribesmen content with their lot. It provided a logical explanation for the perennial problem of evil, but at the same time impeded the rational investigation of natural phenomena. It likewise discouraged the individualist, the social 'outsider', the man who preferred to think for himself and pit his own conscience against tribal tradition. The witch-doctor, the king-pin of traditional thought, could not however cope with the more serious kinds

---

[1] See Gelfand, M. *Proud record: an account of the health services provided for Africans in the Federation of Rhodesia and Nyasaland.* Salisbury, Federal Information Department, 1960

of disease; his pharmacopeia might contain a few useful herbs, but he could not successfully treat the more difficult cases, so that European-run hospitals gradually became filled with African patients, many of whom first sought the *nganga*'s advice until their respective diseases progressed to such an extent that white doctors could no longer do any good. European medicine—like the Christian religion and the white man's school-learning—made gradual progress, proving a powerful solvent of ancient beliefs, and native dispensary assistants joined the African vanguard of a new philosophy.[1]

To sum up, Southern Rhodesia was beginning to develop a new class— as yet humble and undistinguished, without much social cohesion and devoid of political strength. Few Europeans as yet took account of the few thousand black village schoolmasters and clergymen, the hospital dispensers in native clinics, the handful of clerks and interpreters in government offices. But slowly the influence of new ideas began to make itself felt, and educated Africans helped to spread them afield. Teachers and evangelists preached of a heavenly kingdom where all men were equal in the sight of God; the Europeans' own newspapers informed literate Africans of the social surging that stirred the masses overseas. Black men witnessed the tremendous advances made through the application of experimental science; they saw the conquest of the air and the transmission of sound across undreamt distances; they marvelled at the internal combustion engine, but realized that none of these inventions took their origin in magic. Africans at last stepped into a new society which—for all its harshness—safeguarded human life to an extent unknown before. White dominion in the end presented Africans with much greater opportunities and a much richer variety of choice than the tribesmen knew of old. Since first having set foot in Africa a generation ago, concluded the Rev. John White, a profound change had taken place in the outlook of the native people, a 'racial' awakening, and a new dissatisfaction with their social, industrial and political status that marked nothing less than 'a nation in its birth throes'.[2] European rule itself called forth a dawning African race and class consciousness, and this loomed forth as a greater challenge to white Rhodesians than any faced by the Pioneers.

---

[1] Based on Gelfand, M. *Medicine and magic of the Mashona.* Cape Town, Juta and co., 1956, also an unpublished paper by Professor Gelfand, kindly supplied to the author. In this Professor Gelfand, writing in 1962, records that about 35 per cent of chronic illnesses complained of by African patients at the Harari Hospital, Salisbury, are attributed to witchcraft. He holds this to be a true indicator of the extent to which the general population still believes in magic. No comparable figures are available for the earlier period, but the percentage was probably much higher in the 'thirties.

[2] Presidential address by the Rev. John White (in *Proceedings of the Southern Rhodesia missionary conference held at Salisbury, Southern Rhodesia, 2nd to 5th August, 1926.* Salisbury, the Conference, 1926, p. 15)

Note on sources and treatment

The bulk of Colonial Office archives at the Public Record Office, London, are open to the public fifty years after their creation. The same period applies to material of Imperial provenance preserved in the National Archives of Rhodesia (formerly in the National Archives of Rhodesia and Nyasaland). Rhodesia permits access to nearly all its files thirty years after their creation, but the correspondence of the Governor and the minutes of the Executive Council are only accessible to the public after fifty years, and no source references to this and similar material have been given. Cabinet papers remain closed indefinitely and have not been utilized.

UNPUBLISHED SOURCES OF OFFICIAL PROVENANCE

Imperial Records

Material of Imperial provenance in the National Archives of Rhodesia used by the author includes correspondence of the High Commissioner for South Africa (HC), and files accumulated in the office of the Resident Commissioner (RC), an Imperial officer stationed at Salisbury between 1898 and 1923.

Rhodesian Public Archives

These include material created during the regime of the British South Africa Company which governed Southern Rhodesia from 1890 to 1923, and material produced under Responsible Government (both symbolized by 'Nat. Arch. SR'). The majority of the open material has been fully described in *A guide to the public records of Southern Rhodesia under the regime of the British South Africa Company 1890–1923*. Central African Archives, 1956. The main groups include Administrator's Office (A); Administrator, Matabeleland (AM); Defence and Police (B); Education Department (E); Chief Native Commissioner (N); Chief Native Commissioner, Matabeleland (NB); Public Health Department (H); Agricultural Department (G); Attorney-General's Department (J); Land Settlement Department (L); Commercial Branch and Estates Office,

Bulawayo (LB); Mines Department (M); British South Africa Company's Cape Town office (CT); British South Africa Company's London office (LO); The post-Company material is described in a separate inventory which is available in the National Archives and has not yet been published.

UNPUBLISHED SOURCES OF PRIVATE PROVENANCE

The Historical Manuscripts Collection of the National Archives contains a considerable body of material relevant to Rhodesia. References to this collection are marked 'Nat. Arch. MS'. Particularly interesting are papers concerned with or derived from: Alderson, Sir E. A. H., soldier (AL 1); Baines, J. T., artist, explorer (BA 7–8); Bertodano, F. R. de, Marques del Moral, soldier, diplomatist (BE 3); Blakiston, J. L. L., storekeeper, telegraph official (BL 1); Bruce, G. W. H. Knight —, bishop (BR 8); Capell, A. E., soldier (CA 1); Carnegie, D., missionary (CA 3); Chamber of Mines, Salisbury (CH 6); Chamber of Mines of Rhodesia (CH 7); Chaplin, Sir F. P. D., Administrator (CH 8); Coghlan, Sir C. P. J., politician, lawyer (CO 8); Colenbrander, J. W., pioneer (CO 4); Cripps, A. S., missionary (CR 4); Cripps, L., farmer and politician (CR 1); Dawson, J., trader (DA 1); Downie, J. W., politician (DO 1); Fairbairn, J., concession agent (FA 1); Fry, I., concession agent (FR 2); German Federal Republic (Cape Town Consular files) (GE 2); Giese, A., prospector (GI 1); Grey, A. H. G., 4th Earl Grey, Administrator (GR 1–2); Heyman, Sir H. M., soldier, company director (HE 1–2); Hole, H. M., civil servant (HO 1–2); Jameson, Sir L. S., Administrator (JA 1–2); Jarvis, Sir W. A., soldier (JA 4); Frank Johnson and Company Ltd (JO 4); Johnson, Sir F. W. F., pioneer leader, soldier and politician (JO 3); Leask, T. S., trader (LE 2); Leggate, W. M., politician and farmer (LE 3); Livingstone, D., doctor, explorer, missionary (LI 1–2); Lobengula, chief (LO 1); McChlery, J., politician (MA 15); Machiwanyika, J., teacher (MA 14); Mauch, C., explorer (MA 17); Meikle, T., trader (ME 1); Mitzeki, B., evangelist (MI 2); Moffat, H. U., politician, mining manager (MO 13); Moffat, J. S., Imperial civil servant (MO 1–2); Moffat, R., missionary (MO 5–6); Moodie, G. B. D., trekker and farmer (MO 11–12); Newton, Sir F. J., civil servant and politician (NE 1); Pelly, D. R., clergyman (PE 3); Pioneer Corps Association (1890 Mashonaland) (PI 2); Rawson, O. C., farmer (RA 4); Rhodes, C. J., politician, mining magnate (RH 1); Rhodesian League, political organization (RH 7); Rhodesian Party, political organization (RH 8); Sapte, H. L., soldier (SA 10); Selous, F. C., hunter, soldier (SE 1); Tati Company Ltd., mining concern (TA 1–2); Wilson, B., prospector, concession agent (WI 6). The author was also given access by Lord Malvern to his private papers which have been deposited in the National Archives but which are closed for public use until they are 30 years of age. Access was also granted to the papers of Lieutenant-Colonel T. Nangle, a former Reform Party candidate.

PUBLISHED SOURCES

The library of the National Archives at Salisbury has fairly complete files of all Rhodesian newspapers, with only a few gaps here and there. These papers include the *Bulawayo Chronicle, New Rhodesia, Rhodesia Herald, Rhodesian Railway Review* and numerous others. The Library holdings are equally comprehensive regarding departmental and commission reports, the *Debates* of the local Central African legislatures and so forth. The Library owns a fairly complete set of relevant Colonial Office Confidential Prints, prepared by the Colonial Office for its own use, and containing correspondence bearing on Southern Africa. These have been quoted under their reference 'African' or 'African South' followed by the relevant number. They are open to public inspection when they are fifty years old.

The Library also has a considerable body of secondary literature. This forms the world's largest collection of Rhodesiana and has been fully catalogued. A selective bibliography is appended.

SELECT BIBLIOGRAPHY

1. Books, Pamphlets and Periodical Articles and Theses (including Official Publications by Individual Authors)

Abraham, D. P. 'Monomotapa dynasty' (in *NADA*, v. 36, 1959, p. 59–84)

Abraham, D. P. 'Maramuca: an exercise in the combined use of Portuguese records and oral tradition (in *Journal of African history*, v. 2, 1961, p. 211–225)

Abraham, D. P. 'The early political history of the kingdom of Mwene Mutapa (850–1589)' (in *Historians in tropical Africa: proceedings of the Leverhulme inter-collegiate history conference held at the University college of Rhodesia and Nyasaland, September 1960*. Salisbury, the college, 1962, p. 61–91)

Alderson, E. A. H. *With the Mounted infantry and the Mashonaland field force*. Methuen and co., 1898

Amery, L. S. (ed.) *'The Times' history of the war in South Africa*. Sampson Low, Marston and co., 1900–1909. 7 v.

Axelson, E. *South-East Africa, 1488–1530*. Longmans, Green and co., 1940

Axelson, E. *The Portuguese in South-East Africa, 1600–1700*. Johannesburg, Witwatersrand University Press, 1960

Baines, T. *The northern goldfields diaries of Thomas Baines* . . . ; ed. by J. P. R. Wallis. Chatto and Windus, 1946. 3 v. (Oppenheimer series, no. 3)

Baldwin, W. C. *African hunting and adventure from Natal to the Zambezi*. . . . Richard Bentley, 1863

'Bamangwato' (i.e. Broderick, M.) *To Ophir direct; or, the South African goldfields*. Edward Stanford, 1868

Beit, Sir A., and Lockhart, H. G. *The will and the way: being an account of Alfred Beit and the trust which he founded*. Longmans, Green and co., 1957

Bekker, P. *Path of Blood: the rise and conquests of Mzilikazi*. . . . Longmans, Green and co., 1962

Bocarro, A. 'Extracts from the decade . . . of the performances of the Portuguese in the East' (in Theal, G. M., ed., *Records of south-eastern Africa*. . . . Cape Town, the Government of the Cape Colony, 1896–1905, v. 3, p. 342–435)

Boxer, C. R. *An African Eldorado: Monomotapa and Mocambique, 1498–1752*. Salisbury, Historical association of Rhodesia and Nyasaland, 1959 (Local series, no. 2)

Boxer, C. R. *Race relations in the Portuguese colonial empire, 1415–1825*. Oxford, Clarendon Press, 1963

Boxer, C. R., and Azevedo, C. de. *Fort Jesus and the Portuguese in Mombasa, 1593–1729*. Hollis and Carter, 1960

Brown, D. D. 'Pioneers of Rhodesian tobacco' (in *Rhodesian tobacco journal*, Aug 1953, p. 63–67; Oct 1953, p. 105–109; Nov 1953, p. 89–92; Dec 1953, p. 79–82; Jan 1954, p. 70–75)

Brown, R. 'The Ndebele succession crisis, 1868–1877' (in *Historians in tropical Africa: proceedings of the Leverhulme inter-collegiate history conference held at the University college of Rhodesia and Nyasaland, September 1960*. Salisbury, the college, 1962, p. 159–175)

Bruce, G. W. H. Knight-. 'The Mashonaland mission of Bishop Knight-Bruce, 1888', ed. by C. E. Fripp (in *Gold and the Gospel in Mashonaland, 1888, being the journals of 1. The Mashonaland mission of Bishop Knight-Bruce; 2. The concession journey of Charles Dunell Rudd*. Chatto and Windus, 1949. Oppenheimer series, no. 4, p. 1–145)

Bruce, Sir M. *Tramp royal*. Pan books, 1957

Bullock, C. *The Mashona and the Matabele*. Cape Town, Juta and co., 1950

Burbridge, A. 'Missionary attitudes toward heathen customs' (in *proceedings of the Southern Rhodesia missionary conference*. . . . 1926, p. 40–44)

Burke, E. E. *A bibliography of Cecil John Rhodes (1853–1902)*. Salisbury, Central African archives. 1952 (Bibliographical series, no. 1)

Capell, E. A. *The Second Rhodesia regiment in East Africa*. Simson and co., 1923

Carbutt, C. L. 'The racial problem of Southern Rhodesia' (in *NADA* 1934, v. 12, p. 6–11)

Central African archives. *A guide to the public records of Southern Rhodesia under the regime of the British South Africa company, 1890–1923*. Cape Town, Longmans, Green and co., 1956

Chapman, J. *Travels in the interior of South Africa*. Bell, Daldy and Stanford, 1868. 2 v.

Clay, H. *Report on industrial relations in Southern Rhodesia*. . . . Salisbury, Government printer, 1930 (C.S.R. 3–1930)

Clements, F., and Harben, E. *Leaf of gold: the story of Rhodesian tobacco*. Methuen and co., 1962

Coghlan, *Sir* C. P. J. *Responsible government, the draft constitution: an explanatory address*. . . . Bulawayo, Responsible government association, 1922

Colquhoun, A. R. *Dan to Beersheba*. William Heinemann, 1908

Colvin, I. *Life of Jameson*. Edward Arnold and co., 1912. 2 v.

Cripps, A. S. *An Africa for Africans: a plea on behalf of territorial segregation areas and of their freedom in a South African colony*. London, Longmans, Green and co., 1927

Cronjé, J. M. *En daar was lig: die sending van die Ned. Geref. Kerk in die O.V.S. na Noord—en Suid-Rhodesië, gedvrende die jare 1899–1947*. Bloemfontein, Sinodale algemene sendingskom-missie van die N. G. Kerk in die O.V.S., 1948

Darter, A. *The pioneers of Mashonaland*. Simpkin, Marshall, Hamilton, Kent and co., 1914

[D'Erlanger, E. B.] *The history of the construction and finance of the Rhodesian transport system*. Privately printed, 1939

Desai, D. M. *The Indian community in Southern Rhodesia*. Salisbury, the author, 1948

Doke, C. M. *Report on the unification of the Shona dialects* . . . . Salisbury, Government of Southern Rhodesia, 1930 (C.S.R. 25–1930)

Drew, J. D. C. 'The four Southern Rhodesia referendums: their organization and social and political background' (in National archives of Rhodesia and Nyasaland. *Occasional papers*, no. 1, 1963, p. 42–57)

Du Plessis, J. *A history of Christian missions in South Africa*. Longmans, Green and co., 1911

Du Plessis, J. *Life of Andrew Murray of South Africa*. Marshall brothers, 1920

Duignan, P. *Native policy in Southern Rhodesia, 1890–1923*. Stanford University, Ph.D. thesis, 1961.

Edwards, J. A. 'Southern Rhodesia and the London daily press, 1890–1923' (in National archives of Rhodesia and Nyasaland. *Occasional papers*, no. 1, June 1963, p. 58–70)

Fage, J. D. *The achievement of self-government in Southern Rhodesia, 1898–1923*. Cambridge University, Ph.D. thesis, 1949

Finaughty, W. *The recollections of William Finaughty, elephant hunter, 1864–1875*. Cape Town, A. A. Balkema, 1957

Fox, H. W. *Memorandum . . . on the position, policy and prospects of the company, including an investiga-tion of the company's title to land in Rhodesia*. British South Africa company, 1907

Fox, H. W. *Memorandum . . . on problems of development and policy*. British South Africa company, 1910

Fox, H. W. *Memorandum on constitutional, political and financial and other questions concerning Rhodesia*. British South Africa company, 1912

Fox, H. W. *Memorandum . . . containing notes and information concerning land policy*. British South Africa company, 1912

Fox, H. W. *Memorandum . . . upon land settlement in Rhodesia*. British South Africa company, 1913

Frankel, S. H. *Capital investment in Africa*. Oxford University Press, 1938

Gann, L. H. 'The Southern Rhodesian land apportionment act, 1930: an essay in trusteeship' (in National archives of Rhodesia and Nyasaland. *Occasional papers*, no. 1, June 1963, p. 71–91)

Gann, L. H. *A history of Northern Rhodesia: early days to 1953*. Chatto and Windus, 1964

Gelfand, M. *Tropical victory: an account of the influence of medicine on the history of Southern Rhodesia, 1890–1923*. Cape Town, Juta and co., 1953

Gelfand, M. *Medicine and magic of the Mashona*. Cape Town, Juta and co., 1956

Gelfand, M. *Livingstone the doctor; his life and travels*. Oxford, Basil Blackwell, 1957

Gelfand, M. *Shona ritual with special reference to the Chaminuka cult*. Cape Town, Juta and co., 1959

Gelfand, M. *Proud record: an account of the health services provided for Africans in the Federation of Rhodesia and Nyasaland*. Salisbury, Federal information department, 1960

Gelfand, M. 'Migration of African labourers in Rhodesia and Nyasaland (1890–1914)' (in *Central African journal of medicine*, v. 7, 1961, p. 293–300)

Gelfand, M. *Shona religion with special reference to the Makorekore*. Cape Town, Juta and co., ltd, 1962

Glass, S. *The background of the Matabele War.* University of Natal, M.A. thesis, 1959

Godlonton, W. A. 'The journeys of Antonio Fernandes...' (in Rhodesia scientific association *Proceedings and transactions*, v. 40, 1945, p. 71–103)

Goodall, E., and others. *Prehistoric rock art of the Federation of Rhodesia and Nyasaland.* Salisbury, National publications trust, 1959

Gray, R. *The two nations: aspects of the development of race relations in the Rhodesias and Nyasaland.* Oxford University Press, 1960

Hamilton, J. A. L. Agar-. *The road to the north: South Africa, 1852–1886.* Longmans, Green and co., 1937

Hammond, F. D. *Report... on the railway system of Southern Rhodesia.* Salisbury, Government printer, 1926. 3 v. (C.S.R. 2–1926)

Hancock, W. K. *Smuts: the sanguine years, 1870–1919.* Cambridge University Press, 1962

Harris, Sir J. H. *The Chartered millions: Rhodesia and the challenge to the British Commonwealth.* London, Swarthmore Press, ltd [1920]

Hickman, A. S. *Men who made Rhodesia: a register of those who served in the British South Africa Company's Police.* Salisbury, British South Africa company, 1960

Hindley, G. L. *Fifty years with Ford.* Salisbury, Duly and co., 1961

Hole, H. M. *The making of Rhodesia.* Macmillan and co., ltd, 1926

Hole, H. M. *Old Rhodesian days.* Macmillan and co., ltd, 1928

Hole, H. M. *The passing of the black kings.* Philip Allan, 1932

Hollemann, J. F. *Shona customary law with reference to kinship, marriage, the family and the estate.* Cape Town, Oxford University Press, 1952

Hone, P. F. *Southern Rhodesia.* George Bell and son, 1909

Hughes, A. J. B. *Kin, caste and nation among the Rhodesian Ndebele.* Lusaka, Rhodes-Livingstone institute, 1956 (Paper no. 25)

Hugo, H. C. 'A brief review of the Mashona marriage problem' (in *Proceedings of the Southern Rhodesia missionary conference...* 1926, p. 26–33)

Jackson, M. V. *European powers and south-east Africa: a study of international relations on the south-east coast of Africa, 1796–1856.* Longmans, Green and co., 1942

Johnson, F. *Great days: the autobiography of an Empire pioneer.* G. Bell and son, ltd, 1940

Jollie, E. M. Tawse-. *The real Rhodesia.* Hutchinson and co., 1924

Jones, J. F. *Report upon the present condition of Rhodesia....* The British South Africa company, 1903

Keigwin, H. S. *Report... on the suggested industrial development of natives.* Salisbury, Government printer, 1920 (A. 7–1920)

Lacerda e Almeida, F. J. de. *Lacerda's journey to Cazembe in 1728; translated and annotated by R. F. Burton. Also journey of the pombeiros, P. J. Baptista and A. José, across Africa from Angola to Tette on the Zambeze: translated by B. A. Beadle, and a résumé of the journey by M. M. Monteiro and Gamitto by C. T. Beke.* Royal geographical society, 1873

Lansdown, G. N. 'Zimbabwe's discoverer' (in *United empire: the journal of the Royal empire society,* v. 25, 1934, p. 598–599)

Leask, T. *The Southern African diaries of Thomas Leask, 1865–1870;* ed. by J. P. R. Wallis. Chatto and Windus, 1945 (Oppenheimer series, no. 8)

Leonard, A. G. *How we made Rhodesia.* Kegan Paul, Trench, Trübner and co., 1896

Leys, C. *European politics in Southern Rhodesia.* Oxford, Clarendon Press, 1959

Lockhart, J. G., and Woodhouse, C. M. *Rhodes.* Hodder and Stoughton, 1963

Long, B. K. *Drummond Chaplin: his life and times in Africa.* Oxford University Press, 1941

Lovett, R. *The history of the London missionary society, 1795–1895.* Henry Frowde, 1899. 2 v.

Lucas, Sir Charles P. (ed.) *The Empire at war, v. 4 [Africa].* Oxford University Press, 1925

McGregor, R. *Native segregation in Southern Rhodesia: a study of social policy.* London University, Ph.D. thesis, 1940

McHarg, J. *Influences contributing to the education and culture of the native people in Southern Rhodesia from 1900 to 1961.* Duke University, Ph.D. thesis, 1962

Mager, E. *Karl Mauch: Lebensbild eines Afrikareisenden.* Stuttgart, W. Kohlhammer, 1895

Margolis, W. *The position of the native population in the economic life of Southern Rhodesia.* University of South Africa, M.A. thesis, 1938

Mason, P. *The birth of a dilemma.* Oxford University Press, 1958

Mauch, C. 'Reisen im Inneren von Süd-Afrika, 1865–1872' (*in Petermann's geographische Mittheilungen,* Ergänzungsheft no. 37, 1874, p. 28–52)

Millais, J. G. *Life of Frederick Courtenay Selous, D.S.O.* Longmans, Green and co., 1918

Moffat, J. S., and others. *The Matabele mission: a selection from the correspondence of John and Emily Moffat, David Livingstone and others, 1858–1878*; ed. by J. P. R. Wallis. Chatto and Windus, 1945 (Oppenheimer series, no. 2)

Moffat, R. *Missionary labours and scenes in southern Africa.* John Snow, 1842

Moffat, R. *The Matabele journals of Robert Moffat . . .* ; ed. by J. P. R. Wallis. Chatto and Windus, 1945. 2 v. (Oppenheimer series no. 1)

Moffat, R., and M. *Apprenticeship at Kuruman: being the journals and letters of Robert and Mary Moffat, 1820–1828*; ed. by I. Schapera. Chatto and Windus, 1951 (Oppenheimer series, no. 5)

Mohr, E. *Nach den Victoriafällen des Zambesi.* Leipzig, Ferdinand Hirt und Sohn, 1875

Monclaro, Fr. 'Account of the journey made . . . with Francisco Barreto in the conquest of Monomotapa in the year 1569' (in Theal, G. M., ed., *Records of south-eastern Africa.* . . . Cape Town, the Government of the Cape Colony, 1896–1905, v. 3, p. 202–253)

Muller, C. F. J. *Die Britse Owerheid en die Groot Trek.* Johannesburg, Simondium, 1963

Neumark, S. D. *Economic influences on the South African frontier, 1652–1836.* Stanford University Press, 1957

Norris, F. *The roll call: a record of the part Rhodesia took in the Transvaal war—1899, 1900, 1901.* Bulawayo, the author, 1902

Odlum, G. M. *Agricultural and pastoral Rhodesia.* British South Africa company, 1909

Olivier, Baron. *White capital and coloured labour.* Hogarth Press, 1929

Parker, F. *African development and education in Southern Rhodesia.* Columbus, Ohio State University Press, 1960 (International education monographs, no. 2)

Rademeyer, J. J. *Die land noord van die Limpopo in die ekspansiebeleid van die Suid-Afrikaanse republiek.* Cape Town, A. A. Balkema, 1949

Ranger, T. O. *State and church in Southern Rhodesia, 1919–1939.* Salisbury, Historical association of Rhodesia and Nyasaland, 1961 (Local series, no. 4)

Ranger, T. O. 'The organisation of the rebellions of 1896 and 1897' (in *History of Central African peoples conference 28 May–1 June 1963.* Rhodes-Livingstone institute, Lusaka)

Ranger, T. O. 'Traditional authorities and the rise of modern politics in Southern Rhodesia: 1898–1930' (in *History of Central African peoples conference 28 May–1 June 1963.* Rhodes-Livingstone institute, Lusaka)

Ritter, E. A. *Shaka Zulu: the rise of the Zulu empire.* Longmans, Green and co., 1955

Robinson, R., and Gallagher, J., with Denny, A. *Africa and the Victorians: the official mind of imperialism.* Macmillan and co., 1961

Rolin, H. *Les lois et l'administration de la Rhodésie.* Brussels, Etablissement Emile Bruylant, 1913

Rudd, C. D. 'The concession journey of Charles Dunell Rudd'; ed. by V. W. Hiller (in *Gold and the Gospel in Mashonaland, 1888, being the journals of 1. The Mashonaland mission of Bishop Knight-Bruce; 2. the concession journey of Charles Dunell Rudd.* Chatto and Windus, 1949, Oppenheimer series, no. 3, p. 146–246)

Schreiner, O. *Trooper Peter Halket of Mashonaland.* T. Fisher Unwin, 1897

Selous, F. C. *A hunter's wanderings in Africa.* Richard Bentley, 1881

Selous, F. C. *Sunshine and storm in Rhodesia.* Rowland Ward and co., 1896

Sim, T. R. *Tree-planting in South Africa.* Pietermaritzburg, Natal witness ltd, 1927

Smith, E. W. *The way of the white fields: a survey of Christian enterprise in Northern and Southern Rhodesia.* World Dominion Press, 1928

Summers, R. 'Carl Mauch on Zimbabwe ruins' (in *NADA*, v. 29, 1952, p. 9–17)

Summers, R. 'The military doctrine of the Matabele' (in *NADA*, v. 32, 1955, p. 7–15)

Summers, R. *Inyanga: prehistoric settlements in Southern Rhodesia.* Cambridge University Press, 1958

Summers, R. 'Environment and culture in Southern Rhodesia: a study in the "personality" of the land-locked country' (in *Proceedings of the American philosophical society*, v. 104, 1960, p. 266–292)

Summers, R. 'The Southern Rhodesian iron age' (in *Journal of African history*, v. 2, 1961, p. 1–13)

Sykes, F. W. *With Plumer in Matabeleland.* Archibald Constable and co., 1897

Tabler, E. C. *The far interior: chronicles of pioneering in the Matabele and Mashona countries, 1847–1879.* Cape Town, A. A. Balkema, 1955

Theal, G. M. *The Portuguese in South Africa with a description of the native races between the river Zambesi and the Cape of Good Hope during the sixteenth century.* T. Fisher Unwin, 1896

Thomas, O. *Agricultural and pastoral prospects of South Africa.* Archibald Constable and co., 1904

Thomas, T. M. *Eleven years in Central South Africa.* John Snow and co., 1873

Thompson, L. M. *The unification of South Africa, 1902–1910*. Oxford, Clarendon Press, 1960
Tracey, H. *Antonio Fernandes: descobridor do Monomotapa, 1514–1515*. Lourenço Marques, Arquivo historico de Moçambique, 1940
Van der Merwe, P. J. *Trek: studies oor die mobiliteit van die pioniersbevolking aan de Kaap*. Kaapstad Nasionale pers beperk, 1945
Van der Merwe, P. J. *Nog verder noord: die Potgieter-kommissie se besoek aan die gebied van die teenswoordige Suid-Rhodesie, 1856*. Kaapstad, Nasionale boekhandel beperk, 1962
'Vindex' (i.e. Verschoyle, J.) *Cecil John Rhodes: his political life and speeches, 1881–1900*. Chapman and Hall, 1900
Wadia, A. S. N. *The romance of Rhodesia: being impressions of a sightseeing tour of Southern and Northern Rhodesia*. J. M. Dent, 1947
Walker, E. A. *A history of Southern Africa*. 3rd. ed. Longmans, Green and co., 1957
Wallis, J. P. R. *One man's hand: the story of Sir Charles Coghlan and the liberation of Southern Rhodesia*. Longmans, Green and co., 1950
Warhurst, P. R. *Anglo-Portuguese relations in South Central Africa, 1890–1900*. Longmans, Green and co., 1962 (Imperial studies, no. 23)
Warhurst, P. R. 'The scramble and African politics in Gazaland' (in *History of Central African peoples conference 28 May–1 June 1963*, Rhodes-Livingstone institute, Lusaka)
Whiteside, J. *History of the Weslyan Methodist Church of South Africa*. Elliot Stock, 1906
Williams, B. *Cecil Rhodes*. 2nd ed. Constable and co., 1938
Wills, W. A., and Collingridge, L. T. *The downfall of Lobengula*. . . . 'The African review', 1894
Wills, W. H., and Hall, J. *Bulawayo up to date*. Simpkin, Marshall, Hamilton, Kent and co., 1899
Wise, C. D. *Report on land settlement in Southern Rhodesia*. British South Africa company, 1906

2. Official Publications

British South Africa Company

Directors' reports and accounts . . . [for the period 29 Oct 1889—]. The company, 1889
Letter, dated 21st July 1897 from the British South Africa company to Her Majesty's Under-secretary of state for the colonies covering despatch and annexures from the Administrator, Earl Grey . . . dealing with Sir R. Martin's report on the native administration. . . . The company, 1897
Proposals for the encouragement of land settlement and immigration. The company [1913]
Report of the . . . general meeting . . . [1891–1941]. The company, 1891–1941
Reports of the conferences between the Chartered co. directors and the representatives of public bodies held at Bulawayo, during October of 1907. Bulawayo. Argus printing and publishing company ltd, 1907
Reports on the administration of Rhodesia, 1889/92–1900/02. The company, 1892–1902. 9v.
Reports on the native disturbances, 1896–1897. The company, 1898
Southern Rhodesia: free gift of land to retired and discharged soldiers and sailors. The company [c.1918]
Southern Rhodesia mining handbook, 1909. The company, 1909
Statement of policy of the British South Africa company. Salisbury, the company, 1913

Government of the Federation of Rhodesia and Nyasaland

An agricultural survey of Southern Rhodesia. Part 1: Agro-ecological survey. Salisbury, Government printer, 1961

Southern Rhodesia Government

Board of enquiry . . . upon the public service in Southern Rhodesia. Cape Town, Cape times, 1909
Commission to enquire into . . . certain matters in dispute between the Beira and Mashonaland and Rhodesia Railways and the employees of the said Railways. *Interim report* and *Final report*. Salisbury, Government printer, 1928 (C.S.R. 4–1928 and 12–1928)

Commission to enquire into the cost of administration of the Colony of Southern Rhodesia. *Report.* Salisbury, Government printer, 1924 (C.S.R. 20–1924)

Committee of enquiry into the economic position of the agricultural industry of Southern Rhodesia. *Report.* Salisbury, Government printer, 1934 (C.S.R. 16–1934)

Committee of enquiry to investigate the question of the defence system of Southern Rhodesia, 1917. *Report.* Salisbury, Government printer, 1918 (A. 3–1918)

Copy of correspondence, opinions by counsel, documents and returns relating to the question of the ownership of the mineral rights in Southern Rhodesia. Salisbury, Government printer, 1933 (C.S.R. 18–1933)

Correspondence and memoranda relating to the Ministers' negotiations in London in connection with the 'Railways bill, 1926'. Salisbury, Government printer, 1926 (C.S.R. 29–1926)

Correspondence relating to the native tax ordinance, 1903. Salisbury, Argus printing and publishing co., 1904 (A. 2–1904)

Correspondence respecting the operation of the jury system in Southern Rhodesia. Salisbury, Government printer, 1909 (A. 12–1909)

Cost of living committee, 1921. *Report.* Salisbury, Government printer, 1921 (A. 2–1921)

Customs agreement between the Union of South Africa and Southern Rhodesia, 1930. Salisbury, Government printer, 1930 (C.S.R. 21–1930)

Customs union convention provisionally entered into between the governments of the Cape of Good Hope, Natal, the Orange River Colony, the Transvaal and Southern Rhodesia, 1903. Salisbury, Argus printing and publishing co., 1903 (A. 1–1904)

Department of agriculture. *Southern Rhodesia handbook of tobacco culture.* Salisbury, Argus printing and publishing co., 1913

Draft scheme of administration under the proposals for amalgamation of the territories of Southern and Northern Rhodesia. Salisbury, Government printer, 1916 (A. 13–1916)

Education commission, 1929. *Report.* Cape Town, Cape Times limited, 1929 (C.S.R. 27–1929)

Education committee, 1908. *Report.* Salisbury, Argus printing and publishing co., 1908 (A. 5–1908)

Education committee, 1916. *Report.* Salisbury, Government printer, 1917 (A. 2–1917)

Land commission, 1925. *Report.* Salisbury, Government printer, 1926 (C.S.R. 3–1926)

Maize enquiry committee, 1930. *Report.* Salisbury, Government printer, 1930 (C.S.R. 2–1931)

Native affairs committee of enquiry, 1910–11. *Report.* Salisbury, Government printer, 1911

Native education commission, 1924. *Report.* Salisbury, Government printer, 1925 (C.S.R. 20–1925)

Native labour enquiry committee, 1906. *Report.* Salisbury, Argus printing and publishing co., 1906 (A. 1–1906)

Native labour enquiry committee, 1921. *Report.* Salisbury, Government printer, 1921 (A. 16–1921)

Ottawa conference. *Report of the committee appointed to investigate and report to the government on certain matters relating to the natural resources and industries of Southern Rhodesia.* . . . Salisbury, Government printer, 1932 (C.S.R. 1–1933)

Railway court of enquiry, 1929. *Report.* Bulawayo, Government printer, 1929 (C.S.R. 17–1929)

United Kingdom Government

C. 4643 (1886) *Transvaal: further correspondence respecting the affairs of the Transvaal and adjacent territories*

C. 4839 (1886) *Transvaal: further correspondence respecting the affairs of the Transvaal and adjacent territories*

C. 4956 (1887) *Bechuanaland: further correspondence respecting the affairs of Bechuanaland and adjacent territories*

C. 5070 (1887) *Bechuanaland: further correspondence respecting the affairs of Bechuanaland and adjacent territories*

C. 5237 (1887) *Bechuanaland: further correspondence respecting the affairs of Bechuanaland and adjacent territories*

C. 5363 (1888) *Bechuanaland: further correspondence respecting the affairs of Bechuanaland and adjacent territories*

C. 5524 (1888) *Bechuanaland: further correspondence respecting the affairs of Bechuanaland and adjacent territories*

C. 5904 (1890) *Correspondence respecting the action of Portugal in Mashonaland and the districts of the Shire and Lake Nyasa*

C. 5918 (1890) *Bechuanaland: further correspondence respecting the affairs of Bechuanaland and adjacent territories*

C. 6046 (1890) *Correspondence respecting the Anglo-German agreement relative to Africa and Heligoland*

C. 6048 (1890) *General act of the Brussels conference, 1889–90; with annexed declaration*

C. 6370 (1891) *Papers relating to the Anglo-Portuguese convention signed at Lisbon, June 11, 1891*

C. 6375 (1891) *Treaty between Her Majesty and His Majesty the King of Portugal defining their respective spheres of influence in Africa, signed at Lisbon, June 11, 1891*

C. 7032 (1893) *Agreement between Great Britain and Portugal relating to spheres of influence north of the Zambesi*

C. 7171 (1893) *South Africa: copies of extracts of correspondence relating to the British South Africa company in Mashonaland and Matabeleland*

C. 7190 (1893) *South Africa: the British South Africa company in Mashonaland: copies of two telegrams omitted from [C. 7171], September 1893*

C. 7196 (1893) *South Africa: copies and extracts of further correspondence relating to affairs in Mashonaland, Matabeleland and the Bechuanaland Protectorate*

C. 7284 (1894) *South Africa: correspondence respecting the death at Tati of two indunas in October 1893*

C. 7290 (1894) *South Africa: further correspondence relating to affairs in Matabeleland, Mashonaland and the Bechuanaland Protectorate*

C. 7291 (1894) *Agreement between Great Britain and Portugal prolonging the modus vivendi of 1893*

C. 7383 (1894) *South Africa: papers relating to the administration of Matabeleland and Mashonaland*

C. 7555 (1894) *Matabeleland: report by F. J. Newton ... upon the circumstances connected with the collision between the Matabele and the forces of the British South Africa company at Fort Victoria in July 1893*

C. 8130 (1896) *Matabeleland: report of the land commission of 1894 and correspondence relating thereto*

C. 8141 (1896) *South Africa: correspondence relating to the rinderpest in South Africa in March 1896*

C. 8547 (1897) *British South Africa company's territories: report by Sir R. E. R. Martin on the native administration of the British South Africa company, together with a letter from the company commenting upon that report*

C. 8732 (1898) *British South Africa company's territories: correspondence relating to proposed changes in the administration of the British South Africa company*

C. 8773 (1898) *British South Africa company's territories: (i) Charter of the British South Africa company, October 29, 1889; (ii) Order in council, May 9, 1891; (iii) Order in council, July 18, 1894*

C. 9138 (1899) *British South Africa company: papers relating to the British South Africa company....*

C. 9323 (1899) *British South Africa company: correspondence with Mr. C. J. Rhodes relating to the proposed extension of the Bechuanaland railway*

Cd. 1200 (1902) *Southern Rhodesia: correspondence relating to the regulation and supply of labour in Southern Rhodesia*

Cd. 2028 (1904) *Southern Rhodesia: correspondence relating to the introduction of indentured Asiatic (Chinese) labour into Southern Rhodesia*

Cd. 7264 (1914) *Southern Rhodesia: correspondence relating to the constitution of Southern Rhodesia*

Cd. 7509 (1914) *Southern Rhodesia: papers relating to a reference to the Judicial committee of the Privy council on the question of the ownership of land in Southern Rhodesia*

Cd. 7970 (1915) *British South Africa company: supplementary charter to the British South Africa company dated 13th March 1915*

Cd. 8674 (1917) *Southern Rhodesia: papers relating to the Southern Rhodesia native reserves commission, 1915*

Cmd. 547 (1920) *Southern Rhodesia: correspondence with the Anti-slavery and aborigines' protection society relating to the native reserves in Southern Rhodesia*

Cmd. 1865 (1920) *Forestry in Southern Rhodesia: statement prepared for the British Empire forestry conference, London, July, 1920*

Cmd. 1042 (1920) *Southern Rhodesia: despatch to the High commissioner for South Africa, transmitting the Order of his Majesty in Council of the 9th November 1920*

Cmd. 1129A (1921) *Southern Rhodesia: papers relating to the Commission appointed to take account of what would have been due to the British South Africa company if the administration of Southern Rhodesia by the company had been determined on the 31st March 1918; correspondence and report*

Cmd. 1129B (1921) *Southern Rhodesia: minutes of proceedings of the Commission.* . . .

Cmd. 1273 (1921) *South Africa: first report of a committee appointed by the Secretary of state for the colonies to consider certain questions relating to Rhodesia*

Cmd. 1471 (1921) *South Africa: second report of the committee appointed by the Secretary of state for the colonies to consider certain questions relating to Rhodesia*

Cmd. 1573 (1922) *Southern Rhodesia: despatch to the High commissioner for South Africa transmitting draft letters patent providing for the constitution of responsible government in the colony of Southern Rhodesia and other draft instruments connected therewith*

Cmd. 1914 (1923) *Rhodesia: correspondence regarding a proposed settlement of various outstanding questions relating to the British South Africa company's position in Southern and Northern Rhodesia*

Cmd. 1984 (1923) *Rhodesia: agreement between the Secretary of state for the colonies and the British South Africa company for the settlement of outstanding questions relating to Southern and Northern Rhodesia, dated 29th September 1923*

Cmd. 3076 (1928) *Southern Rhodesia: papers relating to the Southern Rhodesia Native juveniles employment act, 1926, and the Southern Rhodesia Native affairs act, 1927*

Cmd. 3234 (1929) *Report of the commission on closer union of the dependencies in eastern and central Africa*

Cmd. 4174 (1932) *Imperial economic conference at Ottawa, 1932: summary of proceedings and copies of trade agreements*

Cmd. 4175 (1932) *Imperial economic conference at Ottawa, 1932: appendices to the summary of proceedings*

Cmd. 5218 (1936) *Despatch from the Governor of Southern Rhodesia relating to the proposed amendment of the Southern Rhodesia constitution*

INDEX